An A to Z of the Middle East

Alain Gresh and Dominique Vidal
Translated by Bob Cumming

Zed Books Ltd
London and New Jersey

An A to Z of the Middle East was first published in French
under the title *Les Cent portes du Proche-orient* by
Editions Autrement, 4, rue d'Enghien,
75010 Paris, in 1987

It was first published in English in an updated edition by
Zed Books Ltd, 57 Caledonian Road, London N1 9BU, UK and
171 First Avenue, Atlantic Highlands, New Jersey 07716, USA, in 1990

Copyright © Alain Gresh and Dominique Vidal 1990
Translation copyright © Bob Cumming 1990

Cover design by Sophie Buchet
Typeset by Opus 43, Cumbria
Printed and bound in Great Britain by
Biddles Ltd, Guildford and King's Lynn

British Library Cataloguing in Publication Data

Gresh, Alain
    An A — Z of the Middle East.
    1. Middle East.
    I. Title II. Vidal, Dominique III. 100 portes du Moyen -
orient. *English*
    956

    ISBN 0-86232-880-2
    ISBN 0-868232-881-0 pbk

Library of Congress Cataloging-in-Publication Data

Gresh, Alain
    [Cent portes du Proche-Orient. English]
    An A to Z of the Middle East / Alain Gresh and Dominique Vidal :
translated by Bob Cumming.
        p. cm.
    Translation of: Les cent portes du Proche-Orient.
    Includes bibliographical references (p.).
    Includes index.
    ISBN 0-86232-880-2 (cloth). -- ISBN 0-86232-881-0 (pbk.)
    1. Middle East--Dictionaries. 2. Jewish-Arab relations-
-Dictionaries.   I. Vidal, Dominique, 1950- . II. Title.
    DS43.G7413 1990
    956--dc20
                             90-12983
                                   CIP

st

dal

Contents

Introduction

'Crazy', 'absurd', 'inexplicable', 'incredible', 'incomprehensible': these are the words that are most often used to describe the bloody conflicts that rend the Middle East. Is such an opaque picture really the best we can achieve, however surrealist the latest twist in the Lebanese civil war, the Arab-Israeli conflict, the confrontation between Iran and Iraq, or Iraq's invasion of Kuwait?

Do journalists, or, *a fortiori*, specialists, have the right to give up trying to understand or to make others understand what is happening in this part of the world, and why people are dying there ? The warm reception the first (French) edition of this book received seems to indicate a growing desire to grasp the whys and wherefores of the tumult in this region full of martyrs. Hence the need for reference points, not in order to hide the complexity of Middle Eastern reality, but to provide a way of approaching it. This is precisely what we have tried to do in this book: to provide as much information as possible given the limits of space; to make it accessible without distorting reality; to offer an overall view while respecting the specificity of certain situations; to knit together the past and the present, concentrating on current events but avoiding the ephemeral.

History sometimes moves forward in spurts. Since the first edition of this book, the *intifada*, that unprecedented Palestinian uprising, has shaken up the whole Middle Eastern scene and set new challenges to all and sundry, once again bringing to centre stage the question, avoided for the last forty years, of the partition of Palestine between the two peoples who lay claim to it.

In 1986, the Palestinians 'of the interior' seemed as if paralysed by the crisis of the PLO. The reunification of the PLO in 1987 no doubt helped catalyse the 'revolution of the stones' which has dominated the last three years. Hussein of Jordan, who in 1986 was still envisaging a possible return of the West Bank to Hashemite control, has been forced officially to break off his country's links with the territory. In those days, Arafat was still hesitating to move from the implicit to the explicit in terms of his relations with the state of Israel. Three years later, while proclaiming their own state, he and his friends recognized the right of Israel to exist, on the basis of UN resolutions 181, 242 and 338. As a result, the United States, who in 1986 would have nothing to do with the PLO, accepted the need to engage in a substantial dialogue with the organization, a dialogue which was suspended in June 1990, following a Palestinian commando's attempt to land on an Israeli beach. Israel had a coalition government in those days. Now, Shimon Peres, who was prepared to envisage an international conference, is no longer close to the centre of power. Itzhak Shamir is in full control and stubbornly resists all the international pressure pushing him towards negotiations between Israel and the Palestinians, even if, in January

1989, he was forced to grant that the UN had a role to play.

The Arab—Israeli conflict was not the only one to evolve rapidly during the last three years. In 1986, the Iran—Iraq war was at its peak. In 1990, despite the millions of victims of their bloody conflict, Teheran and Baghdad came closer together, thanks to the Gulf crisis. Saddam Hussein had launched into another military adventure, aiming, as always, to establish himself as the leader of the Arab world. In August 1990 he invaded and annexed Kuwait. His campaign, with overtones of a 'holy war' waged in the name of an Arab nation abandoned by the oil-rich monarchies, soon became an anti-American crusade when, to enforce the UN embargo, the US sent more than 150,000 troops, a war fleet, fighter aircraft, ultra-modern tanks, and anti-tank helicopters to the Gulf. All this hardware was required to deal with an Iraqi army armed to the teeth by the West itself.

And what can be said about Lebanon which, three years ago, we thought was about to emerge from its nightmare thanks to the efforts of those who sought to move away from confessionalist confrontation? Today it has sunk even deeper into that nightmare and now, with its two governments, verges on implosion. Or of South Yemen, where a long power struggle degenerated, in January 1986, into a full scale civil war. Or of Sudan, where the victorious general strike of spring 1985, finally forcing General Numeiry from power, raised so many hopes — only to end in an Islamic military dictatorship. And so on, and so on....

Even the profile of the two superpowers has shifted considerably. The US, whose influence had been declining, has returned to the region in force. The Soviet Union no longer opposes American initiatives and remains deaf to Arab criticisms of the massive emigration of Russian Jews to the Holy Land. This is the background against which the current US-Soviet rapprochement, one might even say honeymoon, is influencing events; after Afghanistan, the Gulf War, Cambodia, Namibia, and the Western Sahara, the detente initiated by the November 1987 agreement on intermediate missiles should also benefit the Middle East. The Soviet-American consensus over the Gulf crisis is another example.

The insertion of the main events of the last four years is not the only way in which this edition has been enriched. Thanks to Alexandre Darmont, we have been able to add many more maps. We have also tried to take account of the suggestions and reviewers' comments about the first edition. Above all, we have extended the book's scope. A dozen new headings now cover problems and personalities which were not so prominent in 1986.

These extensions are not merely for the sake of completeness. We still believe, as we did in 1986, that the Palestine question is the very eye of the storm. The partition of Palestine having been strangled at birth with the tacit agreement of the British, their Arab 'allies' and the young Israeli state, the Israeli-Palestinian conflict became the Arab-Israeli conflict, shaping the entire region. This is not simply a question of endless wars — five in forty years, with their accompanying cortège of death and destruction and hatred transmitted from generation to generation. The Palestine question has been internalised as a holy cause by popular opinion throughout the Arab world. It has given a boost to nationalism and exercised great pressure on governments already disposed to move away from the west and to draw closer to the Soviet Union. It has destabilized countries that have had to accommodate hundreds of thousands of refugees. Finally, it has accentuated the burden of military spending on impoverished economies. Not one of the wars, the economic or political developments or the ideological tendencies the Middle East has known over the last forty years is completely separate from the Israeli-Palestinian conflict. It has given rise to new conflicts and has fanned old ones.

The example of Lebanon does, however, show how much care is needed to distinguish specific internal and external factors, in this case concerning the reasons for the outbreak and acceleration of the civil war. Of course, the influx of refugees to the land of the Cedars, and then the arrival of the PLO, pushed out of Jordan after Black September in 1970, the alliance between the Palestinian resistance and the Lebanese National Movement, not to mention the escalating Israeli military operations, all lit the fuse. But the powder-keg was indisputably Lebanese; without the determination of the old Maronite Christian bourgeoisie to preserve its economic and political privileges, in a country which now had a Muslim majority, the explosion would have been if not impossible, then at least much smaller. In short the Israeli-Palestinian conflict destabilized Lebanon because the internal equilibrium of this Switzerland of the Middle East had broken down and had not been replaced by an alternative better suited to the new balance of power. One could say as much of many other centres of tension; understanding the roots and solutions of conflicts requires a particularly fine grasp of the respective roles of endogenous and exogenous factors.

The nature of our endeavour has not changed. We are seeking to de-mystify the myths of the Middle East, to disentangle its knots, to decode its codes. How? Above all, by looking at the issues from many angles, the national, the regional and the international; the social, the political and the ideological; the religious, the strategic and the military; the ethnic and the confessional, the geographical and the historical. It is the historical viewpoint that concerns us most, for the present, in the Middle East more than in any other part of the world, cannot be understood separate from its past. It lies at the crossroads of three continents, the linchpin between east and west, north and south, and has been the scene of so many migrations, the cradle of writing and of some of the most prestigious civilizations, the living heart of three great monotheistic religions. It is a region where every plot of land, every stone, every face carries within it millennia of human creation and destruction. To ignore this is to lose any hope of understanding the contemporary reality.

Muhammad's prophecy in the 7th Century, the great Umayyad and Abbasid empires that dominated the world till the 13th Century, then the Ottoman Empire still mark the people of today in a thousand ways.

Without going so far back, the defeat of the Turkish Empire in 1918, and its break-up by the victorious powers, principally Britain and France, were to fix the frontiers of the main states of the Middle East, lastingly and often arbitrarily. While Egypt has roots going back several thousand years, Lebanon, Syria, Palestine, Iraq and Jordan were born in the western chancelleries. The frontiers of Saudi Arabia were determined by force of arms. These partly artificial national structures ran counter to the aspiration for one great Arab nation which was then current among many intellectuals, yet they have lasted. The only change has been the birth of the state of Israel in 1948 and, in 1990, the unification of the two Yemens.

Until then, between the two world wars, the peoples of the region reacted less to the territorial carve-up than to a barely camouflaged colonial domination. Turkish and Muslim supremacy had given way to western and Christian hegemony. In the 1920s and 30s, the nationalist movement clashed again and again, in country after country, with rulers linked to the west. It was during these struggles that were forged the ideas and the men who would bring about genuine independence.

The end of the Second World War was a turning point. France was pushed to the side-lines. Britain, albeit victorious, had been bled white. Jewish — Arab confrontation was already raging in Palestine. The birth of the state of Israel and the defeat of the Arab armies accelerated an already ineluctable process. In less than ten years, most of the regimes linked to the west collapsed: in Cairo, in 1952, the Free Officers seized power; in Syria one coup followed another; the Iraqi monarchy fell in 1958. The last French and British attempt to reconquer their lost positions — the Suez expedition of 1956 — ended in fiasco. Paris and London faded out of the Middle East, to make room for a new power, the United States.

'Arab unity', 'anti-imperialism', 'socialism'; these three slogans sum up the thought and action, from the late 1950s to 1967, of Nasser in Egypt, the Ba'athists in Syria, and the nationalists in Iraq. Their ideals mobilised not only the peoples of the three countries mentioned but everybody in the region. Movements inspired by their example threatened ruling regimes, in Jordan in 1956–57, in Lebanon in 1958 and even in ultra-conservative Saudi Arabia. Some regimes actually fell, as in North Yemen in 1962. Those who embraced these ideals found the Soviet Union a useful ally against western 'imperialism'.

The June 1967 defeat of the Arabs by Israel at first seemed to accentuate radicalism. The Ba'ath seized power in Baghdad, Qadhaffi in Tripoli and Numeiry in Khartoum. Lebanon's contradictions grew more acute. The Palestinian resistance installed itself in Jordan. But in fact, nationalism's hour had passed, ushering in the era of Islamicism.

Although in power in the three great capitals of the Arab world, Cairo, Baghdad and Damascus, Arab nationalist forces were in fact losing their power to convince and mobilise people. Their achievements no longer measured up to their rhetoric.

Arab unity? The United Arab Republic, the fusion of Egypt and Syria in 1958, fell apart within three years. National states, even if artificial, proved resistant to the call for unity. Divergences between leaders were in the end stronger than the mystique of the Arab nation.

Anti-imperialism? Inasmuch as it was identified with the struggle against the old colonial powers and Israel, it helped in the quest for genuine independence. But in order to achieve what? Successive defeats cast doubt on the promised liberation of Palestine. Economic dependence grew worse.

Socialism? True, agrarian reform had dismantled the old feudal order, the main founts of wealth had been nationalised and industry taken into state ownership. But despite progress in education and health care, social inequalities were growing. The governments had neglected agriculture — the agrarian balance of trade of all these countries was very much in the red — to the point that people flooded into the towns, where not enough industrial or tertiary employment had been created. Thousands of the under- or unemployed crowded together in the cities — the shock troops of the hunger riots which would from then on periodically shake the Arab capitals, from Cairo to Rabat.

On top of all the unkept promises, there were the various restrictions on democracy, all in the name of the struggle against the 'enemies of the revolution'. The regimes had grown more authoritarian. All forms of economic, social or political opposition were banned. Those in power muzzled the press, turned the trade unions into puppets, and society into a barracks. The political police became the central cog of the state.

The Arab defeat of 1967 was thus only part of a much deeper failure. The death of Nasser in 1970 crystalised the end of these illusions: once again the 'Arab dream' had been broken. A twofold process then began. On the one hand, the leadership of the Arab world passed to the moderates, led by Saudi Arabia. Thanks to their oil resources, these countries, allied to the west, imposed their own vision of the world, supported Sadat's *Infitah* in Egypt and its imitators throughout the Arab world, and turned to Washington for a solution to the conflict with Israel.

On the other hand, Islamic fundamentalism became the main political force. The failure of the attempt to modernise, be it capitalist or socialist, was blamed on imported ideologies. In the context of systematic repression, the mosque became the only locus of self-expression, organisation and protest. The universities provided a spectacular example of the phenomenon; until then bastions of the left, they suddenly shifted over to the Islamic groups. The movement found its most committed support amongst the small bourgeoisie of the cities. By 1979, Khomeini's victory in Iran gave a boost to a movement which was already threatening to spread like wildfire throughout the Arab world.

And yet, ten years later, one is struck by the Islamicists' relatively slow advance. Apart from in the Sudan, they seem condemned to the role of eternal opposition. Arab popular reaction to the 1990 Gulf crisis further illustrates the contradictions of these popular movements financed by the oil Emirates, as well as the lasting strength of Arab nationalism.

An approach to the Middle East has to be multidimensional. That is why we have opted for a very varied system of headings, so that the reader can find his or her own way as simply as possible. A brief chronology of the main events in the region since the Second World War, 112 topics arranged alphabetically, appendixes covering the key texts of the Palestine issue, from the Balfour Declaration of 1917 to the 1988 Palestinian National Council, a bibliography arranged thematically and by country and, finally, an index.

In the original introduction, we expressed the hope that the reader, specialist or novice, would detect 'an effort to go beyond the passions and prejudices that the Arab-Israeli conflict so often arouses'. Recognition of this effort in the reviews of the first edition was one of the things we most appreciated. We have tried to abide by that in this new edition, out of principle and because the hope of peace between Arabs and Jews in Palestine has no better friend than tolerance and mutual understanding.

Let the poet, Paul Eluard, have the last word:

'We have accepted others
as others have accepted us
We need each other.'

Chronology (1947—1990)

1947—1967
1947
29 November   The UN General Assembly adopts the Partition Plan for Palestine by a two thirds majority.
1—9 April   The Palestinian villagers of Deir Yassin are massacred by Irgun troops.
14 May   Proclamation of the birth of the State of Israel. The Arab states have rejected the partition plan, and, on the 15th, their troops move into Palestine.
1948—1949
The Palestine War, which ends with the victory of the Hebrew State. Armistices are signed between Israel and its various Arab neighbours.
1949
11 May   The State of Israel becomes a member of the UN.
1950
24 April   Jordan annexes the West Bank. Egypt seizes control of Gaza.
May   Tripartite British, French and American declaration.
1951
20 July   Assassination of King Abdallah of Jordan.
October   Israel rejects the UN peace plan accepted by Egypt, Syria, Lebanon and Jordan.
1952
The Free Officers take power in Egypt. Two years later, Nasser becomes the uncontested leader in Cairo.
1955
February   The Baghdad Pact is signed. Israeli attack on Gaza (28 February).
April   The Bandung Conference expresses support for 'the rights of the Palestinian people'.
1956
March   Nationalist pressure forces the dismissal of the British General, Glubb Pasha, in Jordan.
26 July   Nationalization of the Suez canal.
October/November   French, British and Israeli attack on Egypt.
1957
January   Exposition of the Eisenhower Doctrine.
1958
1 February   Egypt and Syria unite to form the United Arab Republic.
14 July   The Iraqi monarchy falls, triggering 'preventive' interventions by the British in Amman and by the Americans in Beirut.

1959

October   Fatah, recently established in Kuwait, holds its first Congress.

1961

28 September   Syria secedes from the UAR.

1962

September   Revolution in North Yemen.

1963

March   A military coup brings the Ba'ath to power in Damascus.

June   Levi Eshkol takes over from David Ben Gurion as head of the Israeli government.

1964

January   The Bourguiba plan for peace in Palestine is presented.

13–17 January   First summit meeting of Arab leaders in Cairo.

29 May   Creation of the Palestine Liberation Organization.

1965

1 January   First Fatah military operation against Israel.

After 1967

1967

5 June   Israel attacks Egypt, Syria and Jordan. Following a six-day lightning war, Israeli forces occupy Sinai, the Golan Heights, the West Bank, Gaza and East Jerusalem.

22 November   The UN Security Council adopts Resolution 242.

1968

21 March   The battle of Karameh between Israeli troops and Palestinians.

10–17 July   The fourth Palestine National Council meets and adopts the Palestine National Charter.

July   The Ba'ath seize power in Baghdad.

1969

1–4 February   The fifth Palestine National Council is held. Yasser Arafat becomes President of the Executive Committee of the PLO.

25 May   Numeiry takes power in Khartoum.

1 September   Qadhaffi takes power in Tripoli.

November   The Lebanese Government and the PLO sign the Cairo Accords, following numerous incidents in Lebanon.

1970

February   Major clashes between the PLO and the Jordanian Government.

30 May–4 June   The seventh Palestine National Council sets its sights on a democratic Palestine.

July   Nasser and Hussein accept the Rogers Plan based on the implementation of UN resolution 242.

September   Confrontation between the PLO and the Jordanian army. Black September.

28 September   Death of Nasser.

16 November   Hafez Al Assad takes power in Damascus.

1970—1971

The PLO is expelled from Jordan. The leadership of the Palestinian resistance moves to Lebanon.

1972

5—6 September   Murder of Israeli athletes during the Munich Olympic Games.

1973

April   Three key leaders of the PLO are assassinated by an Israeli team in Beirut. Major demonstrations expressing solidarity with the PLO are held in Lebanon.

August   The Palestine National Front is set up in the occupied territories.

6 October   Egyptian and Syrian troops attack Israeli forces. Beginning of the October or Yom Kippur war.

22 October   The Security Council adopts Resolution 338. The fighting stops a few days later.

26—28 November   Arab summit in Algiers. The PLO is recognized as the 'sole representative of the Palestinian people'. Jordan abstains when the vote on this motion is taken.

1974

At the twelfth Palestine National Council, the PLO accepts the idea of a national authority over 'any part of liberated Palestine'. A few weeks later, the Rejection Front is set up.

26—29 October   Arab summit in Rabat. Jordan rallies to the majority viewpoint and recognizes the PLO.

13 November   Yasser Arafat addresses the UN. The UN recognizes Palestinian rights to independence and self-determination. The PLO gains observer status.

1975

April   Beginning of the Lebanese Civil War.

1976

January   First Syrian armed intervention in Lebanon.

30 March   The Day of the Land in Galilee. Huge demonstrations are severely repressed and six Palestinians die.

April   The PLO handsomely wins the municipal elections in the West Bank.

June   Syrian troops in Lebanon mount a major offensive against the PLO and the Lebanese National Movement.

12 August   The Palestinian refugee camp at Tal Al Zatar finally surrenders, after a siege of 57 days.

6 September   The PLO is admitted as a full member of the Arab League

1977

10—20 March   The PLO holds its thirteenth Palestine National Council in Cairo. The idea of an independent Palestinian state in part of Palestine is accepted.

3—4 May   First official meeting between the PLO and the Israeli Communist party in Prague.
17 May   Begin wins the Israeli elections and becomes Prime Minister.
20 June   The European Summit in London recognizes 'the need for a home-land for the Palestinian people'.
1 October   Joint Soviet-American declaration on peace in the Middle East. The PLO endorses its proposals.
19—21 November   Sadat goes to Jerusalem.
2—5 December   The 'Steadfastness Front' is set up in Tripoli, bringing together Libya, Algeria, Syria, South Yemen and the PLO.
1978
14 March   Israel invades South Lebanon
17 September   The US, Israel and Egypt sign the Camp David Accords.
5 November   The Baghdad Arab Summit comes to an end, having con-demned the Camp David accords.
1979
February   Khomeini returns to Teheran.
26 March   Egypt and Israel sign a peace treaty in Washington.
6 July   Arafat, Brandt and Kreisky meet in Vienna.
1980
2 June   Attempts are made on the lives of three Palestinian mayors. The Mayors of Nablus and Ramallah are seriously wounded.
30 July   The Knesset votes through a fundamental law making 'reunited' Jerusalem Israel's capital.
September   Beginning of the Iran-Iraq war.
1981
June   Israeli attack on the Osirak nuclear reactor at Tamuz in Iraq.
July   Palestinian-Israeli war on the Lebanese frontier. Israeli bombardment of Beirut.
7 August   A peace plan is put forward by Prince Fahd, Crown Prince of Saudi Arabia.
6 October   Assassination of President Sadat.
1982
25 April   The Fez Arab Summit comes to a deadlock and is suspended *sine die*.
6 June   The Israeli invasion of Lebanon begins. A few days later, Beirut is under siege.
21 August   The PLO starts to evacuate Beirut, under the protection of the multinational force.
1 September   President Reagan presents his peace plan.
9 September   The final resolution of the Arab summit in Fez is adopted.
14—18 September   Bashir Gemayel is assassinated. The Israelis enter West Beirut. Hundreds of Palestinians are massacred in the refugee camps of Sabra

and Shatila. Leonid Brezhnev outlines his peace plan.

20 September King Hussein proposes a Jordanian-Palestinian Confederation.

21 September Amin Gemayel is elected president of Lebanon.

1983

January Arafat, Avneri and Peled meet in Tunis.

February The sixteenth Palestine National Council in Algiers adopts the Fez Plan and the Soviet proposals.

April Abortive negotiations between Arafat and King Hussein.

10 April Issam Sartawi is assassinated in Portugal while attending a Congress of the Socialist International.

17 May Israeli-Lebanese peace agreement.

25 May Beginning of dissidence within Fatah.

August—September The civil war starts up again in Lebanon. The Druze seize control of the Shouf mountains. In Israel, Begin resigns and is replaced by Shamir.

November The Syrians and their dissident Palestinian allies begin the siege of Tripoli.

24 November 6 Israeli soldiers are exchanged for nearly 1,500 Palestinian prisoners held by the Israelis.

20 December Yasser Arafat and 400 loyalists leave Tripoli in Greek ships under French protection.

22 December Meeting between Arafat and Mubarak.

1984

February In Lebanon, the Wazzan government resigns. West Beirut is taken by the Amal militia. Walid Jumblatt's Progressive Socialist Party fighters seize Mount Lebanon. The US marines leave Beirut, followed by the British and Italian contingents.

7 March Amin Gemayel abrogates the Israeli-Lebanese accords of 17 May 1983.

19 March The Shamir government falls after a vote of no confidence in the Knesset.

27 March Aden accords between Fatah, the PFLP, the DFLP and the PCP.

1 April The French contingent of the multinational force leaves Beirut.

1 May A national unity government is set up in Beirut.

24 July The result of the elections in Israel are so close that the two main parties are forced to form a national unity government, after several weeks of negotiations.

22—29 November The seventeenth Palestine National Council is held in Amman, without the participation of the DFLP, the PFLP, the PCP or the pro-Syrians. A week later, Yasser Arafat, re-elected President of the Executive Committee, is granted an audience with the Pope.

1985

January   The Falashas, the Jews of Ethiopia, are moved to Israel.

15 January   Israel announces the staged withdrawal of its troops from Lebanon.

11 February   In Amman, King Hussein and Yasser Arafat present a joint declaration, known as the Jordanian-Palestinian accords.

Further massacres at Sabra, Shatila and other Palestinian refugee camps, this time at the hands of the Amal militias.

6 April   Numeiry falls.

June   The Israelis complete their withdrawal from Lebanon, apart from a border area in the south controlled by the South Lebanese army led by the pro-Israeli General Lahad.

24 September   3 Israelis are assassinated in the port of Larnaca, in Cyprus.

1 October   The Israeli air force bombs the headquarters of the PLO in Tunis, killing seventy people.

7 October   The 'Achille Lauro' is hijacked. One person is killed.

23 November   An Egypt Air Boeing is hijacked and lands at Malta, where an assault by Egyptian security forces results in 60 deaths.

27 December   Terrorist attacks at Vienna and Rome airports.

1986

19 February   Palestinian-Jordanian negotiations fail to convince the PLO to accept resolution 242, for lack of US guarantees about the resistance movement's participation in the proposed international conference. King Hussein abrogates the Palestinian-Jordanian accords.

15 April   American raid on Tripoli and Benghazi, followed by European sanctions against Libya, accused by Washington of organizing anti-Western terrorism.

29 May   The Shi'ite Amal militia launches a new 'war of the camps' against the loyalist Palestinians.

September   A wave of terrorist attacks hits Paris. The trail seems to lead to Iran.

5 October   The London *Sunday Times* publishes revelations by the Israeli atomic physicist Vanunu, according to whom Israel has already made 100–200 atomic bombs. Vanunu is kidnapped and taken back to Israel where he is condemned to 18 years in prison — the maximum penalty being 20 years.

1987

22 February   The Syrian Army returns to West Beirut, which it had been forced to leave in 1982.

4 March   Ronald Reagan recognizes that the secret arms deliveries to Iran were a mistake and promises better collaboration with Congress. The Irangate scandal is at its height.

20–26 April   The PLO (Fatah, DFLP, PFLP, PCP) reunites in the course of the eighteenth Palestine National Council, which is held in Algiers.

1 June The Lebanese Prime Minister, Rashid Karamé, is killed by a bomb in his helicopter. Selim Hoss takes over.

31 July 475 people die in the clashes between Iranian pilgrims and the Saudi police in Mecca.

8—11 November The Arab Summit in Amman condemns Iran. The Palestinian question drops from the top of the agenda.

December In the occupied territories, first in Gaza, and then in the West Bank, the Palestinian *intifada* begins. The Israeli repression it encounters is condemned by the Security Council of the United Nations on 22 December.

1988

23 February During a tour of the Middle East, George Schultz launches his peace plan. It runs aground, vetoed by Israeli Prime Minister Itzhak Shamir.

9 April Mikhail Gorbachev receives Yasser Arafat in Moscow and urges the PLO to 'recognize the State of Israel and take its security interests into account'.

16 April An Israeli commando team assassinates the PLO second-in-command, Abu Jihad, in Tunis.

4 May Three French hostages are freed in Beirut.

7—9 June The Arab Summit in Algiers reaffirms its support for the PLO as the 'sole legitimate representative of the Palestinian people in their struggle to establish an independent Palestinian state', and calls for an international conference.

31 July King Hussein announces on television that he is breaking off his country's 'administrative and legal ties' with the West Bank, annexed by his grandfather, King Abdallah in 1950 and occupied by Israel since 1967.

August After eight years of war, Iran and Iraq call a cease-fire.

1 November Elections in Israel strengthen the hand of the religious parties. Itzhak Shamir remains prime minister of a national unity government formed in mid-December.

13-15 November The nineteenth Palestine National Council meets in Algiers. The PLO proclaims the State of Palestine, recognizes resolutions 181, 242 and 338, and reaffirms its condemnation of terrorism.

15 December The United States agrees to start 'substantive talks' with the PLO after Yasser Arafat has explicitly recognized the right of the State of Israel to exist and formally condemned all forms of terrorism.

1989

4 January—3 March Tension between Libya and the US.

14 March In Lebanon, General Aoun declares a 'war of liberation against Syria'. His forces clash with those of Syria and its allies repeatedly during the next 12 months.

7 April Itzhak Shamir presents his four point plan based on the holding of elections in the Occupied Territories.

2—4 May   Yasser Arafat visits Paris where he declares the Palestine National Charter 'caduque' ... no longer relevant.

30 June   In Sudan, General Omar Hassan El Bechir seizes power in a coup which significantly reinforces the grip of the Islamicists.

4 September   President Mubarak of Egypt presents his ten point proposal responding positively, but conditionally, to the Shamir Plan.

1—24 October   A meeting of Lebanese parliamentarians at Taef (Saudi Arabia) agrees a declaration of 'national understanding' envisaging constitutional reforms promoting greater power sharing between Christians and Muslims. The agreement was ratified on 5 November by the Lebanese parliament, which elected René Moawad as the ninth President of the Lebanese Republic at the same time. General Aoun opposed both decisions. On 22 November, René Moawad was killed by a car bomb in West Beirut. Two days later, the Parliament elected Elias Hraoui to replace him.

10 October   James Baker, the US Secretary of State, presents his five point plan, a synthesis of the Israeli and Egyptian proposals, aiming at a tripartite US, Israeli and Egyptian meeting to set up Israeli-Palestinian negotiations.

1990

January   Jewish emigration to Israel surges. From a figure of less than 15,000 in 1989 (itself a 580% increase over 1988), the Soviet *aliya* hits a record 50,000 for the first six months of 1990. The annual average could, from now on, settle at 150,000 new immigrants, according to the Jewish Agency. This would have serious consequences for Israeli society and the economy. Without the enormous financial resources needed to cope with this upsurge, the arrival of so many *olim* is bound to cause serious employment and housing problems.

February—March—April   In Lebanon, General Aoun's army clashes violently with the Christian militia of the Lebanese Forces. There are several thousand casualties.

15 March   The Labour Part in Israel, angered by Itzhak Shanmir's refusal to respond positively to the American proposal for negotiations, forces a vote of no-confidence in the Government through the Knesset. Shimon Peres having failed to form a government, Itzhak Shamir is once again sworn in on 11 June, this time at the head of government uniting the right, the far right and the religious parties. His first action is to reject the Baker Plan.

22 May   Proclamation of the Republic of Yemen, a fusion of the Northern and Southern Republics, with Sanaa as the capital.

20 June   After the attempted disembarkation of a Palestinian commando in Israel, George Bush announces the suspension of the US-Palestinian dialogue.

2 August   The Iraqi army enters Kuwait, which is annexed by Baghdad six days later. In the meantime, on the 6 August, the UN Security Council decrees an embargo on trade with Iraq, and on 7 August the US decides to send a full scale Armada to the Gulf.

List of Entries

xxi

THE POLITICAL MIDDLE EAST

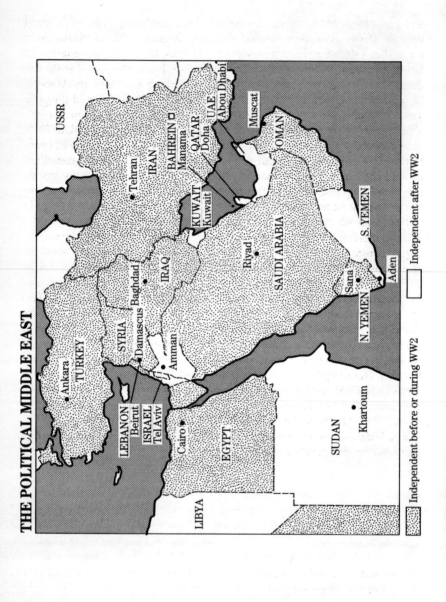

USSR

TURKEY
Ankara

SYRIA
Damascus

LEBANON
Beirut

ISRAEL
Tel Aviv

Amman

IRAQ
Baghdad

IRAN
Tehran

BAHREIN □
Manama

QATAR
Doha UAE
Abou Dhabi

KUWAIT
Kuwait

Muscat

OMAN

SAUDI ARABIA
Riyad

S. YEMEN

N. YEMEN
Sana

Aden

EGYPT
Cairo

LIBYA

SUDAN
Khartoum

Independent before or during WW2

Independent after WW2

Abu Nidal

SABRI AL BANNA (Abu Nidal) was born in Jaffa, in Palestine, in 1937, into a wealthy family possessing several thousand hectares of land. **Refugees** in **Gaza** after 1948, his parents later settled in Nablus. In 1960, Sabri emigrated to **Saudi Arabia**, where he worked as a technician. It was there he first became involved in political activities, first with the **Ba'ath**, then with Fatah. Arrested, he was tortured, then deported. After the **war of 1967**, he rejoined the *fedayeen* in Amman. He was sent by Fatah to Khartoum in 1969, then made representative of Yasser Arafat's organization and of the **PLO** in Baghdad, in 1970.

In 1974, he came out against the 'pragmatic' policy adopted by the PLO and in favour of pursuing an all-out struggle against Israel. He then seceded and created the Fatah Revolutionary Council which at that time drew on the support of Iraqi leaders. Since then, his Arab alliances have evolved according to circumstances; he has been supported in turn by **Iraq**, **Syria** and **Libya**.

The Fatah Revolutionary Council's influence has been limited, though it became more extensive after the **war of 1982**. The organization joined the Popular Front for the Liberation of Palestine, an amalgamation, in Damascus, of opponents of Yasser Arafat. But it is largely due to the efficiency of its terrorist cells that Abu Nidal's group has earned its international reputation. Its 'achievements' include the assassination of several PLO cadres: Said Hammami, Ezzedine Kalak and Issam **Sartawi**. It was also implicated in the Rue des Rosiers attack, in 1982, and the attack on the Istanbul synagogue, in September 1986. On November 8, 1987, the group boarded a ship off Gaza and took as hostage a French woman, Mme Valente, and her children — now released. The group has also been held responsible for the attacks on the *City of Porus* (July 1988) and a Pan Am Boeing 747 (December 1988). In October and November 1989, bloody internal conflicts seriously weakened the organization and in 1990, Abu Nidal left Libya for Baghdad, returning to its roots.

Abu Nidal has been condemned to death by the PLO, some of whose leaders claim that the group is heavily infiltrated by the Israeli intelligence services.

Aliya

THE 'ASCENT' — literal translation from the Hebrew — of the **Jews** into Palestine. After the Dispersion (*Diaspora*) resulting from the Roman crushing of the Bar Kokhba Revolt in 135 AD, the Jewish presence in Palestine remained, for many centuries, extremely limited. The tiny communities of **Jerusalem**, Safad, Tiberiade and Hebron existed, especially from the 18th century onwards, on the charity (*Haloukka*) of the scattered Jews. Towards the end of the 15th century, their ranks were swelled by the many Jews expelled from the Iberian Peninsula. In 1835, however, Palestine harboured only 10,000 Jews.

But, from being a religious idea, the renaissance of **Israel** gradually became a political objective. After the appeals of Napoleon, the Saint-Simonians and Lord Byron, the Zionist movement took up the idea. Even before Theodor **Herzl**, the Russian Leon Pinsker was imagining and organizing, with the Lovers of Zion, the new colonization of the biblical lands. Several *aliyot* were to achieve this.

To the 25,000 Jews — concentrated in Jerusalem, Hebron, Safad and Tiberias — still, in 1880, swamped by almost half a million Arabs, the first *aliya* brought reinforcements numbering 20 to 30,000, virtually all from the Tsarist Empire. The first agricultural enterprises came into being; these, along with the nineteen new settlements created by Baron Edmond Rothschild, were to harbour more than 5,000 pioneers. At the same time, the Jewish bourgeoisie was investing in Palestine, particularly in citrus fruits.

The second *aliya*, basically of Russians with socialist backgrounds, attracted 35 to 40,000 new immigrants between 1903 and 1914. Dozens of additional settlements came into being. Tel Aviv rose from the ground, and Jerusalem and Haifa expanded. Hebrew, once a literary and liturgical language, now became an everyday language. These central European Jews were joined by the first Yemenis, who replaced the Arab *fellaheen* in the agricultural projects; for the *kibbutzim*, the first of which was founded in Degania in 1911, were allowed to employ only Jewish workers. Thus, on the eve of World War I, there were about 80,000 Jews in Palestine — 2 to 3 million left Russia and Poland at the same time for Western Europe and the Americas.

Of the old Jewish communities and the first two *aliyot* there remained, in 1918, only 60,000 members in Palestine, that is to say 10% of the total population. The 'legalization' of immigration by the **Balfour Declaration** was to allow this proportion to triple in twenty years.

The cadence was slow at first. The third *aliya*, from 1919 to 1923, brought 35,000 Jews from the USSR, Poland and the Baltic countries, most of whom were socialists, workers and pioneers. In addition to these, the fourth *aliya*, from 1924 to 1931, with 82,000 participants, brought Jews from the Balkans and the Middle East who were, generally speaking, members of the middle class. By the end of 1931, 175,000 Jews, that is 17.7% of the total population, were present in the Holy Land.

It was the triumph of Nazism in Germany that was to stimulate Jewish immigration to the **Yishuv**, and totally alter its characteristics. From 1932 to

1939, the fifth *aliya* brought an additional 247,000 Jews, that is to say 30,000 a year, four times more than at any time since the end of World War 1. Stemming less from the Zionist option than a flight from the threats of Nazism, this new colonization was mainly German and middle class — the Zionist Organization had concluded a treaty with Berlin in 1933 authorizing the transfer of German Jewish capital.

By 1939, there were exactly 429,605 Jews in Palestine, constituting 28% of the total population. Despite the British blockade (see **Great Britain**), 118,338 others — this was the sixth *aliya* — joined them there between then and the declaration of independence on May 14, 1948. Among these were many survivors of the **holocaust**, often travelling in secret to avoid the tragic fate of the *Exodus*. Thus, when the State of Israel came into being, it comprised 650,000 Jewish citizens, a third of the inhabitants of Palestine.

This number was to increase five-fold over the next twenty-five years, due to the additional numbers brought by numerous, and massive, *aliyot*. These *aliyot*, however, differed greatly from the preceding ones, in the first place concerning the origins of the new Israelis: until the 1970s, the great majority were to be Jews from Africa and Asia.

The Soviet-American detente also encouraged the influx into Israel of Jews from the USSR. After reaching its apogee in 1979, this immigration was to dry up until the arrival in power of Mikhail Gorbachev. By the end of 1988, the rhythm of departures exceeded 3,000 a month. But the percentage of Soviet Jewish immigrants choosing Israel was still only 10 per cent or less, the rest preferring Western Europe or the **United States**.

In 1989, however, the situation changed. The United States made immigration by Soviet Jews much more difficult. On the other hand, the accelerating upheavals in the Eastern bloc, and especially the growing tension in the **Soviet Union**, caused great anxiety amongst the Jewish communities there. Furthermore, relations between Eastern Europe and Israel continued to improve. By early 1990, the number of Jews leaving the USSR for Israel had reached a record 10,000 plus a month, and the Israeli authorities were predicting 500,000, even a million new arrivals over the next few years. While this unprecedented wave of immigration may reinforce Israel in its struggle against the Palestinians and the Arab world, the integration of so many people into Israel poses serious social and economic problems which may well only be resolvable if the peace process comes to fruition.

American Aid

THE MIDDLE EAST has always held an important place in American aid, both civil and military, given its importance as a stake in US strategy.

To summarize a long period, extending from 1967 to 1981, this aid was mainly to the advantage of Israel, the beneficiary to the tune of 6 billion dollars of economic aid and 14.5 billion of military aid. Next comes Egypt with 5.9 and 2 billion, then, far behind, Jordan (1 and 1) and Iran (0.1 and 0.8).

This hierarchy, indicative of the priorities that have been established over the last two decades, including those reflected in the evolution of the region since the Camp David Accords, is also reflected in the distribution of basic American funds in 1988, according to official statistics:

3,000 million dollars to Israel (57.9% as against 48.5% in 1985),

2,116.5 million dollars to Egypt (40.87% as against 46.4%),

46,250 million dollars to Jordan (0.89% as against 2.6%),

13,150 million dollars to Oman (0.25% as against 1%),

2 million dollars to North Yemen (0.04% as against 0.7%),

0.375 million dollars to Lebanon (0.02% as against 0.8%).

In total, with more than 5 billion dollars, the countries of the Middle East, excluding Turkey, receive half the aid America allocates abroad. However, the pressing needs of an evolving Eastern Europe have led US leaders to re-examine these figures and consider a cutback of at least 5 to 10 per cent.

Arab

'ARAB' is used to designate an ethnic group (or a people) made up of individuals who speak one of the variations of the Arabic language, identify with the history and culture that have grown up since the emergence of the great Umayyad and Abbasid empires of the 12th century — one of whose main characteristics is adherence to Islam — and possess a sense of their Arab identity. Though close links exist between Arabs and Islam, the terms are not synonymous. The overwhelming majority of Muslims are not Arabs (but Indians, Pakistanis, Indonesians, etc.) and in Egypt, Lebanon, Syria, Iraq, etc. there are Christian Arabs.

The birthplace of the Arabs was the Arabian Peninsula. From there, they embarked on the conquest of the world in the name of Islam. Gradually, they were assimilated into the populations they dominated — large numbers of whom converted to the new faith — from whom they borrowed many of the traits of what has come to be known as Arabo-Muslim civilization. Today, the zone peopled by Arabs is, roughly speaking, that occupied by member states of the Arab League. Arab minorities continue to exist on the fringes of this area (Turkey, Black Africa, Israel), others have settled in Europe or

America as a result of migrations. Within Arab countries, pockets of non-Arabs remain: Kurds, Armenians, Berbers, etc.

The emergence of an Arab nationalism is recent and has been greatly influenced by European ideas. Between the 15th and 19th centuries, Arabs were content to be subjects of the **Ottoman Empire**, predominantly Turkish but Muslim. The decline of the Sublime Porte and the aggression of the Christian powers — who had conquered Arab countries such as Algeria and Egypt — provoked a crisis among Arab intellectuals. At the beginning of the 20th century, Al Kawakibi, a Syrian Muslim, called for the restoration of an Arab Caliphate. A Syro-Lebanese, Azury, took up these ideas, created a League of the Arab Fatherland and founded a review, *Arab Independence*. His disciple, Rabath, was to write: 'The old, archaic ideal of the Muslim community will gradually be supplanted, under the pressure of events, by the magnificent conception of the rediscovery of Arab unity and greatness.' Already the contradiction between 'Muslim solidarity' and 'Arab solidarity' exists. This explains why, originally, many propagandists of Arabism were Christians. However, it was not until World War I that Arab elites rallied to this new doctrine. The great Arab Revolt that arose in 1916 — in which Lawrence of Arabia won fame — allowed them to envisage in concrete terms the constitution of a united Arab kingdom. London and Paris would finally decide to divide the Middle East into separate states, but the Pan-Arab vision was to remain in the hearts of many nationalists. It must be stressed, however, that alongside this growing Arab nationalism (*Qawmiya*), a local patriotism (*Wataniya*), linked to specific states (Egypt, Tunisia, etc.), remained alive.

After World War II, in the struggle against the colonial presence, Arab nationalism expressed itself with renewed vigour. It acquired, with Ba'athism and Nasserism, a revolutionary character. The 'Arab Voice', broadcast from Cairo, mobilized the various peoples, from the Gulf to the Atlantic. The movement even resulted in Egypt and Syria forming a single state, the United Arab Republic (1958—1961). But this experience, like those of the formation of various federations, was to be short-lived and without sequel: differences existed that were very difficult to overcome. The defeat of June 1967 marked the end of the great dreams of unity. The ideology of Arab nationalism underwent a double attack. Palestinian nationalism — a 'local patriotism'! — and the *fedayeen* were to mobilize the Arab masses for more than ten years. The Islamic 'thrust' that established itself, particularly around the late 1970s, rejected all solidarity not founded on Islam. However, although the organizations calling for it are in profound decline, Pan-Arabism remains an indispensable point of reference in all political discussions in the Mashreq (the Middle East) and the Maghreb, one sign, amongst others, that it retains a great hold on Arab peoples and that it might well, in the near future, rise again from the ashes. The 1990 Gulf crisis is just one example.

Arab League

THE LEAGUE of **Arab** States was created on March 22, 1945, in Alexandria. **Egypt, Iraq, Lebanon, Saudi Arabia, Syria,** Transjordan and **Yemen** (North) stood as godparents at the organization's baptism. With the end of colonial domination, the League was enlarged and today numbers twenty members including Palestine; over and above the founder members are **Libya, Sudan,** Tunisia, Morocco, **Kuwait,** Algeria, South Yemen, the United Arab Emirates, Bahrain, Oman, Mauritania, Somalia and Djibouti, plus the **PLO** which has been a full member since 1976. The re-establishment of diplomatic relations between Cairo and the majority of the Arab states, at the end of 1987, favoured Egypt's return to the organization in May 1989.

The League's headquarters were transferred from Cairo to Tunis in 1979, after the signing of the Israeli-Egyptian peace treaty (see **Camp David Accords**). The secretary general is Chadhli Qleibi, a Tunisian — until 1979, the post was held by an Egyptian. Specialized standing committees have been set up (economy, culture, etc.; of particular importance is the political committee). The Defence Council (made up of foreign secretaries and defence ministers) and the Economic Council (composed of ministers of finance) meet under the aegis of the League. Since 1964, the date when they were officially instituted, the summits of the heads of state have been the supreme authority where conflicts are resolved and major decisions taken. The League has also created many specialized, autonomous agencies. Amongst others, there are the Arab Labour Organization, the Postal Union and the Telecommunications Union.

It was during World War II that the idea of a federation of Arab countries resurfaced. On May 29, 1941, Anthony Eden, British Foreign Secretary, stated in the House of Commons apropos the Arab world: 'It seems to me both natural and just that not only natural and economic links but also political links be reinforced. For its part, His Majesty's Government will give the greatest support to any plan that receives general approbation.' London was trying to gain the sympathies of the Arab countries. Its Hashemite allies of Amman and Baghdad were then trying to set up a unified state of the Fertile Crescent (which would include Palestine and Syria as well as their state). In opposition to this project and the Hashemite hegemony, the Egyptian monarchy initiated counter-measures that led to the meeting in Alexandria.

Although expressing, in a distorted way, the aspiration for Arab unity, the League has never been an instrument for implementing it. Its statutes do not stipulate making efforts in this direction and the various concrete attempts (such as the creation of the United Arab Republic, in 1958) have been made outside the League, which is governed by the rule of unanimity. The organization has above all helped to coordinate the actions of the Arab regimes, particularly on the Palestinian question. It is in this domain that the most significant decisions have been taken: creation of the **PLO** (1964); recognition of the PLO as sole representative of the Palestinian people (1973—1974); adoption of the **Fez Plan** (1982). However, the Gulf crisis in 1990 split and possibly jeopardized the future of the organization.

Arabian Peninsula

CRADLE of the **Arab**-Islamic civilization and **oil** centre of the modern world, the Arabian Peninsula comprises eight states, four of which, **Saudi Arabia**, **Kuwait**, and the two **Yemens**, are listed as separate entries to which the reader may refer. The present entry will therefore give only a brief survey of the remaining four: Bahrain, Qatar, the United Arab Emirates and Oman.

But before examining each of them individually, a few common characteristics, over and above their Arabness, deserve our attention. There is first the fact that they all possess, albeit in varying quantities and qualities, a similar resource: oil. In 1988, 22% of world production, 40% of exports and 62% of reserves were concentrated here. Across the 800 km of the Gulf (470 km at its widest, but only 50 km at its narrowest — the Straits of Hormuz) there still passes 20% of the industrialized world's oil supplies, even if the area is no longer the lungs of the West. This explains the boom experienced by the region's states from the mid-1970s — much earlier for Saudi Arabia and Kuwait — and also the already harsh repercussions of the oil recession in the mid-1980s, and of course the still crucial importance of the zone for the great powers, especially the **United States**.

Until recently, all the states of the peninsula, with the exceptions of Saudi Arabia and North Yemen, were colonies or protectorates of **Great Britain**, installed in the 19th century to pacify all routes to India. The security imposed by the British was based on a simple principle: discourage any project on the part of a state to establish supremacy by encouraging the parcelling up of the region into emirates constituting so many fragile protectorates, of which London, for its own benefit, consolidated the economic bases and state structures. But, a century later, the collapse of its empire and the crisis in its finances led the United Kingdom to disengage; the decision, taken by a Labour government in 1968, was applied on December 1, 1971 by a Conservative government.

'The departure of the British', wrote Raoul Delcorde in *La Sécurité et la stratégie dans le golfe arabo-persique*, 'caused disturbances in the balance of the Gulf and, to fill the gap, two solutions presented themselves: either that one sufficiently strong state take it upon itself to maintain order in the region (which would imply the agreement of the other states) while itself being supported by a great power, or that each state equip itself with a military capacity and an internal cohesion sufficient to guarantee its own security. But facts can prove obstinate: the divisions and troubles that arose on the Arab side of the Gulf and the Soviet presence in Iraq necessarily led to the emergence of a new centre of power, Iran.'

The United States was then bogged down in the Vietnam War. Rather than commit itself militarily elsewhere in the world, it preferred to back the puppet regimes. In the region, the obvious candidate was the Shah. Unlike Saudi Arabia, the other candidate for supremacy in the zone, **Iran** possessed the human means necessary to become the pivot of the American policy of containment of the **Soviet Union** in the region whose importance for the Western economy had been underlined by the Yom Kippur **War of 1973**. Admittedly there was a long-standing rivalry between Persians and Arabs here. But Tehran took advantage of events to sieze the upper hand: though it accepted the independence Bahrain was demanding, it occupied militarily, on the eve of the British departure — and therefore with their complicity — the islands of Abu Musa and the two Tumbs, the keys to the Straits of Ormuz. And it was the Shah's army that crushed the popular guerilla movement in Oman. Despite the fears of **Egypt**, Kuwait, Saudi Arabia and, of course **Iraq**, Iran set itself up as the policeman of the Gulf. In fact, it was in response to the latter's expansionism that the Federation of the United Arab Emirates was formed, which Bahrain and Qatar refused to join, however. Saudi Arabia, while sharing the Shah's hostility towards the threat of both the Soviets and the Arab nationalists, undertook to safeguard its own interests.

The United States, once extricated from the Vietnamese deadlock, tended to involve itself more and more directly in the zone, increasing its imports of hydrocarbons from the Gulf and attracting the main share of the petrodollars, not to mention their fabulous arms sales — Iran alone bought from them, between 1972 and 1976, over ten billion dollars worth. But, in 1978–1979, the Islamic Revolution changed everything. The main outpost of American policy disappeared. Iranian supremacy took on a revolutionary aspect. The sizeable Shi'ite (see **Shi'ism**) minority redoubled unrest in the Emirates. In 1979, even the Saudi regime fell victim to fundamentalist riots from which it narrowly escaped, mainly due to the help of French soldiers (see **fundamentalism**). This was why America decided to reorganize its military disposition, notably with the creation of the **Rapid Deployment Force**.

In order to confront any 'attempt by an external power to take control of the Persian Gulf region', which President Carter considered to be 'an attack against vital American interests', the State Department undertook to guarantee the Pentagon a chain of bases and military 'facilities': Morocco, Turkey, Egypt, Diego Garcia in the Indian Ocean, Oman, Somalia and Kenya. The **Gulf War** between Iraq and Iran, from 1980, would test the newly established system. Whilst the United States, like the USSR, proved to be totally incapable of preventing the massacre, the Emirates feared a possible extension of the conflict. Tehran did not hesitate, furthermore, to apply strong pressure on them, both from outside and — via the Shi'ite minority — from inside. Closely linked to Washington, whose growing intervention they encouraged but with whom they could not openly ally themselves given America's support of **Israel**, the region's leaders agreed to implement an old Saudi project long deferred: the Gulf Cooperation Council (GCC).

The organization, officially formed in May 1981 and composed of Saudi Arabia and the five other emirates (but not the two Yemens), went beyond the idea of a mere Common Market evoked in the 1970s. In economic terms, the GCC coordinates the industrial policies of the countries concerned by preparing them for the post-petrol period; building sites have sprung up and integration is advancing by leaps and bounds. But, politically, it also attempts to eliminate the principal factors tending to destabilize the region's regimes: differences between member states that it tries to resolve peacefully, the Israeli-Arab conflict in which the GCC intervened in favour of a political solution to the Palestinian problem and, above all, the Iraq-Iran confrontation on which it adopted a tougher position after the entry of Iranian forces into Iraqi territory during the summer of 1982.

The 1990 Gulf crisis triggered by Iraq's invasion of Kuwait may well have opened a new chapter in the history of the peninsula. The US is not hiding its desire for a permanent military presence in the area. It is as if Saddam Hussein had given the US a chance to revive the abortive 1955 Baghdad Pact, but this time with Iraq as the enemy. In the meantime the Soviet Union has established diplomatic relations with Oman (September 1985), the United Arab Emirates (November 1985) and Qatar (August 1988), military and financial agreements with Kuwait, bank loans from the Gulf, etc. Even Saudi Arabia announced, in September 1990, the forthcoming reopening of a Soviet embassy.

Bahrain is composed of thirty-three islands with a total surface area of 1,000 square kilometres, but its population (less than 500,000 inhabitants, of whom 200,000 are foreigners) is concentrated into two of these: Bahrain itself and Al Muharraq. From its two centuries of Persian domination, before the British colonization, it retains a sizeable minority proclaiming its Iranian origins, speaking Persian and firmly attached to Shi'ism. Tehran had tried to annex Bahrain when, in 1968, London gave up its protectorate, but the conference organized in 1970 under the control of the UN ended in independence, proclaimed in August 1971. The island's life has been characterized by chronic political agitation and by the presence of opposing forces, left-wing and Muslim extremist. The dissolution, in 1975, of the Assembly elected two years previously — a sign, at the time, of a fumbling attempt to democratize this absolute monarchy — and the uncovering of an 'Iranian plot' in 1981 strengthened the regime's repressive character.

The decrease in oil production, which had begun in the 1930s, led Bahrain to diversify early on: apart from traditional activities (fishing and pearls), the country equipped itself with a huge aluminium factory and a petrochemical complex; since the Lebanon **War (of 1982)**, the capital, Manama, has become the principal financial power in the region; it also possesses an airport and a seaport equipped with a dry dock. But the Gulf War curbed this boom. Since 26 November 1986, Bahrain has been linked to Saudi Arabia by a bridge 25 kilometres long.

Qatar, with a surface area of 11,000 square kilometres, most of it desert, is inhabited, according to the census of 1986, by 372,000 people, 217,000 of whom live in the capital, Doha, and 70% of whom are foreigners (Iranians, Asians and other Arab countries) — the oil recession has already caused the departure of several thousand of them. From being an economy based on animal husbandry, fishing and pearls, Qatar leapt, with the exploitation of its hydrocarbons, to a high level of development: refineries, petrochemistry, cement factories, steel-works, communication networks on both land and sea, health and education systems, etc. The political life of the country, independent since 1971, takes the form of internal struggles within the ruling Al Thani family. Ahmed Ibn Ali was supplanted in 1972 by his cousin and Prime Minister, Khalifa Ibn Hamad, who, in 1977, named his son Hamad Ibn Khalifa as crown prince.

The Federation of United Arab Emirates was, on the eve of its independence (1971), meant to combine all the emirates of the one-time Pirate Coast. But Qatar and Bahrain having turned down the offer, it numbers only seven members: Abu Dhabi, Dubai, Sharjah, Ras Al-Khaima, Umm Al-Qaiwain, Ajman and Fujaira — a total of 84,000 square kilometres and 1.4 million inhabitants, of whom almost 80% are foreigners. The massive influx of Arab immigrants, but also of Pakistanis and Indians, is obviously explained by the oil boom of the 1970s, which made the United Arab Emirates one of the richest countries in the world.

Its political life nonetheless remains troubled by power struggles between emirates, notably those between Abu Dhabi, whose emir, Sheikh Zayed, is president of the Federation, and Dubai, whose emir, Sheikh Rashid, occupies the post of prime minister. Thus its provisional Constitution (from absolute monarchy) has regularly been extended since its adoption in 1971, when agreement could not be reached on a definitive text. Similarly, the dissolution of the armed forces of each emirate and their fusion into a single army, the cause of numerous crises, has not been accomplished. In June 1987, Sharjah was shaken by a *coup d'état* against the Emir, Sheikh Sultan, overthrown by his brother until pressure from the other emirates and Saudi Arabia reinstated the Emir and made his brother the crown prince and vice-governor. The emirates, like many others, had a bone to pick with Iran, which had forcibly annexed the larger Tumb, whose position in the heart of the Gulf had proved strategic.

At the entrance of the Gulf proper, *Oman*, former Sultanate of Muscat and Oman, stretches over an area of 300,000 square kilometres — including Dhofar, pacified in 1975 following lengthy fighting led by the Oman forces, backed by Saudi Arabia and a strong contingent of Iranian soldiers, against the Popular Front for the Liberation of Oman supported by South Yemen. The country being essentially desert, with mountains reaching over 3,000 metres, it is in the capital, Muscat, and along the narrow coastline that one finds most of its 1.3 million inhabitants, of whom 20% are Pakistanis, Indians and Iranians — though here, too, many of the latter were obliged to leave by to the oil recession. From the beginning of the 1960s, oil had given Sultan Qabus — who came to power in 1970 after ousting his father, Ibn Taimur — the means of modernizing an extremely backward country: the development of petroleum derivative industries, construction of seaports and airports, the development of infrastructure and public services. However, the regime has undergone little democratization, with the exception of the timid creation, in 1981, of an Advisory Council.

Inter-state conflicts weigh heavily on relations between the Gulf monarchies, no doubt because every square kilometre is rich in oil. One can distinguish between 'major conflicts' and smaller, less important disputes that nonetheless lead to political splits. In the first category, the struggle between Iraq and Iran over the Shatt Al Arab, which served as the pretext for Iraq's August 1990 invasion of Kuwait; the Iranian demands for Bahrain followed by Iran's occupation of three small islands belonging to the United Arab Emirates in the Straits of Hormuz; not to mention the difficulties emerging from the delimiting of the frontiers between Iraq, Iran, Kuwait and Saudi Arabia. Mention could also be made of the major dispute between Saudi Arabia and Yemen over the Saudi provinces of Asir and Najran in the north and over the border lines in the south.

In the second category, in 1986 a minor war between Bahrain and Qatar concerned the control of the island of Fasht Al Dibel; the two countries also disputed the Hawar Islands, and Bahrain demanded a coastal zone of Qatar. Abu Dhabi, Qatar and Saudi Arabia fought over the zone of Khaur Al Ubaiyid; more important was the United Arab Emirates' claim to the Mussadam Cape, which controls the Straits of Hormuz and which belongs to

Oman, although separated from it physically. Various territorial conflicts engage the rival monarchs of the United Arab Emirates. Finally, mention should be made of the battle of the oasis of Buraimi between Saudi Arabia, Oman and Abu Dhabi, a conflict that goes back to the 1950s and was only partially resolved in 1974.

All these antagonisms which, from a distance, resemble something from musical comedy, play an important role in defining the relations between the Gulf countries and often express diplomatic and economic differences — within OPEC for example — and the obstinate mutual mistrust between states united by a similar ideological vision.

Arafat (Yasser)

BORN on August 24, 1929, in Cairo, where most of his childhood was spent, Yasser Arafat is nonetheless Palestinian and related, on his father's side, to the powerful Al Hussein family, who played an important political role in Jerusalem during the period of the British Mandate. He gave up Cairo University, in 1948, to take part in the fighting in Palestine. He was disarmed by Arab troops who invaded the country after the proclamation of the State of Israel: a memory he was to carry forever. After the defeat, he took refuge in Gaza, then returned to Cairo in 1950 to continue his studies, which qualified him to become a public works engineer.

It was in the Egyptian capital that he met the men with whom he was to found the Fatah, and who would become his right-hand men in the leadership of the PLO: Khalil Al Wazir (Abu Jihad) and Salah Khalaf (Abu Iyad). Together, they were active in the Palestinian Students Union — Yasser Arafat was president from 1952 to 1956 — and edited a magazine, *The Voice of Palestine*. Arafat was arrested and jailed for several days in October 1955, at the time of Nasser's liquidation of the Muslim Brothers organization (although Arafat was not a member of it). During the Suez War of 1956, he fought as a sub-lieutenant in the Egyptian army.

It was in the Nile Valley that the first foundations of what was to become the Fatah doctrine were shaped: a decided mistrust of Arab leaders who refused to arm the Palestinians and hoped to keep them under strict control; a profound belief in armed struggle, for which the guerilla campaign mounted at Gaza in 1956-1957 against Israeli troops, which he helped coordinate with Abu Jihad, served as a model.

Threatened again with being arrested, Arafat (whose *nom de guerre* was

Abu Ammar) — settled in **Kuwait**, one of the few countries where, despite the British Protectorate that lasted till 1961, Palestinians enjoyed a certain freedom of action. It was there, in 1959, that he founded the Fatah (the name made up of the Arabic initials of Movement for National Liberation) and published *Our Palestine*. The central point of this new organization's doctrine stipulated that the liberation of Palestine was primarily the business of Palestinians, and should not be entrusted to Arab regimes or postponed until the establishing of some problematic Arab unity. This doctrine, at the time of all-conquering Pan-Arabism, virtually amounted to heresy. However, the failure of the United Arab Republic and the dissolution of the Syro-Egyptian alliance in 1961 strengthened Fatah's ideas.

The victory of the Algerian Revolution, in 1962, confirmed Arafat's belief in the soundness of the principle 'rely on your own strength'. Preparations for armed struggle were accelerated and, on January 1, 1965, the first military operation against Israel took place. But Fatah, a movement without ideological references, had difficulty asserting its authority. It was condemned by virtually all the Arab governments. Even the Ba'athist Syrian regime, usually prompt to help the organization, was quick to condemn its militants; thus Arafat was imprisoned in May, 1966. It was not until after 1967, with the defeat of the Arab regimes, that the *fedayeen* became the focus of Palestinian mobilization.

Two days after the end of hostilities, a Fatah congress was held in Damascus. After lengthy debate, it was decided, at Yasser Arafat's instigation, to take up armed struggle again. He went several times into the occupied **West Bank** to this end. He also established his first contacts with **Nasser** (November 1967) whose help was to be decisive to him. On March 21, 1968, he took part in the Battle of Karameh (Jordan) where Palestinian commando units confronted the Israeli Defence Forces (IDF). This battle, which demonstrated the determination of the Palestinians and had repercussions throughout the Arab world, was to give Fatah and Arafat the authority necessary to take over the reins of the old, ailing PLO. In February, 1969, the latter was revived and a new executive committee elected. Yasser Arafat became president. From this moment, his life became inextricably linked with that of the PLO.

Arms (sales of)

THE MIDDLE EAST has long been the number one client of those selling arms to the Third World. But its share of the market has increased since the

Arab-Israeli conflict and the other conflicts of which it was, and in some cases still is, the theatre. The **Iraq-Iran** war (see **Gulf War**), in particular, accelerated and diversified this escalation in arms purchases. Over and above the increase in conventional weapons, it has opened up two new and alarming categories: **missiles** and chemical weapons. In total, from 1971 to 1985, the region has consumed 45.9% of all arms sold to the Third World. For the arms dealers, it is at once an economic, political and strategic affair — although, as events have shown, in the cases of **Egypt** and Iran, influence born out of military cooperation can prove precarious.

In the total of heavy weapons imported by the Third World, the Middle East's share went, from the late 1960s to the 1970s, from a little over 30% to almost 45%, way ahead of Africa (16% to 22%), the Far East (31% to 13%), Latin America (8% to 11%) and South Asia (14% to 9%). Today the proportion is over 50%.

On the other hand, statistics showing how the principal dealers cut up the cake are less easy to come by. The **Soviet Union** remains the principal supplier, with a great quantity of arms being supplied to several countries: a little over a third of the Middle East market. Another third of the market is taken up by the **United States**, whose clients, less greedy, are much more numerous. In overall terms, the shares of the United States and the USSR in arms sales to the Middle East fell from 86% in the period 1971–1975 to 66% during 1981–1985. This was because other suppliers had appeared on the scene. In particular, there was **Great Britain**, back in full swing after signing its 'contract of the century' with **Saudi Arabia**: in 1987 and 1988 it delivered, amongst other things, 110–130 Tornado aeroplanes, 90 Hawks and 30 Pilatus DC–9s, 80 Blackhawk helicopters and 6 Sandown minesweepers, all in exchange for 400,000 barrels of oil a day. The region also accounts for almost two-thirds of **France**'s arms sales. But new competitors now challenge the old ones, from both the communist side (China, North Korea) and within the Third World (Argentina, Brazil).

Out of the ten major Third World importers from 1971 to 1985, seven were from the Middle East: Iraq (8%), Iran (7.7%), **Syria** (7.2%), Egypt (7.2%), **Libya** (7.1%), then — after India (6%) — **Israel** (5.3%) and Saudi Arabia (4.3%) — followed by Vietnam (3.1%) and Argentina (2.5%).

Each supplier has its 'portfolio'. From the American side, Israel is slightly ahead of Saudi Arabia, followed by Egypt, the United Arab Emirates and **Lebanon** — five Middle Eastern countries amongst the eleven foremost buyers of American arms. Major contracts are also under discussion (but blocked by Congress) with **Jordan**. From the Soviet side, the major buyers have been Libya, Syria and Iraq, followed by South **Yemen** and, recently, certain of the Gulf states, notably North Yemen and **Kuwait**. Jordan, too, has signed contracts with Moscow. As for France, it does its best business with

Iraq and Saudi Arabia, but also has outlets in Egypt, the Gulf, **Lebanon**, and even, it is now known, in Libya. For its part, China deals with Saudi Arabia, Syria, Libya and, of course, Iran.

The war between Iran and Iraq created a new, bitterly contested market: if Iraq, over and above its traditional Soviet and French suppliers, like the Arab countries, deals with Austria, Belgium, Brazil, Chile, North Korea, Spain, Hungary, Italy, Morocco, Poland, Portugal, GDR, FRG, Switzerland, Czechoslovakia and Yugoslavia, Iran has been able to procure arms from Algeria, Argentina, Brazil, Chile, North and South Korea, Great Britain, **Israel**, Libya, Syria, Taiwan and Vietnam.

Irangate revealed how the United States and Israel delivered arms to Tehran in order to obtain the release of hostages, gain the favour of 'moderates' there, and subsidize the Nicaraguan Contras. From 1980 to 1988, 53 countries sold the two belligerents 50 billion dollars' worth of military equipment, a fifth of the arms sold to the Third World during this period. The war over, Iraq and Iran themselves are now trying to re-sell part of their provisions, even if it means slashing prices.

The diversity of sources of supply of most Middle East countries — with the exception, basically, of Israel, Syria and South Yemen — stems also from the various trump cards held by each seller. In modern tanks, the USSR offers its T—72 and soon perhaps its T—80, France its AMX—30 and 30 B 2, the FRG its Leopard, and the United Kingdom its Chieftain. The French and the Americans offer self-propelled guns and 150 or 203 mm mortars, the USSR has a 240 mm version. In the domain of **missiles** — see the alphabetical listing for more details — the race is on between, on the one hand, Israel, and on the other, Syria, Iraq, Egypt, Saudi Arabia and Libya. Competition is fierce, on this level, between the American Lance, the Israeli Jericho II, the Soviet FROG 7, Scud—B and SS—21, the Chinese M—9, CSS—2 and Silkworm. As for chemical weapons, used by Iraq against Iran and against the **Kurds**, they could have been manufactured by Iran, Israel, Syria, Libya and, possibly, Egypt.

In the air, supremacy belongs to the American electronic surveillance plane AWACS E3—Sentry, the British Hawk and Tornado, the French Mirage F—1, 2000 and 4000, the American F—15, F—16 and FIA 18, the Soviet Mig—23, Mig—25, Mig—27, Mig—29 and Sukhoi—22, 24 and 25. In matters of air defence, it is the USSR, with its SAM—2, 5, 6, 8, 9 and 11 (supplied to Syria) which has the edge, but the United States offer their Hawk and the famous Stinger. Helicopters are one of France's strengths, with its Gazelle, its Puma, its Dauphin and its Alouette, despite competition from the Anglo-American Blackhawk. At sea, the United States, the USSR, France, Great Britain and Italy share the market.

However, arms imports into the Middle East decreased as a result of the development of independent local arms industries. This is particularly true of Israel, which manufactures, amongst other things, its own machine pistol (the Uzi), its own assault rifles (the Galil), its own tanks (Merkava), aircraft (Kfir, plus helicopters and transport planes), missiles (AIM 9—L and AIM 7), patrol boats (OSA, Komar, Reshef and Alya), etc. Not only does Israel equip its own army, it also sells its arms to countries like South Africa, Argentina, Ecuador, Guatemala, Haiti, Honduras, Kenya, Liberia, Salvador and Venezuela. Israel has thus become the world's fifth leading arms exporter, with total annual proceeds estimated at a billion dollars, almost 15% of the country's total exports. Egypt, over and above assembling the Mirage 2000, the Alpha-Jet trainer, and the Chinese F—7 fighter, produces a missile with a 700 km range in cooperation with Argentina and Iraq.

According to the statistics for 1986 in *The Military Balance 1988—1989* (The International Institute for Strategic Studies, London), in percentages of gross national product devoted to defence, Iraq leads (31.7%), just ahead of Iran (30.4%), followed by Oman (28.4%). Next comes Saudi Arabia (22.4%), then Israel (18.9%), Jordan (15.5%), Syria (14.5%), and North Yemen (12.5%). Last, in a bunch finish, come the Emirates (8.8%), Egypt (8.3%) and Kuwait (8.1%). Libya spends only 6.8% and Bahrain 3.4%.

For Nadia Benjelloun-Ollivier, 'there is a decided gap between Israel and its traditional enemies, the former forging ahead alone, probably using a different yardstick to measure its strength than that hitherto, given a strategy that is no longer entirely defensive or that combines defence and supremacy'. The great powers' passing on of their most up-to-date technology in conventional matters, increasing the suppliers' hold over their clients, also increases — notes the analyst — the advantage possessed by Israel, more independent, thanks to its own arms manufacturing industry. In short, she concludes, 'surrounding Israel, the Arab powers no longer constitute a real threat'.

The 1988 edition of *Report on the Balance of Power in the Middle East*, published each year in Israel, without denying this 'qualitative advantage' of the Jewish state, nonetheless notes that it 'has been reduced' due to Arab acquisition of missiles, aircraft, tanks and chemical weapons.

Assad (Hafez Al)

BORN on October 6, 1930, at Kardaha in northern **Syria**, Hafez Al Assad belongs to the Alawite minority — a sect of Shi'ite origin (see **Shi'ism**), considered by many Muslims to be heterodox, members of which are to be found only in **Lebanon** and, above all, Syria, where they represent slightly over 10% of the population. Assad grew up in a family of well-to-do peasants. His secondary education took place at the *lycée* in Al Lattakieh. During this period, he belonged to the **Ba'ath** party and took part in student demonstrations against the French occupation. In 1952, he entered the military college at Homs where he met Mustapha Tlass, the current minister of defence. A fighter pilot, he did several training courses in the **Soviet Union** before being sent to **Egypt** during the ephemeral United Arab Republic (1958—1961). There, along with several other Syrian officers, amongst whom was Salah Jedid, he formed the Ba'athist Military Committee which was largely instrumental in bringing the Ba'ath to power in Damascus in 1963.

Appointed Commander-in-Chief of the air force in 1965, the following year he helped Salah Jedid to eliminate the regime in power, judged to be too right-wing. But as head of the air force and Minister of Defence, he was quick to oppose the radicalization imposed by Salah Jedid as well as his adventurism. Thus, during the events of September 1970 (**Black September**) in Jordan, he refused to supply air cover to Syrian tanks trying to give assistance to the **PLO**. Internal squabbles intensified and, on November 16, 1970, a *coup d'état* carried Assad to the presidency of the Council. In the months that followed, he was elected Secretary General of the Ba'ath Party, then President of the Republic.

In a few years, Assad consolidated a power which became authoritarian and depended on the army and the defence brigades — a Praetorian guard led by his brother Rifa'at. He has been behind all the major decisions taken since 1970: participation in the October **War of 1973**, negotiations with **Kissinger** in 1974—1975, intervention in Lebanon in 1976, rejection of the **Camp David Accords** in 1978. A formidable enemy, possessed of an iron will, he also knows how to be flexible when necessary; the vicissitudes of his relations with his neighbours, or with the White House, give ample proof of this. In domestic affairs, he has pitilessly eliminated all opposition, including that within the Ba'ath Party and the army.

In November 1983, after a serious cardiac attack which kept him out of public life, a war of succession took place between his brother Rifa'at and the generals of the army, amongst whom was Shafik Fayyad. After a period of unrest and armed clashes, the return of Assad — who temporarily exiled the protagonists — brought an end to the discord. The president took advantage of the situation to reorganize power, undermine the strength of his brother — who, after having been appointed vice-president alongside Abdel Halim Khaddam, Minister of Foreign Affairs responsible for the Lebanese portfolio, was once again exiled — and confirm his supremacy at the 8th Party Congress in January 1985. But it was to be a precarious victory: physically burnt out, surrounded by aides who, with an eye to succeeding him, are concerned above all with enlarging their circle of followers, Hafez Al Assad seems unable to impose an ambitious strategic project on his country.

President Assad leads an austere life, in contrast with the corruption that has largely set in inside the corridors of power, despite regular campaigns aimed at raising the moral standard.

Ba'ath

THE BA'ATHIST MOVEMENT (from the Arabic word *ba'ath*, renaissance) was created in Damascus in the 1940s by the Orthodox Christian, Michel Aflak and the **Sunni**, Salah Al Din Bitar.

The party's first congress was held in 1947 in the Syrian capital. In 1953, it merged with Akram Hourani's **Arab** Socialist Party and took the name Arab Ba'ath Socialist Party. It was the first to consider the Arab world as a whole as its field of action, and regional sections were created in Transjordan (1948), **Lebanon** (1949–1950) and **Iraq** (1951) But the Syrian region remained the most substantial. It reached its peak in the 1960s, and became, along with Nasserism, one of the principal expressions of revolutionary Arab nationalism.

An extremely ideological party, the Ba'ath adopted as its watchword 'Unity, liberation, socialism'. Arab unity is at the centre of its doctrine and has priority over all other aims. According to its founder, Michel Aflak, the Arab peoples form a single nation aspiring to form a state and play a unique role in the world. Secular in sensibility — it rejects the denominational or confessional division of seats in the Syrian parliament (see **confessionalism**) — it nonetheless accepts the role **Islam** has played as a constituent element of Arabism. The call to socialism in the 1950s remained vague, and the Ba'ath came out in favour of a pluralist democracy and free elections. Lastly, the Palestinian question is far from being the central point of its ideology, if it concerns the Ba'ath at all.

The Ba'ath very quickly came to the fore in political life in **Syria**, where military and civilian leaders succeeded one another in power after independence. But the turning point in the party's history dates from 1958 and the creation of the United Arab Republic (UAR) by **Egypt** and Syria. The Ba'ath, who shared **Nasser**'s analysis of Arab and international politics, agreed to dissolve its Syrian branch. Its members were involved in decision making but, increasingly marginalized, resigned from office at the end of 1959. The self-dissolution of the organization, followed by the collapse of the UAR in September 1961, provoked a long internal crisis. This grew worse even when the party came to power in Iraq in February 1963 and in Syria in March of the same year.

Following long periods of clandestine existence, a change took place in the ideology and the very organization of the party. It stepped up its attacks against liberal democracy, and the military element played an increasingly important role in the machinery of the organization. Demands were put forward that were socialist in character. Above all, the failure of the UAR caused certain cadres to question the dogma of Arab unity. In Syria, those referred to as regionalists — Dr Atassi, Hafez Al Assad, Salah Jedid — as opposed to the nationalists, in favour of an Arab plan, increasingly affirmed their control following the Ba'ath's coming to power in 1963 and then, by a *coup d'état*, expelled their Ba'athist rivals from power in February 1966. The party's founders, including Michel Aflak, were forced into exile. Two separate Pan-Arab leaderships, each with regional branches, were established: one in Damascus, the other in Baghdad (after the Ba'ath took power in July 1968). The initial ideological differences grew blurred, to be succeeded by bitter political antagonism. The two parties were now transformed into political instruments of the state.

Paradoxically, it was at the height of its power, with the leadership of two major states, that Ba'athism began to decline as an ideology. The defeat of 1967 had exacerbated the crisis of Pan-Arabism, and there was a swing towards, firstly, supporting the Palestinian resistance, then towards Islamicization. The regional policies of Iraq and Syria, dictated by state interests, attracted no great following in the Arab world. However, Ba'athism has made its own mark on domestic politics, with the application of socialist measures (or rather the establishment of state capitalism) and a degree of secularization.

Balfour Declaration

THE NAME given to the letter of November 2, 1917, in which Lord Arthur James Balfour, British Foreign Secretary, made it known to Lord Walter Rothschild, the representative of British Jewry, that 'His Majesty's Government views with favour the establishment in Palestine of a national home for the Jewish people' — the full text can be found in Appendix 1. This document represents the reopening, for the first time since the Roman crushing of the last Jewish rebellion, in 135 AD, of the idea of a Jewish state in the Holy Land. 'One nation', Arthur Koestler was to write, 'solemnly promised a second nation the territory of a third.'

The reasons that brought **Great Britain** to this agreement involved both long- and short-term factors.

In the short term, London, in the throes of a world war, hoped to improve its position by conciliating the Zionist movement which, since its creation in 1897, had grown in power and influence within the Jewish communities of Europe and America. The promise of a 'national home', thought British strategists, might turn the **Jews** into a trump card: in Palestine where they would support Allenby's troops, in the **United States** where they would bring their weight to bear in favour of entering the war against the central empires, in Germany and Austro-Hungary where they would break away from their government, and in Russia where they would slow down the radicalization of the revolution — many Bolshevik and Menshevik leaders were of Jewish origin — and would prevent the defection of the oriental ally.

But Britain's aims went beyond mere contingency. Obsessed by the security of its colonial system, it feared the ascendancy of a major European power in Palestine — **France**, obviously — who 'so close to the Suez Canal would be a permanent and formidable threat to the Empire's essential lines of communication' (Sir Herbert Samuel, future first British High Commissioner in Palestine). From then on, the Zionist project became all the more attractive in that it was presented with such skill: 'A Jewish Palestine', explained Haim Weizmann, the Zionist Organization's principal leader, 'would be a safeguard for England, particularly in matters concerning the **Suez Canal**.'

The affair was concluded with the Balfour Declaration. There were no illusions on either side: the Zionists were well aware of Great Britain's reasons for involving itself thus, and therefore of the necessity of never relaxing the pressure needed to ensure it kept its word; but the British game seemed to be, by far, the most profitable. For its part, London was well aware that the Zionist movement was using British 'cover' to realize its dream. Here is Lord Curzon, Balfour's successor: 'While Weizmann tells you one thing, and you are thinking in terms of a "national Jewish homeland", he has something quite different in mind. He envisages a Jewish state, and a subject Arab population, governed by the Jews. He is trying to bring this about screened and protected by the British guarantee.' To London it mattered little, as long as its hold on Palestine was assured.

But it was essential, in winning the Jews, not to lose the Arabs who, for the moment, constituted the overwhelming majority of the Palestinian population, not to mention most of the countries of the Middle East colonized, directly or indirectly, by the British. Did the Balfour Declaration ostensibly contradict the assurances given to Sherif Hussein and Ibn Saoud? Diplomats thought so: the efforts undertaken by the British authorities to promote the 'national Jewish homeland' were tempered, in the text, by the need to do nothing 'that would prejudice the civil and religious rights of the non-Jewish communities in Palestine'. Such artistic licence was to prove expensive.

Begin (Menachem)

LEADER of the Israeli right wing which he brought to power for the first time in 1977, he held the post of prime minister until his resignation as a result of the war in **Lebanon**.

Menachem Begin was born on August 13, 1913, in Russia, at Brest-Litovsk, a town with a Jewish majority where the Zionist movement was already very active. From the age of twelve, he was a militant member in the organization, first on the left (with Hashomer Hatzair), then on the right with Betar, a revisionist paramilitary youth organization — an offshoot of **Zionism**, ultra-nationalist, authoritarian, not to say fascist in character — created in the 1920s by Zeev Jabotinsky. When he was sixteen, Begin made the acquaintance of the man nicknamed by his socialist adversaries Vladimir Hitler, who preached the 'the transformation of this country (including Transjordan) into an independent state under the leadership of a well established Jewish majority' (Z. Jabotinsky, *Basic Principles of Revisionism*). A fervent enthusiast, he became the leader of Betar whilst studying law in Varsovie, then the organization's permanent representative. But then came the German invasion, and Begin fled to the east; arrested by the Soviet secret police and interned in a labour camp in the polar circle, he was to owe his release to the agreement signed by Stalin with the Polish government, now exiled in London — Brest-Litovsk was Polish in the inter-war years.

Having enlisted into General Anders' Polish army, Begin, in the spring of 1942, rejoined his wife in Palestine, where he was appointed commissar of Betar and head of the revisionist secret army, the Irgun. With his troops, in 1944 he joined his own secessionists from the Lehi, the Stern Gang (formed in 1943), in armed struggle against the British occupying forces. The attacks he organized led him into serious clashes with the organizations in the majority, notably the Haganah, which he denounced for its 'wait-and-see policy'; from November 1944 to September 1945 the latter, under the name of Operation Season, conducted a veritable witchhunt of Begin supporters. Alliance, however, triumphed (May 15, 1948) when in its turn the Haganah turned to violence against the British representatives, and especially after 1947 as clashes escalated with the Arabs in Palestine (see the **war of 1948–1949**).

During this period, Menachem Begin's Irgun was responsible for some of the operations most condemned by public opinion, Jewish included: the attack of July 22, 1946, on the King David Hotel in Jerusalem, seat of British Headquarters, that resulted in 200 dead and wounded, many of whom were Jews; the massacre in the Palestinian village of Deir Yassin on April 9, 1948, where 200 civilians lost their lives and which led to the massive flight of the Arab populations; and the *Altalena* affair — a ship chartered by the Irgun to procure arms in large quantities — described by the Prime Minister, Ben Gurion, as 'an attempt to overburden the army and destroy the State'.

This reputation for adventurism, hysterical nationalism and distinctly factious tendencies counted heavily against the Irgun. The war over, Begin therefore dissolved his military organization to turn his attention to the political arena: he founded the Herut ('Freedom', in Hebrew) Party. In the spring of 1947, Begin moved into a flat in Tel Aviv, and it was in this same flat that, thirty years later, he heard the news of his victory. Between these two events, there was a long haul, patiently conducted on four fronts: violent polemic — going as far as rioting in front of the Knesset — against the reopening of relations with West Germany; denouncing the socialist strangle-hold on the state and the often scandalous failures; the unification of all discontented elements, particularly the Oriental Jews; and, of course, the chauvinist dialogue on the Jewish people's right to all land on both sides of the Jordan. But Menachem Begin's rise to power owed less to his own efforts than to the gifts that Labour kept handing him on a plate.

The best of these was undoubtedly the mentality of conflict and occupation in which socialist governments were caught up. 'Henceforth', wrote Eytan Haber in his biography of Begin, 'anything Begin advocated no longer seemed to smack of extremism. The apparently unbridgeable gulf that had been opening up between Begin and his opponents no longer existed .... The national consensus had broadened considerably, and Menachem Begin had pride of place within it.' Traumatized by the shock of the Yom Kippur War which cast doubts on the policy followed for twenty-five years, and tired moreover of a Labour regime in power for as long, Israeli society saw no other solution than to experiment. From being a pariah, the man whose name never passed the lips of Ben Gurion had become respectable and respected and, what is more, considered to be the best orator in Israel. Indeed, the socialist Prime Minister, Levi Eshkol, had offered him a ministerial portfolio on June 1, 1967. Ten years later, he was prime minister, the Likud having gained in 1977 33.4% of votes, whereas the Herut of 1949 had collected barely 11.5%.

The firm silence in which Menachem Begin has wrapped himself since his departure from the political arena, in 1983, nonetheless says a great deal about the failure of his access to power. After the success of Camp David, he had in fact launched into desperate action prompted by a double failure: that of the Israeli economy and that of the Lebanese War. In 1938, during a congress, Begin had challenged his master, Jabotinsky, and obtained a modification of Betar's solemn oath: 'I shall make ready my weapons for the defence of my nation and I shall bear them only in its defence' had, at the request of the young Zionist from Brest-Litovsk, become: 'I shall make ready my weapons for the defence of my nation and the conquest of my country'. Hardly a slight difference.

Ben Gurion (David)

BORN in Plonsk (Poland), on October 16, 1886, David Grin emigrated in 1906 to Palestine where, having become leader of the Mapai and president of the Zionist Executive under the name of Ben Gurion, he was to proclaim, 42 years later, the **independence** of the State of **Israel**, whose prime minister he was to be for a considerable period.

Son of one of the founders of the Lovers of Zion, which organized the first Jewish *aliya* to Palestine, David Grin in 1905 espoused the Zionist-socialist doctrine of the Poalei Zion (Workers of Zion). The following year, he went to Palestine. An agricultural worker for four years, he joined the editorial staff of the socialist journal *Ahdut* (Unity) in 1910; there he wrote his first articles, which he signed as Ben Gurion — after the leader of the independent Jewish government at the time of the revolt against Rome. But soon the young man sailed to Salonika, then on to Constantinople. He hoped to achieve his objective, the renaissance of a Jewish state, by the Ottomanization of Palestine. World War I shattered this dream. Banished from the Ottoman Empire, Ben Gurion embarked for the **United States**.

After a vain attempt there to raise an army of Jewish pioneers, he published his first book, *Eretz Yisrael* (The Land of Israel). It was after his marriage to Paulina Mombaz that he learned, on November 2, 1917, of the famous **Balfour Declaration**. While most Zionists celebrated this as a victory, Ben Gurion warned: 'Only the Hebrew people can turn this right into a tangible reality and it alone must, by its body and soul, by its strength and its capital, construct its "National Home" ' — this quotation, and others below, is drawn from Michel Bar-Zohar's remarkable biography, *Ben Gurion*.

On his return, at the end of 1918, to a Palestine liberated by the British, Ben Gurion resumed his struggle for the unification of socialists and, to get round sectarian obstructions, chose to work in the union sector. Rising swiftly through the ranks of the Histadrut (Israel's Labour Federation), he proved to be a leader. Not only did he increase the membership of the Histadrut ten-fold, but he also considerably widened its sphere of influence, notably through the creation of a network of enterprises and services linked to it.

In 1929, the members of the various socialist parties approved unification. Ben Gurion became secretary general of Mapai (Workers' Party of Israel), which gained 42.3% of the **Yishuv**'s votes in 1934, then half the votes of the 19th Zionist World Congress in 1935. Its leader thus became president of both the Zionist Executive and the Jewish Agency.

From isolated incidents in 1920, 1921 and 1929, Arab resistance to the establishment of the Jewish National Home escalated, in 1936, to the level of generalized rebellion. **Great Britain** now backtracked and proposed the partition of Palestine. The Yishuv unanimously rejected this, but Ben Gurion, for his own motives, accepted. 'A partial Hebrew state is not an end but merely a beginning. . . . We shall take there all the Jews we possibly can. . . . We shall create a diverse economy. . . . We shall organize a modern national defence . . . and then I am sure we shall not be prevented from settling in other parts of the country, either by agreement with our neighbours, or in any other way. . . .'

Three years later, this watchword of the Jewish state would be imposed on the movement by the president of the Executive. The British White Paper of 1939 and the outbreak of World War II had helped persuade it: it was no longer on Great Britain, but on the United States that Zionists now had to count. Having crossed the Atlantic at the end of 1941, Ben Gurion organized the Biltmore Conference which, in May 1942, recommended the constitution of a 'Jewish Commonwealth'. Within six months, all the Zionist authorities, even those in Palestine, had ratified the change, despite the influence of those who believed in a bi-national solution. Alternating between fundamentalists engaged in anti-British terrorism and opportunists ready to comply with conditions laid down by London, Ben Gurion imposed his person and his policy at the head of the movement, gaining acceptance for the change which he orchestrated: the partition proposal. Formulated in August 1946 by the Executive of the Jewish Agency, it was the inspiration for the **Partition Plan** adopted by the UN in November 1947.

Ben Gurion now held all the reins in his hands. As president of the Executive, he drafted and, on May 14, 1948, delivered the declaration of independence. As prime minister, he imposed the new state's authority, including the use of force when the Irgun became factious. As defence minister, he was in charge of the Jewish forces during the **war of 1948–1949**. With arms reinforcements from Prague, he launched the spring counter-offensive in 1948, then created Zahal, the Israeli Defence Forces (IDF), securing victory for it. His strategy, based on a tacit agreement with Abdullah of **Jordan**, was the following: take advantage of the Arab attack to prevent the birth of the Palestinian Arab state, extend to its detriment the territory of the Jewish state and rid the latter of the majority of its Arab population. 'We liberated a very large territory, much more than we expected', he confided in 1949. 'Now, we shall have to work for two or three generations. As for the rest, we shall see later.' The timing was to be altered, but not the programme.

From 1949 to 1953, the prime minister therefore applied himself to the transformation of Israel: he doubled the population by organizing the arrival of 700,000 new immigrants, set in motion a vigorous economic development, created an entire education system, and ensured the increase in numbers of **settlements**, including those in the Negev. Indeed, it was there, in the Sde Boqer *kibbutz*, that Ben Gurion retired in 1953, after having handed over the reins to Moshe Sharrett. But the Lavon Affair — named after the minister of Defence who was forced to resign — brought back the Old Man, as he was then called, to public life.

From 1955, he organized the **war of 1956**, the Suez War. From 1949, Israel had abandoned its original neutrality to become involved in the nascent Cold War. 'We must explain', admitted Ben Gurion in 1952, 'that the whole of Israel . . . is available as a base for the free world.' But this time, alliance with the West was sealed militarily: after the operations at Kibya (1953) and Gaza (1955), Tel Aviv launched its army against Egypt, figurehead of the Arab nationalist movement, against whom London and Paris were also sending their forces. The aim? 'To eliminate Nasser, of course', Ben Gurion had claimed at the Franco-Israeli-British Conference at Sèvres, some days earlier.

Pressure from two sides — American and Soviet — forced the IDF to withdraw. 'Israel, after the Sinai campaign, will never be the same', Ben Gurion told the soldiers. The failure of the adventure nonetheless pushed him to try, in vain, to make secret contact with the Arab leaders. At the same time he took care to have the IDF reinforced, with, in particular, valuable aid from France which even assisted the Jewish state in the construction of a nuclear reactor. For 'personal reasons', the Old Man resigned in 1963. On bad terms with his successor, Levi Eshkol, and the principal leaders of Mapai, he went as far as creating a schism, in 1965, with the founding of Rafi.

After the **War of 1967**, for which he criticized Israel for having taken the initiative, Ben Gurion held aloof from the reunification of Labour factions. He strongly recommended the return of all occupied Arab territories — except East Jerusalem. During the elections of 1969, he again headed a 'State List', which gained only four seats. This setback precipitated his definitive retirement, the following year, at Sde Boqer. He died there on December 1, 1973.

Black September

THE TERM is used to designate both the events of September 1970 that ended in the crushing of the PLO by the Jordanian army and a Palestinian organization that was created as a result of those events.

After the Six Day War of 1967, the *fedayeen* had established their bases in Jordan, and it was from there that they conducted their actions against Israel. But, very quickly, the problem of relations between the Palestinian resistance and King Hussein's regime reared its head. Jordan had suffered harsh Israeli reprisals. The king disapprovingly watched the rise of a counter-power which undermined his authority and opposed his attempts at political settlement. Confrontations between Jordanian and Palestinian forces increased. Crisis was unavoidable. The pretext was to be the Rogers Plan — named after the American secretary of state — which restated the broad outlines of Resolution 242. Nasser and King Hussein accepted it during the summer of 1970, whilst the PLO unanimously rejected it. George Habash's PFLP thought confrontation should be hastened and Amman taken over. On September 7, 1970, his commandos hijacked three planes from international airlines to the town of Zarka, in north Jordan. The airport was declared a liberated zone. Although the PFLP had, at Yasser Arafat's request, been suspended from the PLO, the trap closed on the entire organization, which King Hussein wanted to see eliminated. On the 16th, he formed a military government and the army received the order to intervene. The fighting, of indescribable violence — and causing thousands of Palestinian civilian victims — continued until September 27. Less than a year later, the PLO had been completely ousted from Jordan.

On November 28, 1971, a Palestinian commando squad assassinated the Jordanian Prime Minister, Wasfi Al Tal; the Black September organization was born. Created by Fatah, it carried out some forty operations outside Israel, of which the most spectacular was to be the massacre of Israeli athletes at the Munich Olympic Games in 1972. For Abu Iyad, one of the leaders of Fatah, 'the organization acted as an auxiliary to the Resistance, at a time when the latter was no longer able to fulfil its military and political duties to the full. . . . Its members reflected the profound feelings of frustration and anger felt by the entire Palestinian people faced with Jordan's butchery and the complicity that made it possible. . . .' The Black September group disappeared after the War of 1973. It contributed to the long-standing identification, in public opinion throughout the world, of Palestinians with terrorism.

Camp David Accords

CAMP DAVID is the name of the summer residence of the president of the USA, where, on September 17, 1978, Jimmy Carter succeeded in getting Anwar Al

Sadat and Menachem **Begin** to sign two draft treaties, one involving the 'concluding of a peace treaty' between their two countries, the other setting out a 'framework for peace in the Middle East', the text of which may be read in Appendix 7.

The Camp David Accords represent the culmination of a long march towards a separate **Egypt-Israel** peace, at the initiative of the United States. Shortly after the Yom Kippur **War of 1973**, the Geneva Conference, under the co-presidency of Henry **Kissinger** and Andrei Gromyko, broke down. The *Rais*, the Egyptian head of state, who had launched the October conflict to force the opening of international negotiations, then chose the 'one step at a time' policy proposed to him by the American secretary of state, offering Egypt an 'honourable solution', with the prospect of finally alleviating the unbearable economic burden of a thirty-year conflict. All tendencies joining together, Israeli leaders were delighted, for their part, at the hope of peace between their country and an Arab country, which involved no concessions on the Palestinian question. Methodically, 'Dear Henry' advanced: the agreement referred to as the Kilometre 101 in November 1973, the arrangements for the disengagement from the canal in January 1974, and finally, on September 1, 1975, the first comprehensive agreement. The state of war betwen Israel and Egypt was abolished, Tel Aviv withdrawing to a distance of 50 kilometres from the Suez Canal and handing back the oil wells of Sinai, Cairo discontinuing its sea blockade and reopening the **Suez Canal** to Israeli ships. United Nations' troops were stationed in a demilitarized zone.

After another abortive attempt at international negotiations, which the **USSR** and the United States, by their common declaration of October 1, 1977, had set in motion, Anwar Al Sadat resumed his search for a bilateral solution. 'We had to find' — he explained in his autobiography — 'an entirely new method, able to short-circuit red tape.' The Egyptian president's visit to Jerusalem, on November 19, 1977, was in fact nothing if not innovative, both in form and substance. Not enough, however, to overcome the Israeli prime minister's obstinacy. Carried to power on May 17, 1977, by a reactionary wave, the first since 1948 to have beaten the Labour Party, Menachem Begin personified the touchy nationalism of his supporters. The acceleration of the establishment of Jewish settlements on the **West Bank** was at the centre of the plan destined, in the long term, to rebuild 'Greater Israel'. But Sadat decided to force the hand of the leader of the Likud, as he had decided to disregard the harangues of those who denounced the Egyptian treason: 'I shall carry the peace negotiations to their conclusion, even if the other Arab states refuse to associate themselves with it', the Egyptian president claimed. The skill, and pressure, of American diplomacy would do the rest.

The first of the two draft treaties drew up the peace between Israel and

Egypt. Scheduled to be formulated in three months, the treaty was not in fact signed until March 26, 1979. On April 25, 1982, in accordance with its provisions, and when the last Israeli settlements had been dismantled, the Sinai was liberated: for the first time since 1967, Egypt had re-established its sovereignty over its entire territory, with the exception of the disputed zone of Taba. Israel, for its part, could congratulate itself on gaining normal diplomatic relations, for the first time since 1948, with an Arab country, and a major one at that. The second text — see Appendix 7 — confided the fate of the West Bank and **Gaza** to Egypt-Israel-Jordan-Palestinian negotiations that were to lead to an autonomy governed by an elected authority, as a prelude to a definitive statute, also to be negotiated by the four. These negotiations were never to get beyond the tedious debates of an Egyptian-Israeli commission.

This flagrant contradiction, between one agreement applied and one that remained a dead letter, is hardly surprising. The child of Camp David was still-born for several reasons. A separate solution, it did not involve any of the other Arab countries, *a fortiori* the PLO; the broadening of the process launched by Tel Aviv and Cairo was doomed from the outset. Made up of two parts, it did not link the two; forced to put the first into operation to regain the Sinai, Egypt had no way of imposing on Israel a real solution to the Palestinian problem. Conceived by the United States without the Soviet Union, the Camp David document naturally aroused the hostility of Moscow and its allies in the area. But, more importantly, the solution envisaged for the occupied territories was also impracticable, involving either too much or too little for those concerned. Too much for Begin who, his signature scarcely dry on a document calling for Israeli withdrawal from an area destined for autonomy, not to mention a definitive statute of independence, once again pronounced his refusal to entertain any idea of giving back the West Bank, Gaza and East Jerusalem, or accepting any independent Palestinian state! Too little for the Palestinians, who had to renounce any idea of a future state, their representative having already been barred from the negotiations.

Aborted or not, Camp David had, at all events, significant consequences for the Middle East, whose landscape it completely overturned. The most densely populated, the most economically powerful, the strongest military power of the Arab countries, Egypt, now found itself isolated, excluded by its 'peers'. Israel, on the other hand, with its southern flank now safe, felt its hands free to act in the north and east. At the same time, the Palestinians now faced a foe more sure of itself, since its allies were divided. In short, with hindsight, it seems clear that the Camp David Accords delayed the hour of a global solution more than they advanced it, as was frequently claimed at the time.

Confessionalism

THIS TERM designates the political system in force in **Lebanon** whose roots go far back in history. Under the **Ottoman Empire**, as early as the 16th century, we find the formation of the *millet* system: different lateral 'cities' (Christian, Jewish) were recognized alongside **Islam**. Their religious leaders enjoyed numerous privileges and directed the lives of their flocks. But it was the direct intervention of the European powers that was to speed up the genesis of confessionalism. After the events of 1860 and the French intervention, the Lebanese question became a European one. A 'comprehensive settlement' was imposed on Mount Lebanon (Lesser Lebanon) (4,500 square kilometres, less than half the present country) which henceforth was directly answerable to the Sublime Porte. An administrative council was formed, comprising representatives of the six principal religious groups: **Maronite, Druze, Sunni, Shi'ite**, Greek Orthodox and Greek Catholic. Lesser Lebanon, with a large Maronite majority, was divided into seven *mudiriyaat* : four Maronite, one Druze, one Greek Orthodox and one Greek Catholic. The sectarianism thus established was reinforced by the mission taken on by each of the European powers: Paris defending the Maronites, London the Druze, Saint Petersburg the Greek Orthodox.

In 1920, **France** established its mandate over the region and separated Greater Lebanon (with its present borders) from what was to become **Syria**. Three factors contributed to the establishment of confessionalism. Within the new frontiers, the Christians were barely in the majority; but, determined to maintain their hegemony, the fear of being submerged by Islam revived their sense of unity. At the beginning of 1926, the status of political community was accorded the Shi'ites who, until then, had been part of the Sunni legal sphere. Finally, Article 95 of the Constitution of 1926 stipulated: 'As a temporary measure, and with the intention of establishing justice and harmony, communities will have equal representation in public office, and in the composition of ministries. . . .' This temporary measure is still in force today. In the meantime, seventeen religious persuasions or 'confessions' have been officially recognized, each of which has an administration based on tribal relations.

In matters of personal status (marriage, divorce, inheritance), each community has autonomy; civil marriage therefore does not exist. In the field of politics, the rules were laid down by the pact of 1943: Maronite president, Sunni prime minister, Shi'ite parliamentary speaker, etc. In parliament, 6 out of the 11 seats belong to Christians and 5 to Muslims with an internal repartition, for each of the two religions, between the different sub-groups.

Thus, in 1972 — the date of the last parliamentary election — out of 99 MPs, 30 were Maronite and only 19 Shi'ite. The same breakdown exists for all administrative and army posts.

The presidential nature of the regime has accentuated the large hegemony of the Maronites. The overall system is being called into question by the interminable civil war which, ironically, has reinforced the solidarity of the various confessional groups.

Still more serious, 'the occupation of the territory by Lebanese groups has undergone radical changes leading to the homogenization of each region' (Elizabeth Picard). The Christians left Tripoli and now number less than 50,000 in West Beirut — as against 500,000 ten years ago. The Jbeil Mountain, Kesruan and almost all of Metn are now exclusively Christian. The Shouf became Druze following the flight of the Christians between 1983 and 1985. The country has thus been divided into virtually homogeneous cantons, each cosily withdrawn into its own community solidarity.

Curiel (Henri)

HENRI CURIEL was born in Cairo on September 13, 1914, the son of a rich Jewish banker. His secondary education took place at a Jesuit college, after which he left for France where he obtained his degree in law. On his return to Egypt, he was active in anti-fascist movements and then, in 1943, founded the Egyptian National Liberation Movement (ENLM), a communist organization that was to play a decisive role when World War II was over. Repeatedly arrested, Henri Curiel was once again taken into custody on May 15, 1948, both as a Jew and as a communist who had supported the Partition Plan of Palestine. Freed at the beginning of 1950, he was deported from his country in September and deprived of his nationality.

Living in hiding in France, from 1956 onwards until his arrest in 1960 he helped organize support for the Algerian FLN. Freed in June 1962 following the signing of the Evian Accords, he set up the solidarity network whose aim was to supply concrete support to Third World struggles. Concurrently, he campaigned for an Arab-Israeli *rapprochement* and a peace based on the national rights of all the peoples of the region. He helped to organize the Bologne Conference of 1973, in which both Arabs and Israelis took part, and, especially, the Paris negotiations of July 1976 that brought together, under the aegis of Pierre Mendès-France, Issam Sartawi, General Peled and Uri Avnery.

Denounced by the newspaper *Le Point* and Georges Suffert as 'the leader of the aid networks of terrorism', he was assassinated on May 14, 1978, by a mysterious commando squad called Delta. The assassins were never found.

Druze

A SECT originating from one of the branches of **Shi'ism**, its roots can be traced back to the Fatimid caliphate established in Cairo in the 10th century. The Caliph, Al Hakim, tried to have himself recognized as a god. After his death, his supporters were persecuted, but his former vizier, having taken refuge in **Syria**, managed to convince several tribes of the divine nature of his late master. It is to him that the sect owes its name. Some years later, in 1043 AD, the new preaching was declared 'accomplished', and proselytism and conversions forbidden: 'The veil is drawn, the door is closed, the ink is dry and the pen broken.' The doctrine, maintained by a small caste of initiates highly influenced by Greek and Hindu philosophy, is so esoteric that, contrary to the Shi'ites, the Druze are mainly considered by other Muslims to be apostates.

There are Druze communities in **Lebanon**, Syria and **Israel**. In the last of these, they number around 70,000 and receive different treatment from other Arabs, Christian or Muslim. In particular, they are liable to military service, which gives them certain privileges; in recent years however, an upsurge of insubordination has developed amongst Israeli Druze which the occurrence of the Intifada has strengthened. But it is mainly in Lebanon that the Druze play a political role.

The first Druze emirate was created in the 12th century at Mount Lebanon. At the end of the 16th century, Fakhreddin II unified under his sceptre the territories of what is now modern Lebanon. From this date, Maronites and Druze were to assert their power over the Lebanese mountain.

The Druze community represents only about 7% of the Lebanese population, but compensates for its numerical weakness by a high degree of unity, a strong territorial concentration in Mount Lebanon (the Shouf, Metn, Harbaya) — which was accentuated in the period 1983–1985 by the exodus of many Christians from the region — and great fighting qualities. A long-standing split has set the Yazbaki clan (headed by the Arslane family) against the **Jumblatts**, who have nevertheless maintained their supremacy. One man, Kamal Jumblatt, was to be, from 1943 until his assassination by Syrian agents in 1977, both the most prestigious Druze representative and the leader of the Lebanese left wing. His son, Walid, succeeded him, both as head of the Jumblatt clan and the Progressive Socialist Party (PSP) founded by his father. The PSP, although recruiting certain cadres from other religious denominations, is mainly identified with its Druze base.

Egypt

FOLLOWING the failure of Napoleon's famous expedition, Mohammed Ali, an Albanian officer in the Turkish army, seized power in Cairo. He was the founder of modern Egypt and his descendants would reign for a century and a half. The strategic importance of the country's geographical situation, accentuated by the cutting of the Suez isthmus, plus the expansion of cotton growing, made what was still theoretically a province of the **Ottoman Empire** into a prime target for the European powers. In 1882, **Great Britain** occupied Egypt and, after the declaration of World War I, the English established their protectorate.

At the end of the war, a handful of nationalists, headed by Saad Zaghloul, formed a delegation (the Wafd) to go to London to negotiate for **independence**. Britain's refusal aroused great anger and violent demonstrations, prompting His Britannic Majesty, in a unilateral declaration of February 21, 1922, to recognize Egypt as an independent sovereign state. It was a bogus independence, the real power remaining in the hands of the British High Commission. Henceforth, political life would revolve around three poles: the Palace, the British proconsul and the Wafd, which had become a political party with a popular membership — but feudal in leadership — carrying the day in all elections (those that were not heavily rigged, that is). The treaty of 1936, signed by the Wafdist government of Nahas Pasha, led to several minor concessions (such as the withdrawal of British troops to the **Suez Canal** zone) but did not live up to the expectations of the nationalists. Furthermore, Nahas was dismissed by the Palace in 1937. In 1942, London foisted on King Farouk, who had been flirting with Nazi Germany, the reinstatement of the Wafd to government; Nahas Pasha and his administration lost much of their prestige in the process.

After 1945, the anti-English movement became more radical and in February 1946 a wave of demonstrations swept through Egypt. Despite the War of Palestine and martial law, the movement gained strength and carried the Wafd to power again in 1950. Prompted by the general radicalization of consciousness, Nahas Pasha unilaterally repealed the treaty of 1936 that he himself had signed. Guerilla warfare was stepped up against British troops in the Suez Canal zone. The burning of Cairo, in January 1952, was used as the pretext for a brutal 'return to order'. The Wafdist cabinet was dismissed by the King and the Wafd, uncertain, divided, faint-hearted, discredited itself. The way was now open for the Free Officers who seized power on July 13, 1952, and established the Republic on June 18, 1953.

Nasser, the central figure of the new regime, refused to return to the multi-party system, established a single party, embarked on agricultural reform and, above all, opened negotiations with London. On October 19, 1954, he signed a treaty by whose terms British troops would withdraw over an eighteen-month period; in an emergency, however, their return was envisaged. The Suez expedition of 1956 rendered this clause null and void: after 75 years of foreign occupation, Egypt was once again free. It even became the centre of the Arab world, the Mecca of revolutionary nationalism. The Arab Voice, broadcast from Cairo, would contribute to the upheavals that were to shake the Middle East between 1956 and 1967. But though a powerful wind of change was sweeping through the traditional structures, greatly damaging the colonial presence, it was not to prove capable of realizing the dream of unity. The United Arab Republic (UAR), made up of Egypt and Syria, was to have only an ephemeral existence (1958–1961). The beginning of the 1960s ushered in a new period of 'radicalization': the nationalizing of industry, phase two of the agricultural reforms, the creation of the Arab Socialist Union. The alliance with the USSR — symbolized by Nasser's and Krushchev's inauguration of the Aswan Dam in 1964 — was strengthened. However, dreams of an independent economic development were to be shattered against General Dayan's tanks. With the defeat of 1967, Egypt became a conquered nation, partially occupied, crushed by the burden of the war. The *Rais* (title of the Egyptian head of state) tried to rally his country, refusing to accept the facts: he reconstructed his army with the help of the USSR and decided to give support to Yasser Arafat's *fedayeen* organizations; he undertook a war of attrition over the Suez Canal in 1969–1970 all the while claiming his readiness to negotiate a political solution (the Rogers Plan).

When Sadat succeeded Nasser, in 1970, he had already chosen an orientation poles apart from that of his predecessor. It was not until after the October war of 1973 that he was able to apply it: an *infitah* (open) economy and alliance with the United States 'which holds 99% of the cards' to resolve the Arab-Israeli conflict. The new direction followed by Sadat was to be brilliantly vindicated by his trip to Jerusalem in November 1977, followed by the signing, the following year, of the Camp David Accords. Through it, Egypt won peace, the Sinai and considerable American aid. It lost its relationship and credibility with virtually the entire Arab world. The population, who had enthusiastically welcomed the end of a painful war, were soon to be disappointed. The economic crisis, far from being resolved, worsened. Public liberties were constantly being whittled down. And when, in 1981, four men assassinated the *Rais*, few Egyptians wept.

A new phase then opened, marked by a more balanced policy. Mubarak consolidated the Camp David Accords, but made peace with Jordan, Iraq and the PLO, then renewed relations with the majority of Arab countries. He had maintained preferential relations with the USA but normalized those with the USSR. The opposition enjoys greater freedom of action, but the governmental party maintains its hold on the state apparatus. The *infitah* policy is still followed, but the new president is trying to combat corruption and to extend productive activities. After achieving some success, this policy based on pragmatism and expediency has run up against serious obstacles: worsening of the economic crisis, pressure from fundamentalists (particularly apparent during the parliamentary elections of April 1987), and tension with Israel concerning the **intifada**.

With a national debt estimated at more than 50 billion dollars and a population explosion, it is economic problems that most concern the government led by Atef Sidki since November 10, 1986. Egypt's economic crisis has now been accentuated by the return of some 1.2 million Egyptian workers whose foreign currency earnings from Iraq and Kuwait used to provide for 7 million Egyptians, but who now find themselves dependent on their families as a result of the Gulf crisis. The government fears a social outburst of the type that took place in January 1977. The police revolt in Cairo, in February 1986, reminded everyone of the abject poverty of millions of Egyptians.

Egypt stretches over a million square kilometres, of which only a tiny part is cultivable. With more than 50 million inhabitants in 1988, it represents more than a third of the population of the Arab world. Egyptians are either Sunni Muslims or Christian Copts (about 15%). The country's main financial resources come from oil, the **Suez Canal**, tourism and money sent home by the 3 to 4 million Egyptians working abroad. Egypt, whose agricultural balance is in the red, exports cotton. The political system is characterized by a strong reliance on the power of the president.

Fez Plan

THE FEZ PLAN was a set of proposals for the settlement of the **Arab**-Israeli conflict adopted on September 9, 1982, by the summit of Arab sovereigns and heads of state, convened at Fez in Morocco. Its importance stems from the context of this summit, the new content of the plan and the implications of the principles it proposed.

The **Lebanon War of 1982**, whose first phase ended shortly before the Fez summit with the departure from Beirut of the **PLO** and its fighters, had posed with unparalleled force the question of the fate of **Palestinians**. Objectively, this new conflict upheld the argument according to which the Middle East will never have stability as long as the Palestine question remains unsettled, all the more so since the resistance had lost, in Lebanon, its last autonomous base. Western opinion, traditionally pro-Israel, had been so shocked by pictures of the Israeli invasion and particularly the siege of Beirut — not to mention the massacres of **Sabra and Shatila** that it learned of shortly afterwards — that it pressed for a lasting solution. Already, on September 1, the president of the United States had referred to this in a speech; the **Reagan Plan** admittedly returned to the prospect of 'autonomy', but admitted that it was a question of solving the problem, not of 'refugees', but of 'a people'.

Arab leaders therefore found themselves obliged, a few days after the White House, to formulate a coherent plan. This need was all the more pressing in that their passivity in the face of the tragedy experienced by Palestinians and Lebanese had profoundly shocked their fellow citizens, Palestine remaining for most Arabs a central part of their own identity. Any attempts at renewing the unrealistic and demagogic proposals for the 'liberation of the whole of Palestine', implying the 'destruction of the Zionist presence', were now unacceptable. As was the acceptance of the American project, a by-product of the **Camp David Accords**.

Between these two extremes, the summit ended up opting for a return to sources: for the first time in their history, in fact, Arab states came out, on September 9, 1982, in favour of the coexistence of two states, one Israeli and the other Palestinian, 'with Al Quds (**Jerusalem**) as its capital'. This change of direction was made particularly clear by Article 7 of the Fez Plan — whose entire text can be found in Appendix 9: 'The Security Council guarantees peace between all the states of the region'. If Israel is not explicitly mentioned, this declaration, according to all observers, nonetheless constituted in effect a recognition of the existence of the Jewish state (with the frontiers it possessed prior to the Six Day **War of 1967**). Such was not, and is not, the opinion of Israeli leaders, who saw in this plan nothing but a 'new declaration of war'.

The fact remains that the Fez Plan, despite the lapse of time and the events that have taken place since its adoption, remains, at least on the level of basic principles, the most serious framework for any international negotiations aiming at establishing a lasting peace in the region. Its similarity to the United Nations Resolution partitioning Palestine (see **Partition Plan**, the fact of its being constructed around the idea of the coexistence of the two peoples and their respective states, the Arab consensus it aroused, its positive reception by virtually every country in the world, are all points in its favour.

Foreign Trade

AN IMPORTANT political and strategic pawn, the Middle East also constitutes a substantial economic target. Its population is considerable: more than 150 million men and women. Its needs of all kinds, in keeping with this population, are accentuated by the dependent nature of its economies: mostly oriented towards exports of raw materials, the population has to import its basic needs in manufactured goods. The great majority of states in the region have little difficulty in affording such imports thanks to the resources to be found in their subsoil, first and foremost being oil. Furthermore, a surplus is created which, lacking the opportunity, or desire, to invest locally, many countries of the region choose to place abroad.

To give some indication of the scale of the factors summarized above some statistics are called for. In 1986, the combined imports of the countries concerned (**Saudi Arabia**, Bahrain, **Egypt**, United Arab Emirates, **Iraq, Iran, Jordan, Kuwait, Libya**, Oman, Qatar, Syria, and **North and South Yemen**) exceeded 90 billion dollars, of which 70 to 80% went on manufactured goods. Their total exports, on the other hand, reached 85 billion dollars, of which 75 to 85% was raw materials. As well as oil, one also finds in the Middle East gold, phosphates, sulphur, asbestos, coal, lignite, iron, chromite, copper, manganese, lead, zinc, antimony, nickel, etc.

Oil and its derivatives, such as gas, lacking in Israel, Jordan and Lebanon, represent 70% of the exports of Egypt, 50% of Syrian exports, 85% of Kuwait's, 90% of Bahrain's, 75% of the Emirates', of Iran, Oman, Qatar, Saudi Arabia, Iraq and Libya. This explains the growing importance up to 1982 of oil resources: 2.8 billion dollars in 1966, 4.6 in 1970, 13.5 in 1973, 89 in 1977, 177 in 1981, approximately 100 in 1984. As for the surplus, it rose, between 1974 and 1984, to almost 450 billion dollars, of which 5% went to international financial institutions, 15% to developing countries, and 80% to the developed countries — the United States having tapped 65% to 70% of these various investments.

However, the oil recession and the fall in oil prices checked many illusions: the combined exports of the countries of the Middle East, excluding Israel, fell to 159 billion dollars (of which oil accounted for 130) in 1982 and 79 billion (56 being oil) in 1986.

The five main importers of the Middle East are Saudi Arabia (19.1 billion dollars in 1986), Iran (11.6), Iraq (10.2), Egypt (9.5), the Emirates (7.4). As for the five largest exporters, they can be classified as follows: Saudi Arabia (20.1), Iran (13.4), Iraq (about 11), United Arab Emirates (9.9) and Libya (6).

There are three main holders of foreign investments: Saudi Arabia, far in the lead, with more than 160 billion dollars, followed by Kuwait with 80 and the United Arab Emirates with 40 — the figures are from 1983.

As for the Middle East's partners, it is the developed market economies that lead (63% of imports, 50% of exports), followed by developing market economies (29% and 46%), with planned economies bringing up the rear (8% and 4%).

For the United States in particular, commercial relations with the Middle East are strategically significant, but also important economically: it is one of the rare regions with which, although in recession, they have a healthy balance. In 1986, their exports to the Middle East (8.4 billion dollars, that is 4% of total American exports) surpassed their imports from the region (7.9 billion, that is 2% of the total). In 1987, however, there was a slight deficit. Moreover, slightly in the red in 1987, the balance of Arab-American commerce showed, in 1988, a deficit of 2.1 billion dollars. Acccording to figures given in the *Statistical Abstract* of 1988, Washington's largest clients in the Middle East were, in 1986, Saudi Arabia (3.5 billion dollars), Israel (2.2), Egypt (2) and Iraq (0.5). And its principal suppliers were then Saudi Arabia (3.6 billion dollars), Israel (2.4) and Iran (0.6). If Arab-American exchanges tend to be diminishing, commerce between the United States and Israel has increased enormously, following the agreement of a free exchange negotiated between the two countries.

The USSR, although a more modest economic partner, has nonetheless expanded its commercial dealings with the Arab world, despite the setbacks experienced in the 1970s, and excluding all contact — until 1988 — with Israel. According to figures for 1986 given by the United Nations, the Soviet Union sold 1.3 billion dollars worth of goods to Arab countries, and bought from them 1.8 billion. The USSR's clients in the Middle East are headed by Iraq, Egypt and Syria (each around the 0.4 billion mark); first place amongst its suppliers goes to Libya (1 billion dollars), followed by Iraq (0.5), Egypt (0.4) and Syria (0.25). A fair amount of these exchanges concerns the importing of oil and the exporting of arms. But the USSR's commercial relations, like its political relations, have expanded somewhat, in particular regarding Saudi Arabia, Egypt, Iran, Kuwait, Lebanon and North Yemen, coupled with the growing cooperation it maintains with Iraq, Libya, Syria and South Yemen.

Overall, in 1986, the United States constituted the leading supplier to Bahrain, Egypt and Israel. Japan surpassed it in Saudi Arabia, the Emirates, Kuwait, Qatar and North Yemen. In Jordan, Saudi Arabia was the main supplier, and in Oman it was the Emirates. For its part, Syria gets most of its supplies from Iran, as does Libya from Italy.

If the EEC, the United States, Japan and the USSR figure among the

The Middle East in Figures

	Area km² thous.	Population thousands	Birth Rate per thousand inhabitants	GNP per inhabitant in $	Average Annual Growth Rate 85-86 (%)	Average Yearly Inflation Rate 80-86 (%)
Bahrein	1	0.431	?	8 510	?	−1.8
Egypt	1 001	49.7	34	760	3.1	12.4
Iran	1 648	45.6	41	?	?	?
Iraq	435	16.5	44	?	?	?
Israel	21	4.3	22	6 210	2.6	182.9
Jordan	98	3.6	39	1 540	5.5	3.2
Kuwait	18	1.8	32	13 890	−0.6	?
Lebanon	10	?	40[2]	2.6[1]	?	?
Libya	1 760	3.9	44	?	?	?
North Yemen	195	8.2	49	550	4.7[1]	13.1
Oman	300	1.3	45	4 980	5	3.6
Qatar	11	0.317	?	13 200	?	?
Saudi Arabia	2 150	12	42	6 950	4	−1.3
South Yemen	333	2.2	49	470	?	4.8
Sudan	2 506	22.6	45	320	−0.2	32.6
Syria	185	10.8	45	1 570	3.7	6.2
United Arab Emirates	84	1.4	28	14 680	?	−1.4

(1) Different period   (2) In 1965
Unless otherwise indicated all figures refer to 1986.

Breakdown of GNP			Exports ($ million)	Imports ($ million)	Exchange Rate (1980 * 100)	Debt as % % of GNP[2]	Defence Spending (as % of total spending)[2]	Life Expectancy (years)
Agr.	Ind.	Serv.						
?	?	?	?	?	?	?	?	70
20	29	51	4 617	9 517	76	58.8	17.7	61
26[2]	36[2]	38[2]	13 435[1]	11 635[1]	?	?	?	59
18[2]	46[2]	36[2]	?	10 190	?	?	?	63
?	?	?	7 136	10 737	96	72.1	30.1[1]	75
8	28	63	733	2 432	97	68.9	26.7[1]	65
73[2]	3[2]	27[2]	7 383	5 845	47	?	12.8	73
12[2]	21[2]	67[2]	500	2 203	?	?	?	?
5[2]	63[2]	33[2]	6 006	4 511	39	?	?	61
34[1]	16[1]	50[1]	20	1 033	99	41.1	28.8	46
61[2]	23[2]	16[2]	2 527	2 401	37	38.3	41.9	54
?	?	?	?	?	?	?	?	69
4	50	46	20 085	19 112	46	?	?	63
?	?	?	645[1]	1 543[1]	78	189.7	?	50
35	15	50	497	1 138	70	95.9	24.1[1]	49
22	21[1]	58	1 325	2 703	74	17.7	?	64
?	?	?	9 900	7 447	53	?	45.3[1]	69

principal partners of the countries of the region, the share of the rest of the Third World in exchanges with the Middle East is far from negligible: more than 30% of its imports and almost 50% of its exports. The developing countries rank first among suppliers to South Yemen, second among suppliers to Oman, Iran, Libya, Lebanon, and third to Egypt and Israel. But they rank first among the clients of Saudi Arabia, North Yemen, Iran, Iraq and Kuwait, second among those of Oman, South Yemen, Egypt, Libya, the United Arab Emirates and Qatar, and are third-best clients of Israel and Syria.

France

THE FIRST Western power to entrench itself in the Middle East, a long-standing rival of **Great Britain** in the fierce struggle for supremacy in the region, France was also the first to be expelled from it. It took General de Gaulle to restore its prestige, and its markets, in the region.

It was in 1535 that Francois 1 obtained from the Sultan the 'capitulations': this involved certain privileges for France and its nationals within the **Ottoman Empire**. This first step was complemented by interventions in favour of Lebanese Maronite Christians (see **Maronites**), whose defence it officially undertook in 1639. The capture of **Jerusalem** by the Crusaders, on July 15, 1099, also heralded the era, in Palestine, of France, which was recognized as the protector of Catholic holy places. With Napoleon's Egyptian Expedition (1798–1799) a new period of French interest in the Middle East began: the colonial period.

To **Egypt**, whose Gallicizing was to be spectacularly signified by the construction of the **Suez Canal** (1869), were added French conquests in North Africa: Algeria, beginning in 1830, then Tunisia, which became a French protectorate in 1881, as well as Morocco in 1912. At the other end of the Ottoman Empire, the territory of Obock, the future French Somaliland, was occupied from 1862. Paris even began to dream of a *pashlik* dependency stretching from Morocco to the Sinai, and of a Syro-Egyptian state.

If such projects did not materialize, France's position, on the eve of World War I and the dismantling of the Ottoman Empire, was nonetheless very strong. Apart from the areas it had colonized or in which it had established supremacy, it had great importance in Ottoman economic, social and cultural life. Most of the foreign capital invested in the Empire was French, accounting for 11% of French capital exported — that is, more than the whole colonial Empire. This domination was based on state loans as well as shares and bonds in private companies. French capital dominated the banking system, railways, ports, roads, urban public utilities and certain mining operations, not to mention the world of commerce. The principal creditor of the Empire and of Egypt — in British hands since 1882 — the French state would see its control of their economic policies strengthened by the bankruptcy of 1875—1876. Even in the cultural domain French influence prevailed, primarily in education — French being the principal means of communication, after Turkish, from one end of the sultan's dominions to the other.

That was how the Oriental question looked at the outbreak of the first world conflict, in terms favourable to France, despite its weak miltary presence in the region during and after the war. This is clear from the **Sykes-Picot Agreement** and its implementation into the peace treaties and conventions of 1923 and 1924. Paris, retaining North Africa of course, obtained a mandate for **Syria** (including **Lebanon**), Cilicia and the *Vilayet* of Adana, and the oil region of Mossul, which, in 1918, Clemenceau retroceded to the British in exchange for 25% of the Turkish Petroleum Company.

For France, the decades which followed amounted to a futile attempt to combat the **Arab** national movement on the one hand and British competition on the other. Division and repression: such was the French tactic during its mandate. Faisal, elected king by the Syrian National Council on March 8, 1920, was forcibly expelled by the troops of General Gouraud who, on July 24, occupied Damascus. And the first task of the mandatory power was to divide the country into six: a Greater Lebanon, with a Christian majority, the Alawite State, the State of Aleppo, the State of Damascus, the Druze *Jebel* and the *Sanjak* of Alexandretta. The states of Aleppo and Damascus were combined, in 1925, to become the Syrian state. Then, in the Druze *Jebel*, insurrection broke out that spread to the whole mandated area: the dismantling of the country and the takeover of its government by the high commissioner provoked the overwhelming majority of the country. It would take a year and a half — and the bombing of Damascus by General Sarrail — before the French expeditionary force, reinforced for the occasion, finally put down the rebellious nationalists.

After repression came negotiations. In 1926, Lebanon was granted a republican parliamentary constitution attached to France. Ten years later, the Popular Front offered France a treaty granting Lebanon independence in exchange for military bases and facilities for the French army. But, like the one promised to Syria, this treaty was never to be signed since, in the meantime, Paris had undergone a change of heart. Obviously, France's prestige among the people it was governing, and the people of the region in general, suffered as a result of such methods; their desire for unity made them oppose the parcelling up that was being attempted by the occupying power, their religious feeling as Muslims was outraged by the privileges reserved for

Christians (and, to a lesser extent, the **Druze**), they found their democratic aspirations trampled underfoot by brutal repression and their hopes of independence mocked by French prevarications.

The final stroke came during World War II. Caught in pincers between the German offensive in Libya heading for Egypt, and that of the Caucasus towards Iraq, Great Britain had, at all costs, to defend its rear. Now, Vichy had allowed the Germans to help themselves to Lebanon and Syria; London therefore decided to occupy them, in July 1941, with the help of the Free French forces, after short but bloody battles in which Moshe Dayan took part, losing his right eye in the process. In the name of de Gaulle, General Catroux declared independence. Too late: the nationalist movement turned against him. The Lebanese (1943) and Syrian (1944) parliaments ended by abolishing French privileges. France's attempt to land troops was to no avail; the British, backed up by American and Soviet guarantees, lost no time in accepting the two countries, with no regard whatsoever for France's position, into both the Arab League and the United Nations, of which they were founder members of course. On December 31, 1946, the last French soldiers left the Levant.

Was it hoped in Paris to regain a footing in the Middle East by forming an exclusive alliance with **Israel**? The fact is that Franco-Israeli ties became increasingly close, to the extent that French experts would pass on to their Israeli colleagues the secrets of nuclear power, the bomb included, and help them to make the Jewish state a major power in this field too. The guilt felt by France, like the other Western states, after an extermination that it had allowed to take place, and the sense of brotherhood felt by socialists in power in both countries no doubt had a bearing on this trend, which was to be intensified, from 1954 onwards, by the conflict that started between the French government and Algerian nationalists. In supporting Israel against its Arab adversaries, French leaders apparently thought they could win in the Middle East the war they seemed unable to win in Algeria. This is manifestly the reason for French involvement in the Suez **War of 1956**. The fiasco of the venture was to have serious consequences: in Algeria, where it aggravated the uprising, and the Levant, where Paris, like London, was condemned to an irreversible decline by the hostility it had aroused in an Arab nationalist movement at the height of its power — and by the rivalry of the United States which was taking over the reins in the region.

It was to General de Gaulle that France owed its return to power. Right in the middle of the Six Day **War of 1967**, for which he held Israel responsible, the President of the Republic drastically altered the traditional viewpoint of the French Foreign Office. After having condemned the occupation of Arab territories and the annexation of Jerusalem by the Jewish state, he penalized the latter by an embargo on arms sales to the 'belligerent countries'. It is from this period that the controversial phrase 'a self-confident and dominant people' dates. The General's successors, Georges Pompidou then Valéry Giscard d'Estaing, remained faithful to this realignment in Middle East policy — but not to the embargo on arms destined for Israel, modified in 1969, abolished in 1974: the French diplomatic service agreed with its Arab counterparts regarding the conditions of a lasting peace, authorized the PLO to open an office in Paris and pressured the EEC to recognize 'Palestinian national rights', meanwhile getting involved once again in the Lebanese imbroglio. As for the Israelis, they took great pleasure in pointing out the economic perks of the Gaullist U turn: fabulous contracts with Iraq, Egypt, Saudi Arabia, Libya and Iran, oil being exchanged for arms, advanced technology, particularly nuclear civil technology, and many consumer goods.

The Mitterrand view differed somewhat from this, situated somewhere between the traditions of the SFIO (French section of the Workers International), whose friendship with Israel it maintained along with a pro-USA policy, and the Gaullist tradition from which it retained a fondness for the grand principles so dear to the Arab peoples. With hindsight, it is difficult to distinguish any trace of the left in the region, it having proved so contradictory, not to say incoherent.

The Arab world, uneasy about the Zionism attributed to Francois Mitterrand, was at first reassured: there was the president of the Republic's support of the Fahd Plan and statements about the Palestinian state made by the foreign secretary, who even met with Yasser **Arafat**. Then came the cold shower of the visit to Israel, in March 1982, that allowed Menachem **Begin** to reduce his diplomatic isolation — aggravated by the annexation of the **Golan** — without having to make any concessions; he even dealt sharply with his French guest, when the latter dared to speak of the rights of Palestinians. The tricolour flew again in Arab skies; it was France that allowed the PLO to leave Beirut when under siege by the Israeli Defence Force (IDF).

The negative side of the military presence in Lebanon was that France was to become involved in the conflict between the Phalangists — and their American allies — and the opposition supported by Damascus. The French contingent would find itself reproached for both its absence at Sabra and Shatila when the massacres took place and its involvement against Muslim forces, in particular during the bombing of Baalbek. Before leaving Lebanon, the French army would, for the second time, save the Palestinian resistance, this time from the trap of Tripoli. There then followed a period of relative calm, Paris taking a back seat to Washington and the **Reagan Plan**, not daring to take the Franco-Egyptian resolution before the UN Security Council, and abandoning all action, be it national, bilateral, multilateral or European. Neither the improvement in relations with Israel, nor the reopening of relations with Syria, dramatically symbolized by Francois Mitterrand's visit to Damascus in December 1984, brought about any new dynamics.

On the other hand, as Iraq's principal arms supplier after the USSR, France was to become enmeshed in the Gulf War — which led to the kidnapping and lengthy imprisonment of diplomats Marcel Carton and Marcel Fontaine, then of researcher Michel Seurat and journalist Jean-Paul Kauffmann, and other journalists. The new majority led by Jacques Chirac would inherit this unhappy problem, to which was added, in September 1986, a dreadful wave of terrorist attacks.

After mounting tension that ended in the breakdown of diplomatic relations between Paris and Tehran, negotiations were resumed. The French hostages were dramatically freed right in the middle of a presidential election, in the spring of 1988, opening the way for a normalizing of relations between the two countries. Two years later, in Summer 1990, France's friendship with Iraq and repeated calls for a peaceful solution to the Gulf crisis did not stop French citizens being detained amongst the other 20,000 western hostages taken by Suddam Hussein. Whilst condemning the invasion of Kuwait and supporting the embargo, France still called on the UN to guarantee a peaceful solution to the crisis.

Anxious not to lose any of France's acquisitions in the Middle East, the successive governments of Pierre Mauroy and Laurent Fabius, then of Jacques Chirac and finally of Michel Rocard succeeded in preserving and, to a certain extent, in taking advantage of the heritage (economic and political) of the preceding governments of the Vth Republic. On the other hand, despite France's commitment to the principle of mutual Israeli and Palestinian recognition of each other's right to a country, a principle which François Mitterrand has often reiterated, notably during Yasser Arafat's visit to Paris in May 1989, France has never been able to push the peace process forwards towards a settlement of the Arab-Israeli conflict along these lines.

Franjiyyeh (Suleiman)

SULEIMAN FRANJIYYEH was born on June 15, 1910, in North Lebanon, of a feudal Maronite family. In June 1957, during a clash between opposing Maronite factions, several dozen people were killed; Suleiman had to take refuge in Syria where he established close relations with numerous military men, including a certain Hafez Al Assad. These relations were to remain constant: true, the Maronites of the north have sometimes looked towards Damascus and, unlike those of Mount Lebanon, they assume their Arabness naturally.

Elected to parliament in 1960, replacing his brother, the real politician of the family, Franjiyyeh filled various ministerial offices. In 1970, he was elected president of the Republic, defeating his opponent, Elias Sarkis, supported by the Chehabists. During the first part of his mandate — marked by nepotism and corruption — he tried, with some success, to break the opposition movement and gain control of the PLO which, since leaving Jordan, had withdrawn into **Lebanon**. But, on April 10, 1973, his hopes of maintaining the country's old structures crumbled.

On that day, an Israeli army commando unit made a raid right into the centre of Beirut. Several important PLO leaders were assassinated. Saeb Salam, the Sunni prime minister, was forced to resign whilst tens of thousands of Lebanese and Palestinians demonstrated against the army's negligence. In May, there were violent clashes between the army and Palestinian commandos. The situation continued to deteriorate and even the formation of a coalition government, in the autumn of 1974 — where Kamal **Jumblatt**, Camille Chamoun and Pierre **Gemayel** sat side by side — did not halt the process that ended in the **Lebanese Civil War** of 1975–1976.

On April 13, 1975, when this war broke out, Franjiyyeh still had eighteen months of his electoral term before him. At first, with Syrian support, he tried to maintain a neutral position. On February 14, 1976, he presented a 'programme of national action' which, while retaining the **confessional** political system, proposed certain reforms: an equal Muslim/Christian repartition; the abolition of confessionalism in public office; the election of the prime minister by the Assembly. But it was already too late: the conflict had become more extreme and Suleiman Franjiyyeh was not considered a man 'above the fray' (his own militia, the Marada, took a prominent part in the clashes).

The president then joined up again with the Lebanese Front. He remained in office only through Syrian military intervention. By the time he handed over the highest office in the state to Elias Sarkis, in 1976, Franjiyyeh was only war-lord, like his rivals and allies.

But, unlike other elements of the Lebanese Front, he was firmly committed to alliance with Damascus and hostile to any *rapprochement* with Tel Aviv. When an overturning of the alliance was proposed in Lebanon — the Maronite right wing was increasingly banking on Israel, while Syria made its peace with the PLO and the Lebanese National Movement to combat **Sadat's** open policy during his visit to **Jerusalem** — Suleiman Franjiyyeh left the Lebanese Front (May 11, 1978). On June 13, his son Tony, Tony's wife, their little daughter and several of his followers were assassinated, at Ehden, by a Phalangist commando squad. Franjiyyeh's rupture with the right was complete. In 1988, he was Syria's candidate in the Lebanese presidential elections.

At almost eighty years of age, Suleiman Franjiyyeh has become one of the symbols of a closed political system in which clan allegiance and gerontocracy prevail.

Fundamentalism

BY A SIMPLISTIC and not very plausible comparison with Catholicism, the term Fundamentalism designates — particularly in the media — Muslims for whom Islam is the central focus of their political action. The term has been much in fashion since the upheavals in Iran. It couples phenomena that are often contradictory, dispenses with any need for analysis and reinforces the clichés and simplifications from which racism and fear of others are seldom free.

It is important, however, to try to be clear-sighted regarding this important phenomenon of our time: the political mobilizing, in the name of religion, of tens of millions of men and women. In the 19th century, Islam had been a driving force in the resistance to colonial violence. Later, when the new national states saw the light of day, the economic and political models set up were based on western societies or, later, on the societies of socialist countries. Islam then became only a vague political reference, particularly at state level. However, something that has gone largely unnoticed by observers, it did greatly influence civil society and the individual citizen.

It is difficult to draw up an overall balance sheet for the Arab world for that period extending from the end of World War II to the beginning of the 1970s. It would call for a detailed study, country by country. Two main features, however, stand out: the consolidation of political independence; the failure of attempts at modernization. Basic problems — hunger, poverty, illiteracy — are far from being solved. At the same time, formidable upheavals have affected the life of the individual. Can one measure what chaotic urbanization has meant for the tens of thousands of peasants uprooted from their villages? What are we to make of the 'modernization Sadat-style' which saw Cairo's population soar to 12, 13 or 14 million (no one knows for sure), the intensification of social inequalities and the breakdown of community life? The entire fabric of the old social life has been ripped into shreds. In a world and a society that are destructive, where responsibility for problems is quickly attributed to imported ideologies — whether western or socialist — people see in Islam a last resort; they seek political solutions to their problems in religion. That is the real significance of the 'Islamic Revival'.

This awareness is also linked to the political vacuum that was created in the Arab world as a result of various forms of repression; political parties had been banned, unions reduced to petty Prussianism, popular organizations sucked dry of all substance. In such conditions, the mosque becomes the only place where one can meet, discuss things, make political decisions. The use of religion — and of certain groups like the Muslim Brothers — in the struggles of 'moderate' regimes against the left, Nasserism and Ba'athism, is a factor that must not be ignored, even though it may not be a decisive one. Thus it was **Sadat** himself who encouraged the reconstitution of the Muslim Brothers, freed their leaders, gave them freedom of action and expression denied other factions of political life.

In this troubled context a multitude of organizations and movements developed, claiming Islam as their authority. Their often contradictory visions, their choices of conflicting political tactics, only go to show that there is no *one* Islamic vision of the world, that one cannot find in the Qu'ran — any more than one can in the Bible or the Gospels — a comprehensive answer to current questions. The Amal movement in Lebanon, the Muslim Brothers in Egypt, the Islamic Tendency in Tunisia; so many diverse projects despite their common sources. It should also be noted that, contrary to established notions, the cadres of these movements are young, urban and educated, and that their attitude cannot be reduced purely and simply to a refusal of modernism — even if the western version is generally rejected.

The Muslim Brothers are the oldest movement in this mutation. Founded in 1927 by an Egyptian school teacher, Hassan Al Banna, it was very powerful in the 1940s and 1950s, before being broken by **Nasser** in 1954—1955. Today it is enjoying a new lease of life in different Arab countries, though it now finds itself in competition with more radical groups — like the one that assassinated Sadat in 1981.

Galilee

THE GALILEE is the northern region of Palestine, assigned by the **Partition Plan** of 1947 to the **Arab** state and annexed by Israel at the end of the **war of 1948—1949**. It is where the majority of Israeli Arabs live today, though the considerable Jewish colonization of the area has altered its demographic balance.

The Galilee is rich in religious history: it was the centre of Judaism and, above all, with the town of Nazareth, the site of Christ's preaching.

As a border region adjoining **Lebanon**, it has frequently been the target of Palestinian attacks. It was in the name of Peace for Galilee that **Begin** launched the invasion of Lebanon in 1982.

Gaza

A STRIP of land 330 kilometres square, the territory of Gaza was part of Palestine under the British Mandate, adjoining **Egypt**. After the **war of 1948—1949**, Gaza came under the administration of Cairo but was not annexed. It retained an autonomous status. It is a much poorer region than the **West Bank**, with only a few agricultural resources (citrus fruits, vegetables), where more than three-quarters of the population is made up of refugees.

With the **Suez War of 1956**, Gaza underwent its first Israeli occupation. It was to be the only direct confrontation between **Palestinians** and Israelis during the period 1949—1967. It was in this conflict that Palestinians acquired experience in armed resistance. It was here that most of the Fatah leaders hammered out their ideas and the rebirth of Arab nationalism began.

Evacuated in 1957, Gaza was once again occupied in June 1967. The territory then had 390,000 inhabitants. Contrary to the West Bank, and although possessing only rear bases, the population launched itself recklessly into armed struggle. It was not until 1971, with General Sharon — who used every means at his disposal — that the Israelis managed to put an end to it.

The military victory led, as on the West Bank, to the establishment of Jewish **settlements** and the integration of Gaza into the Jewish economy: almost half the active population of the area crosses, every day, into the Jewish state to work in industry, building trades or public services. The population, extremely young, is highly educated thanks to the United Nations Office for Palestinian refugees. But those with qualifications cannot find work and have to emigrate. This phenomenon, already perceptible on the West Bank, has assumed greater proportions in Gaza.

From 1972—1973, contacts between the elites of the West Bank and Gaza increased, and it was as a united effort that, after the **October War of 1973**, they supported the **PLO** and the idea of a state constructed inside the occupied territories. In the Gaza Strip, however, the movement has been less organized (numerous refugees, absence of traditions, deficiencies in the social structures). The Muslim Brothers, whose roots in the region are long-standing, are powerful and were frequently used, in the 1970s, by the occupying authorities to counterbalance the influence of PLO partisans. It was in Gaza that, on October 8, 1987, the **Intifada**, or Palestinian uprising, began.

Gemayel (Family)

PIERRE GEMAYEL was born on November 6, 1905, into an eminent Maronite family, at Bikfaya, in the heart of Mount Lebanon. He studied at a Jesuit school in **Egypt**, then qualified as a pharmacist. In 1936, he created the **Phalangist Party**, which he headed for almost half a century. His position strengthened notably during the civil war of 1958, at the end of which he took part in the government of national reconciliation. Elected as a member of parliament to Beirut in Ashrafieh in 1960, he took an active part in political life, held various ministerial offices and twice stood as candidate, in 1964 and 1970, for the presidency of the Republic: without success. A fierce opponent of **Arab** nationalism and socialism, he was in the vanguard of the struggle for liberation, the upholding of the Maronite hegemony and, after 1967, against the PLO's presence in **Lebanon**. He called again and again for army intervention against the Palestinian Resistance then, when this failed to materialize, prepared his party to fight. During the civil **war of 1975–1976**, he was the key figure in the right-wing coalition. But the initiative gradually passed into the hands of armed factions and his son, Bashir. Pierre Gemayel nonetheless maintained a certain hold over the Political Office of the Phalangists, which he continued to direct up to his death, on August 29, 1984. Along with Chamoun and **Franjiyyeh**, he had dominated Maronite political life. Like them, he symbolized conservatism, but also the gerontocracy of the leaders.

Bashir Gemayel was born on November 10, 1947, the younger of Pierre Gemayel's two sons. He studied with Jesuits, then trained as a lawyer and spent a year in the **United States**. Involved in politics early on, he nonetheless held no important post at the outset of the civil war in 1975 — neither in the Phalangist Party nor in the Assembly. Assistant to William Hawi at the head of the military forces of the Kataeb, he succeeded him on his death, on July 13, 1976. Some days later, he acceded to the command of the Lebanese Forces (LF), the combined militia of the Right. His career had now really begun. A great fighter and a charismatic leader, he made himself loved by his men, who had confidence only in him. He forcibly established autonomy for the LF *vis-à-vis* political authorities. On two occasions, and in a bloody manner, he used them against his allies: in 1978, with the Ehden operation against the Franjiyyeh family, which confirmed the split with **Maronites** of the north; and in 1980 when, after bitter clashes that left a hundred dead, he liquidated the militia of Camille Chamoun's National Liberal Party (NLP), though Chamoun was president of the Lebanese Front. Elected president of the Republic on August 23, 1982, following the Israeli invasion, he never actually held office. He was assassinated on September 14. The Israeli government lost an essential card in its Lebanese policy.

Amin Gemayel, eldest son of Pierre, was born on January 22, 1942, at Bikfaya. Educated by Jesuits, he became a lawyer and business man. He was elected to parliament in 1970 in the North Metn and was involved in the Political Office of the Phalangist Party. Considered more diplomatic and moderate than his brother — he did not agree with the latter's various military campaigns against their allies — he nonetheless had to take a back seat to him and it was Bashir who became president. After his assassination, Amin replaced him. Elected to the Magistrature Supreme on September 21, 1982, he also benefited from a sudden upsurge of national unity. This was not to last. Allied with the United States, Amin at first played the Israeli card. On May 17, 1983, he signed a treaty with Israel, provoking the anger of Damascus and a broad front of Lebanese leaders, including Franjiyyeh, **Jumblatt**, Berri and Karameh. He suffered massive defeats and even lost control of West Beirut. He then changed course, repealed the May 17 agreement and formed a government of national unity headed by Karameh.

But Amin was to prove incapable of unifying the various factions around a national project. His term in office ended, in September 1988, in confusion: the president had no successor, and two governments would henceforth represent the Lebanese legality. At the beginning of October 1988, Samir Geagea's Lebanese Forces ousted Gemayel from his fiefdom in the Metn, and thus unified the Christian camp.

Golan Heights

THE NAME of the Syrian plateau situated to the north-west of **Israel**, which occupied it in June 1967, just after the Six Day War, then annexed it in December 1981.

The Golan's importance has been appreciated since earliest times. The caravan route from Damascus and Baghdad to the Mediterranean, it was occupied by the Greeks, who named it Gaulanitide. The Romans incorporated it into the province of Peraea, whose governors had their headquarters at Kuneitra, currently the plateau's principal town. Then, in the 7th century, the Arabs conquered it under the name of Al Joulan. In accordance with the **Sykes-Picot Agreement** of 1916, the treaties that concluded World War I made the Golan an integral part of the Syrian mandate accorded to **France**, a status that would be confirmed by the circumstances that emerged from World War II.

The plateau's importance is above all strategic: from an altitude of 1,000 metres it dominates the Hauran Plain in **Syria** and the **Galilee** valley in Israel; on the Lebanese side, it overlooks the Anti-Lebanon and the Hermon. Its fortress character is strengthened by mountainous terrain which the Syrians, after the creation of the State of Israel, would dot with bunkers, trenches and artillery deadly to the Israeli lines situated beneath them. It is also in the Golan that one of the sources of the River Jordan is to be found. But the region is equally remarkable for the richness of its agriculture: in 1966, according to Syrian sources, the Golan had 37,000 (horned) cattle, 1 to 2 million sheep and goats, 1,300 horses, 7,000 draught animals, 200,000 poultry, etc.; it produced cereals (over 100,000 tons), market-gardening produce (13,000 tons), milk, meat, honey, eggs, wool and, finally, 4,000 hectares of orchards containing 2.7 million fruit trees yielding 22,000 tons of fruit a year. Another of the plateau's assets are its hydraulic resources, whose discharge reaches 3,300 litres/second.

It was these three assets that Israel coveted when, on June 8, 1967, once the battles had ceased on the Egyptian and Jordanian fronts, the Israeli Defence Forces (IDF) attacked the Golan, which fell in two days. The area occupied had increased by 510 square kilometres at the end of the **war of 1973**, at all events until May 31, 1974; the Syrian-Israeli withdrawal agreement, brought about by the American Secretary of State, Henry **Kissinger**, allowed Damascus to regain the new pocket invaded during the Yom Kippur War and a small part of the Golan, including Kuneitra. But the problem of the plateau remained, coupled with that of its 170,000 refugees.

In fact, once installed, Israel intended to remain. The installations inherited from the Syrian army were augmented. Settlements multiplied — 50 constructed between 1967 and 1988. The occupiers took control of the soil's richness, particularly the water. The 15,000 inhabitants who had remained after the Six Day exodus, all Druze, had to resist Tel Aviv's wish to impose on them Israel's citizenship and laws. Unrest, already rife in the spring of 1981, was redoubled when, on December 14, 1981, one day after General Jaruzelski's *coup d'état* in Poland, Menachem **Begin**, transforming the *de facto* annexation into an official annexation, obtained from the Knesset a vote 'applying Israeli law to the Golan Heights'. The affiliation of the Golan to *Eretz Israel*, the protection of Jewish settlers and Damascus's refusal to negotiate were not enough to justify the Israeli decision; it was declared 'null and void' by the UN General Assembly, on December 17, by a vote that was unanimous apart from two voices (Israel and the United States).

Condemned by the international community, the Jewish state is nonetheless, up to the present time, master of the Syrian Golan. But no-one can possibly believe that Damascus and the Hafez Al Assad regime is ready to renounce its Alsace-Lorraine; the subject of the Golan will certainly come up again in any future peace talks.

Great Britain

FOR A LONG TIME the most influential Western power in the Middle East. The attraction of the region for London was based on economic, political and, above all, strategic considerations. From the time of the British Empire, the region's land and sea routes (including, from the end of the 19th century, the **Suez Canal**) constituted a vital lifeline between London and India in particular. From 1800 on, British strategy was therefore aimed at creating, first of the **Ottoman Empire** then, after its dismembering, of Palestine and its neighbours, a 'buttress to defend the main routes leading to India' (Fernand L'Huillier).

It was during the 19th century that Great Britain ensconced itself in the Middle East. It seized in succession Malta (1815), the Pirate Coast and the emirates of the Arabian-Persian Gulf (1820), **Egypt** (1882) and the **Sudan** (1898). During the same period, London took over the Suez Canal Company (1875) and secured the protectorates of the south coast of Arabia (1886 to 1914). In Persia, a sharing of dominance was negotiated with Russia (1907), followed by the Anglo-Persian Oil Company's acquisition of the first oil concession, extraction beginning in 1900.

From its position of strength, the British Empire was able to grab the largest slice of the Ottoman cake, after the defeat of the Turks and their German allies. In accordance with the **Sykes-Picot Agreement**, the territories allocated after World War I to British administration, either directly or indirectly, comprised both what is nowadays called **Iran**, **Iraq**, and **Jordan**, the ports of Haifa and Acre in Palestine as well as a mandate for the latter, to which must be added England's possessions in Egypt, Sudan, the **Arabian Peninsula** and the Gulf.

But this extraordinary expansion was based on contradictory promises that London, with some difficulty, would have to put into practice. 'Better to win and perjure oneself than lose', as the so-called **Lawrence of Arabia** had said. Victory achieved, decisions now had to be made. To the French, Great Britain had promised **Syria** and **Lebanon**; it held to this agreement. But to the Arabs, to ensure their participation in the war against the Sultan, it had claimed 'to recognize and support Arab **independence**'. This promise, given to both the Wahabite Ibn Saud and the Hashemite Hussein, was not respected — neither in the case of Syria nor Lebanon to whom Paris would refuse any real independence until 1941, nor of Palestine where London had promised Zionist leaders to promote the creation of the 'Jewish national homeland' envisaged in 1917 by the **Balfour Declaration**, nor even of the other territories under British influence whose leaders were to see their dream of a great independent Arab state fade away. Under cover of the mandate — aimed, as a French high commissioner declared, 'at allowing populations who, in political terms, are still minors, to educate themselves so as to attain self-government one day' — the British government did its utmost to avert the mounting wave of Arab nationalism.

Roughly speaking, it succeeded in this until World War II, adapting different means for the various countries. In Iraq, faced with a powerful nationalist movement, it had to grant independence in 1930, but meanwhile retained its economic, political and military influence. As for the **West Bank**, it would remain an emirate constitutionally linked to Great Britain. In Egypt, a cunning game played out between the king and the Wafd Party guaranteed London the perpetuation of its interests, particularly in the canal zone, and this despite a formally recognized independence. As for the Arabian Peninsula and the Gulf, English predominance there remained undisputed, even if the **United States**, through its oil concessions, was beginning to gain a footing in the region, particularly in Saudi Arabia.

The situation was more complex in Palestine where Great Britain had to face both a Zionist movement that insisted Lord Balfour's promise be kept, a promise included in the text of the mandate, and the Arab Nationalist Movement, which opposed the influx of Jewish immigrants. This Palestinian revolt was to take the form of increasingly long and violent uprisings which the British authorities, while brutally putting them down, had to take into account. Hence the successive White Papers of 1922 and 1930 which modified, though only verbally, the promises given to the Zionist Executive and, in particular, that of 1939 which drastically reduced Jewish immigration and land purchase. But this tardy revision was not enough to spare London from paying, and highly, for its double game

From being a pawn of British power, Palestine became in effect, after World War II, the catalyst of its decline. Submitted to the terrorism of extremist Zionist groups, to the pressure of world opinion stunned by the holocaust and Arab demands, Great Britain had to turn to the UN (see **Partition Plan**). The partition of Palestine was no sooner decided than London set out to sabotage it, but in vain. The State of **Israel** unilaterally declared its own independence, on May 14, 1948, and the invasion of the Arab states' armies, distinctly pro-British, launched on the 15th, failed. This humiliation was promptly turned against the instigator of the conflict; henceforth Great Britain would be the prime target of the Arab national movement, in whose eyes it was responsible for the Palestinian tragedy. Neither attempts to hide behind the cloak of Pan-Arabism, nor efforts to seek the support of regimes it controlled, would spare it the bitter setbacks brought by the 1950s: the nationalization of the Anglo-Iranian Oil Company by Doctor Mossadegh in Iran (1951), the nationalization of the Suez Canal (1956), revolution in Iraq (1958), etc.

The final straws for the British authorities, the Suez fiasco of 1956 and the withdrawal from Aden and the Gulf after 1967, would bring to an end, virtually definitive as it happened, more than a century and a half of predominance in the Near and Middle East. Victim of the Zionist movement on which it had thought it could count, of the Arab National Movement which, like Lawrence, it had hoped to coax round, London would have to bear the cost of competition, not from **France** who was also being ousted from the region, but from the United States; the latter's rise in power would be in inverse proportion to Britain's decline.

Gulf War

NAME given to the war which, from 1980 to 1988, was fought between **Iran** and **Iraq**, threatening the oil artery constituted by the Arabian-Persian Gulf and, more generally, peace in the region, or even on a global level.

It was, wrote the *Guardian*, 'the most expensive and the most futile war in Middle East contemporary history'. Expensive: the figures are frighteningly eloquent. The victims numbered at least a million between the two countries, Iran officially declaring 300,000. If many of these dead were soldiers — including adolescents of fifteen recruited into the Iranian army — many others were civilians killed in military operations aimed at towns and civilian populations. In economic terms, the damage was no less enormous: according to the most realistic estimates, the two belligerents must each have spent between a third and a half of the national budget.

In all, additional military expenditure, losses in gross domestic product and non-invested capital would reach 500 billion dollars between the two countries. Iran has officially (over)estimated the cost of reconstructing its economy at 300 billion dollars. Iraq has evaluated its similar operation at 50-60 billion. On top of this, Tehran is 10 billion in debt and Bagdad 60 billion. What is more, close to 700 ships were damaged or destroyed — amounting to two billion dollars — in the zone where 25% of western oil supplies is in transit, and in which is concentrated 30% of Iraq's hydro-carbon resources and 90% of Iran's.

For all that, was the Gulf War, to use the *Guardian*'s adjective, 'futile'? Clearly, its origins go far back in history. From the 16th century on, the Safavid Shi'ite dynasty, which had restored the Persian Empire, coveted Mesopotamia, then a province of the **Ottoman Empire**. This rivalry between the two empires, complicated by the intervention of the colonial powers, led to clash after clash. Already, the stake was the control of certain territories, in particular of Shatt Al Arab, the meeting place of the Tigris and the Euphrates which, 200 kilometres long, flows into the Arabian-Persian Gulf. Numerous treaties have marked this historic battle, the most recent having been signed in 1913 and 1937. The whole business was sparked off again by the Iranian revolution in 1958: the evolution of the two regimes diverged, Iran under the Shah establishing itself firmly in the western camp and Ba'athist Iraq gradually forging links with the Soviet Union. Aggravated by the Kurdish question, the dispute had to wait until 1975 before a temporary solution was reached: on the initiative of the Algerian President, Boumedienne, the Shah and Saddam **Hussein** made their peace. Both gave up their demands; Shatt Al Arab was shared between them; free navigation in the Gulf was guaranteed; the Kurdish uprising was cut off from its bases.

But the calm was not to last. The year 1979 saw the triumph of the Islamic Revolution. The ayatollahs and the mullahs succeeded the Shah, toppled from the throne by a formidable popular movement. Tehran's new leaders did not hide their ambition: to overthrow the Baghdad regime by supporting Iraq's Shi'ites — the majority of the population. The Iraqi Ba'ath Party, for its part, made no bones about its desire to see the last of **Khomeini**. In September 1980, after months of border incidents, Saddam Hussein denounced the 1975 treaty and launched his troops in an attack on Iran. Tehran not only repulsed the attack but, from 1982, carried the war into Iraqi territory.

The absurdity of the war became all the more apparent when deadlock set in. Only one type of logic seems to fit perfectly, the logic of Orwell. In *1984*, George Orwell envisages a situation where 'war is a purely domestic affair'. In the three empires he describes, war is waged by each group in power against its own subjects, and the object of the war is not to make or prevent territorial conquests, but to keep the structure of society intact. This prophetic vision is singularly apt when applied to Iraq and Iran.

Why, in 1980, did Baghdad's Ba'athist regime take military action? Clearly, its aims were multiple. No doubt it wanted to regain the Shatt Al Arab and the Iranian Khuzistan. It also hoped to deal a definitive blow to the Islamic Revolution, which it believed ready to fall. And it aimed to break its own regional isolation, even hoping — taking advantage of Egypt's isolation following Camp David — to gain a certain supremacy in the Arab world. So much is clear from its rapid veering from the 'Rejection Front', of which it had been the centre, to alliance with **Saudi Arabia** and the emirates of the Arabian Peninsula.

However, Saddam Hussein's decision was almost certainly based on motivations internal to Iraq. In 1980, his regime was in difficulties. A powerful opposition was drawn up against him: communists excluded from the National Front and harshly repressed, **Kurds** once again in revolt, fundamentalist Shi'ites encouraged by their co-religionists' victory in Tehran. A real guerilla force was taking shape. It was also, perhaps even especially, to break this eruption, by welding the population together in battle against the 'hereditary enemy', that Baghdad embarked on the venture. Not without success, if not at first, at least when the battle turned against them; the enthusiasm of the 'defenders of the fatherland' allowed the Ba'ath to split the opposition, by separating part of the Kurdish movement from the communists and their allies.

The thinking was the same in Tehran. The need to face up to the Iraqi attack remobilized a disillusioned population and put a worried army back on its feet. The priority given to national defence was used to justify breaches of civil liberties and the freezing of any change in the structure. It served as a pretext for reactionary clergy to take control of the country. First the 'liberals', then President Bani Sadr, were ousted. Repression spread and turned first on the *mujahedeen* and the *fedayeen*, and then on the communists of the Tudeh Party. The great promised reforms were bogged down in parliamentary commissions. So true was all this that, from 1982, although Iran had repulsed Baghdad's troops, Khomeini decided to continue the hostilities. He rejected both the ceasefire proposals from Iraq and the countless mediations (UN, Non-Aligned, Islamic Conference, Algeria, Saudi Arabia, etc.).

The final, equally strange aspect of the Iran-Iraq conflict was manifested by the contortions of the great powers. The Gulf War did not fit into the East versus West framework, each of the belligerents having allies and enemies in both camps. Paris and Moscow found themselves side by side, as Baghdad's principal arms suppliers. Irangate revealed that Washington, humiliated by Tehran over the embassy hostages, was still delivering to the Islamic Republic many of the arms it needed. And Israel, supposed to be taking a stand against this extremist Islam, was the first to supply Iran, with the aim of weakening its Iraqi Arab enemy. No doubt this 'exteriority' of the Gulf War, which clearly does not obey the traditional laws of the genre, also explains its interminable quality.

Why then did it end when it did? Tehran's decision, after refusing for six years, to accept the UN's ceasefire proposal, was based on a combination of four reasons. First, the military defeats it had undergone: on all fronts, particularly in the south, with the Iraqis' recapture of the Fao Peninsula, the mullahs' army had been forced to relinquish the territory it had conquered since 1982. Then there were the effects on the morale of the home front — particularly that of the capital hitherto spared fighting — caused by the new weapons employed by Baghdad: missiles and chemical weapons. There is no doubt that the 'war of towns' was a significant factor in the ayatollah's about-face. The tragic end of the Iranian Airbus, shot down by an American ship in July 1988, must also be mentioned. The fourth and last factor, which was probably the decisive one: the evolution of the political balance of power within the Iranian leadership. President Rafsanjani assumed a central role. In August 1990, Iraq renounced all claims to the Shatt-al-Arab, and Iran's military defeat turned into a political victory overnight.

Habash (George)

BORN on August 2, 1926 in Lydda (Palestine), George Habash comes from a family of Greek Orthodox merchants. In July 1948, during the Palestine **War of 1948—1949**, his family was driven out of his birthplace. Having made his home in Beirut, he studied pediatrics at the American University, completing his studies in 1951. He was already very active politically, but it was not until the next year that he founded the **Arab** Nationalist Movement (ANM). From that moment on, his life became inseparable from that of his organization.

It was in the same year that George Habash opened a people's clinic in Amman. It was from there that he took part in the leadership of the ANM whose aim was defined as follows: 'As long as no united state exists, unifying **Iraq**, **Jordan** and **Syria** (as a first step), any confrontation with the **Jews** and the Western alliance will be virtually impossible.'

Arrested in 1957, he took refuge in Damascus, at the time of the formation of the United Arab Republic of **Egypt** and Syria. Converted to Nasserism, George Habash and the ANM evolved theories dissimilar to those of Fatah. According to them, what was essential for the liberation of Palestine, was not the mobilization of the **Palestinians** themselves, but the intervention of Arab countries against **Israel**. The role of Palestinians would be confined to being a 'catalyst'. In 1964, the ANM created a Palestinian section which operated out of Beirut, where Dr Habash had settled. It carried out its first armed operation in 1966.

The **war of 1967**, which dealt a serious blow to Nasser's prestige, devastated the ANM. It disappeared, carried under with the wreck of the idea of Arab unity personified by the Egyptian *Rais*. The ANM gave birth to various regional sections, the most famous of which were the **South Yemen** branch, which seized power at the end of 1967, and the Popular Front for the Liberation of Palestine (PFLP) directed by George Habash.

Established in Jordan with the other *fedayeen* organizations, the PFLP was extremely militant in the field and attracted international attention by its hijacking of aircraft, the first of which involved, on July 23, 1968, an El Al plane. Weakened in February 1969 by a split instigated by Nayef **Hawatmeh**, the PFLP nonetheless continued to play a subversive role within the Hashemite kingdom, where it called for the overthrow of the regime. 'The liberation of Palestine will come through Amman', it trumpeted, drawing the PLO into the confrontation of September 1970 (**Black September**), which would see the elimination of the resistance in Jordan.

After this serious defeat, the PFLP changed tack. In 1972, it renounced external operations, preferring to concentrate its attacks on Israel, but without establishing any distinction between military and civilian targets. It adopted Marxism-Leninism as its theory. It split with its more extreme elements, like Dr Wadih Hadad. Nonetheless, after 1973, the PFLP was still at the heart of the opposition to new orientations within the PLO. George Habash condemned the idea of a mini-state made up of the **West Bank** and **Gaza**; he was opposed to the holding of the Geneva Conference and Yasser **Arafat**'s visit to the United Nations; he violently attacked the **USSR**, guilty in his eyes of setting the PLO on the path to surrender. His only ally on the international scene, at the time, was Iraq.

After the signing of the **Camp David Accords**, Palestinian solidarity was re-established but the PFLP, which had left the PLO Executive Committee in 1974, did not rejoin it until 1981. Having undergone a serious brain operation at the end of 1980, Dr Habash remained on the sidelines for many months. Differences between the PFLP and Fatah remained critical, and came to a head once again after 1982.

George Habash once again found himself at the centre of an anti-Arafat coalition, the Palestine National Salvation Front, in which the dissidents of Fatah, Saika and the PFLP–General Command of Jibril also took part. But, unlike these groups, he did not refuse to take part in the Algiers Palestine National Council (PNC) of April 1987 — after which he rejoined the executive organs of the PLO — and December 1988. If he rejected certain of the latter's decisions — in particular the acceptance of Resolution 242 — he claimed to be in favour of maintaining Palestinian solidarity.

An uncompromising leader, Dr Habash has retained great influence within the PLO, with both friends and enemies. He made the PFLP the second most important organization after Fatah, particularly influential in the refugee camps. Finally, he has been able, whatever his alliances with Arab regimes, to preserve the **independence** of the PFLP. Closely linked to Damascus, the PFLP has also strengthened its relations with the USSR.

Hawatmeh (Nayef)

BORN on November 17, 1935, at Salt, on the East Bank of the Jordan, into a Greek Catholic peasant family, Nayef Hawatmeh began his higher education in Cairo in 1954 and, the same year, joined George **Habash**'s **Arab** National Movement (ANM). Back in **Jordan** in 1956, his revolutionary activities resulted in his being condemned to death *in absentia*. In 1958, he took part in the **Lebanese Civil War**, then took refuge in **Iraq**, where he directed the ANM section for five months. From 1963 to 1967, he was in South **Yemen** where he played a part in the anti-British liberation struggle. After the Six Day **War of 1967**, he took advantage of an armistice and returned to Jordan where he joined the PFLP. He became the head of the organization's left-wing faction, which had Marxist-Leninist leanings, and was critical of the Arab lower middle classes. The split became final in February 1969, and Hawatmeh formed the Popular Democratic Front for the Liberation of Palestine (PDFLP), which became the DFLP in August 1974.

If the DFLP adopted the same adventurist attitude that had characterized the PFLP in Jordan in the period 1969–1970, the political differences between the two could not have been more marked. As early as 1969, at Hawatmeh's instigation, the PDFLP denounced the chauvinist slogans of the 'kick the Jews into the sea' type. In 1970, it opened a dialogue with the Israeli extreme left organization, Matzpen. Furthermore, from 1973 on, it became — along with Fatah and the communists — one of the most ardent defenders of the idea of a Palestinian mini-state. On March 22, 1974, Hawatmeh gave an interview to the Israeli newspaper, *Yediot Aharonot*, that aroused wide interest: 'I believe', he said, 'that it would be a very good thing if Israeli society, with all its different components, become aware of a revolutionary Palestinian position regarding the Arab-Israeli conflict. . . . I do not see why we must accept that Arab reactionary forces conduct a dialogue with Israel's most extreme tendencies while forbidding progressive forces doing the same with progressive Israeli forces. Admittedly, such a dialogue would represent a threat both for Zionism and Arab reactionaries '

This frank, restrained language is not in contradiction, at least in the eyes of the DFLP, with ruthless armed operations, such as the one undertaken at Maalot, in May 1974, which left sixteen Israelis dead, many of them school-boys. The period 1974–1977 witnessed a strengthening of the alliance between the DFLP and the socialist camp, as well as its adoption of most of the traditional communist analyses. On the Arab front, its main support was South Yemen, with whom Hawatmeh had retained important contacts.

From 1977 on, the DFLP dissociated itself from Fatah, whom it accused of making compromises with 'Arab reactionary forces'. Hawatmeh nonetheless tried to maintain a middle ground between **Arafat** and the Rejection Front. Fervent defender of the **Fez Plan** of 1982, he nonetheless condemned the PLO's *rapprochement* with Cairo and Amman. In favour of alliance with **Syria**, he disagreed with the latter on numerous occasions and refused to join the Palestine National Salvation Front (PNSF). In April 1987, at the

Palestine National Council (PNC) in Algiers, he and Arafat were reconciled. A year later, in November 1988, he gave his approval to the new direction taken by the PLO: proclamation of the Palestinian state, acceptance of Resolution 242, a fundamental resolution to create a provisional government when the time was ripe.

By the originality of his analyses and the independence he was able to maintain vis-à-vis the Arab regimes, Nayef Hawatmeh made the DFLP one of the most exceptional organizations in the Palestinian movement.

Herzl (Theodor)

THE FOUNDER of **Zionism**. Born in Budapest in 1860, he settled with his family in Vienna at the age of eighteen. Having completed law studies and become an attorney, Herzl turned his attention to literature and the theatre. At the age of thirty-one, separated from his wife and scarred by the suicide of his best friend, he left for France, where he was appointed correspondent for the *Neue Freie Presse*, a new Austrian daily.

Until that time, Theodor Herzl, like most West European Jewish intellectuals, believed the solution to the Jewish problem lay in the assimilation of his co-religionists into the populations among whom they were living. The emancipation of the **Jews** and the recognition of their equal rights, initiated by the French Revolution, seemed to him an irreversible historical trend. Jacob Samuel, the main character of his play, *The New Ghetto*, written in 1894, dies crying: 'I want to come out of the ghetto. . . .'

But the martyrdom of Captain Alfred Dreyfus, himself a believer in assimilation, and the wave of anti-semitism that accompanied it, were to change Theodor Herzl's outlook entirely. Already, in 1882, his predecessor, Leon Pinsker, had summed up the Jew, in *Self Determination*, in this striking portrait: 'seen by the living as dead, by the indigenous population as a foreigner, by the settled as a tramp, by the wealthy as a beggar, by the poor as an exploiter, by patriots as a stateless person, and by all classes of society as a competitor to be hated'. Taking as starting point the existence of a Jewish people and the impossibility of its assimilation, Herzl saw as the only solution the creation, if possible in Palestine, of a Jewish state. This was the purport of his 1896 work, *The Jewish State*, and of the meetings he solicited and obtained from the German emperor, a Turkish sultan, Pope Pius X, the King of Italy, British and Russian ministers (including one who had organized pogroms), etc.

To each of the foregoing, he emphasized the far-reaching significance of his project: for the English, the strategic role of a Jewish Palestine that would protect the 'vital line' of the British Empire, for the Germans and Russians the possibility of bringing to an end their 'Jewish problem', and for the Turks a bargain exchanging the redeeming of the Ottoman Empire's enormous debt for the concession of Palestine. Conditions were right for the realization of the plan adopted, at Basle, on August 29 and 30, 1879, by the first Jewish World Congress, convoked by Theodor Herzl who became its president.

'At Basle', he wrote in his *Journals*, 'I created the Jewish state. If I said that publicly today, it would be met by general laughter. Perhaps in five years, certainly in fifty, everyone will understand.' Indeed, fifty years and nine months later, the state of **Israel** saw the light of day. But Herzl was not to know the outcome of his 'vision'; after fighting in vain for the foundation of his Jewish state, whether in Argentina, in the Sinai or in Mozambique, he died on July 3, 1904.

Holocaust

BIBLICAL name given to the destruction of the **Jews** of Europe by the Nazis during World War II. Many authors prefer the term genocide, so as not to give the attempted extermination of the Jews any connotation of religious sacrifice.

Anti-semitic racism was, from the outset, an important element of Hitlerian Fascism. The Nazi 'bible', *Mein Kampf*, is permeated with it. Up until 1933, the Brown Shirts' anti-semitism was mainly expressed verbally: the Jew served as scapegoat, depicted   so as to fuel the discontent of the population which it polarized — with the features of the 'Judeo-Bolshevik' or the 'Judeo-plutocrat'. With Hitler's arrival in power the 'legalization' of anti-semitism began: the Law of April 7, 1933, then the Nuremberg Laws (September 15—16, 1935) establishing strict segregation aimed at preventing all contact between Aryans and Jews, particular emphasis being placed on banning mixed marriages and excluding Jews from a number of professions, etc. At the same time, acts of violence increased, ranging from the compulsory boycott of Jewish businesses to the imprisonment of thousands of Jews, by way of the third degree treatments that were a speciality of the SA and the SS.

The assassination, in Paris, of embassy attaché von Rath by one Grynspan, in November 1938, seved as a pretext for the unleashing of a veritable anti-semitic reign of terror. A pogrom extending over the whole of Germany, organized by Goebbels and Himmler, with the help of the Gestapo, the

Kristallnacht, the 'Night of Broken Glass', November 9, ended with a dreadful toll: 191 synagogues set alight, fifty of which were destroyed, 7,500 Jewish shops demolished and pillaged, 91 Jews savagely murdered. . . . 'We must arrest as many Jews, especially the rich ones, as existing prisons can hold. On their arrest, immediate contact must be made with the appropriate concentration camps, in order to intern them as quickly as possible,' specified the message sent by the SS number two, Reinhard Heydrich, to all high-ranking police officers. In actual fact, on November 10 and 11, 20,000 Jews were rounded up to join the communists, social democrats and Christians already imprisoned, some since 1933. But those remaining at liberty were by no means let off: a collective fine of a billion marks was imposed on German Jews as punishment for their 'abominable crimes', not to mention the cost of their destroyed possessions — the insurance claims were confiscated by the government! On top of this, anti-semitic legislation was intensified, Jews being henceforth totally eliminated from the German economy, by making over their businesses and possessions to 'Aryans'.

'The main problem remains: it consists of chasing the Jews out of Germany,' Heydrich had declared. At first, the solution resorted to was fee-paying emigration: from 1933 to October 31, 1941, 537,000 Jews legally left Germany, Austria and Bohemia-Moravia, at a cost of 9.5 million dollars paid out by their co-religionists abroad. After having toyed with the idea of deporting the Jews to Madagascar, then begun to assemble them in Poland, high-ranking Hitlerians came round to the 'final solution' long prophesied by Hitler. No one was left in any doubt on the matter. Thus, on January 30, 1939, the Chancellor once more stated before the Reichstag: 'I'll make a prophecy. If Jewish capital, in Europe and elsewhere, manages one more time to plunge peoples into a world war, the consequence will not be the bolshevizing of the world, and consequently a victory for the Jews, but on the contrary the destruction of the Jewish race in Europe.'

Decided on during the summer of 1941, finalized at a meeting in Wansee, Berlin, on June 20, 1942, the final solution involved the deportation of all the Jews of occupied Europe to existing concentration camps and, more especially, to new camps under construction: extermination camps. Thus were born, among others, Auschwitz, Treblinka, Belzec, Sobibor and Shelm-no, where the installation of gas chambers allowed the daily annihilation of thousands of men, women and children. 'The definitive solution to the Jewish problem in Europe concerns approximately 11 million Jews,' Heydrich had estimated at Wansee; if one includes the victims of the wholesale massacres on the Eastern Front, those of the ghettos and the death factories, he achieved more than half of his objective. Six million.

The genocide of the Jews by the Nazis does not stand alone in the history of humanity: the Indians of Latin America and North America, the Armenians and, more recently, the Cambodians are tragic proof of this. But the holocaust stands out from all of them by its sheer scale — more than half the targeted population; by the extent of the technical means employed — from the transport wagons to the crematoriums; and by its purely racial character, excluding all other motives (territorial gains, economic advantage, rise in social status, etc.). In the middle of a century seen as representing human progress, its effect was all the more devastating on communities who had seen their assimilation as a guarantee against the renewing of the persecution of the past. It was a wound that was never to heal.

Ever since then, the extermination of the Jews, more than forty years ago, has continued to exert a crucial influence: decisively, in 1947, in favour of the creation of the State of Israel; then, during the various Israeli-Arab conflicts, in the form of a 'natural' sympathy of Western opinion with Israel. One cannot dispute the claims of the Arab peoples, **Palestinians** above all, when they complain of paying in the stead of Europeans for the crimes committed or tolerated by them against the Jews. 'We are', wrote Marguerite Duras in *La Douleur*, 'from that part of the world where the dead are piled up in an inextricable charnel-house. This is happening in Europe. It is here that Jews are being burned, millions of them. Here they are being mourned.' That being the case, surely it is not difficult to understand that Israelis live with the memory of that horror, from which they protect themselves by a justifiable quest for security. More generally speaking, the memory of the holocaust makes up a substantial part of Jewish identity throughout the world, even where they have once again been integrated into the nations where they live. And even when they do not feel implicated in Israeli policy, that memory gives birth in them to a certain feeling for Israel seen as a refuge, just in case.

However much the genocide may therefore have been used as an argument, or even more as a pretext for some affair or other, it would be absurd to underestimate its political, ideological and cultural importance.

Hussein Ibn Talal

THIRD KING of **Jordan**, Hussein was born in 1935 in Amman. He underwent a dual education, classical **Arab** and Western, which he completed at Sandhurst Military Academy in **Great Britain**. He was at the side of his grandfather, King Abdullah, when the latter was assassinated in 1951. After a short reign by his father Talal — who maintained an anti-British policy and was forced to abdicate on grounds of insanity — Hussein was crowned king. By the time he came of age, on May 2, 1953, he wielded the real power in the land. King

Hussein has now been reigning for almost 36 years, a longevity unequalled in the Middle East.

The dynasty has, however, been through many crises, the first of which erupted in the mid-1950s. Nasserism was then in full swing and exerted a profound influence on those of the population of Palestinian origin. The king, committed to alliance with the West, was in favour of joining the Baghdad Pact. But the opposition of his people was too strong; he gave up the project and even had to dismiss Glubb Pasha, the English commander of his army, in March 1956. In October of the same year, a particularly bloody raid — 48 dead — by the Israeli Defence Forces (IDF) against the little town of Qalqilya further hardened the climate of opinion. On October 21, the nationalist parties won the elections and Suleiman Nabulsi was appointed prime minister. After the Suez expedition, the king even denounced the alliance treaty with London, but, feeling his power threatened, reacted by turning to the army, composed of Bedouins faithful to the Hashemites. In April 1957, he dismissed the government, dissolved parliament and banned political parties. His authority restored, the king was nonetheless constrained, in July 1958 — following the collapse of the Hashemite monarchy in Iraq — to bring in British parachutists.

In 1964, following a *rapprochement* with Nasser and in the face of the Israeli decision to divert the flow of the River Jordan, King Hussein sponsored the creation of the PLO in Jerusalem. However, its leader, Shukairy — supported by the *Rais* — was against the Hashemite king: at the heart of the crisis lay the problem of controlling the West Bank Palestinians. After the war of 1967, the conflict surfaced again, but this time with the *fedayeen* organizations which the king eliminated with great brutality in 1970–1971, during the events of Black September.

Hussein tried to regain the initiative in the Palestinian question and strengthen Palestinian loyalty to the crown. He also hoped, by an agreement with Israel, to regain the West Bank. On March 15, 1972, he set out his plan for a United Arab Republic, in other words the transformation of the kingdom into a federal state, composed of two regions: the West Bank which would be called Palestine, and the East Bank which would retain the name of Jordan. But his proposals had little success and were rejected by Arab countries and the PLO as well as Israel.

The October 1973 offensive of Egypt and Syria, in which Jordan took no part, represented the prelude to the PLO's diplomatic breakthrough. A year later, in October 1974, at the Arab summit in Rabat, the king concurred in the general consensus that made the PLO the sole representative of the Palestinian people, the only agent entitled to negotiate the future of the West Bank and Gaza.

The king remained faithful to this commitment, and he condemned the

Camp David operation initiated by **Sadat** in 1977—1978. The Israeli invasion of **Lebanon** and the departure of the PLO from Beirut in the summer of 1982 created conditions that were propitious for a new role for King Hussein. The sixteenth Palestinian National Council (PNC) in Algiers ratified, on February 1983, the idea of a Jordano-Palestinian federation. But, under pressure from the Palestinian *intifada*, Hussein renounced, on July 31, 1988, all rights to the West Bank. The following year, he committed his country to a process of democratization, including the first free elections for thirty years.

The King has managed to safeguard his throne under the most difficult circumstances. The great question mark hanging over him, and the new Jordanian identity he has managed to create, remains the Palestinian issue. The Gulf crisis exposes him to military threat on both sides, from Iraq and from Israel, with a rising tide of Arab nationalism to cope with as well.

Hussein (Saddam)

A SUNNI MUSLIM, born on April 28, 1937, at Takrit, a village to the north of Baghdad, into a peasant family, Saddam Hussein has ruled **Iraq** for twenty years. More than any other leader, he has made a mark on the contemporary history of his country, for better or worse. Late in starting his education, he entered a Baghdad secondary school in 1955. He became politicized there and, in 1957, joined the **Ba'ath** Party. Shortly after the uprising of July 14, 1958, which brought the monarchy to an end, his party went into opposition. In October 1959, he took part in an abortive assassination attempt against General Kassem; wounded, he was forced to flee, first to **Syria**, then to **Egypt** where he completed his secondary education. It was there that he learned of the success of the *coup d'état* of February 1963 which overthrew Kassem and in which the Ba'ath had participated. He therefore returned to Baghdad and joined the party leadership. But the Ba'ath was ousted from power in November 1963; Saddam went into hiding.

Arrested in October 1964, he spent two years in prison. On his release, he was elected deputy secretary-general of the party. But it was the Ba'athist army officers, lead by Hassan Al Bakr, who organized the *coup d'état* of July 17, 1968, then went on, on July 30, to eliminate certain of their allies. From this date the inexorable rise of Saddam Hussein began. With Al Bakr as ally, he developed the political wing of the Ba'ath — whose influence was reduced — and was particularly successful in Ba'ath-izing the armed forces: before the end of 1970, 3,000 political commissars stiffened the officer corps. In November 1969, he became vice-president of the Revolutionary Command

Council (RCC), the real centre of power. Through the elimination — sometimes by political assassination — of their rivals, the duo Saddam Hussein—Al Bakr definitively confirmed its power at the end of 1971. Saddam Hussein stood out as the real man of strength. Brutal but pragmatic, he took the major decisions that put a stamp on Iraq, from the nationalization of oil to the attack on Iran.

Al Bakr's function was above all to ensure the loyalty of a maximum number of officers. Little by little, his usefulness declined: on July 16, 1979, he resigned from his position as president of the Republic and of the RCC, to be replaced immediately by Saddam, who promoted around himself an increasingly grandiose cult. A few days later, several highly placed leaders were tried and executed on charges of conspiracy and complicity with Syria. More than ever, the RCC became, for Saddam, a reliable tool, dominated by Sunni elements from Takrit (like the president) and members of his own family.

The end of the Gulf War, in 1988, presented him with a new challenge. Saddam Hussein, largely responsible for this disastrous war — it had cost his country hundreds of thousands of human lives and caused incalculable financial losses — may now encounter more active opposition. His August 1990 invasion of Kuwait, defying both the West and moderate Arab opinion, may be a last ditch response to these difficulties. Winner take all ...

Immigration

THE MIDDLE EAST has always been a land of migrations. But, in recent decades, the phenomenon has taken on a new dimension. The reason for this is simple: the region is comprised on the one hand of countries that produce oil, hence capable of large-scale investment but sparsely populated, and on the other, densely populated countries which produce no (or very little) oil, with the exception of Iraq which is alone in holding both these assets.

As a result of this inconsistency, large-scale immigration has come about to reinforce the insufficient work forces, particularly in the Arabian Gulf. At first, these new workers were from Arab countries, such as Egypt, Jordan, the Yemen, Syria, Lebanon or Iraq and, of course, Palestine. But, since 1970, the entrepreneurs of the Gulf have cast their net further afield: into Asia. It was in India, the Philippines, South Korea, and even in China, that henceforth an increasingly large percentage of this auxiliary work force would be recruited. True, the wages vary, some workers receiving up to three or four times as much as others, depending on whether they are Asians or Arabs.

Elizabeth Longuenesse has supplied important statistical details on immigration in the Gulf. Overall, in 1980, it represented 54% of the active population, varying from 42% in **Saudi Arabia** to 89% in the United Arab Emirates. In **Kuwait**, until the Iraqi invasion, foreigners constituted 78.6% of workers, and were dispersed between agriculture and fishing (1.4%), mining and oil (1.2%), industry (9.9%), electricity-water-gas (1.6%), building trades (25%), business (14.2%), transport and communications (5.9%), and services (40.6%). But this distribution also stemmed from the presence of 300,000 **Palestinians**, often integrated into local society. This is not the case for most of the Gulf's immigrant workers, who often have to pay a forfeit of several months' wages to the labour contractor to obtain work and a visa, and all this to live alone — only rarely do families follow, and always much later — on miserable pay, at the mercy of the despotism of the emirs.

The result of a political decision, this massive immigration is obviously not without political consequences. Many Gulf regions prefer to call in Asian labour to avoid the risks that would be incurred, according to them, by an Arab immigration more sensitive to democratic and nationalist under-currents. But the wave of immigration that has resulted from all this has profoundly destabilized the backward societies of the Gulf, striking a blow against traditional Arab culture and identity, and, at the same time, giving rise to feelings calculated to stimulate the upsurge of fundamentalism. It has not, however, hindered the development of a more or less revolutionary opposition movement, local Arabs and foreigners even sometimes joining forces. Contrary to certain prophecies of catastrophe, the oil recession affecting the Gulf countries has not had a significant effect on immigration, which has continued to increase. But the differentiation has become accentuated between Arab immigrants, whose numbers have stabilized but who tend to settle, and Asian immigrants whose numbers are increasing but who are subjected to a rapid turnover.

Independence

INAUGURATED by the dismantling of the **Ottoman Empire**, immediately after World War I, the era of independences (i.e. the attaining of independence by the subject peoples) lasted, in the Middle East, into the 1970s. Needless to say, the process took place within the framework of frontiers, often arbitrary, defined by the victors.

The first country to win its independence, **Egypt** was also, in this region so often carved up at the whim of the colonizers, one of the few nations established centuries before. On top of this, a powerful nationalist movement had developed, centred around the Wafd Party. Since 1918, disturbances had been so violent that London chose, on February 28, 1922, to concede independence unilaterally. But the British reserved enormous privileges for themselves in matters of communications, defence and protection of their foreign interests — just as they did in **Sudan**. The same went for the new treaty which the British were forced to sign on August 28, 1936, following a long test of strength with the Wafd: in it they benefited in particular from facilities in the event of war, and the recognition of their interests in the **Suez Canal** zone where they maintained a force of 10,000 men. Admitted to the United Nations in 1937, Egypt would not gain real independence until 1954, when **Nasser**, succeeding Neguib, managed to force the former mother country to evacuate the canal zone before going on, in 1956, to nationalize the Suez Canal Company.

Iraq was also the scene of a vigorous campaign for independence. The announcement of the British Mandate, in 1920, unleashed an uprising there which was put down, not without great difficulty, by His Majesty's troops. The coronation of Feisal, chased out of **Syria** by the French army, did not bring the turbulence to an end. With the result that, constantly on the retreat and having failed to honour three different treaties, **Great Britain** finally acknowledged that of 1930, which granted total independence to Iraq, in exchange, here too, for military facilities, including bases. What was once Mesopotamia thus entered the League of Nations on October 3, 1932.

At that time, what is now **Saudi Arabia** was already independent. True, it was with Ibn Saud that Sir Percy Cox, British resident in the Gulf, had concluded the first Anglo-Arab agreement in 1915: the organization of the anti-Turk revolution in return for independence. Having failed, as we have seen, to grant this immediately after the war, as promised to the whole Arab world, London gave it, in 1926, to 'the King of Hedjaz and Sultan of Nedj and his dependencies'. The Wahabite leader had in fact triumphed, in the meantime, over the Hashemite Sherif, Hussein; Arabia was his ... on condition that he recognize the British positions, in the south in the Gulf, and in the north in Transjordan.

In 1921, London had detached from the Palestine Mandate, entrusted to it by the League of Nations, the territory to the east of the Jordan, to construct there the Emirate of Transjordan. At its head would be Abdullah, brother of Faisal and, like him, a son of the Sherif, Hussein. Probably the most artificial of the brain-children of Sykes and Picot, Transjordan, entirely lacking a people conscious of it own identity, gave little trouble to its protector. Though its frontier was recognized in 1927 by Ibn Saud, and its organic law and a treaty sanctioning its British character were adopted in 1928, the emirate did not manage to obtain its (formal) independence until 1946. And in

1950, following the annexation of **Jerusalem** and the **West Bank**, the King imposed the term the Hashemite Kingdom of **Jordan**.

Shortly before this, **Lebanon** and Syria had in their turn attained independence. Yet their French 'mandatory' had done everything in its power to delay the eventuality. In 1920, it was by means of force that Faisal, proclaimed King by the General Syrian Congress, was expelled from Damascus. Then began a long series of territorial 'fiddling'. 1920: the Mandate is divided into four states, Greater Lebanon, Damascus, Aleppo and an Alawite state. The last three were federated in 1922, the **Druze** Jebel becoming autonomous. 1924: creation of the Sandjak of Alexandretta, ceded to Turkey in 1939. Further carving up in 1925: Greater Lebanon, Syria and Druze Jebel, where an uprising broke out that extended to the whole country, before being put down by the French army. It was not until 1936 that independence, in exchange for a military alliance, bases and 'facilities', would be promised to Lebanon and Syria in a treaty . . . never to be ratified, for the very good reason that the Popular Front had just ended! Vichy having allowed the Axis powers to make military use of the two countries, Great Britain occupied them in July 1941, with the Free French forces. Their leader in the field, General Catroux, de Gaulle's representative, proclaimed the independence of Lebanon and Syria. But it was late in the eyes of the national movement, which was granted admission to the UN without the slightest reference to France's special position. The last French soldiers left the Levant on December 31, 1946.

However, Great Britain's enjoyment of its rival's misfortunes was to prove short-lived: 30 years after the **Balfour Declaration**, 25 years after the Mandate, its Palestinian policy had reached a dead end. The UN, to whom it had referred the matter, decided on the **partition**. On May 14, 1948, Sir Allan Cunningham, the seventh and last British High Commissioner in Palestine, boarded ship at Haifa. That very day Israel declared its independence: 'On this day when the British Mandate ends and in virtue of the natural and historic right of the Jewish people and in compliance with the resolution of the UN General Assembly, we proclaim the creation of a Jewish state on the soil of Israel.' The Arab state, also provided for by the UN, was never to see the light of day. The fatal spiral of Israeli-Arab conflicts began.

Ousted from Palestine, then Egypt (1954–1956), from Sudan (1956) and Iraq (1958), the British, for a while, held on in the **Arabian Peninsula**. Admittedly, Saudi Arabia was independent, as was **North Yemen** which, by a skilful game of alliances, had always preserved its freedom. But all the other emirates, sultanates and principalities were in the hands of the British. **Kuwait** was the first to break free from London, in 1961. Six years later, it was the turn of the Federation of South Arabia, which would become the Peoples' Republic of Yemen in 1970. Oman would gain independence in 1970,

Qatar and Bahrain in 1971, the same year as the United Arab Emirates, formerly the Pirate Coast. But the key date was undoubtedly 1967: that year, Great Britain decided to withdraw all its troops then east of Suez.

Thus, the state structures born out of the dismantling of the Ottoman Empire led to the independence of most of the peoples it had governed in the Middle East. With the exception of three: the Palestinians, the Kurds and the Armenians.

Infitah

AN ARABIC TERM meaning 'opening', *infitah* refers to an 'open door' or liberal economic policy that broke with the socialism of **Nasser** and the first Syrian Ba'athist leaders. The new trend was put into practice by **Sadat**, on his coming to power, and also by President **Assad**, though on a more limited scale and under much stricter state control — and by Iraq (around 1977—1978).

Begun in **Egypt** after 1971, the *infitah* got into full swing after October 1973. The *Rais* then defined its major principles: encouragement of the private sector and foreign investment, opening up to non-Egyptian banks, liberalization of foreign trade, curtailing the role of the public sector. A series of decrees and laws made possible the concretization of this new economic philosophy.

Fifteen years later, the balance sheet remains inconclusive. Private and foreign capital have invested above all in the non-industrial and agricultural sectors, where profits are immediate and substantial: import—export, real estate, banks, tourism. Speculation and corruption have reached hitherto unknown heights. Social inequalities have been aggravated, and the insolent wealth of the *nouveau riche* flouts the eternal poverty of the Egyptian people. Egypt's dependence on external aid has increased (particularly in terms of agriculture and finance) and millions of its labourers, technicians and executives have gone off to work in the oil-producing countries. But the public sector, which was to be reformed, has proved sacrosanct: for social reasons, but also because there is no go-ahead private capital capable of assuming the management of crucial industries such as steel and arms.

Admittedly, the overall picture is not so bleak, and certain successes have been achieved: Egypt has become an exporter of oil and certain sectors of agriculture and industry have acquired a new efficiency. But Egypt's example has highlighted the difficulties of imposing a liberal model on an under-developed economy without giving rise to profound distortions and social upheavals. The demonstrations of January 1977 in Cairo are still remembered as symbols of this.

International Conference

FRAMEWORK proposed by the USSR and most of the **Arab** countries to negotiate an agreement over the Arab-Israeli conflict, accepted by the **PLO** and European Economic Community, long rejected by the **United States** which, however, proposed an alternative plan in 1986. The Israeli Prime Minister, Itzhak **Shamir**, on the other hand, has remained extremely hostile to the idea.

The Arab-Soviet conference proposal differs from the traditional Israeli-American policy on three points. The international conference presented itself as a global transaction, as opposed to the 'separate peace' type of agreement of the **Camp David** Accords: it aimed to bring together, not two states or a group of states, but every one of the parties concerned — including, the Soviets specified, the PLO; in the same way, it put on its agenda, not this or that element of the conflict, but the entirety of all its aspects, including **Lebanon**.

Secondly, it was international, the Soviets insisting on the fact that the United States and the USSR, 'as states who have been led to play a considerable role in the affairs of the Middle East . . . must also participate in the Conference', as well as, they added vaguely, 'certain other states in the near Middle East and neighbouring regions capable of making a positive contribution'. To the **Kissinger** notion of peace under solely American auspices, the international conference therefore opposed the model of an international forum initiated by the **United Nations** and placed under the sponsorship of the UN Security Council.

The third and last obstacle was, of course, the very contents of the proposed solution, the USSR declaring itself in favour of the coexistence of a Palestinian state on the **West Bank** and in **Gaza** (including East **Jerusalem**) and the State of **Israel** returning to the borders it possessed prior to the Six Day **War of 1967**, a plan that both Israel and the United States of course rejected.

The international character of the conference, its UN framework, the Soviet-American stamp, even the very proposals presented by the USSR for a 'just and lasting peace' were based, it is true, on a certain legal precedent. It was the UN, aided by an agreement between the two principal allies of World War II, which decided on the **partition** of Palestine, a partition that was never realized, with the consequences we all know. It was therefore naturally the United Nations which continued to take charge of the problems of the Middle East, be it the Palestine question to which it devoted numerous **resolutions** or the successive conflicts between Israel and its neighbours. At the end of the

Yom Kippur **War of 1973**, a first international conference was even opened, in Geneva, in December 1973, with Henry Kissinger and Andrei Gromyko as co-presidents. However, it did not last long, the Israeli delegates banning any participation by the PLO and refusing all territorial concessions, strengthened by the prospect — then at the planning stage and soon to materialize — of an agreement between Cairo and Tel Aviv. After ten years of unsuccessful attempts at the 'American peace', Moscow was now proposing, in short, a return to the point of departure.

But did the circumstances really justify such a return? The debate centred less on the principle of an international conference than on its conception. For the United States and the Israeli Labour Party, it would have to be an umbrella for direct negotiations between Israel, a Jordanian-Palestinian delegation and representatives of the other Arab countries. The USSR, without rejecting the idea of bilateral negotiations, still insists on the multilateral character of the conference, to which, accordingly, the PLO has to be invited as such. No doubt the Soviet-American detente, which has already brought the points of view closer, will help this already old project to take shape. The USSR has relaunched several proposals for an international conference in the context of the Gulf crisis. Whether Washington's, and even more so, Israel's reservations on the subject can be overcome remains to be seen.

Intifada

IN ARABIC, uprising: the name given to the Palestinian revolt that broke out, early in December 1987, in **Gaza** and on the **West Bank**. On a larger scale and more determined than any previous movement in the occupied territories, the 'revolution of stones' profoundly altered the landscape of the Middle East.

It was on December 7, 1987, that a traffic accident — a collision between an Israeli vehicle and a Palestinian shared taxi, two of whose occupants died — sparked matters off. Two days later, the first confrontations took place between young **Palestinians** and Israeli soldiers, in the camp of Jabalya. Within a week, the uprising had spread to the whole of the Gaza Strip and the West Bank, despite the state of siege decreed by the occupying powers. Taken by surprise, the Israeli government, all tendencies united, adopted a single priority: 'Crush the subversion', in the words of the Defence Minister, General Rabin, whose membership of the Labour Party would not prevent him from directing, with an iron hand, the repression of the *intifada*.

Thus, the escalation of demonstrations, strikes and confrontations was met by a spiral of repression. The army multiplied the curfews, fired on teenagers who taunted them, put them through the third degree, arrested tens of thousands of them and interned (often without trial) thousands more, did not stop short at 'ill-treatment' during its raids against the villages or in the prisons, deported several score of Palestinians, etc. Openly flouting the stipulations of the Geneva Convention, this violent conduct shocked public opinion, Jewish included, which, the world over, proved susceptible to the flood of pictures diffused by the mass media. The attempt to bury alive by bulldozer four villagers of Salem and the scene in which two youths from Nablus were battered during a live broadcast by CBS cameras particularly moved consciences. One thousand days after the start of the uprising, the statistics were as follows: more than one thousand dead, tens of thousands wounded, 9,000 prisoners — which, with the 4,000 already in detention, made a total of 13,000 detainees from a population of 1.7 million inhabitants.

However, this massive use of force did not deter the rebels. Their determination, over and above the combination of circumstances — hope raised in April 1987 by the reunification of the PLO at the Palestine National Council (PNC) in Algiers, anger in November following the overlooking of the Palestine question at the Amman Arab summit in November — had plunged its roots into fertile soil. Obviously, resistance to the occupation had been there from the outset, in June 1967. The progressive expansion of the Israeli annexation of the West Bank and Gaza, in particular the increase in Jewish **settlements**, had met with growing opposition which found expression both in demonstrations and acts of violence and in the municipal elections of 1976 where PLO supporters won hands down. But, this time, we were witnessing the explosion of the pent-up frustrations of an entire generation, born under the occupation, which was surmounting the relatively resigned attitude of previous generations, and dragging them, by its example of dignity regained, into action for independence. Never, even in 1981 and 1982, had the 'Palestinians of the inside' made their presence so vigorously felt.

In fact, the scale of the *intifada* exceeds that of preceding uprisings in many respects. Its duration: by December 1990, three years. Its scope: the whole of the occupied territories, including **Jerusalem**, Bethlehem and the villages, traditionally relatively unaffected. Its form: massive meetings, general strikes and confrontations combine with self-determination in everyday life and acts of civil disobedience. Its participants: the young rub shoulders with their elders, the refugees of 1947–1949 mingle with those born in the territories, labourers and peasants find themselves side by side with tradesmen, professionals and intellectuals.

Born spontaneously, as all observers, including Israelis, have pointed out, from an explosive mixture of ingredients — shanty-town poverty, massive unemployment, the humiliation of national feeling and daily repression — the revolution of the stones quickly became organized. Local people's committees organized the street fighting — without fire-arms — against the Israeli army, but also supplied teaching, medical back-up and other basic services — to the extent that observers began to speak of 'liberated zones'. Autonomous, the local committees also met up in a United Patriotic Leadership which included, relatively united despite their differences, Yasser **Arafat**'s Fatah, George **Habash**'s Popular Front, Nayef **Hawatmeh**'s Democratic Front, the Palestinian Communist Party and the Islamic groups — excluding their most extreme fringe, the Islamic Resistance Movement known after its initials as Hammas (in Arabic, zeal). Only this last movement remained outside the general consensus of the *intifada's* purpose: the creation of an independent Palestinian state on the West Bank and in Gaza, the State of **Israel** withdrawing to the borders it possessed prior to the Six Day War. Like a resurrection, 40 years after its abortion, of the **Partition Plan** voted by the UN General Assembly.

The uprising, placing its strength at the service of this purpose, caused a reshuffling of the cards in the Middle Eastern pack, and challenged many of the principal players. The first to react was King **Hussein** of **Jordan**. He, whose grandfather Abdullah had annexed the west bank of the River Jordan and who had always hoped to reconquer it after 1967, saw his dream fade; on July 31, 1988, he announced a breakdown of relations between his country and the West Bank. 'Jordan is not Palestine', he declared, 'and the independent Palestinian state will be established on Palestinian land occupied after its liberation.' The 'Jordanian option' having thus evaporated, the PLO now became Israel's inevitable partner in future peace negotiations. The political opportunity presented by the revolution and the conditions to be met in order to sit down at the negotiating table forced Arafat and those close to him — as the United Patriotic Leadership of the *intifada* did not hesitate to point out — to define a concrete peace programme. Approval of the **Fez Plan**, the **Soviet Plan** or 'all the UNO resolutions' was no longer enough. The PLO found itself forced to recognize the State of Israel, in order to obtain reciprocal acknowledgement. The Palestine National Council of mid-November 1988 had in any case taken the first steps in this direction, by proclaiming an independent Palestinian state while accepting Resolution 181 of 1947 as well as Resolutions 242 and 338 of the UN Security Council (see **United Nations, Resolutions of**), and by reaffirming its condemnation of terrorism.

Brain-teasers for both sides. Apart from Israel's image, severely damaged by its repression of the uprising, the very certitude of its citizens seemed shaken by the *intifada*. They were forced to give up the Zionist movement's cherished idea, according to which 'time is on our side'. The *status quo* established in June 1967 was slipping away. To prolong it artificially would mean taking a considerable risk, knowing that in the future, despite Russian Jewish immigration, the Arabs will constitute a sizeable majority in Greater Israel (in other words Israel of 1967 plus the West Bank, Gaza and the **Golan Heights**). A dreadful dilemma. To remain Jewish, would Israel have to cease being democratic? Or should it abandon its Judaism to remain democratic? Or again, would it be better to give up the territories to safeguard both of these characteristics?

Avoided for forty years, the Palestinian question now became as unavoidable for the majority of Israelis as the Israeli question for Palestinians. In addition, it provoked in Jewish thinking a double radicalization. On the one hand, the increasingly numerous partisans of the annexation of the West Bank and Gaza responded to the 'demographic threat' by calling for 'transfer' — a euphemism coined to avoid using the terms expulsion or, even worse, deportation — of the majority of the Palestinian population. At the other end of the political spectrum, the upholders of a negotiated Israeli-Palestinian peace, implying withdrawal from the territories, were also gaining ground. Confused, the silent majority hesitated: witness the surveys according to which, if one Israeli out of every two approves of dialogue with the PLO — on condition that it recognizes Israel and renounces terrorism — one in three claim they can envisage transfer.

This confusion characterized the campaign for the parliamentary elections of November 1, 1988. Chasing the floating votes, Likud and the Labour Party both shirked addressing the problem in any depth. Shimon **Peres** avoided openly calling for withdrawal from the territories, just as Itzhak **Shamir** avoided calling for their annexation. Both preferred, through a desperate 'mouth to mouth' operation, to resuscitate the defunct 'Jordanian option'. Labour banked on dialogue with a 'Jordano-Palestinian delegation' within the framework of the international umbrella-conference of the Shultz Plan to achieve a 'territorial compromise'. The Likud, for its part, opted for the negotiations with Jordan and **Egypt** stipulated by the **Camp David Accords** to bring about 'autonomy'. Confused, the electorate ended up dismissing both of them, only the religious parties finally making any progress — along with the Civil Rights Movement (Ratz). 'Even if Israelis voted for the repeal of Newton's Law of Gravity, apples would still fall', was the ironic comment of the former Minister of Foreign Affairs, Abba Eban, after the polls.

Under enormous pressure from world public opinion, the National Unity Government of Itzhak Shamir proposed, on May 7 1989, a plan to hold elections in the occupied territories, though without giving up claims to Israeli sovereignty over the West Bank and Gaza.

However, by the Autumn, Egypt's rather positive response to the proposal, with the Mubarak plan and the PLO's acceptance of the elections, had led the Israeli authorities to backtrack. It took full-scale pressure from the Americans, who were themselves engaging in 'substantial discussions' with the PLO, before the Israeli government accepted the Baker plan in November 1989. Talks continued, in an attempt to set up the conditions for negotiations, under US aegis, between Israel, Egypt and a Palestinian delegation, the composition of which proved to be the main point of dissension. The plan finally fell foul of Mr Shamir's intransigence, provoking the Labour Party's withdrawal from government and the formation of a right-wing cabinet in June 1990. Even so, despite the ascendency enjoyed by Mr Shamir thanks to the support given to his new government by the small religious parties, some form of direct dialogue seemed inevitable until the 1990 Gulf crisis led Washington to relieve its pressure on Israel, making a settlement even more unlikely. However, the Gulf crisis has itself helped to revive the idea of an international conference to resolve the problems of the area.

Iran

THE FIRST Persian Empire goes back to Cyrus, in the 6th century BC. The reign of the Sassanids, followers of Zoroaster who ruled from the 3rd century AD, would last over 400 years. Weakened by incessant wars with the Byzantine Empire, they were defeated by the Arabs in 637 AD, at the battle of Qadissiyya. Converted to Islam, the Iranians contributed greatly to the cultural glory of the Abbasid Empire, but Persia did not re-emerge as an independent political entity until the 16th century.

It was at the beginning of the same century that the foundations of the Safavid Empire were laid by Ismail Safavi. He declared Persia's autonomy vis-à-vis the Ottoman Empire and made use of Shi'ism, decreed the state religion, as a means of forging a national identity. The Empire started to decline in the 18th century when Persia was invaded by Afghanistan and threatened by the Tsars and the Turks — who conquered Tabriz in 1725.

At the end of the century, Great Britain, whose influence in India was growing, established itself as a decisive actor in the Persian drama, whilst a new dynasty, the Qajars, came to power — it would last until 1925. Under attacks from the Ottoman Empire and Russia, as well as meddling from London, Persia played on the rivalry between these great powers. Despite the loss of much of its territory, it maintained its independence. The discovery of oil increased the country's importance.

In 1905–1906, a movement in favour of a constitution developed in opposition to the Shah, but he was not finally removed, with Russian help, until the eve of World War I. Although neutral during the war, Persia's sympathies were with the Ottoman Empire. But the dissolution of the latter and the advent of the Bolsheviks to power in Russia left the field open for London which, for over 40 years, would turn the country into a virtual protectorate. The Qajars were overthrown in 1925 by a *coup d'état* organized by an officer, Reza Khan, who had attracted attention four years earlier as defence minister; the reign of the Pahlavis began.

The new sovereign, who styled himself Reza Shah, encouraged economic development and Westernization — but at a much slower pace than in Turkey, under Mustapha Kemal, and never for a moment relinquishing his despotic power. There was repeated conflict with Britain which still had a predominant influence in the region — particularly through the Anglo-Iranian Oil Company, which extracted oil and operated the giant refinery of Abadan. In an attempt to rid himself of this oppressive custodian, the Shah developed cordial relations with the USSR and, to an even greater extent, with Germany, which took an active part in the country's economic development: in 1939, it accounted for 41% of Iranian trade.

At the outbreak of World War II, Tehran proclaimed its neutrality. But, after the launching of the Nazi attack against the **Soviet Union** in June 1941, Iran became the only feasible route by which Great Britain could send supplies to its new ally. Moscow and London now demanded that the Shah get rid of his German advisers. On his refusal, Soviet and British troops were sent into the country; the Shah was forced to abdicate in favour of his son, Mohammed Reza.

After the conclusion of the world war and the elimination of the Kurdish Republic of Mahabad in northern Iran, Great Britain became the favourite target of the nationalists. The refusal of the Anglo-Iranian Oil Company to even discuss the question of sharing its profits with the state led to a radicalization of public opinion. It was this that brought about, on April 28, 1951, the appointmemt of Mossadegh as Prime Minister and the nationalization of oil. 'Oil is our blood, oil is our freedom', yelled demonstrators. In August 1953, a *coup d'état*, organized by the CIA in collaboration with London, brought an end to Mossadegh's government. The Shah confirmed his dictatorial power and brutally eliminated all secular opposition. The **United States** replaced Great Britain as the tutelary power in Iran.

The 1960s and 1970s saw the confirmation of both the dictatorial character of the regime and Iran's commitment to economic Westernization. In the countryside, the White Revolution gave rise to the disturbances of 1963, in which **Khomeini** won fame. The great industrial projects were considerably helped by the rise in oil prices in 1973. The creation of a formidable military machine transformed Iran into the 'policeman of the Gulf': Tehran intervened against the rebellion in Dhofar (Oman) and, in November 1971, took forcible control of the three islands of Abu Musa, the small Tumb and the large Tumb.

The Shah degenerated into megalomania; in October 1971 in Persepolis he celebrated 2,500 years of the Persian Empire. In 1973, Prime Minister Hoveyda declared that 'the last thing Iran needs is a Western-style democracy'. All secular opposition was hunted down by the secret police, the Savak. As for the proposed modernization, it took the form of an anarchic urbanization, the destructuring of the countryside and growing poverty. The presence of 30,000 American advisers and numerous foreign bases outraged the population's sense of nationalism.

The sole force to survive the dreadful political repression, the Shi'ite clergy was the only channel for the people's aspirations towards dignity, sovereignty, liberty and independence. The whole of 1978 was marked by popular demonstrations and by dreadful repression. The latter proved futile; on January 16, 1979, the Shah was forced to leave the country and, on February 1, Khomeini triumphantly returned to the capital. The Islamic Revolution had triumphed; 25 years earlier, this same revolution had been secular and democratic, but the Western powers had crushed it, clearing a path for the *mullah*.

In February 1979, it was another liberal, Mehdi Bazargan, who was appointed prime minister. He fell from power nine months later, when the revolution became more radical and, on November 4, students in 'the line of the Imam' occupied the United States Embassy — whose staff were not released until January 20, 1981. The new constitution formalized the immense powers of the Guide, in other words Khomeini. In 1980 and 1981, the regime seemed on the brink of disaster — the Kurdish uprising, the move of Massoud Radjavi's *mujahedeen* to take up armed opposition, the flight of the president-elect Bani Sadr who took refuge in France in the summer of 1981 — when Iraqi aggression of September 1980 and the outbreak of the Gulf War inspired an outburst of patriotism. In 1983, Iran managed to chase all Iraqi troops from its territory and invaded its neighbour. The war, thanks mainly to Khomeini's stubbornness, was to last until August 1988.

This long conflict allowed the leaders to disguise their differences and postpone certain crucial decisions. For if Iran was using the oil income to pay for its imports, no actual course of development had been decided on. And with reason: the power was profoundly split between conservatives, in favour of private property, and radicals, defenders of a larger role for the state. Similarly, in international matters, after the radicalism of the first year, pragmatism dominated: Tehran did not hesitate, as Irangate made clear, to turn to Israel and the United States for its arms supplies. If its relations with Saudi Arabia were bad, those with other emirates, like Oman, remained cordial. The 1990 Gulf crisis has also made some rapprochemnt with Iraq possible.

Iran has a surface area of 1.65 million square kilometres, three times the size of France. According to the census of October 1986, the population numbers more than 51 million people. Aside from Persians, who speak Farsi and represent around half the inhabitants, the principal ethnic groups are the Turks, the **Kurds**, the Baluchs and the Arabs; there are also slightly over 1 million nomads. Iran accommodates around 2 million foreigners: 1.5 million Afghans — mainly refugees who fled the Soviet intervention of 1979 — and 500,000 Iraqis, expelled from their country because of their Iranian origins. The country's main wealth is oil, production of which reached 2 million barrels a day in 1987, as against 3.17 million in 1979 and 1.32 million in 1981. Oil accounts for around 90% of exports, the rest being made up of agricultural produce, minerals and rugs.

Irangate

THE NAME given — by analogy with Watergate, which cost Richard Nixon the presidency — to the scandal involving the secret sales of American arms to **Iran** from 1985 to 1987, in which many high-ranking American officials were implicated, including President Reagan himself.

In fact, it all began in October 1984, with the **United States** Congress's adoption of the Boland Amendment, which forbade for one year 'all other agencies or entities of the United States engaged in intelligence activities' to 'support, directly or indirectly, military or paramilitary operations in Nicaragua'. Immediately, the heads of the National Security Council — in particular the Director of the CIA, William Casey, and the National Security Adviser, Robert McFarlane — attempted to get round the decision in order to continue supplying aid to their Nicaraguan friends in difficulty.

Over and above the contributions they received from the Saudis (32 million dollars between July 1984 and February 1985), from the Sultan of Brunei (10 million dollars), and, apparently, from the South Korean dictatorship, certain people in Washington came up with the idea of selling to Tehran arms whose profits would go to the Nicaraguan counter-revolutionaries. The project tied in with the strategy of those who continued to see Iran, with or without **Khomeini**, as an indispensable base for the United States.

And it was only natural that they should turn to Tel Aviv. In fact, the Israelis were qualified specialists on two counts: for some time they had been supplying arms to both the Contras and Iran. Having established links with the Central American regimes, including that of Somoza, **Israel** had been sending supplies and training officers for the anti-Sandinista guerilla forces, according to some from as early as 1979. At the same time, true to the precept according to which 'my enemy's enemies are my friends', Israel had, at the outbreak of the **Gulf War**, taken Iran's side, fighting as it was against one of the bastions of the **Arab** world, **Iraq** — 500 million dollars worth of Israeli arms were delivered to Tehran between 1980 and 1983, according to the Institute of Strategic Studies in Jaffa.

The key men in this dual traffic — David Kimche, Director General of the Ministry of Foreign Affairs (a post occupied at the time by Itzhak **Shamir**), Amiram Nir (adviser in counter-terrorism to Prime Minister **Peres**), who died in a plane accident in late 1988, Yaacov Nimrodi (former Mossad agent and ex-military attaché in Tehran), and their Iranian friend Manucher Ghorbanifar (a former agent of Savak, the Shah's secret police) — set up the deal in January 1985. In exchange for American-made missiles delivered by Tel Aviv, the Americans would obtain the liberation of the hostages held by **Lebanon**, would turn into reality their hope of a moderate — and therefore anti-Soviet — replacement for Khomeini, and recoup juicy profits for their Contra protégés.

Through this channel, two deliveries took place: in August-September 1985, 508 Tow anti-tank missiles; then, in November, Hawk anti-aircraft missiles. But only a single hostage, the Reverend Benjamin Weir, was set free. Disillusioned, McFarlane resigned on December 11, 1985. Israel, however, had no intention of giving up the Iranian connection: Shimon Peres therefore sent Amiram Nir to Washington in early January 1986, the bearer — as North and Poindexter explained in a memorandum — of a 'plan by which Israel, with a limited assistance from the USA, can create conditions to aid the advent of a more moderate government in Iran'. The proposal to exchange the hostages for the delivery of 3,000 Tow missiles was accepted, on February 17, by Ronald Reagan.

There was only one major difficulty: the Irangate men intended, this time, to despatch the arms themselves to Tehran. To achieve this, Lieutenant-Colonel North called on certain old campaigners, notably ex-General Richard Secord. Formerly with the Pentagon and the CIA, he had proved himself against Cuba and in the secret war in Laos, was an expert in arms deals with the Middle East and had gone into partnership with Albert Hakim as head of the company Stanford Technology Trading Group International, whose aircraft were often used in secret operations. Already involved in the previous Israeli transaction, Secord had for some time been organizing the collection of funds and the transport of arms whose profits went to the Contras. In all, he and Hakim would handle three strictly American deliveries: Tow missiles and spare parts for the Hawks, a quarter of which North himself took to the Iranian capital at the end of May 1986, plus a Bible bearing a dedication from President Reagan in person.

But in the meantime the latter, floundering in his denials and admitted 'oversights', preferred to cut his losses; the Irangate scandal hit the headlines. Triple scandal, in fact:

- Firstly, these arms sales were in direct contradiction to the official US policy towards Iran: surely operation Staunch, in progress at the time, was aimed precisely at dissuading US allies from supplying arms to Iran?
- Secondly, they had taken place outside the normal institutional processes and in violation of the Constitution, and of laws and regulations in force in the United States — to the extent that the journalist Theodore Drapper, in a famous series of articles in the *New York Review of Books* in 1987, could describe Irangate as the rise and fall of an 'American Junta'. Thus the first two arms deliveries took place without the required authorization of the president of the United States; the minutes of most of the crucial meetings are lacking, never written up or, worse, destroyed; and no one is unaware of the opposition put up by the Secretary of State, George Schultz, and the Defence Secretary, Caspar Weinberger. In fact, a small group of men — Casey, McFarlane, North, Poindexter — had, with the agreement of a Reagan admittedly weakened by illness and the after-effects of an attempt on his life, seized the real power, in the name of the higher interests of the country but without ever reporting to Congress;
- Thirdly, in violation of the decisions of the said Congress, these arms sales allowed the illegal transfer of a total of 30 to 50 million dollars not only to the Nicaraguan guerillas, but also to Afghan and, apparently, Angolan guerillas. On the first 1,000 Tow missiles alone that were delivered to Iran, Secord had earned 5.5 million dollars, Ghorbanifar 3 to 4 million and Khashoggi 2 million.

At the beginning of October 1986, an American plane, crammed with equipment destined for the Contras, crashed in Nicaragua. One of the pilots survived. Eugene Hasenfus was picked up by the Sandinista army, spilled the beans and denounced those in charge. And, on November 3, the pro-Syrian Lebanese weekly, *Al Shira'a*, recounted McFarlane's sad journey to Tehran. With the result that, in a televised press conference on November 25, 1986, Ronald Reagan — after having claimed that he 'had not been totally informed of the nature of the activities undertaken in connection with this initiative' towards Iran — had to announce that he was relieving Poindexter and North of their duties. The Tower Commission was charged with clearing up the matter.

From its months of hearings and its report, little came. Proof of the changing times: whilst a third-rate burglary had cost Richard Nixon the presidency, Ronald Reagan came out of this extraordinary accumulation of official abuses virtually unscathed, not to mention Vice-President George Bush, who, also implicated, was nonetheless, in November 1988, triumphantly elected president of the United States.

No doubt the stakes involved in Irangate outweighed its apparent objective: behind the support of the Nicaraguan counter-revolutionaries and the creation of a moderate alternative to Shi'ite **fundamentalism**, the very essence of Reagan's doctrine was under threat, namely the strategy of 'low intensity conflicts'. A recognition of the limits of American power, this strategy was nonetheless fundamentally offensive. In effect, it advocated a combination of 'direct intervention' (as in Grenada in 1983, or against Libya in 1986), the 'covert action' dear to the CIA (from Iran in 1953 to the Congo in 1961, from Brazil in 1954 to Chile in 1973) and 'support to freedom fighters' (such as the Contras, the Afghan *mujahedeen* and UNITA). In the Middle East, in particular, it took the form of creating a **Rapid Intervention Force** capable of intervening against any attempt at aggression or destabilization. And, on this chess board, Iran was clearly an irreplaceable piece.

Iraq

ALTHOUGH Baghdad was the capital of the Abbasid Empire from the 8th to the 13th centuries, Iraq, with its present frontiers, did not come into being until after World War I. Chased out of **Syria** by French troops in 1920, Emir Faisal — son of Sherif Hussein, the leader of the **Arab** revolt — was crowned in Iraq on August 23, 1921, by the British. The mandate that London had obtained from the League of Nations in 1920 was to endure for over ten years. The country gained independence in 1932, not without having to sign a treaty of alliance with **Great Britain** which retained its military bases and a decisive influence in important matters. During World War II a *coup d'état* by General Al Kailani, who had nationalist leanings but sought support from Nazi Germany, was crushed by British intervention.

The end of the war saw the confirmation of the strength of the national movement which was anti-monarchist and anti-British. Attempts in 1948 by the regime's leading figure, Prime Minister Nouri Said, to sign a new treaty with London resulted in massive popular demonstrations. The Palestine **War of 1948—1949** allowed the authorities to put their house in order, while Iraqi contingents took part in the fighting and the defeat of the Arab armies.

After **Nasser**'s coming to power, King Faisal II and Nouri Said took the leadership of the pro-Western Arab coalition. Iraq joined the Baghdad Pact in 1955 then, in 1958, formed a federation with **Jordan** to counter that of the United Arab Republic.

But it was too late: on July 14, 1958, a group of officers, led by General Kassem, overthrew the monarchy and established the Republic. Kassem opposed the Arab nationalists who favoured union with **Egypt**, undertook progressive reforms and sought the backing, at first, of the powerful Iraqi Communist Party (ICP). But the regime's hesitancy, the increasingly personal character of the leadership and the renewal of the Kurdish uprising brought Kassem down; he was overthrown on February 8, 1963. After a relatively uneventful reign by the Aref brothers, Nasserian in tendency, the Ba'ath seized power in July 1968. It is still there today.

The regime, whose leading figure, from 1970 on, has been Saddam Hussein, has become increasingly radical. In 1972, it signed a friendship treaty with the Soviet Union and nationalized the IPC, the oil company controlling the extraction of the black gold of which Iraq is one of the world's principal producers. In 1973, a progressive National Front, with which the communists were associated, came into being. The recognition, in 1970, of the autonomy of the Kurdish people also marked a turning point, even though negotiations with their leader, Barzani, broke down. The war resumed and ended with the crushing of the Kurds in 1975, after the signing of an agreement between Tehran and Baghdad. Lastly, on the Palestine question, the Iraqi Ba'ath Party adopted a radical vocabulary (which had no effect whatever on the attitude of the Iraqi troops stationed in Jordan in 1970 — they remained in their barracks during Black September) and gave its support to the Rejection Front as well as Abu Nidal's group from 1974.

From 1978, a change of direction took place in Ba'athist policy. Saddam Hussein made overtures to the conservative leaders of the Gulf, broke off his alliance with the ICP and extended his relations with the USSR. He also opposed the Islamic Revolution and, in September 1980, unleashed an attack against Iran. After some initial victories, Baghdad's troops had to retreat and fight on their own territory. The fighting, which caused hundreds of thousands of deaths, destroyed a large part of the economic potential of both countries and was used to justify Iraqi inaction when Israel invaded Lebanon in 1982. The moderate states — those of Jordan and the Gulf — supported Baghdad which, in return, made a spectacular reconciliation with Cairo and the PLO.

The last two years of the war were marked by a recovery of Iraq's situation: super-armed, its forces were able to retake the territories occupied by Iran — including Fao — and did not hesitate to use chemical weapons. New pipelines — across Turkey and Saudi Arabia — have made it possible to increase oil exports and augment state earnings. The power of Iraq's army worries its neighbours, and rightly so, as the invasion and annexation of Kuwait in August 1990 shows. This new adventure is not just about the financial and oil resources seized by Saddam Hussein; it is inseparable from his ambition to become the leader of the Arab world.

With a surface area of 440,000 square kilometres, Iraq has around 16.5 million inhabitants, about a third of whom are Kurds. Shi'ites (see Shi'ism) represent more than half the Arab population, and there is also a small

Christian minority. The country's principal resource is oil. The possibility of Saddam Hussein failing in his latest adventure may at least give his opponents the chance they have been waiting for. The economic gains of the 1970s have been largely wiped out by the war with Iran, and the country's national debt has risen to more than 60 billion dollars. The cost of reconstruction is estimated at 60 billion. The Ba'ath Party's powers, especially those of Saddam Hussein, are virtually unlimited. The opposition is heterogeneous, with communists, Islamic Shi'ite forces and, above all, Kurdish organizations who have once again taken up armed struggle in the north of the country.

Islam

ISLAM (in Arabic, submission to God) is one of the three great monotheistic religions. Followers of this faith are called Muslims. Islam also designates a civilization and a culture established over the centuries, and in which the Christians of the Orient also recognize themselves.

The Prophet Mohammed preached in Arabia in the 7th century of our era. He unified, by the word and the sword, a large part of the **Arabian Peninsula**. After his death in Mecca, in 632 AD, his successors, the caliphs, were endowed with a dual mission, religious and political. They were both the guides of the faithful and the initiators of conquests. This overlapping of religion and state was to be a millstone in the history of Islam — though of course it also characterized Christianity over a long period. A crisis in the succession brought about the two great Islamic schisms: **Shi'ism** and Kharijism. The orthodox were designated by the term **Sunni**.

In a century, the Muslim Arabs extended their rule to the borders of China and Spain. Two great empires organized the administration and control, and conversion, of the conquered populations. The Umayyad Empire, which foundered in 750 AD, and the Abbasid Empire which succeeded it and ended under the onslaught of the Mongols in 1254 AD. **Arab** domination was replaced by that of the Turks and the **Ottoman Empire**, which survived until World War I. The constitution of Mustapha Kemal's Turkish Republic brought to an end the institution of the caliphate, a symbol, at times precarious and disputed, of the unity of the **Umma**, the community of Muslims. Today there are 700 million Muslims in the world, of whom less than 150 million are Arabs. The majority are to be found in Asia (Pakistan, Bangladesh, Indonesia, India). An extremely dynamic Black Islam has also been solidly established in Africa.

For its followers, the Islamic religion is the natural continuation of Judaism and Christianity from which it borrowed various elements. Thus, it reveres Moses and Jesus, but teaches that Mohammed brought to a close the cycle of prophets, that he is 'the seal of the prophets'. The word of God, contained in the sacred book, the Qur'an, was imparted to Mohammed by the Archangel Gabriel. The Sunna, a recension of the deeds of the Prophet and his close companions, is the second source of Law. Using these texts as a basis, juridical schools were created — four for the Sunni — which established the social and religious duties of all good Muslims. Five ritual obligations, called the 'pillars of religion', are the basis of religious life: the profession of faith ('I testify that there is no God but Allah and that Mohammed is His Prophet'); the five daily prayers; fasting during the month of Ramadan; institutionalized charity (zakat); the pilgrimage to Mecca. Islam has no clergy as such and thus no official Church; no one intercedes between God and his creature. But a special task is allotted to the Doctors of Law, who must define the manner in which the principles defined in the Qu'ran are to be applied.

Islam is not a fixed doctrine and, throughout the course of history, has known many modifications. As Biancamaria Scarcia has written: 'Just as in the past, where it was used to achieve extremely contradictory ends, Islam today can as easily justify a progressive policy as a reactionary one. Today, no more than in the past, there is no one political Islam, in the sense that there is no single ideology or single Islamic vision of things.' One therefore cannot find in Islam an 'analytical grid' allowing one to grasp the situation in **Saudi Arabia**, **Libya** or **Iran**. To borrow another of Mme Scarcia's ideas, civil society 'reserves ... the possibility of elevating to the level of religion rules and solutions that have been imposed on it by circumstances and not by principles'.

The fact that adherence to religion is still very widespread in the masses of Islamic countries is an important phenomenon. The religious disaffection that has marked the West 'was checked in Islam in the 11th century by vigorous efforts on the part of the Sunnis, efforts whose success was made easier by internal evolution within societies and changes in their situation vis-à-vis the exterior' (M. Rodinson). Amongst these changes were the crusades, colonization, and confrontation with an increasingly dominant West. Islam then became 'the driving force of resistance to colonial violence'. In Europe, the struggle against the Church constituted one of the rallying points of those who fought for civil liberties in the 19th century; but the colonized masses rose up against oppression in the name of Islam, in which intellectuals and thinkers such as Jamal Al Din Al Afghani (1838—1897) and Muhammed Abdu (1849—1905) sought answers to the immense traumatism that colonization had come to represent. Islam's presence remained strong up to **independence**; from then on it tended to become blurred in the political sphere. It was not until the 1970s — with the emergence of what has too hastily been called

fundamentalism — that the Arab masses again looked to Islam for political answers to their problems.

In conclusion, it should be remembered that Islam is also a culture and a civilization. It has contributed crucial advances in the fields of the various sciences, from astronomy to mathematics, from medicine to chemistry. It produced thinkers as important as Ibn Khaldun, Avicenna and Averroes. It has, in a word, participated in the development of the world we know today.

Israel

'ON THIS DAY that sees the end of the British Mandate and in virtue of the natural and historic right of the Jewish people and in accordance with the Resolution of the United Nations General Assembly (see **United Nations, Resolutions of**), we proclaim the creation of a Jewish State in Palestine.' These were the words with which, at 4 p.m. on May 14, 1948, David **Ben Gurion** announced to the world, from the foyer of the Museum of Tel Aviv, the birth of Israel. Thus, in a single phrase, he affirmed the new state's double claim to legitimacy: that of the Jewish people's right, according to **Zionism**, to Palestine — based on the the promise made, almost four thousand years before, by Jehovah to Abraham (Genesis, IX, 18) — and that of the international law decreed by the UN following the Hitlerian genocide.

No sooner was it created than Israel found itself at war with its neighbours, whose armies, the very next day, May 15, invaded Palestinian territory. The **Arab**-Israeli **war of 1948–1949** was to be but the first in a long series. Israel's very history has been punctuated by these conflicts. David Ben Gurion was prime minister from 1948 to 1963, with a brief interlude from 1953 to 1955, when he went into retirement only to have it interrupted by the Lavon affair. The Old Man's long term in office was characterized by the country's demographic, economic and social expansion, by Israel's shift from its early policy of non-alignment to an increasingly open pro-Western commitment, but also by the preparation and realization, in 1956, of the intervention against **Nasser**'s **Egypt**. On the other hand, Ben Gurion, having resigned in 1963, did not sanction the **war of 1967**, launched much against his will by his successor, Levi Eshkol, surrounded by a government of National Unity. After Levi Eshkol's death, in 1969, Golda Meir presided over the coalition until 1970, the date of the retreat of the Right. It was to be a Religious-Labour coalition — like all Israeli governments from 1948 to 1967 — that suffered the full shock of the 'surprise' of the **war of 1973**. The consequences of the latter would lead Labour to its downfall: after one final Rabin government, in 1976, the Right, reformed within Likud, won the general elections of 1977, for the first time in Israel's political history. After the Lebanon **War of 1982**, Menachem **Begin** was forced to hand over the leadership of the government to Itzhak **Shamir**. The elections of 1984 having seen the dismissal of the two major parties in confrontation, a government of national unity was set up, with Shimon **Peres** and Itzhak Shamir undertaking in turns the role of president, until the elections of November 1988, right in the middle of the Palestinian *intifada*. This brief summary gives some idea of how much the development of the Jewish state has been marked by that first conflict with the **Palestinians** and, as a result, with the Arab world. We will return to this in more detail.

Admittedly, Israel's balance sheet, four decades after its foundation, appears impressive in many respects. In demographic terms: from 716,000 in 1948, its Jewish population had increased to over 3,600,000 by 1988 — this is, however, less than a third of the Jews registered in the world. This increase owes much to the organization of the *aliya*, through which, in forty years, some 1,800,000 immigrants have settled in Israel — though 300,000 to 500,000 emigrated again. The economic balance sheet, too, is impressive: less than a billion dollars in 1948, the Gross Domestic Product today is more than 30 billion; as for the Gross National Product per capita, it has risen from less than 1,500 dollars in 1948 to more than 8,000 in 1988 — one should also point out, amongst the capital invested in this expansion, the substantial payments constantly being made by the Diaspora, the billion dollars paid out by the German Federal Republic in reparations and, above all, the 50 odd billion dollars of aid received by Tel Aviv from the American government. There is also a cultural balance sheet: the 3.6 million Israeli Jews consume annually, for instance, 13 million books, 3.5 million theatre tickets and 180 classical music concerts with 40,000 season-ticket holders.

But these examples, and there are many more, of undeniable achievements that demonstrate the vitality of the Jews who chose Israel in which to rebuild their lives after the tragedy of World War II, cannot conceal the effects of the Israeli-Palestinian conflict on all aspects of the country's life. It is, in fact, the decisive element that has structured the young Jewish state, whose economy, social and political life, culture, ideology and, of course, defence have been organized around this continuous struggle. This, in turn, has fanned all the contradictions of Israeli society, sometimes stretching them to breaking point and even giving rise to new, still more dangerous ones. If the Israel of 1990 is generally agreed to bear little resemblance to either the ideal dreamed of by the pioneers or the society visualized by Theodor **Herzl**, it is first and foremost because of the state of war, inevitable if truth be told, between Zionism itself and Palestinian nationalism. The founder of the Zionist movement and his successors chose to ignore Palestinian national rights, just as, until the 1970s, the Palestinian movement denied Israeli identity. The

ISRAELI EXPANSION

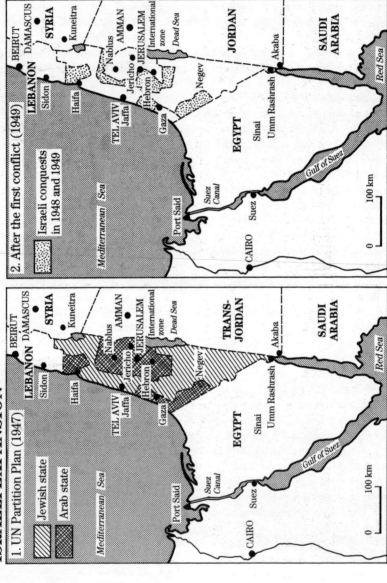

1. UN Partition Plan (1947)

Jewish state

Arab state

Mediterranean Sea

BEIRUT
LEBANON
Sidon
Haifa
TEL AVIV
Jaffa
Gaza
Port Said
Suez Canal
CAIRO
Suez
EGYPT
Sinai
Umm Rashrash
Gulf of Suez
Red Sea
SAUDI ARABIA
Akaba
TRANS-JORDAN
Negev
Dead Sea
International zone
JERUSALEM
Hebron
Jericho
Nablus
AMMAN
Kuneitra
SYRIA
DAMASCUS

0   100 km

2. After the first conflict (1949)

Israeli conquests in 1948 and 1949

Mediterranean Sea

BEIRUT
DAMASCUS
SYRIA
Kuneitra
Nablus
AMMAN
JERUSALEM
International zone
Dead Sea
LEBANON
Sidon
Haifa
TEL AVIV
Jaffa
Jericho
Hebron
Gaza
JORDAN
Negev
Akaba
SAUDI ARABIA
EGYPT
Sinai
Umm Rashrash
Gulf of Suez
Suez
Suez Canal
Port Said
CAIRO
Red Sea

0   100 km

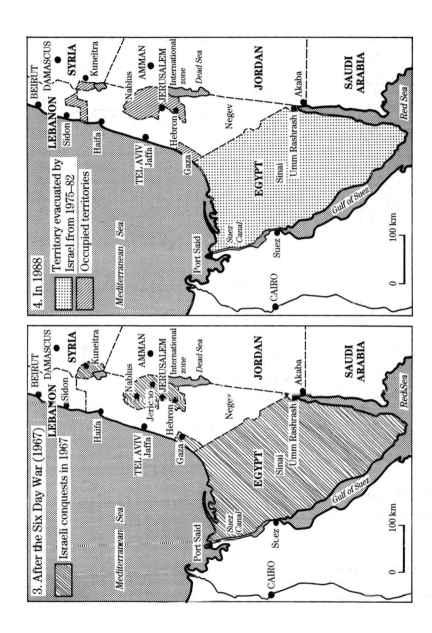

4. In 1988

Territory evacuated by Israel from 1975–82

Occupied territories

BEIRUT
DAMASCUS
SYRIA
Kuneitra
LEBANON
Sidon
Nablus
AMMAN
JERUSALEM
International zone
Dead Sea
JORDAN
SAUDI ARABIA
Akaba
Red Sea
Haifa
TEL AVIV
Jaffa
Negev
Hebron
Gaza
Umm Rashrash
Sinai
EGYPT
Gulf of Suez
Mediterranean Sea
Port Said
Suez Canal
Suez
CAIRO
100 km
0

3. After the Six Day War (1967)

Israeli conquests in 1967

BEIRUT
DAMASCUS
SYRIA
Kuneitra
LEBANON
Sidon
Nablus
AMMAN
Jericho
JERUSALEM
International zone
Dead Sea
Hebron
JORDAN
SAUDI ARABIA
Akaba
Red Sea
Haifa
TEL AVIV
Jaffa
Negev
Gaza
Umm Rashrash
Sinai
EGYPT
Gulf of Suez
Mediterranean Sea
Port Said
Suez Canal
Suez
CAIRO
100 km
0

contrast between project and reality could not be more striking.

'We wish to be in the vanguard of all that is in the interest of humanity, and represent, as a new country, a country of experimentation,' wrote Herzl. And in fact, the socialist Zionists, adopting this conception and 'Marxizing' it, were able — thanks to their overwhelming influence in the Yishuv and subsequently in the young Israel — to give free rein to the most generous of utopias: collective ownership of land, a system of communes (*kibbutzim*, around 30% of the Jewish rural population and 3% of Israelis in general) and cooperatives (*moshavim*, accounting for 70% of agricultural production and, in a wider sense, a trade union economy representing up to 28% of the Gross National Product, 66% of agricultural employment and 66% of salaried employment. All these are achievements, and there are others, of Israeli socialism which, however, was unable to resist the forced Americanization of a society at war and facing crisis: financial speculation breaking all records, many agricultural settlements on the brink of calling in the auditors, and the principal trust of the Histadrut trade union organization, Koor, laying off thousands of workers and selling off several of its subsidiaries in a bid to avert bankruptcy.

'We will strive to find, for all age groups, for all levels of society, happiness in work,' wrote Herzl. Israel has long since ceased to see this as a social priority. Furthermore, how is the rise in the standard of living to be maintained and important social needs satisfied when more than a third of the state budget is being devoted to defence, to 'maintaining law and order' in the occupied territories and to colonizing them? Rather than make drastic cuts in these expenses, the country — particularly since the victory of the Likud, in 1977 — has embarked, in view of the crisis affecting the Israeli economy like all Western economies, on a path of austerity for the workforce and drastic cuts in public service budgets, accelerated, what is more, by privatization. Educational standards have dropped dangerously, the health service finds itself on the brink of collapse, transport is in a state of disorganization, etc. Despite an undeniable decline in inflation, which had rocketed to more than 1,000% in the middle of the decade, buying power continues to diminish. Unemployment, on the other hand, has climbed to the (official) record level of 7% — what a paradox, for a state that offers a welcome to Jews from anywhere in the world! And more than half a million Israelis (one Jewish inhabitant in seven) lives, according to statistics, beneath the poverty threshold. In short, Israel too is familiar with the joys of 'rampant liberalism'.

'We are a people, an indivisible people,' claimed Theodor Herzl. In fact, a people profoundly divided, at least in Israel, and on an ethnic basis, the dividing line between the haves and the have-nots being, roughly speaking, the dividing line between Western Jews and Oriental Jews. Forming the majority of the Israeli population since the 1950s, Jews from Arab countries make up — after the Israeli Arabs — the main body of the poor, the un-employed, the illiterate and criminal offenders. Contrary to expectations, these discriminations have been reproduced, even intensified, from gene-ration to generation, with political repercussions that (Western) Labour leaders, in power since 1948, did not foresee. To gain revenge for more than three decades of injustice, the Oriental Jews, *en masse*, went over to the Likud, enabling it to come to power and stay there — in November 1988, 70% of them again voted for Itzhak Shamir's party.

'I cannot believe that the Jewish state I want to establish will be narrow-minded, orthodox and reactionary,' affirmed Theodor Herzl. Forty years after the proclamation of the Jewish state, then dominated by the social-democrats, flanked by a powerful left wing, made up of Zionists and communists, the Right, the extreme Right and the religious groups picked up (in November 1988) almost 53% of the votes. Whereas Ben Gurion and his friends had attacked, and marginalized, the fundamentalist Right, one Israeli in two would henceforth declare themselves tempted by the prospect of the annexation of the **West Bank** and **Gaza** and of the 'transfer' of the main body of their Arab population — a 'solution' which, hitherto, only Rabbi Kahane had dared to defend publicly: 'There is', he roared in December 1987 in the Knesset, 'no remedy to the epidemic that is spreading and which threatens to exterminate us, by war or by demography. No other remedy but that of Joshua: "And you will chase out all the inhabitants of the country before you". Chase out, transfer, deport, expel. With no inferiority complex, no sense of guilt.' Kahane found himself expelled from parliament, but several new members took up the torch. Will Israeli democracy show more clemency towards the heirs of Jabotinsky than those of Judah Magnes? Based on the model of the Algerian 'gangrene', we now see anti-Palestinian repression being turned against Israelis: an atomic scientist kidnapped and secretly imprisoned for having revealed that Israel was producing and stockpiling atomic bombs; militant pacifists condemned for the 'crime' of dialogue with the PLO; journalists concerned about the truth on the West Bank and in Gaza thrown into prison and mistreated on the pretext of treason; pacifist publications and information centres muzzled.

'Will we, in the long run, become a theocracy? No! . . . We will not allow the theocratic tendencies of our religious leaders to intensify. We will confine them to their temples.' In fact, they very quickly left them. With a percentage of votes varying from 10% to 15%, they succeeded, by acquiring a pivotal role and applying skilful pressure on the **Israeli political parties**, in gradually imposing their rule. Already, Ben Gurion had yielded to them in 1948—1949, when he renounced the idea of endowing the Jewish state with a constitution — the only law a Jew must obey, explained the religious sector, is divine law

— and accepted a compromise, a so-called *status quo*, in matters of education. Not only were the Rabbinical tribunals to reign as masters over the personal life of Israelis — Judaity, marriage, divorce and inheritance depend entirely on them: 'It is legally impossible', explained the Israeli jurist Claude Klein for example, 'to contract in Israel a marriage between a Jewish person and a non-Jewish one' — but the synagogue managed to have its own education system recognized and financed, while obtaining control of the religious education given by state schools. The rabbis would squeeze still more from Menachem Begin, who needed them, in 1977 and 1981, to defeat his Labour adversary. New subsidies to religious schools followed and, more importantly, a stricter application by all state agencies of the *Shabat*, the religious law by which Saturday is a day of rest, and the *Kashrut*, the religious code governing food. The ultra-orthodox would once again turn to the attack after the elections of 1988, promising their support to whichever of the main parties would best satisfy their demands, particularly concerning the revision of the law regarding 'Who is a Jew' — along with the 'Law of Return', it forms the basis for the attribution of Israeli nationality — in order to reduce the possibility of conversion to Judaism. Thus Israelis — 25% of whom declare themselves detached from all religious practices, 45% of whom are non-religious although continuing to observe certain traditions — are subjected to a sort of theocracy, and of the most backward kind.

'The barracks is the place for professional soldiers' who, like the 'ministers of the faith' — said Herzl — 'have no right to interfere in affairs of state, for their meddling would provoke internal and external problems.' In defiance of this judicious advice, Israeli political life swarms with generals, from Peled (on the extreme Left) to Eytan (on the extreme Right) by way of Sharon (in the Likud), Rabin, Bar-Lev and Weizmann (Labour), not forgetting the pacifists Harkabi and Yaariv. The army, in the broadest sense of the word, represents a third of the Gross National Product, half of research and development, half also of imports and an increasing percentage of exports. For Israel exports more than a billion dollars of arms a year: Kfir aircraft, Merkava tanks, AIM—9L and AIM—7 missiles, Osa, Komar, Reshef and Aliya patrol boats, Uzi machine pistols and Galil assault rifles are sold all over the world. Israel, furthermore, manufactures or assembles arms in cooperation with Argentina, Chile, Columbia, Federal Republic of Germany, Switzerland, South Africa and the **United States**. The major budgetary outlay, principal economic power (after the Histadrut sector) and principal exporter, the Israeli Defence Force (IDF), also constitutes a major ideological force, its own educational network taking advantage of the time at its disposal to train young Israelis — including those in the occupied territories.

'We shall be an outpost of civilization against barbarism', Herzl used to argue before the Great Powers to whom he presented his Palestinian project.

On this point, his successors, at the time of the Yishuv and since the birth of Israel, have scrupulously abided by his ideas. And herein no doubt, a result of the very logic of the venture, lies one of the keys to the Israeli impasse. By exclusively seeking its security in alliance with the great powers, especially — after a brief 'honeymoon' with the **Soviet Union** — with the United States, the Jewish state has sacrificed its chances of a peace with Palestine and the Arab world. How can Israel fully take its place amongst the nations of the Middle East, rather than remaining a North American outpost in the region? And what state, furthermore, would safeguard its very sovereignty — 'the first aim is sovereignty', Herzl used to say — by depending each year on 3 billion dollars (more than 800 dollars per Israeli, man, woman and child) of economic and military aid paid out by the United States, to whom it also owes a large part of the 19 billion dollars (more than 60% of the GNP for one year) of Israel's foreign debt?

'In adversity, we shall remain united and we shall suddenly discover our strength. And it is that strength that will allow us to form a state, even a model state,' wrote Herzl. And indeed, the Zionist movement owes much of its success to the extremely strong motivation, political, ideological and moral, of its members. Many Israeli veterans nostalgically recall this, as the Israeli crisis — and it is probably the most serious dimension — spreads to affect values themselves. 'When they hear the word values, they get out their cheque books,' says one of Rachel Mizrahi's characters. And another adds: 'What oppresses me in this country is not the fear of dying in the next war, it is the lack of any quality of life. Everything is false. Lies, rackets, speculations, fraud, string pulling, theft. Everybody does it and everybody thinks it's normal. It's pathetic. Do you remember, when we used to talk about morals and integrity?' The majority point of view? Certainly not. But, since the **Lebanese Civil War** and especially since the Palestinian *Intifada*, many eyes have been opened. Liberating in the eyes of the ghetto Jews and the survivors of the death camps, Zionism has become an occupier. Pacifist in its declared intentions, it has become military. The promised equality is nothing but a red herring in the eyes of the misfits of Israeli society, those Blacks despised by the Whites. The austerity of the pioneers has been tainted by all sorts of scandals. The much-vaunted democracy, for and by the Jewish citizens, is showing its limitations. And a CBS news report was enough to turn Israeli soldiers, the heroes of wars considered defensive, into torturers in the eyes of the world. Hard enough to take in times of easy victories, this becomes unacceptable during difficult defeats. A sign of the times is the fact that the number of emigrants (*yordim*) has, for almost ten years now, outstripped the number of immigrants (*olim*). This has now been dramatically reversed by the accelerating 'aliya' of Soviet Jews, which may lead to the immigration of a million people by 1995! It is a godsend for Israel, but also a terrible burden on its economy.

There are so many ills and their cure depends, in one way or another, on peace, as a growing number of Israelis now believe. At the beginning of 1989, more than 50% of them declared themselves in favour of negotiations with the PLO, on the condition that was explicitly satisfied at the Algiers Palestine National Council that it recognize the state of Israel and end hostilities with it. For, as Professor Leibowitz has pointed out, 'the basic fact, over and above ideology, theory and faith, is that this country belongs to two peoples. Each of them is profoundly convinced that the country belongs to it. In other words, one is forced to opt either for partition, or for war to the death.'

Israel has more than 4.2 million inhabitants — of which 3.55 million are Jewish as against 645,000 Arabs — and has a surface area, based on its frontiers established prior to the Six Day War of 1967, called the Green Line, of 21,000 square kilometres, to which has since been added the annexed territories: the Syrian **Golan Heights** (2,000 square kilometres), **Jerusalem**; and the occupied territories: the West Bank (5,440 square kilometres), the Gaza Strip (330 square kilometres) and the so-called security strip in South **Lebanon** (850 square kilometres). The Gross Domestic Product rose, in 1986, to 29.46 billion dollars, with 7.136 billion dollars of exports and 10.737 of imports, i.e., a commercial deficit of 3.6 billion dollars, to be added to an external debt then amounting to 23.775 billion dollars. It is true that Israel possesses few natural resources: no oil, some phosphates and potash. The basis of the country's development lies in an agriculture whose success is due to the ultra-modern techniques employed — but which furnishes scarcely 10% of exports — and in an industry that imports raw materials and exports products of greatly added value, like diamonds, electronics, arms, chemical products, etc. More than half the country is taken up by the Negev Desert, which receives only 100 to 200 mm of rainfall. Because of the war, mammoth development projects, based on the cutting of a canal between the Mediterranean and the Dead Sea, have not been implemented.

Israeli Arabs

ISRAELI ARABS are those **Palestinians** who were not part of the forced exodus during the **war of 1948—1949**: 160,000 then, more than 645,000 by 1987. For the most part, they are to be found in three regions: the **Galilee**, The Triangle around Umm Al Fahm and The Little Triangle around Taibeh. In 1949, **Israel** annexed these zones which the **Partition Plan** had allocated to the **Arab** state, and their inhabitants became Israeli citizens, but second-class ones, in a state that wanted above all to be Jewish. Up until 1966, Israeli Arabs lived under a military government that subjected them to carrying passes, to curfews and house arrest, and which furthered Jewish colonization by confiscating Arab land.

The population's social structure has undergone drastic changes in the last thirty years. More than 75% rural in 1960, it is, in the late 1980s, largely urban. More than 50% of the Palestinian workforce is employed in the construction industry. Over 13% of Israeli Arabs are Christian and around 10% **Druze**. The latter enjoy special treatment since, alone amongst the Arabs, they are obliged to do military service. The Israeli government has always made use of religious divisions. But this has not been enough to halt the development of Palestinian national feeling. After 1967 it gained strength and asserted itself magnificently on March 30, 1976, on Land Day, during which tens of thousands of Palestinians demonstrated. Bloody reprisals followed, leaving six dead and dozens of wounded.

It is the Israeli Communist Party that has gradually become the mouthpiece of this national minority fighting for its rights: 40% of the Arab population votes for its candidates in the various elections, and it controls most of the major Arab towns, including Nazareth. The CP has also come to symbolize the cultural renaissance of the Palestinians through its Arab language press (*Al Ittihad, Al Jadid*) and its intellectuals (Emile Habibi, Emile Touma, Tawfik Zayad). Another, less powerful force that expresses this nationalism is Miari and Peled's Progressive List for Peace.

Obviously, the *intifada* has accentuated the radicalization of Israeli Palestinians. Thus, after their massive strikes and demonstrations following December 1987, they contributed decisively, on November 1, 1988, to the results of those parties favourable to the establishment of a Palestinian state alongside Israel: the Communist Party (4 seats), the Progressive List (1 seat), the New Arab Democratic Party (1 seat) and the Civil Rights Movement (5 seats instead of 3).

Israeli Political Parties

ISRAELI political life has always been characterized by the existence of a multiplicity of groupings, the reflection of **Zionism**'s innumerable currents all of which, with the exception of the CP, claim kinship, within the framework of a proportional system which lends itself to diversity. This phenomenon intensified during the elections of 1984, the two major coalitions (of the Right and the Left) both losing ground to smaller groupings. The elections of November 1, 1988, were to confirm this trend, both Labour and the Likud losing ground while religious groups, and the Civil Rights Movement, flourished.

The principal party of the **Yishuv** between the two world wars, then of **Israel** until 1977, was the Labour Party, created in 1930 under the name of **Mapai** (the Labour Party of Eretz Israel) from an amalgamation of two Zionist socialist groups. Reformist, advocating alliance with **Great Britain** and the Zionist Right, it increased its vote from 42.3% in 1931 to 59.1% in 1944. After the creation of Israel it held the posts of presidency and prime minister, but underwent a deterioration that reduced it — along with its allies — from 53.4% in 1949 to 26% in 1977, with a recovery in 1981 (36.6%). In 1988, it stabilized at 30%.

This reversal is all the more striking in that Mapai, having become the Labour Party, benefited after 1969 from the backing of Mapam, within the Labour alignment (Maarakh). Heir to the Hashomer Hatzair (the Young Guard) and the Poalei Zion Smole (Left-wing Workers of Zion), Mapam carried on their original traditions after the war: the project of a bi-national state, friendship with the **Soviet Union**, commitment to the *kibbutzim*. But its entry into government (1967) and the Maarakh (1969) diverted it, and brought it under the wing of the Labour leadership, with whom it nonetheless split in 1984. It paid dearly for this rupture in 1988: it then possessed only three representatives in the Knesset, as against six in 1984.

Still on the Left, but in rupture with the general consensus, there are other minority tendencies. The only organization uniting Arabs and **Jews**, the Communist Party, created in 1922, underwent numerous splits of which the last, in 1965, considerably weakened it amongst the Jewish population. Anti-Zionists in a Zionist nation, pro-Soviet in an anti-Soviet country, advocates of a Palestinian state rejected by their fellow citizens, Israeli communists have yet to achieve 5% of the votes, four-fifths of what they receive from the Arab electorate. The Democratic Front for Peace and Equality (Hadash), which they operate, today has four members in the Knesset. Two other members from the extreme left wing were elected in 1984 — only one remained after the elections of 1988 — on the Progressive List for Peace of the Palestinian nationalist Mi'ari, and the pacifist Israeli general, Peled, heir of Meir Pail's Sheli, Uri Avnery's Haolam Hazeh and of Moked. For its part, Shulamit Aloni's Civil Rights Movement is making great strides: it has increased its seats from one in 1981 to three in 1984 and five in 1988.

Electorally marginal, these movements were nonetheless able, during the **Lebanese Civil War**, to contribute to the expression of a powerful pacifist movement formed by Shalom Achshav (Peace Now), the Committee Against the War in Lebanon and the soldiers' organization, Yesh Gvul (There is a Limit). Inactive after the Israeli withdrawal from **Lebanon**, the pacifist movement once again expressed itself, this time in solidarity with the

Palestinian *intifada*. The great majority of intellectuals, in particular, were to be found involved in demonstrations and signing petitions calling for a halt to repression and for negotiations with the **Palestinians**. But, in 1988 as previously in 1984, this militant group was unable — no doubt due to the alternative offered by the Labour Party — to make any deep impression at the ballot box.

As for the Israeli Right, it has two main components: the 'revisionist' Zionism founded by Zeev Jabotinsky and personified by Menachem **Begin**, and the liberal movement which pre-war and until 1961 was composed of general Zionists who later divided into liberals and independent liberals. Long opposed to each other — a faction of liberals even participated in the coalition government headed by Labour — these two wings underwent a spectacular rise when they united, first in 1965 within Gahal (Herut—liberal bloc), then in 1973 within the Likud (coalition). This combined vote rose from 16.7% in 1949 to 35.3% in 1977. Thus, on June 20, 1977, Menachem Begin became Israel's first non-Labour Prime Minister, before ceding his place, in 1983, to Itzhak **Shamir**, who was to head the government of national unity in 1986 after the changeover with Labour's Shimon **Peres**. He maintained this position after the elections of November 1, 1988.

From the end of the 1970s, Israel experienced an increasingly active extreme Right, born out of the rejection of the **Camp David Accords** and nourished by the colonization of the **West Bank**, the prevailing chauvinism, the severe economic, social and moral crises, all taking place against a background of religious fundamentalism. The best known figure in all this is Rabbi Kahane, member of the Knesset from 1984 to 1988 — the Supreme Court then banned his candidature — whose movement, Kach, has as its aim 'the expulsion of all Arabs from Greater Israel'. But other groups are equally powerful. Apart from the common background, Gush Emunin (Bloc of the Faithful), firmly entrenched in the West Bank **settlements**, shares with Kach a two-fold demand: the annexation of the occupied territories and, to a greater or lesser extent, the expulsion of their Palestinian inhabitants. Called 'transfer', this project was once defended only by Kahane. But fear of the *intifada* brought a considerable section of public opinion round to the idea of expelling the Palestinians, so that Tehiya (Renaissance), Moledet (Fatherland) and Tsomet (Zionist Revival) have had seven members in the Knesset since November 1, 1988. According to surveys, their following amongst the young is around 35%.

The existence of relatively powerful religious parties constitutes another Israeli characteristic. Some are Zionist: the pre-1948 Mizrahi (The Orient, founded in 1902) gave birth to the Mafdal (National Religious Party) which has since been in almost all governmental coalitions. A splinter group developed within it in 1988, under the name of Meimad, reacting against what it considered a swing to the right on the part of Mafdal; Meimad obtained no seats on November 1, 1988. The others are non-Zionist: there is the Agudat Yisrael (The Community of Israel), founded in 1911, and the Poale Agudat (The Workers of the Community of Israel). Agudat has undergone three splits: the **Oriental Jews** regrouped in 1984 within the Shas Party, from which the Yemenis formed Yahad Shivtei Yisrael in 1988; and, in the same year, the anti-Hassidic Ashkenazim of the Agudat founded Degel Tora.

With the number of members of Knesset varying from 13 to 15 (out of 120), the religious parties constitute a real **lobby**, exerting increasing pressure. Thus they made the Likud pay a high price for their support in 1977, without

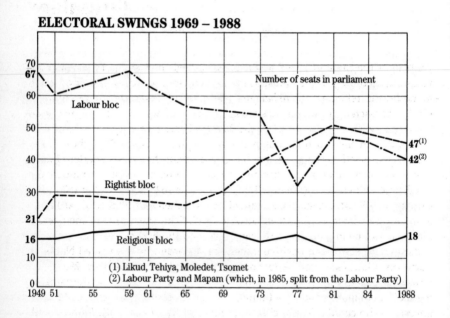

ELECTORAL SWINGS 1969 – 1988

Number of seats in parliament

Labour bloc

Rightist bloc

Religious bloc

(1) Likud, Tehiya, Moledet, Tsomet
(2) Labour Party and Mapam (which, in 1985, split from the Labour Party)

which, it is true, Menachem Begin could not have governed. If Israel has never actually been a secular state, it is only recently that it has become a theocratic one, where religion intrudes into the daily life of every citizen, and where the rabbis are equally responsible for the granting of nationality, for marriage and divorce, or for the subject matter of education. The spectacular progress made by the religious parties in 1988 — Shas: 6 seats (plus 2); Mafdal: 5 (plus 1); Agudat: 5 (plus 3); Degel: 2 (plus 2) — may, in the event of national unity breaking down, lead to an increase in the burden of duties imposed on all citizens: strict observance of the *Shabat*, subsidies to religious institutions, exemption from national service for pupils of the *Yeshivot* (rabbinical schools), even the revision of the Law of Return, etc.

Over a long period, the three major political groups in Israel have undergone — in terms of seats held in the Knesset — the evolution reflected in the table on page 98.

Jerusalem

CAPITAL of the State of **Israel** according to Israelis and of the future state of Palestine according to the **Palestinians**, sacred city for each of the three great monotheistic religions, *Yerushalayim* (the City of Peace) for some, and *Al Quds* (the Sacred) for others, has always been — in other words, for over four thousand years — at the heart of the Middle-Eastern storms.

Founded in the 3rd millennium before our era, a Canaanite tribe having established itself on one of its hills, Jerusalem has since undergone a multitude of occupations: it became, amongst others, Jewish (around 1,000 BC), Egyptian (925 BC), Roman (63 BC), Byzantine (629 AD), Muslim (638 AD), Christian (1099 AD), **Arab** once again (1187 AD), then Ottoman (1517 AD) and, four centuries later, British, from 1917 to 1948. 'The *status quo* of the Sacred Sites will not be impaired in any way,' specified the Berlin Treaty in 1885.

Its modern status is a positive minefield. According to the United Nations' **Partition Plan** (see also Appendix 3), adopted on November 29, 1947, Jerusalem was to constitute a '*corpus separatum* under a special international regime', demilitarized and administered by a trusteeship council and a governor who could not be a citizen of either of the two specified states, and who would guarantee the interests of the Sacred Sites of the three religions and peace between them; finally, the city was to be included in the Palestinian Economic Union. But the first **war (of 1948–1949)** ended with Jerusalem being effectively divided between Transjordanians, who occupied the eastern part, and Israelis, who annexed the western part which they declared, contrary to the armistice conditions, capital of their state. The decision taken by the UN, on December 19, 1949, to internationalize Jerusalem, was never to be put into practice. This situation lasted until the **war of 1967**, during which the Israeli army took from the Hashemite troops the Arab Old City; it was annexed in July 1967. Finally, in June 1980, the whole of Jerusalem was proclaimed 'capital of the State of Israel' by the Knesset, a vote immediately condemned by the UN. Two years later, the Arab **Fez Plan** adopted the slogan calling for an 'independent Palestinian state with *Al Quds* (Jerusalem) as its capital'. A few days earlier, Ronald Reagan, in his speech of September 1, had referred only to the 'indivisible' nature of Jerusalem, leaving the rest to the negotiators. The Soviets, on the other hand, were strongly in favour of partition; the eastern part, they wrote, 'must be restored to the Arabs and become an integral part of the Palestinian state. Freedom of access for believers to the sacred sites of the three religions must be guaranteed throughout the town.'

Two imperatives which, on the face of it, contradict each other.

Sacred city for the Mosaic, Muslim and Christian religions, Jerusalem, in the eyes of believers, is hard to split up. Especially since, as experience has proved, the right to visit the shrines of one's faith in the divided city is often restricted, or even completely flouted — and the UNO has recorded over a hundred sacred sites, amongst which the most important are obviously: for Christians, the Holy Sepulchre; for Muslims, the Omar and Al Aqsa Mosques; and, for **Jews**, the Western Wall of the Temple (called the 'Wailing Wall').

But unifying the town means dashing the hopes of either Israelis or Palestinians, or both, to make it the capital of their state. And Israel, to make this claim irreversible, has occupied the eastern part of the town, traditionally Arab, and encircled it with densely populated housing estates where tens of thousands of Israelis are packed in. If ever the problem is resolved, it will probably be through a concept modelled on that of the Partition Plan of 1947 but containing fresh proposals.

Jew

A NOUN whose very definition has long been the object of extremely complex debates, so numerous and often contradictory are conceptions of 'Jewishness'. Indeed, the question: 'What is a Jew', elicits many responses. 'Can we establish how many of us there are?', wonders Richard Marienstras in *Etre un peuple en Dispora*. And he replies: 'Clearly not, since we don't know who we are.' Lengthy controversial discussions have naturally developed around this theme, in **Israel**. There, the 'right of return', adopted in 1950, stipulates that 'every Jew has the right to come to Israel'. This right was complemented by the Law on Nationality, voted in 1952, which automatically grants Israeli nationality to any immigrant taking advantage of the Law of Return and thus, Jewish. But who is to be considered as such? 'Anyone born of a Jewish mother or who has converted to Judaism', replies Talmudic law, and the ultra-orthodox insist, so far in vain, that the converts in question must have done so in accordance with the strictest conception of Jewish law.

Several famous affairs have brought the legal aspect of the question to the public eye. Thus the case of Daniel Rufeisen, a Polish Jew converted to Catholicism, who asked the Ministry of the Interior to enter him in the register of the Israeli population as Catholic under the heading marked religion, but as Jewish under 'ethnic group': the ministry, and the Supreme Court to which he subsequently applied, refused him the right of return, considering that his conversion made him a non-Jew. On the other hand, Benjamin Shalit, whose wife was not Jewish, managed to have their children registered as Jews under the 'ethnic group' heading. Following these affairs, the religious parties imposed a modification of Article 42 of the Law of Return: 'A Jew', specifies the definitive text, 'is a person born of a Jewish mother or converted (to Judaism) and who does not belong to any other religion.' Clearly, in matters of religion and ethnicity, a certain ambiguity remains.

The religious criterion is certainly indisputable. The first major monotheistic religion, the Mosaic faith, with its sacred texts, its law and rites, unites millions of believers across the world. Its influence is all the greater in that, after the Diaspora, it was religious faith that 'took up the idea of the survival of the people outside of the state-based political forms of national existence' (Ilan Halevy). But the Jewish religion, like many others, has not been spared, in Israel and especially elsewhere in the world, the phenomenon of religious disaffection characteristic of modern times. Many of those one calls — or who call themselves — Jews are atheists. Others, even more numerous, although apparently still attached to their faith, are not practising its rituals. Except at major holidays and festivals, synagogues are as poorly attended as churches and temples. Religion is therefore not a sufficient reference point to embody all Jews.

The alleged common origin — the Hebrews — is no more conclusive. True, in ancient Palestine a Jewish nation-people had been formed. But the collapse of the Jewish kingdoms under the successive blows of the Assyrians and the Babylonians, the Roman Conquest and, above all, the crushing of the Bar Kokhba revolt, in 135 AD, caused its dispersal. While a small nucleus remained in the Holy Land, the main body of the Jewish population was

scattered all over the Mediterranean, often assimilated into the host country. Others, with a profound sense of their own identity, even managed to convert their hosts, sometimes *en masse*. Thus the work of historians indicates that, contrary to the thesis that the Jewish religion does not proselytize — one cannot, it says, 'join' a 'chosen people' — the Jewish state of Southern Arabia, in the 6th century, or again the Jewish state of the Khazars in South-West Russia in the 8th century, were established by winning over the sovereigns and their subjects. Arthur Koestler, in *The Thirteenth Tribe*, thus claims that most of the Jews of Central Europe are descended from the Khazars, therefore from converted Turco-Mongols then dispersed into Slav territory. The same goes for North Africa, Spain, Gaul, Germany, Asia, etc. The majority of modern Jews have therefore, apparently, no direct links with the Hebrews; yet the anthem of the *Hatikvah* nonetheless continues to claim that 'our dream of two thousand years is not lost, to return to the country of our fathers, the land of Sion, Jerusalem'.

All of which goes to show how much the call to the concept of 'race' depends on both the despicable and the ridiculous. The old anecdote of the French Jew who goes off to China in search of his 'brothers' reflects, on a humorous level, this pseudo-theory. Arriving at last in Shanghai, our man, in a dark side street, discovers the synagogue and enters. The Chinese Jews, at prayer there, are at first astonished, then gradually turn threatening. Finally he calls out to them: 'But I'm a Jew, like you.' And they, showing him their slanted eyes, retort: 'Well you certainly don't look like one!' A simple visit to Israel will convince the most doubtful reader of the extraordinary diversity of Jewish 'types', as extensive as those of the hundred and fifty odd countries from which Israelis have come.

The very concept of the Jewish people is, in this respect, unscientific to say the least. With no ethnic reality and aware that the religious angle has proved limited, on what elements would the concept rely? If it is true that, up to World War II, Central European Jews formed a sort of coherent national minority (territory, language, culture, organizations, demands) — in *A History of the Jews*, Ilan Halevi speaks of 'material conditions of nationalistic existence', echoing Zvi Graetz who, in his *Histoire des Juifs* shows how conditions in Poland, for instance, 'led the Jews to live as a state within a state, with their own religious, administrative and legal institutions' — it is no longer true today. The *shtetl*, Central Europe's Jewish 'little town', disappeared in the crematoriums after having undergone the **pogroms**. Scattered into dozens of countries, the majority of post-**holocaust** Jews no longer speak either Hebrew, Yiddish or Judeo-Spanish, and their common culture has been reduced to a minimum. The assimilation initiated on a large scale in the West in the 19th century is once again under way.

This assimilation did not, however, reaffirm itself equally, after the holocaust, from one country to another. The **United States**, with its powerful Jewish **lobby** and **France**, with its Jewish community extremely deep-rooted in the population, offer two extreme examples. In France, in fact, notes Richard Marienstras, 'the prestige of the French revolution was such that the only desirable fate one could envisage, for the millions of Yiddish speaking Jews of East Europe, was assimilation. Very quickly, French Jews became an example to the world, and the value of this example was not diminished for them after the Dreyfus Affair. The "solution" to the "Jewish question" had to be integration. They therefore vehemently rejected the national or nationalistic dimensions of Jewish existence.' And one is familiar with the letter in which Leon Blum, in 1950, endorsed the 'admirable effort' of Israel which 'henceforth guarantees a homeland worthy of all those Jews who have not had like me the good fortune to find it in the land of their birth'.

And yet, even assimilated, the Jews exist, whether they are designated as such: 'It is anti-semitism that creates the Jew,' stated Jean-Paul Sartre — or whether they are conscious of being so. To our way of thinking, 'anyone who feels Jewish, is Jewish', for whatever reasons of their own. For many, it is a long history of persecution culminating with the holocaust, of which even the most assimilated of Jews retain, whether they were affected directly or not, tragic memories. The condition of life of the Jewish man, explained André Neher in *Existence juive*, is 'that of the persecuted man'. For some, as we have seen, it is having the same faith, with the ways of life it still implies, to varying degrees, including a basic understanding of Hebrew. For others again, it is the practice of one of the Jewish languages of the Diaspora, insertion into one of the Jewish cultures — themselves very varied. For yet other Jews, it is a certain affinity with the State of Israel, which, without wishing to settle there — the great failure of **Zionism** lies in having attracted to Israel only one Jew in four — and without necessarily supporting its policy, they nonetheless see as a last resort, 'just in case'. Jewish identity, at the end of the 20th century, no doubt draws mainly on these four sources, which even assimilation has not completely dried up.

'I envy him', wrote Maxime Rodinson of one of his most virulent critics, 'for having straightaway found the definitions and terms necessary to designate an entity that at the same time brings together King David, Einstein, Jesus of Nazareth, Maimonides, Moses, Mendelssohn, Karl Marx, Menachem Begin, Jacques Offenbach, Benjamin Disraeli, Michel Debré, Tristan Bernard, etc., not to mention him and me. . . .'

Jordan

IN 1922, the territories under the British Mandate, situated to the east of the River Jordan, were established as a semi-autonomous principality under the leadership of Emir Abdullah. The latter was a son of the Sherif of Mecca, Hussein — of the powerful Hashemite family — who had raised the standard of the **Arab** revolt against the **Ottoman Empire** during World War I. In 1930 the Arab Legion was created, the backbone of the emirate's armed forces, which would be directed by a British officer, Glubb Pasha, until 1956.

A founding member of the **Arab League** in 1945, Transjordan gained independence in March 1946. However, **Great Britain**'s influence there remained predominant. Immediately after World War II, the question of Palestine galvanized the Hashemite sovereign. Making no bones of his territorial ambitions, Abdullah, encouraged by Britain, ordered his troops into Palestine, alongside other Arab forces, on May 15, 1948. When, in April 1949, Transjordan and **Israel** signed an armistice, the Hashemite king could be well satisfied with the results: he had conquered rich territories — which would become known as the **West Bank** — as well as East **Jerusalem** and the Al Aqsa Mosque, Holy Site of **Islam**. He owed this result to the efficiency of the Arab League and to secret negotiations undertaken with Zionist leaders, which led to his being accused of treachery by his Arab opponents.

The Palestine **War of 1948–1949** profoundly altered the contours of the state. The population, scarcely 500,000 at the outset of the war, tripled in a few months: 500,000 refugees and the 500,000 Palestinians of the West Bank. A destabilizing element was introduced into a hitherto conservative state, with a Bedouin majority. In December 1948, Abdullah took the title of King of **Jordan**; in April 1949, the country's name became the Hashemite Kingdom of Jordan (a name already adopted at **independence** in 1946, but never applied). In April 1950, elections held in Cisjordan (the West Bank) and Transjordan effectively confirmed the annexation of the West Bank. On July 20, 1951, the king was assassinated by a Palestinian at the Al Aqsa mosque in Jerusalem.

His son Talal succeeded him, but lost no time in abdicating in favour of his own heir, **Hussein**, who, proclaimed King, effectively acceded to the throne on his coming of age, on May 2, 1953. The Middle East was then in a state of turbulence with the growth of Arab nationalism and the emergence of the new leader of **Egypt**, Gamal Abdel **Nasser**. Hussein, who had chosen the Western camp, survived various crises: that of 1956–1957 and that of 1965–1966 which found him in opposition to the PLO. He made his peace with Nasser on the eve of the **war of 1967** and his army took part in the fighting, during which the kingdom lost the territories it had conquered in 1948—1949: the West Bank and East Jerusalem.

Threatened by the *fedayeen* between 1967 and 1970, the authorities liquidated the Palestinian armed presence in September 1970 (**Black September**) and June 1971. Since then, the Hashemite dynasty has undergone no serious crisis. Jordan did not take part in the **war of 1973**. Its political leaders were split into two camps: one in favour of retreat into Transjordan; the other retaining its more extensive ambitions. The decision was all the harder in that the territorial designs harboured by a section of the Israeli Right regarding the east bank of the Jordan were well known, and the deadlock could only lead to renewed fighting. On July 31, 1988, in a historic speech, the king settled the matter: he withdrew all demands regarding the West Bank. But this decision, mainly due to the Palestinian *intifada*, did not mean that Jordan had renounced playing a role in the solution of the Middle Eastern conflict. Following the riots that broke out in the Bedouin fiefs during April 1989, the king embarked on a form of democratization. Free legislative elections took place at the end of the year, and were notable for the strong showing of the Muslim Brotherhood.

Considered to be a moderate Arab regime, an ally of Washington, the monarchy nonetheless took a stand against the **Camp David Accords**. It supported **Iraq** in its war with **Iran** and renewed ties with President **Mubarak**'s Egypt.

Spread over an area of almost 90,000 square kilometres, Jordan numbers 3.6 million inhabitants (to which must be added 500 to 700,000 immigrants). Nearly 70% of the population is urban, and the same proportion is of Palestinian origin. Ninety per cent of inhabitants are Sunni Muslims, but there are also a certain number of Christians. Despite genuine development, the country's situation is precarious and depends on Arab and **American aid**, on tourism and on money sent from its expatriates; in 1988 it underwent a serious economic crisis. The country also exports phosphate. The Constitution accords virtually unlimited power to the king, despite the existence of two Chambers, and until recently political parties were banned. On November 8, 1989 the first parliamentary elections for 22 years were held; the results revealed the hidden strength of the Islamic Right.

Jumblatt (family)

KAMAL JUMBLATT was born in 1917 in Moukhtara, in the Shouf (Mount Lebanon), into a feudal **Druze** family. After doing one year at the Sorbonne in Paris, he finished his law degree at the Saint Joseph University in Beirut. Elected an independent member of parliament — on the Druze ticket — he was to be re-elected almost continuously until the outbreak of the civil war in 1975. A minister for the first time in 1947, he founded the Progressive Socialist Party (PSP) in 1949. The party, basically reformist and later to join the Socialist International, became more radical over the years. In 1958, Kamal Jumblatt played an important role in the civil war and in the anti-Chamoun coalition.

After the **Arab** defeat in the Six Day **War of 1967**, Jumblatt came out in favour of the Palestinian resistance. His support to Suleiman **Franjiyyeh's** candidacy for the presidency, in 1970, was more an accident — which none-theless says something of the mysterious workings of Lebanese politics — than a strategic decision and, in 1973, he took the side of the PLO against the Lebanese army.

Kamal Jumblatt was to be one of the central figures in the **Lebanese Civil War** of 1975–1976. He was president of the Lebanese National Movement (LNM), an amalgamation of a dozen or so different parties and personalities calling for the establishment of a democratic, secular **Lebanon**, for extensive reforms in the state and the preservation of the country's Arab character. When, in the spring of 1967, the PLO-LNM alliance felt victory within its grasp, Damascus realigned its relations in favour of the Maronite Right (see **Maronites**). After the failure of attempts at reconciliation, Kamal Jumblatt took military action against the Syrian intervention. But he was helpless against the steamroller that was getting under way: LNM and the PLO were defeated and forced, in the autumn of 1976, to cease fighting without having attained their objectives. Kamal Jumblatt, who remained hostile to the Syrian presence, was assassinated on March 16, 1977, probably on the orders of Damascus.

In losing him, the Lebanese Left lost a federalist, and the Druze community its leader. Kamal Jumblatt was also a philosopher, practised in the spiritual disciplines of India and of Zen Buddhism.

Walid Jumblatt, only son of Kamal, was born on August 7, 1949, in Beirut. Nothing had prepared him to replace his father when he was assassinated but, in accordance with Lebanese tradition, he succeeded him as head of the Druze community and the PSP. On the other hand, he was not elected president of the LNM until 1980.

In 1982, during the Israeli invasion, he refused to take military action against the advancing troops and confined himself, from his fiefdom in the Shouf, to calling for passive resistance. But he quickly became one of President **Gemayel**'s principal opponents, and gathered around him all the malcontents. In September 1983, his men drove the Phalangists from the Shouf and Aley; in February 1984, he took part, along with Amal, in the takeover of West Beirut. In 1985, new outbreaks of fighting, accompanied by massacres, caused the exodus of tens of thousands of Christians; the 'homogenization' of the Druze mountains was virtually complete.

Walid Jumblatt is a key figure in the future of Lebanon. Although he heads a socialist party — part of whose leadership is non-Druze — he is, like all the men who count in Lebanon today, a military commander, a community leader and a businessman.

Khomeini (Ruhollah)

ACCORDING to most sources, Khomeini was born on September 24, 1902, into a religious family living near Isfahan. His education took place at Qom, one of the centres of **Shi'ism**, the majority religion in **Iran** and the state religion since the 16th century. A theologian, he attained the rank of *mujtahid* (one skilled in the interpretation of Islamic Law), then the title of *ayatollah* ('miraculous sign from God') which made him one of the most respected religious leaders in the country. Very early, he showed an interest in politics and published a book refuting secularism; but it was not until 1962 that he really became involved in activism.

An opponent of the agricultural reform — the White Revolution — initiated by the Shah, which encroached on the interests of the Shi'ite dignitaries, he was involved in the disturbances of June 4, 1963, and was imprisoned. Released after having agreed to curb his criticisms, he came to public attention once again through his condemnation of military relations with the **United States** and the granting of diplomatic status to their advisers. He was then expelled from Iran, in November 1964, and took refuge in Najaf, a Shi'ite holy city in **Iraq**. The deaths, in 1961 and 1962, of two important ayatollahs, Mohammed Burujerdi and Abu Al Qassem Kashani, raised him to the pinnacle of the religious hierarchy

He remained in Iraq until October 1978, when the Ba'athist government in Baghdad declared him *persona non grata*. Exiled again, this time in **France**. Khomeini now became a symbol for the Iranian militants who had risen against the Shah's dictatorship. Through his speeches — relayed by cassette — he fuelled the uprising against the regime. On February 1, 1979, he returned in triumph to Tehran; the empire collapsed, the age of the Islamic Republic began.

Khomeini's reasoning hinged on the question of power, the central question for Iranian Shi'ism. According to tradition, on Mohammed's death he was succeeded in turn by twelve Imams ('guides'), the last of whom died in the year 874 AD. After communicating with the outside world through messengers, he definitively withdrew from life, though remaining alive; this is the time of the Great Occultation, while awaiting the end of time and the return of the 'hidden Imam' who will return to restore a reign of justice on earth. But during the Great Occultation, who is to guide the faithful? For Khomeini, the role falls to the *mullah* (theologian) and the *faghi*, the scholar, vicar of the hidden Imam, and delegate of divine sovereignty. This doctrine of the 'government of the scholar' (*velayat faghi*), which accords to the mullah enormous power, has been — and still is — contested by many other ayatollahs.

However, it was to become accepted. But not without difficulty, for the front that had overthrown the Shah was very broad: liberals, religious groups, the *mujahedeen* — members of a revolutionary Islamic organization led by Massoud Radjavi — Kurdish separatists, communists, etc. The war launched by Iraq in September 1980 and the first Iraqi victories provoked an outburst of patriotism, which Khomeini took advantage of to pitilessly crush his erstwhile allies. In 1983, Iran launched a counter-offensive on the front; all opposition — with the exception of the **Kurds** — was crushed. Khomeini's position as absolute ruler of the country was confirmed, but the regime's base had shrunk. The prolongation of the **Gulf War**, due to the ayatollah's obstinacy, alienated many who had sympathized with him, and the agreement, made in August 1988, for a ceasefire constituted a bitter personal defeat. He died on 3 June 1989.

The implementing of the war with Baghdad, the paralysis of the machinery of government under the constant condemnation of the religious community, led Khomeini, at the end of 1987, to make an important revision in his doctrine. 'To claim that the powers of the State are limited to the framework of divine principles is in total contradiction to what I said,' he wrote. 'Government action that is a part of the absolute sovereignty of the Prophet is a basic imperative of Islam, which takes precedence over all others, even prayer, the pilgrimage to Mecca, etc.' In thus wishing to guarantee the government a certain freedom of action, the ayatollah was acknowledging that all internal reforms had been sabotaged, in the name of Islam, by the mullah and that it was necessary — even more so now the war was over — to respond to the formidable economic and social challenges facing the country.

Kissinger (Henry)

AMERICAN Secretary of State Henry Kissinger stamped the Middle East (amongst other places) with his 'step by step' approach, which eventually led to the **Camp David Accords**.

Jewish, born in Furth (Bavaria) in 1923, he fled Nazi Germany with his family, who settled in New York in 1938. Henry Kissinger took part in World

War II, became an American citizen in 1945, then studied at Harvard and went on to teach there until 1969. In the meantime, his political career got off the ground: in 1968 President Nixon appointed him personal adviser for national security. It was in this capacity that he instigated America's *rapprochement* with China (1972–1973), the peace treaty in Vietnam (1973), and the beginnings of the detente with the USSR, which went hand in hand with the reaffirmation of America's tutelage over its allies, manifest in the New Atlantic Charter.

Appointed Secretary of State in August 1973, Henry Kissinger took over the Middle East portfolio, with the Yom Kippur **War of 1973** scarcely ended. His tactics were clear: 'We can' — he declared on November 2, in a speech he was to publish in his autobiography *The Stormy Years* — 'reduce Soviet influence in the region and obtain the lifting of the oil embargo, if we manage to present a moderate programme, and that is what we are going to do. Otherwise, the Arabs will once again be enticed by the Soviets, oil will be lost, we will have everyone against us. . . . We have to prove to the Arabs that they will be better off dealing with us on the basis of a moderate programme than dealing with the Russians on the basis of an extremist programme.'

Kissinger put this line into practice during his tour of the Middle East. The United Nations ceasefire had stipulated negotiations between all the interested parties: convened by Kurt Waldheim, with the American secretary of state and the Soviet minister of foreign affairs as co-presidents, an **international conference** was in fact set up on December 21, 1973 — and immediately adjourned. Kissinger, strengthened by this multilateral setback, proposed his bilateral step by step plan. An initial accord, called the Kilometre 101 Agreement, had been concluded between **Egypt** and **Israel**, concerning the supplying of the Egyptian 3rd Army, the exchange of prisoners and the raising of the blockade on the southern straits of the Red Sea. Then, in January 1974, Kissinger extracted a disengagement agreement whereby the troops of the two countries withdrew to thirty miles from the **Suez Canal**, with the creation of a buffer zone occupied by the Blue Berets of the United Nations. On May 31, there was a new disengagement agreement, this time between **Syria** and Israel, an exchange of prisoners being accompanied by Israel's restitution of the Syrian territory conquered during the war, plus the town of Kuneitra and the surrounding area.

The 'miracle' was repeated in 1975. At the end of another official visit, Henry Kissinger managed to get Cairo and Tel Aviv to sign an unprecedented accord: the two countries officially ended the state of war between them and renounced the use of armed force against each other, Egypt excluding all sea blockades and the Israelis once again giving way to the UN, whose personnel employed electronic detection devices. In exchange for the recovery of his oil wells, the Egyptian head of state agreed to allow the passage through the

Suez Canal of non-military cargoes bound for Israel.

The election, in 1976, of Jimmy Carter, who chose to send the Republican Kissinger back to his studies and assign his post to the Democrat Cyrus Vance, did not prevent 'Dear Henry's' legacy from bearing fruit; the path he had opened up was to lead, in 1978, to the **Camp David Accords**.

Kurds

SCATTERED over **Iran**, Turkey and **Iraq**, the Kurds have a long history: the mythical birth of this people goes back to March 21, 612 BC. Speaking an Indo-European language, converted for the most part to **Sunni Islam**, they inhabit inaccessible mountain regions and have never constituted a unified political entity. Their numbers are the subject of lively controversy, in which the political considerations are obvious — as in Turkey where their existence as a minority is just beginning to be acknowledged. According to Kurdish organizations, there are 10 million in Turkey, 6 million in Iran and 3 million in Iraq, to which must be added the communities of **Syria** (800,000) and the **Soviet Union** (350,000). These figures, no doubt exaggerated, nonetheless give some idea of the scale involved.

Following World War I and the dismantling of the **Ottoman Empire**, the Allies considered creating an independent Kurdistan. On August 10, 1920, the Treaty of Sèvres, signed with Turkey, provided for the creation of an autonomous Kurdistan in western Anatolia and the province of Mossul. But the rebellion and subsequent victory of Mustapha Kemal led to the Treaty of Lausanne in 1923 and the denial of Kurdish rights. Only the new Iraqi state, under British mandate and in accordance with the decisions of the United Nations, was to grant a certain autonomy to Kurds. This promise too was broken. Kurdish revolts broke out — particularly in Turkey, in 1925, 1930 and 1937 — only to be ruthlessly crushed. And, on July 8, 1937, the Saadabad Pact between Turkey, Iraq, Iran and Afghanistan stipulated, amongst other things, a coordination of the struggle against Kurdish subversion and irredentism.

After World War II, and with the support of the USSR, the Kurdish Republic of Mahabad was created in Iran, in January 1946. But, in December, Iranian troops put an end to the experiment. Until the late 1970s, Kurdish rebellion would basically be concentrated in Iraq.

The man who was to symbolize this rebellion was Mustapha Barzani. Born in 1903 in the village of Barzan (Iraq), from a family of religious leaders, he was involved in the abortive experiment of the Republic of Mahabad. A refugee in the Soviet Union for more than ten years, he returned to Iraq after the advent of the Republic, in 1958. When the Kassem regime failed to respect the promises of Kurdish autonomy, he launched, in September 1961, a rebellion in the north of the country, whose slogan was: 'Autonomy for Kurdistan, democracy for Iraq.'

Truces, negotiations and guerilla operations alternated without interruption until 1975. In 1970, an agreement seemed on the cards: the Ba'ath conceded the creation of an autonomous Kurdish region, recognized that the Kurds constituted one of Iraq's two nations and granted them certain rights — one of which was the use of their language, which became the country's second language. However, significant disagreements remained, regarding both the delimitation of Kurdistan — the oil town of Mosul was excluded from it — and the real powers of the local elected representatives. In March 1974, Saddam **Hussein** decided on the unilateral application of autonomy. Spurred on by the Shah of Iran and Henry **Kissinger**, who were alarmed by the pro-Soviet tendencies of the Ba'athist regime, Mustapha Barzani resumed the uprising. It collapsed following the Algiers agreement of March 6, 1975, between Tehran and Baghdad, which ended their dispute over frontiers and brought to a halt all Iranian aid to the Kurdish rebellion.

The outbreak of the **Gulf War**, in September 1980, set off Kurdish protest once again, this time on a larger scale. In Iran, after the fall of the Shah, Dr Abdul Rahman Ghassemlou's Iranian Kurdish Democratic Party (IKDP) took control of Kurdistan; the Islamic Republic's offensive led it to form an alliance with Saddam Hussein's regime. In Iraq too, difficulties created by the war against the 'Persians' encouraged Kurdish irredentism. But unity did not result as a consequence of all this: the DKP, headed since 1976 by Massoud Barzani, Mustapha's son, Jalal Talabani's Patriotic Union of Kurdistan (PUK) and the Iraqi Communist Party allied, split up, became reconciled. Just before the ending of hostilities, in August 1988, they were once again unified and coordinated their activities with the Iranian army.

The Kurdish revival has been equally apparent in Turkey. Since August 1984, the Kurdistan Worker Party (known as PKK) has carried out guerilla operations in the eastern provinces of the country. But if the organization's terrorism has aroused many reservations, it has permitted a new debate, hitherto taboo, in Turkey on the Kurdish question.

The end of the Gulf War allowed the various governments of the region to turn on their own Kurds. Iraq, with particular brutality — including the use of chemical gas — regained control of the north of the country, provoking the exodus of close to a hundred thousand Kurds into Turkey. In Iran, too, less successful offensives were mounted against the IDKP. The assassination in Vienna on July 13, 1989, of Dr Ghassemlou was, however, a serious blow to the organization. But, for the first time since the end of the 1914–1918 war,

Kurdish nationalism was asserting itself simultaneously in the three main countries concerned. It remains, despite its many divisions, an important factor in the future of the region.

Kuwait

IN 1756, from a patch of desert and a few oases on the borders of the Gulf, began the reign of the Al Sabah dynasty which, till August 1990, has survived all the vicissitudes of regional and international politics. In 1899, the reigning sheikh signed a treaty with London by which he delegated part of his powers — notably foreign relations. The discovery of oil, on the eve of World War II, was to totally transform traditional nomadic society. From the beginning of the 1950s, the sovereign used the oil revenue to undertake a programme of public works and improvement in education and medicine — an event unusual enough to warrant mention. On June 19, 1961, Kuwait gained **independence**, the sheikh was transformed into an emir and the country was admitted into the **Arab League** — despite the claims of Kassem's **Iraq** on what it considered a lost province of the mother country.

Kuwait enjoys an economic and social prosperity based on oil and immigrant labour. The population includes barely 40% of nationals; the others are from **Arab** countries — including 300,000 **Palestinians**. From the mid-1970s, Kuwait has tended to replace these migrants, at least as far as unskilled work is concerned, with an Asian workforce that is obliged to undertake everything and anything and is little concerned with the unrest of the Arab world. In a troubled environment, the royal family has tried to remain aloof from inter-Arab conflicts, even to take on the role of mediator. From 1967, it has made a considerable financial contribution to the front line countries and the Palestinian cause. In 1981, Kuwait was a founder member of the Gulf Cooperation Council (GCC) along with the United Arab Emirates, **Saudi Arabia**, Oman, Qatar and Bahrain. It has tended to oppose the hegemony of Riyadh. Relations with the **PLO** — in particular with Fatah — are all the more solid in that the Palestinian community is rich and influential. Finally, in 1964, a Soviet embassy was opened in Kuwait: the only one in the Gulf — apart from Iraq — for twenty years.

The government has also increased its investments abroad, and manages a portfolio estimated at 40 billion dollars with an annual return of 5 to 8 billion. Amongst the companies in which Kuwait owns shares are Daimler-Benz (17%), the German chemical group Hoechst (24.9%), General Motors, General Electric, ATT and various Spanish banking and oil groups. The takeover, in 1988, of 20% of BP shares aroused fierce opposition from the British government. Through this manoeuvre, plus the purchase, in 1987, of the European distribution network of Gulf, one of the oil giants, Kuwait itself disposes of a quarter of its oil production. The scandal of Souk Al Manakh — the collapse of this unofficial financial market in 1983 — seems largely forgotten today.

Oil is the principal source of the wealth and importance of this small emirate, where 10% of world reserves are located. Kuwait, an active member of the Organization of Oil Exporting Countries (OPEC), took control of its own natural resources in 1975.

The victory of the Iranian Revolution and the Gulf War precipitated Kuwait, which had sided with Saddam Hussein, into a state of turbulence. Relations between the Sunni and Shi'ite (see Shi'ism) communities deteriorated, and members of the latter were banned from all sensitive posts. In 1983, the country was shaken by several political disturbances. The authorities took advantage of this, in July 1986, to dissolve the Assembly elected in February which had contained representatives from across the political spectrum, from the Left to the Muslim groups. Freedom of the press is, however, more widespread than in most Arab countries. In early 1990 there were major demonstrations calling for a return to normal parliamentary life.

On 2 August 1990, after mounting a campaign accusing Kuwait of having stolen $2.4 billion worth of Iraqi oil, Saddam Hussein had his army invade the emirate. He annexed it six days later, provoking the United Nations to declare a trade embargo, and the United States to send 100,000 men to the Gulf. The very existence of Kuwait depends on the outcome.

Kuwait has a surface area of 17,800 square kilometres and a population of 1.8 million, almost 60% of whom are foreigners. Around a third of inhabitants are Shi'ites. Oil production has dropped from 3.3 million barrels per day to 1.5 million in 1980 and 1.75 million in 1990.

Lawrence (T. E.)

KNOWN TO HISTORY as Lawrence of Arabia because, during World War I, he championed the Arab Revolt against the Turks, immortalized in his book, *The Seven Pillars of Wisdom*, and the film adapted from it by David Lean.

It was in Cairo, in 1914, that British Intelligence recruited Thomas Edward Lawrence, fresh from Oxford but familiar with the Arab world where archaeological digs had already taken him, passionately fond of literature, young boys and adventure.

The adventure proposed to him by the heads of British Intelligence was a strategic one. In 1914, London feared that Turkey, allied to the central empires, would carry the Arabs in its wake; the sultan, Commander of the Faithful, had declared a holy war (*jihad*). Negotiations were under way: on the one hand between Sir Percy Cox, British Resident in the Gulf and the Wahabite Ibn Saud, and on the other between Sir Henry MacMahon, British High Commissioner in Cairo, and the Hashemite Hussein. Descendant of the Prophet's tribe and leader of the Hedjaz, the latter agreed, during the summer of 1915, to take up arms against the Sublime Porte, in exchange for the promise made by the British to 'recognize and support Arab independence'.

Sent to Hussein to help him organize the revolt, Lawrence worked with his sons, particularly the youngest, Faisal. As Faisal's liaison officer, he took part in the mobilization of the Bedouins, in battles against the Turks, and the capture of important towns, particularly Akaba, in July 1917. Then Lawrence and the Arab troops backed General Allenby's offensive in Palestine (see **Palestinians**) and **Syria**. Lawrence's dream seemed about to materialize: a great pro-British Arab empire, with Hussein at its head controlling the Hejaz, Faisal controlling Syria and **Iraq** and Abdullah Palestine and Transjordan.

But **Great Britain** was bound by other, contradictory promises made to the **French**, the Zionist movement, even to Hussein's Wahabite rival. Before ever seeing the light of day, the Arab Empire was dismembered, Paris and above all London sharing the spoils. Hussein was to make do with the Hedjaz, which Ibn Saud would seize from him; Faisal, chased out of Syria by the French, would find himself on the throne of Iraq, and Abdullah would reign in Transjordan. As for Lawrence of Arabia, he had had enough of this 'epic'; on July 4, 1922, he resigned from the Office of Colonial Affairs.

Other, more mysterious, intelligence missions awaited him in Asia, alongside his new career as a writer, and his activities on behalf of the English fascist Mosley. On May 19, 1935, Thomas Lawrence was killed in an accident (?) a few days before an interview that he had been granted by the German Chancellor, Adolf Hitler.

Lebanese Civil War

THE SECOND civil war (for the first, in 1958, see **Lebanon**) began on April 13, 1975. That day, a bus, bringing back **Palestinians** and Lebanese from **Sabra** camp, was crossing the Ain Al Rummaneh zone, controlled by the Phalangists (see **Phalangist Party**). Suddenly, brisk gunfire broke out: 27 passengers were killed. Reprisals, counter-reprisals, fighting spread throughout the country. But no one imagined at the time that, fourteen years later, it would still be going on, though officially the war ended in September 1976.

The war grew out of a combination of three factors. An economic and social crisis found expression in numerous protest movements against the confessional system (see **confessionalism**) and in an upsurge of left-wing organizations. Confirmation of the Palestinian presence in Lebanon was the second factor. After 1967, the **PLO** had taken control of the refugee camps; since 1971, with its departure from **Jordan**, the **Palestinian Resistance** had found sanctuary in Lebanon. Finally, despite its neutrality, Lebanon had been dragged into the Arab-Israeli conflict in June 1967; indeed, the Israeli army's raids in the south made Lebanon a front line country.

Two coalitions, far from homogeneous, confronted each other during the war's active phase, which was to last eighteen months: the Lebanese Front and the Lebanese National Movement (LNM). Between these two fluctuated a galaxy of forces and personalities, some neutral, some aligned.

The Lebanese Front, which only came into being formally nine months after the outbreak of hostilities, was made up of four components, predominantly Maronite (see **Maronites**): the faction of the President of the Republic, Suleiman **Franjiyyeh**, whose fiefdom was Zghorta, in the north; the faction of ex-president Camille Chamoun, with 3,500 militiamen, the Tigers; the congress of monastic orders led by Father Kassis; and finally, Pierre **Gemayel's** Phalangist Party, whose 15,000 men made up the backbone of the right-wing coalition.

The LNM was an amalgamation of about fifteen parties, ranging from centre to extreme left. Multi-denominational, it had a bedrock of Christians, particularly Greek Orthodox. Its undisputed leader was Kamal **Jumblatt** whose party, the PSP (*Parti socialiste populaire*), and 3,000 militiamen made up the central force of the MNL. Amongst the other components were the Lebanese Communist Party (LCP), the Syrian National Social Party, the Ba'ath, and the Muribatoun — a Nasserian, basically **Sunni** movement.

The respective goals of the two coalitions, to the extent that one can rationalize them, can be defined as follows: on the one hand, to drive out the **Palestinians** and maintain the Maronite bourgeoisie's hegemony over the state; on the other, to form an alliance with the PLO and secularize the state. Between these two camps, there were many who hesitated. There were the traditional Sunni Muslim leaders who would be happy with a redistribution of powers. Certain Maronite leaders, like Raymond Edde, and parties representing other Christian denominations (Armenians, Greek Orthodox). Lastly, special mention must be made of the Shi'ites of the Movement of the Dispossessed, the future Amal, who would fight at the side of the LNM until the Syrian intervention in the summer of 1976.

The first phase of the war, up until January 1976, was roughly equal, with the Lebanese Front having a slight advantage. The PLO — with the exception of organizations belonging to the the Rejectionist Front — avoided committing itself. But, at the beginning of the new year, Maronite forces launched a major offensive against the Palestinian camps. The PLO no longer had a choice. It threw all its weight into the balance and turned the scale in favour of the LNM. It was then that Damascus intervened, at first politically then militarily, against its progressive allies of yesterday. The Syrian leaders who, at the time, were negotiating with Dr **Kissinger**, hoped to reach a compromise with Washington and thus regain the **Golan Heights**. They feared the setting up of a revolutionary regime in Lebanon, a security zone for **Syria**. Finally, they dreamt, for the same reasons and for economic considerations, of strengthening their hegemony over Lebanon. On June 1, 1976, Syrian troops invaded Lebanon in large numbers and, with the help of the Phalangists, crushed the PLO and the LNM. An Arab mini-summit, convoked in Riyadh by **Saudi Arabia** in October, imposed a truce on all belligerents. The civil war, officially that is, was over. It left behind an enfeebled country: 30,000 dead, more than twice that wounded, 600,000 refugees, and grave implications for the country's economic potential.

But Lebanon had not only been more seriously tested than in 1958. The after-effects of the war had undermined the country. The army had not borne up well and had split into rival factions; none of the successive presidents would succeed in forging a new consensus.

Confessionalism had been strengthened by the war, its horrors and massacres. After 1982, this process accelerated. The various communities tended towards self-protection and, for better or worse, grouped themselves in homogeneous zones. Finally, in the south the war continued, characterized by increasingly overt Israeli interference.

The deterioration of the situation in Lebanon would only accelerate that *de facto* explosion of the country that had once been called 'the Switzerland of the Middle East'.

Lebanon

GEOGRAPHY very early dictated to Mount Lebanon its unique qualities. This chain of mountains offers ecological conditions, particularly water in abundance, perfectly adapted for human habitation. Moreover, difficult of access, Mount Lebanon has, on various occasions, served as a natural refuge for different persecuted minorities. It was in the 16th century, with the advent of the **Druze** Maan Dynasty, and especially the reign of Fakhreddine II (1590-1633), that the territory of present-day Lebanon was unified for the first time. It was to be so again during the reign of Bashir II, descended from the great Chehab family, from 1788 to 1840. It was only in this era that the conditions that would make Lebanon a specific entity in the **Arab** world began to take shape: a Christian society in the mountains possessing strong links with Europe; a society of Druze highlanders sufficiently confident in its tribal structures to accept, in its villages, increasing numbers of Christians; a port, Beirut, linking the mountains with the West, with a **Sunni** Muslim presence and the centre, for the whole of the **Ottoman Empire**, of Western learning and ideas; a missionary presence, at first Catholic and then Protestant; a silk industry concentrated in the mountains that promoted exchanges between the hinterland and Beirut.

This double domination — Druze and Maronite (see **Maronites**) — in the Lebanese mountains led, in 1843, to the system of double *kaimakam* or lieutenancies. Two provinces were demarcated in Mount Lebanon: one, Maronite, in the north; the other, Druze, in the south. They remained under the authority of the Ottoman Empire — which had exercised its suzerainty over Lebanon since the 16th century — even if European powers had already arrogated to themselves a right of inspection which encouraged the expansion of **confessionalism**.

1860 was an important year for Lebanon. At its start, a peasant revolt, led by a blacksmith named Tanios Shahine; at its end, inter-denominational massacres. The peasant uprising had degenerated into a religious war. The fate of the Christians served as a pretext for Napoleon III to dispatch an expeditionary force. A comprehensive settlement was negotiated between the European powers and the Sublime Porte; in force until World War I, it sanctioned Lebanese 'uniqueness' with the political representation of the various religious communities.

After the victory of 1918, **France**, under the terms of the **Sykes-Picot Agreement**, gained control of part of the Middle East. It established its mandate for Greater Lebanon (with its present-day frontiers) and institutionalized confessionalism and the Maronite hegemony. When all was said and done, this domination would be short-lived. The Vichy regime having allowed the Axis powers to use Lebanon and **Syria**, **Great Britain** — backed by the French Free Forces — occupied both countries in July 1941. The progression towards **independence** was now inevitable, and it was declared in 1943. Despite troops landings in 1945, Paris was never to regain its authority. Lebanon was to be a founder member of the UN and the **Arab League**.

But independence, proclaimed on March 22, 1943, had not come about simply because of the waning of **France**'s power or the upsurge of the nationalist movement. An unwritten agreement had also been necessary, the National Pact, a compromise agreed between the leading Sunni and Maronite families. Two clauses in the deal: the Christians renounced French protection and accepted independence, the Muslims abjured Arab unity and, above all, the dream of a Greater Syria. Another condition of the birth of the new state was the maintaining of confessionalism.

This precarious balance was frequently to be shaken. The first serious jolt, in 1958, arose from a double crisis, regional and national. The Lebanese president, Camille Chamoun, took up the cudgels against **Nasser**, in the latter's war against the West. In particular, he supported the creation of the Baghdad Pact, in 1955. He therefore could only feel threatened by the establishment of the United Arab Republic (UAR) formed between **Egypt** and Syria on February 1, 1958. On the other hand, the UAR galvanized the progressive parties, as well as Muslims in Lebanon. Disappointed by the lack of reforms — which Chamoun had nonetheless undertaken to put into practice — they could not accept that the president, contrary to the constitution, run for a second term in office. From May 1958 onwards, clashes increased. On July 14, 1958, **Iraq**'s pro-Western monarchy collapsed and Camille Chamoun called on the **United States** to save his regime. The next day, the Marines landed at Beirut. Fighting went on for several more weeks and ended in a compromise: General Chehab, Commander in Chief of the army, succeeded Camille Chamoun and the pact of 1943 was renewed. He and his successor, Helou, were to try, without success, to strengthen the state's authority and eliminate the extreme inequalities, social or sectarian.

During the twenty years leading up to the explosion of 1975, Lebanon underwent a transformation. Its role as regional relay station and linchpin between the Western European and American economies and the Arab world, was galvanized by the boom in oil. Lebanon, where the most basic form of liberalism reigned, acquired capital coming from the **Gulf** states or fleeing the 'socialist yoke' of Egypt, Syria and Iraq. In 1970, the services sector (financiers and banks, commerce, tourism) represented over 70% of the Gross Domestic Product, one of the highest rates in the world. Within this context, the banking sector occupied a central and hegemonic place. The prosperity brought about by this boom was not shared out equally. The absence of a state — noticeable in the economic field — prevented any attempt at social policy. The disparities and inequalities intensified, reflecting — though only partially — denominational divisions.

These domestic tensions were heightened by the impact of the **war of 1967** and the Palestinian presence in Lebanon. Commando units strengthened the resolve of the refugees, of whom there were several hundred thousand in Lebanon. In October 1969, the first serious crisis broke out between the state

WHO'S WHO IN LEBANON

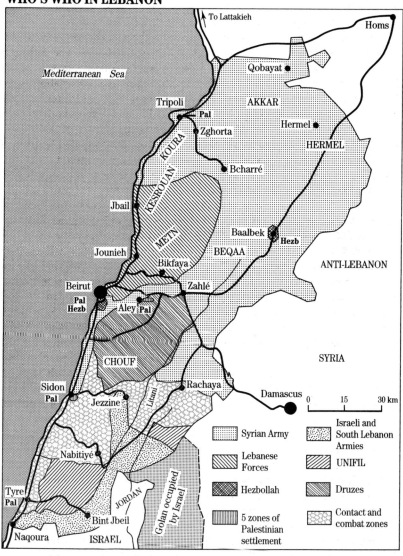

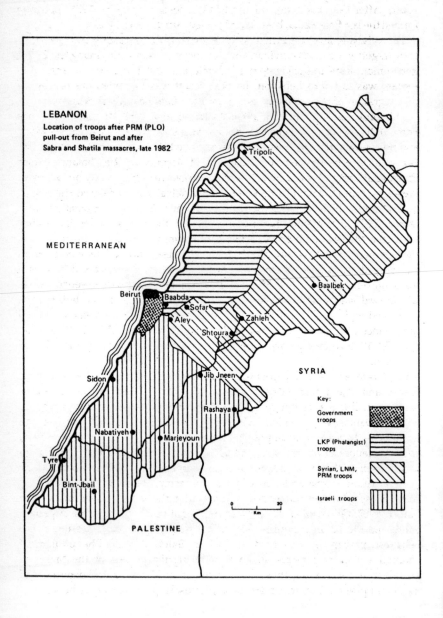

LEBANON
Location of troops after PRM (PLO)
pull-out from Beirut and after
Sabra and Shatila massacres, late 1982

MEDITERRANEAN

Tripoli

Baalbek

Beirut
Baabda
Sofar
Aley
Zahleh
Shtoura

SYRIA

Sidon
Jib Jneen

Rashaya

Nabatiyeh
Marjeyoun

Tyre

Bint-Jbail

PALESTINE

Key:

Government
troops

LKP (Phalangist)
troops

Syrian, LNM,
PRM troops

Israeli troops

0   20
     Km

and the resistance forces. Backed by a Lebanese popular movement which mixed social and nationalist demands, the *fedayeen* succeeded in bringing about the Cairo Agreement which legalized their presence in the camps in the south. After the elimination of the PLO in Jordan, in 1970–1971, Lebanon formed the last Palestinian base. Israel stepped up its reprisal raids.

Tel Aviv was less concerned with destroying the resistance movement — their targets were mostly civilian and Lebanese — than with forcing the Beirut government itself to subjugate the Palestinians. But this tactic, successful in Jordan, was to fail in Lebanon. Its only result was to hasten the process of disintegration of the state and precipitate the Lebanese Civil War.

This broke out on April 13, 1975. When, in June 1982, the Israeli Defence Force (IDF) swept over Lebanon, the country's strength was already sapped and no central authority was able to assert itself. Yet worse was to come. The two years which followed saw the failure of attempts by the Phalangists (see Phalangist Party), backed by Tel Aviv, to impose their hegemony on Lebanon. President Amin Gemayel's regime suffered defeat after defeat: in the Shouf, in September 1983, in West Beirut in February 1984. The opposition front (Amal, PSP, Franjiyyeh, Karameh) extended the zones under its control while the Multinational Force, American Marines at its head, hurriedly left the Lebanese capital. Meanwhile, in the south, resistance to Israeli occupation was spreading; initiated mainly by left-wing parties, it spread and became a mass movement when the Muslim groups joined it. Israel speeded up its withdrawal which was completed in June 1985, apart from the buffer zone controlled with the help of the South Lebanese Army. Gemayel overturned his alliances, repealed the treaty he had signed with Israel in 1983 and, on April 30, 1984, formed a government of national unity under the leadership of Karameh.

In December 1985, a tripartite agreement between Amal, the Lebanese Forces and Walid Jumblatt's PSP seemed to open the way for a lasting agreement. But it was not to be and divisions again took the upper hand, without Damascus — which, with 35,000 soldiers, controlled 60% of the territory — being able to impose its point of view. And in September 1988, after the failure of attempts to find a successor to Amin Gemayel, Lebanon found itself with no president, two governments — one Christian led by General Aoun, Commander in Chief of the army, the other Muslim led by Selim Hoss who had succeeded Karame after the latter's assassination on June 1, 1987. On October 22, 1989, at the initiative of the tripartite Algerian, Saudi and Moroccan committee set up by the Arab League, a session of the Lebanese parliament was held at Taef in Saudi Arabia. The parliament adopted a plan for reforms aimed at reducing the powers of the Maronite president and increasing those of the Council of Ministers and especially of the Sunni prime minister. Under these proposals, parliament was henceforth to consist of Christians and Muslims in equal proportion. As soon as a government of national unity could be elected and formed, the militias would be disarmed and the authority of the state extended. Everyone agreed on the need to end the Israeli occupation, but the Syrian presence proved a more contentious subject. In the end, the Christian deputies hesitantly accepted the Arab proposals envisaging that 'the Syrian forces in Lebanon will cease to play a role in maintaining security within two years at the most (and will then be deployed in the Bekaa). How long the Syrian forces will remain in these areas will be determined in an agreement to be drawn up by the Syrian and Lebanese governments.'

This proposal, accepted by everybody except General Aoun, paved the way for the election on November 5, 1989, of a new president, Rene Moawad. On November 22, he was assassinated, and Elias Hraoui took over. General Aoun's opposition put paid to any real implementation of the Taef Accord. Throughout early 1990, his forces launched bloody assaults on the Lebanese forces of Samir Geagea — an advocate of the Taef Plan. There were hundreds of casualties in the Christian enclaves.

The country, after fourteen years of war, bears little resemblance to the Switzerland of the Middle East, as Western observers had been so fond of describing it. Values, social and political hierarchies and the human geography of the country have been profoundly altered since 1975. The economic system which, up to 1982, had stood up quite well, now collapsed: the pound fell, dragging the country into a spiral of inflation that impoverished the middle classes and all those whose incomes were not payable in dollars. In 1987, it was estimated that 600,000 Lebanese were living below the poverty threshold. Coming as it did on top of the hundreds of thousands of civilian victims of the wars, of the kidnappings, the electricity cuts, the deterioration of the education system, this crisis contributed to the general unbearableness of daily life.

But, the 'new Lebanon' is also the consolidation of confessionalism, the geographic regrouping of the different religious communities. In these new states, 'the patriarchal authority stemming from the family chief and the naive presence of the State have been replaced by the reign of the militias' (Elizabeth Picard). Their power is not only military; they have invaded the economic sphere, levy taxes and customs duties, organize the arms and drug traffic. Their leaders have amassed immense fortunes which, backed up by weapons, make them the new masters.

So, is Lebanon finished? Or is there room to believe, like Elizabeth Picard, in 'a silent majority opposed to the law of force and the exploitation of the "war lords" . . . those unsung heroes who repair the electricity lines, organise the distribution of water, endlessly negotiate local truces and the liberation of hostages, who carry on teaching, nursing, above all who resist the dominant dialogue of hatred and fear of others'?

Libya

THE TERRITORY of present-day Libya, a part of the **Ottoman Empire** since the 16th century, was subjected in the 19th century, like the other countries of North Africa, to the increasing intrusion of European colonialism. With the agreement — at least verbal — of the other powers, Italy began, in September 1911, the conquest of the provinces of Tripolitania and Cyrenaica. Local resistance was particularly fierce, structured by the religious Senoussi Brotherhood, a reforming movement created in the middle of the 19th century. The rebellion lasted right through World War I, at the end of which the socialist Italian government granted greater autonomy to the various regions. Idris Al Senoussi, leader of the brotherhood, was even put in charge of Cyrenaica, but the agreement was short-lived; he had to flee to **Egypt**.

Mussolini's accession to power, in 1922, led to a renewal of hostilities and a new outbreak of resistance to colonialism, under the command of the Senoussis and Omar Al Mukhtar; the fighting lasted nine months. In 1934, Rome unified the provinces of Cyrenaica and Tripolitania, to which it added the province of Fezzan, to constitute Libya, into which, before 1940, poured a wave of more than 120,000 Italian colonists.

During World War II, Idris Al Senoussi, from Cairo, raised forces against the Axis powers. At the close of the war, Cyrenaica and Tripolitania were occupied by **Great Britain**, and Fezzan by Gaullist troops. After long debates at the United Nations on the future of the Italian colonies, Libya gained **independence**, on December 24, 1951. Idris was proclaimed King.

The new regime committed itself to a pro-Western policy: in 1953 and 1954, there were treaties confirming the utilization of important military bases by the British and the Americans. Within the **Arab League**, which it joined in March 1953, Libya championed the conservative bloc against **Nasser**'s Egypt. From the economic point of view, the discovery and exploitation of oil, in 1959, gave the country the resources it lacked. The boom that followed helped to promote urbanization and the development of education and a middle class. In the climate of frustrated nationalist demands prevalent throughout the Middle East, especially after the **war of 1967**, the aging sovereign's despotic regime proved quite unable to cope. On September 1, 1969, a group of young officers, lead by Mu'ammar **Qadhaffi**, a commander of thirty-one, seized power and proclaimed a republic.

Strongly influenced by Nasser, of whom he considered himself a disciple, Qadhaffi set his country on the 'path of socialism': nationalization of foreign banks; increasing pressure on the oil companies; confiscation of the properties of Italian colonists; the constitution of a single party, the Arab Socialist Union. In December 1969, agreements were signed for the evacuation, the following year, of the Wheelus bases by the **United States** and of Tobruk and Al Adem by Great Britain. But relations with Moscow were to prove difficult in these early years; Qadhaffi showed signs of being decidedly anti-Soviet.

From 1975, the regime became more extreme and began to diverge from the Nasserian model. This was the year that saw the publication of the first part of the *Green Book*, the 'solution to the problem of democracy'. In 1976, Qadhaffi proclaimed the 'power of the people', and set up a system of direct democracy through Popular Committees. On March 2, 1977, the Peoples' Socialist *Jamahiriyya* — a neologism coined by combining the Arabic words for republic and masses — was born. After the nationalization of oil, most of the economy passed into the control of the producers. Development was based on importing foreign labour. There were great achievements on the social level, with the introduction of free medical care and compulsory primary education.

There was continued opposition, some of it from abroad. But, divided, it was unable to bring down the regime; in May 1984, Qadhaffi survived an attack on the barracks at Bab Al Aziziyya by armed men from Tunisia.

In international politics, Tripoli drew closer to Moscow, which helped it raise a powerfully equipped army; but the **Soviet Union** distrusted this embarrassing ally and, in October 1985, refused to sign a treaty of friendship and cooperation with Libya. Qadhaffi had developed a violently anti-American policy, extending support equally to revolutionary movements and regimes (South Africa's African National Congress, the Sandinistas of Nicaragua) and terrorist organizations, particularly that of **Abu Nidal**. As of March 1982, the United States imposed a commercial boycott on Libya. On the night of April 14, 1986, the American airforce even launched a raid against Tripoli and Benghazi, aiming to liquidate the colonel; a hundred civilians met their deaths during this attack.

Libya observes a policy of **Arab** unity that fluctuates with changing circumstances. Attempts at unification with other countries have been as numerous as they were short-lived: Egypt (1972–1973), Tunisia (1974), **Syria** (1980) and even Morocco (1984). Extremely radical, it has not hesitated to support the most extreme Palestinian groups; its relations with the **PLO** and **Arafat** have also had their ups and downs. Since 1987, the country has redirected its efforts towards the Maghreb, particularly Tunisia, normalized its relations with the PLO and in 1989 with Cairo.

Qadhaffi has also become interested in his Sahelian environment, which he has almost come to consider as being part of the 'Arab space'. This attitude was spectacularly demonstrated in Chad, where he intervened directly in 1980 — after occupying, in 1973, then annexing, in 1975, the Wuzou Strip, claimed by both countries. This adventure ended in fiasco, Tripoli withdrawing its troops from Chad and, in October 1988, establishing diplomatic relations with Hissene Habre's government.

The new moderation of Libyan foreign policy, noticeable since 1987 and the result of both external setbacks and economic difficulties — between 1985 and 1988, the value of exports dropped by half, as a result of the fall in oil prices — has forced the colonel to soften his domestic options. The authorities are trying to develop industry other than oil by encouraging the formation of agricultural and industrial cooperatives and small family businesses — agricultural or commercial. They facilitate consumerism by opening the frontiers with their neighbours. Even on a political level, a certain detente is being initiated with the 'destruction of prisons' (March 1988), amnesty for the opposition, the abolition of the death penalty. But how long will this Libyan springtime last?

Libya has a surface area of 1,760 million square kilometres (i.e., three times the area of **France**) and has only 4 million inhabitants, most of whom live in the towns, to which must be added half a million immigrant workers. Oil, which represents 90% of exports, is found in abundance; reserves are estimated at more than fifty years of production, at the rate of a million barrels a day. Following the fall in oil prices and the American boycott, the financial balance for 1988 was, for the first time, in deficit. The huge investments of the 1970s had had relatively poor results. An immense artificial river — with a capacity of 2 million cubic metres a year, intended to carry water from an underground lake in the southern desert to the north — has been under construction since 1984.

Lobby

THE NAME GIVEN, in the **United States**, to pressure groups who, to protect particular interests, try to influence the country's policies, at both a congressional and a presidential level. The best known, and certainly the most powerful, is the Jewish lobby, whose pressure on the White House has been pointed out by, for instance, President Harry Truman, in his *Memoirs*.

Its impact stems primarily from the sheer size of the Jewish community in America, the result of massive immigration, notably following the **pogroms** of the late 19th and early 20th centuries: over 7 million, in other words double the number living in **Israel** itself. Since then, this substantial minority has enjoyed a considerable electoral influence, particularly in the states in which it is concentrated: in percentage terms **Jews** represent over 3% of the population in California and Connecticut, almost 4% in Pennsylvania and Massachusetts, over 4% in Maryland, more than 5% in New Jersey and 14% in the State of New York.

The lobby's interventions are coordinated, most efficiently, by the American-Israeli Public Affairs Committee (AIPAC) which, for their implementation, can count on dozens of congressmen, many departmental officials and a whole host of journalists — and chiefs — in the various media.

The Conference of Presidents of the principal Jewish organizations also plays an active role, notably in regard to the White House and the State Department. Amongst other equally influential organizations mention must be made of the American Zionist Council, the B'nai Brith and the famous Jewish Defence League, founded by Rabbi Rahane. Representative of the various political tendencies that make up the American Jewish community, and linked to the corresponding **Israeli political parties**, these groups are particularly successful in making their voices heard since, in general terms, American Jews are responsible for 60% of contributions to the Democratic Party campaigns and 40% to those of the Republicans.

The organization of trips to Israel, briefings, press battles, a network of government personalities and members of parliament, a vital and sometimes decisive vote: all these factors combine to put pressure on the American presidency, particularly when it is at odds with Israel. Already effective in the United States in the defence of the interests of the *Yishuv* emerging prior to World War II, then during and following the war in the winning over of Roosevelt and Truman to the idea of the creation of a Jewish state, the lobby was to intervene with regularity against the supplying of sophisticated weapons to **Arab** countries — including those friendly to the United States; against the prospect of negotiations that included the **PLO** and the **Soviet Union**; in support of getting Soviet Jews on the USSR-USA detente agenda; and, of course, to motivate the massive support given to Israel during its wars against its Arab neighbours.

But the lobby's rigorous organization is not proof against political crises. Already shaken during the Lebanon **War of 1982**, the American Jewish community was again divided by the Palestinian *intifada*, almost half its members disapproving of the Israeli repression and over 70% giving priority to the need for a negotiated solution. Ronald Reagan's undertaking, on December 15, 1988, to enter into a 'substantial dialogue' with the PLO was, generally speaking, well received. However, the Jewish lobby should not forget the fact that the 'strategic alliance' with Israel, strengthened over the decades by different American presidents, also stems from the specific role assigned to the state of Israel by United States policy. Israeli leaders' influence on the White House derives from their awareness of being at the head of the only stable bastion at Washington's disposal in the region. If, in turn, Harry Truman in 1949, Lyndon Johnson in 1967, Richard Nixon in 1973, Jimmy Carter in 1977 and Ronald Reagan in 1982 renounced all or part of their plans in face of Israel's rejection, it was because they could not — or at all events would not — run the risk of a major crisis between the two countries. That is why, for example, in 1979 in the *International Herald Tribune*, Moshe Dayan could afford to take a high hand in the matter: 'You Americans think you will force us to quit the West Bank. But we are here and you are in Washington. What will you do if we maintain our settlements? Protest? What will you do if we keep our army there? Send in troops?'

'Interference in each other's domestic affairs', to quote Joseph Sisco in *Foreign Affairs*, 'has always been a fact in the two countries ever since the establishing of their unique relationship.'

Maronites

THE EARLIEST reference to **Lebanon**'s most prominent Christian community is to be found in the writings of Muslim historians of the 10th century. The Maronites, probably of **Arab** origin, were then concentrated in the Orontes Valley, in **Syria**; since the 7th century, they had professed one of the many heresies that divided Christianity — monotheism. To escape the persecution of the Byzantines, they migrated, towards the end of the 10th century, to Mount Lebanon. In the 12th century, whilst the Crusaders were still in the East, they returned to the bosom of Rome. In the 16th century, they settled in Kesruan (where Shi'ites were in the majority) and in the 17th and 18th centuries in the Shouf (where the Druze were in the majority).

The emergence of modern Lebanon owes much to them and, from 1920 on, they established a pre-eminent position there, thanks to **France** and the **confessional** system. The bourgeoisie and the great Maronite families have developed a strong sense of community, reinforced by ideological justifications (Phoenician origins, non-membership of the Arab world), geographic concentration — particularly in Mount Lebanon — and a system of private education. The Church, the religious hierarchy and the monastic orders play an important role, both economic and political, as do a certain number of great families whose power stems from the possession of extensive landed property, wealth, relations of 'clientship' (a system of patronage), and the 'historic heritage' to which they lay claim. Examples are the **Franjiyyeh**s in Zghorta and the Eddés in Jheilet, in the Beka'a. But the real distinguishing feature of the Maronites lies in the early existence of a party that is both sectarian and new in type and which transcends traditional divisions, the **Phalangist Party**. Finally, it should be noted that the Maronite community was far from united in the 1970s, and that it supplied left-wing parties with many of their cadres. Since 1978, a positive vendetta has existed between the Maronites of the north, allied to Franjiyyeh, and the Phalangists.

Masada

A JEWISH STRONGHOLD, near the Dead Sea, south-east of Hebron, where, in 72 (or according to some 73) AD, **Jews** under siege from the Romans preferred to ritually kill each other rather than surrender.

On September 28, 70 AD, Titus and his troops, charged with putting down the Jewish Revolt, captured **Jerusalem**. 'The army having no one else to kill and nothing left to pillage', recounted Flavius Josephus in *The Jewish War*, 'Caesar, without more ado, gave orders to destroy the City and the Temple from top to bottom, leaving only the highest towers standing.' Bit by bit, the whole country was reconquered. Only one stronghold remained rebellious: Masada. It was held by the Zealots, lead by Eleazar, a descendant, it is said, of Judas. Flavius Silva, the Roman Governor of **Syria**, laid siege to the fortress. A wall was even erected around the fortress to prevent any escape. But the place had great natural defences: the fortress stood on an immense V-shaped rock, surrounded on all sides by deep ravines. Only two narrow paths traversed the precipices. Ramparts and towers completed the defence. Moreover, behind these impregnable walls, the Zealots possessed large quantities of arms and provisions.

The site thus reinforced by King Herod was ideally suited to lengthy resistance. But the Roman soldiers built scaffolds from which they were able, using battering rams and fire, to breach the walls. 'We are sure to be taken', Eleazar then announced, 'but we can choose, beforehand, to die nobly with those we most love.' There followed a long exhortation that ended: 'Let us therefore make haste to bequeath them, in place of the pleasure they hope to gain from our capture, amazement at our death and admiration for our courage.' Thus perished, according to the account of Flavius Josephus — their throats cut by Zealots chosen by lot, the last of whom committed suicide — 960 men, women and children, on May 3, during the great fire lit to annihilate Masada.

This mass suicide made a lasting impression on the Romans and, long after, on subsequent civilizations. The suicide of the besieged of Masada, it was also, at least symbolically, that of the entire Jewish people, abandoned by God. Hadn't Eleazar, in his first death harangue, regretted his companions' inability to 'penetrate the thoughts of God and realize that the Jewish people, that he had once loved, had been condemned by Him'?

The traditional interpretation of Masada sees in it the sign and symbol of the suicidal tendency of the Jewish 'people'. Pushing the historical analysis further and projecting it onto the destiny of the Jews, certain authors see this collective suicide as the result of the stampeding of the advocates of war constituted by the occupants of Masada. Even at this time, others had already chosen peace.

Minorities

A PERMANENT factor in the history of the Middle East, the existence of religious and ethnic minorities once again occupies a central place in the confrontations that are shaking the region.

Their existence is explained by the specific characteristics of this crossroads of three continents, the thoroughfare of innumerable migrations, where some of the greatest civilizations of antiquity appeared and developed. Here too was the cradle of monotheism which found expression in Judaism, then Christianity and finally in Islam.

Neither the appearance of the latter, nor the triumph of its hegemony was to prevent the explosion of minorities. On the contrary: Islam, seeing itself as their continuation, happily coexisted with the People of the Book. This led in the **Ottoman Empire** to a loose, decentralized political system — the *millet*, a sort of 'aggregate of ghettos' — the term comes from Laurent and Annie Chabry, in *Politique et minorités au Proche-Orient*. 'This institutional pluralism', explain the authors, 'had the effect of re-allocating social roles within each community according to a virtually complete hierarchical pyramid scheme and, in theory, of concentrating all social activities within the circle of the community.'

This not always peaceful coexistence was to survive the dismantling of the Ottoman Empire. The 'mandatories' arrogated to themselves by the great powers (**Sykes-Picot Agreement**) in fact incorporated respect for the role of the various communities in the social arrangement. Far from bringing the old *millet* system to an end, they reinforced it by supporting the national demands of certain minorities. Divide and rule was, admittedly, hardly a new precept for Europeans in the Middle East. Hadn't **France** always invoked the 'defence of Christians' to justify its interventions in the Levant? Hadn't it backed the **Druze** or the Alawites, just as **Great Britain** had the Hashemites and the **Kurds**, etc.?

Ethnic and Religious Groups in the Middle East

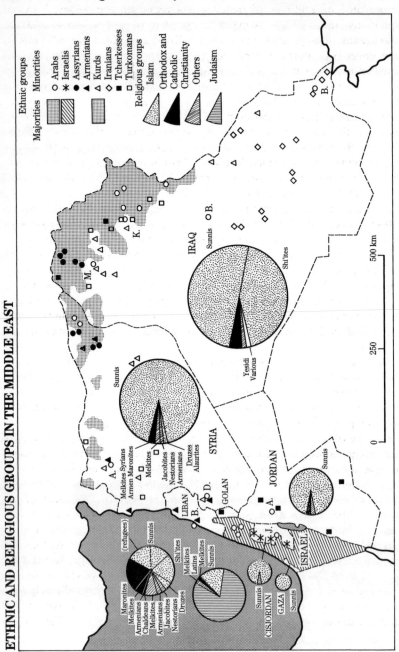

ETHNIC AND RELIGIOUS GROUPS IN THE MIDDLE EAST

Ethnic groups

Majorities   Minorities

Minorities
○ Arabs
✳ Israelis
● Assyrians
▲ Armenians
◁ Kurds
◇ Iranians
■ Tcherkesses
□ Turkomans

Religious groups
Islam
Orthodox and Catholic Christianity
Others
Judaism

IRAQ   ○ B.
Sunnis

Shi'ites

Yesidi
Various

Sunnis

SYRIA

Sunnis
Melkites Syrians
Armen Maronites
Melkites
Jacobites Nestorians
Armenians
Druzes
Alaurites

JORDAN
Sunnis

GOLAN
○ A.

LIBAN
B.
D.

ISRAEL

(refugees)
Sunnis
Maronites
Armenians
Chaldeans
Melkites
Armenians
Jacobites
Nestorians
Druzes

Shi'ites
Melkites
Latins
Melkites
Sunnis

CISJORDAN
Sunnis

GAZA
Sunnis

500 km
250
0

In fact, there was a great temptation to manipulate the contradictions accumulated by centuries of more or less repressed aspirations. National aspirations: those of the Armenians, the Assyrians, the Kurds and the Palestinians, four peoples whose nationalist desires, always under attack, have never been lastingly achieved. Religious aspirations, too: Jewish and Christian minorities in a world dominated by Islam. Within Christianity there were various sects, the Catholic Melchites or Greek Catholics, the Syriac or Syrian Catholics, the Maronites, the Chaldeans, the Catholic Copts, the Catholic Armenians and the Roman Catholics, as well as — separate from Rome — the Greek Orthodox or Byzantine Church, the Syrian Monophysites, the Nestorians, the Copts, the Apostolic or Gregorian Armenians and, of course, the Reformed Churches. Within Sunni Islam, there are the minorities of the Shi'ites (see Shi'ism) and their dissidents, the Zaydites, Ismailis, Druze, Alawite, Baha'is and Yezidis.

Such are the distinguishing features of a region where, as Salah Bechir notes in *Revue d'études palestiniennes* (No. 8), the community 'cannot push its autonomy to the point of identifying with a state. It is either dominant or dominated, allied to the dominant or allied to the dominated; the balance of power maintains this balance that is constantly being imposed and constantly questioned . . . but always negotiated. Hence a state of internal conflict that is sometimes veiled, sometimes overt, but always present. In this perspective, an "international frontier" is indispensable: it establishes the limits of the closed field, of the area where the conflicting forces coexist, where balance is negotiated.'

Stability — as witnessed spectacularly in Lebanon, but also in the region in general — looks all set to be shattered. Why? Obviously it originated with the Israeli-Palestinian conflict which has destabilized the Levant: the creation, for the first time, of a confessional state, the dispossession and dispersion of an Arab people, a succession of bloody wars are so many factors in the resurgence of minority protests. But, equally obviously, this resurgence has been integrated into the strategies of the regional powers, particularly Israel: this was the objective of the Balkanization of the Middle East denounced by some, endorsed by others. On the side of the denouncers, we find the old Lebanese leader Raymond Edde condemning, behind the 'partition' of Lebanon, 'the creation, alongside Israel, of several states of a confessional character, buffer states that would contribute to the security of the State of Israel' (*Le Monde*, November 16, 1975). As for King Hussein's brother, he pointed out that: 'The prospect of a sharing out of Greater Syria between Druze, Maronites, Sunni and Shi'ite fundamentalists coincides with the development of Greater Israel' (*The Times*, September 3, 1983). Which indeed Israeli extremist Oded Yinon had readily admitted in *Stratégie pour Israel dans les années 80*, when he advocated the dismantling of Tel Aviv's neighbours, including **Egypt**, into an endless string of tiny confessional states.

Peace between Israelis and Palestinians therefore constitutes the necessary condition for a new balance between minorities in the Middle East. Necessary but not sufficient in itself: after the Palestinians, there will remain other national identities to be promoted, and the tide of different fundamentalist movements will only ebb within the framework of an autonomous development of the region, unlike the external models whose failures it also sanctions.

Missiles

IT WAS, paradoxically, just as the **Soviet Union** and the **United States** were agreeing to eliminate intermediate-range missiles from their arsenals that the increase in numbers of these devices in the Middle East threatened to upset the military status quo there, with disastrous consequences.

Today, seven countries in the region possess missiles capable of carrying nuclear warheads over 300 km. **Israel** manufactures the Jericho II (range 650 km) and, since 1987, the Jericho IIB (1,450 km) capable of striking any Middle Eastern capital, or even villages in Russia. Both are capable of carrying nuclear warheads, if one is to believe the revelations of the engineer Vannunu regarding their production by Israel since the late 1960s. **Egypt, Iraq, Iran, Jordan, Libya** and **Syria** possess Soviet, Chinese and North Korean Scud-B, with a range of 300 km. As for **Saudi Arabia**, it equipped itself in the spring of 1988 with the Chinese DF–3A (also known as CSS–2); with a range of 2,600 km, they could reach with equal ease Greece, India or the Soviet Union. Israel is particularly worried about the arrival in the Middle East of this weapon, whose performance it knows well since its technicians secretly helped the Chinese convert it from nuclear to conventional power, and perfect its tracking system. In December 1989, Baghdad announced that it had developed a ballistic missile and a ground-to-ground missile with a range of 2,000 kms.

Uneasiness, on both sides, but also among the major powers, has rapidly increased. For the 'war of the towns' into which Iraq and Iran plunged served as a testing bench. For the first time since World War II, civilian populations came under heavy bombing from missiles: during the winter of 1987–1988 alone, Baghdad and Tehran exchanged 200 Scud-B, whose range they had succeeded in doubling, causing over 2,000 victims. And, for the first time since World War I, a belligerent, Iraq, systematically employed chemical weapons against Iran and its own Kurds. It has also threatened to use them against Israel. For the American former Secretary of State, George Shultz, 'the proliferation of longer range missiles and chemical weapons threatens to make future wars even more destructive'.

In fact, the two super-powers shared the same worry: that of a war in which they would find themselves implicated. The days when Washington, Moscow, London and Paris monopolized the manufacture and sales of arms, *a fortiori* of missiles, are gone. New manufacturers, such as Argentina, Brazil, China and North Korea, are carving up for themselves a growing part of the Middle East market where, furthermore, several countries are developing independent arms industries, limiting the super-powers' capacity to prevent a fatal escalation.

Mubarak (Hosni)

SADAT'S successor was born in 1928 in Lower **Egypt**, of a peasant family. He finished his studies at the Military Academy in 1949, then became a fighter pilot, undertaking further training in the USSR. Following the defeat in the **war of 1967** and the reshuffling that took place in the army high command, he was appointed chief of staff of the airforce in 1969 and then, three years later, its commander-in-chief. The more than respectable results obtained in the **war of 1973** led to his being promoted to the rank of general. In April 1975 **Sadat** appointed him vice-president of the Republic, thus confirming the confidence he felt in him and in the abiding role of the army in the political life of Egypt.

During the six years following his appointment, Mubarak was closely associated with the actions of the *Rais* (head of state). In particular, he supported the developments which led to the **Camp David Accords**, although he took no active part in the Egyptian-Israeli negotiations. The day after Sadat's death, October 6, 1981, he received the necessary vote of confidence from parliament and, a few days later, was elected president of the Republic. He has maintained the continuity of Egyptian policy, attempting to modify it without ever really breaking with the legacy left by Sadat.

From the political point of view, the new *Rais* has introduced a state of emergency in the struggle against groups of Muslim extremists, but has defused the climate by freeing political prisoners and engaging in a debate with the opposition which has acquired greater autonomy. But there is no question of undermining the hegemony of the ruling National Democratic Party. In the economic sphere, the new *Rais* has placed the emphasis on productive activities and the struggle against corruption, but without altering the basic foundations of the *infitah*.

At the regional level, a 'cold peace' has been established between Cairo and Tel Aviv since the **Lebanese Civil War**. Concurrently, Hosni Mubarak has initiated a *rapprochement* with the **Arab** world, renewed diplomatic relations with most Arab countries, met with Yasser **Arafat**, and given his support to **Iraq** against **Iran**. If Egypt claims to be loyal to the idea of peace with **Israel**, it is not ready to negotiate the question of 'Palestinian autonomy' laid down by the Camp David Accords. It is searching for another framework for the solution to the Palestinian problem, and has recognized the new Palestinian state.

And finally, on the international level, while maintaining special links with the **United States** — Egypt, which is undergoing serious economic difficulties, received in 1988—1989 close to three billion dollars of aid from Washington — Mubarak has normalized his relations with Moscow, and economic exchanges between the two countries have moved forward in leaps and bounds.

Nasser (Gamal Abdel)

BORN ON January 15, 1918, in Beni-Mor, in the province of Asyut in Upper **Egypt**, Gamal Abdel Nasser was the son of a post office official from a peasant background. Having completed his secondary education in 1934, he began law studies and took part in the massive demonstrations of 1935 against the British occupying forces and the king. The Wafd Party's return to power in 1936 opened the doors of the Military Academy to lower-middle class children, a breach through which the young Nasser promptly stepped. As Anwar Al **Sadat**, one of his companions, would later write : 'To successfully complete the work of renovation, we needed a solid, disciplined force which, prompted by a single desire, would be capable of palliating the absence of authority and of reconstructing the shattered nation. It was the army that furnished this body.' As a sub-lieutenant, he received his first posting, Mukabad, near his birthplace. There he met Sadat and sketched out, in long, passionate talks on Egypt's future, the idea of creating an organization of 'free officers'.

But the road that led to the seizing of power was to be a long one, marked at every stage by humiliation. In February 1942, British tanks surrounded the royal palace and forced the king to appoint a new, pro-British government. When the **war of 1948—1949** broke out in Palestine, Nasser took part in the fighting — he won fame in the Battle of Falujah — and returned from the front with the bitter taste of treachery in his mouth. In 1951, armed struggle developed along the **Suez Canal** against the colonial presence; thousands of young volunteers — trained and armed by the Free Officers — went off to fight. But, in January 1952, the king proclaimed martial law. Nasser's organization numbered at that time about a hundred officers, with an executive committee made up of fourteen members — a broad spectrum ranging from communists to those in sympathy with the Muslim Brothers — united by a hatred of colonialism, of corruption and feudalism. The moment of truth arrived: on July 23, 1952, a *coup d'état* carried them to power. General Neguib, a patriotic, elderly officer who was much respected, served as the movement's figure-head, but Nasser, not yet thirty-four, was its real leader.

As yet he had no clear idea of his role, nor of his aims. In 1952, the Third World was not yet born and the **Arab** peoples lived under the tutelage of London or Paris. The free officers decreed a basic agricultural reform and, on June 18, 1953, proclaimed the Republic, bringing to a close a dynasty that had lasted a hundred and fifty years. But what Republic? After hesitations and clashes, Nasser removed the popular Neguib in the spring of 1954: there was to be no multi-party system in Egypt and the army did not return to its barracks. A similar pragmatism prevailed in foreign policy. On October 19, 1954, a treaty signed with **Great Britain** stipulated the withdrawal of all British troops, but distraining clauses — particularly regarding the return of these same troops should fighting arise — were badly received by many nationalists. Nasser looked to the West for allies. He was fascinated by the **United States**, a power with no colonial past. But Washington could not understand the refusal of Egypt's new master to participate in anti-Soviet pacts. Events then speeded up. Nasser took part in the foundation of the Non-Aligned Movement in Bandung, in April 1955. He bought from Czecho-slovakia the arms the United States had refused him. He nationalized the Suez Canal, on July 26, 1956, and emerged politically victorious from the resulting war. A new leader was born: for Egyptians, free at last, and for Arabs whose struggle against colonialism he would galvanize.

After the failure of the United Arab Republic (the union between Egypt and **Syria**, 1958–1961), Nasser's domestic policy became more radical: the nationalization of much of the private sector, a new phase of the agricultural reform, the adoption of a National Charter, staunchly socialist, and the creation of a new political front, the Arab Socialist Union (ASU). A massive effort in economic development was undertaken with notable success. The reverberations of these measures contributed to a mobilization of progressive forces in the Arab world.

The **war of 1967** served to demonstrate the weaknesses of the Nasserian experiment. The collapse of the army reflected the treachery of those nick-named the 'new class': senior officers, technocrats, newly rich peasants, state bourgeoisie ... all those who had benefited from the revolution and who wanted to see the end of socialism. It was they who dug the grave of Nasserism and supplied the social foundations that allowed Sadat to achieve the 'counter revolution'. Nasser's fear of all autonomous mass organizations (trade union or political), and the bureaucratic nature of the ASU, encouraged the new class. Having resigned after the defeat, called back by popular demand on June 9, Nasser was nonetheless a broken man. When he died on September 28, 1970, Egypt gave him a grandiose state funeral. Whatever his mistakes, they mourned the man who had given them back their dignity. 'Hold your head high, brother' exhorted the streamers hoisted high above Egyptian villages after July 23, 1952.

Oil

PRINCIPAL resource of the Middle East, oil remains one of the essential stakes of power struggles in a region that still produces 25% of the world's oil (and almost 40% of exports of this commodity) and controls almost 60% of its reserves (of which 40% belong to the **Arabian Peninsula** alone).

It was discovered at the beginning of the century; the first extraction operations started in 1909, in **Iran**. It was not forgotten in the bargaining that followed World War I: the British (75%) and the French (25%) shared Mosul between them. It was also through oil that the American penetration took place: after taking a share in Turkish Petroleum in 1927, Standard Oil of California was granted a concession by Ibn Saud in 1933. From 1938 to 1948, the **United States** share climbed from 13.9% to 55.2% of Middle Eastern oil production — which, in the meantime, had tripled. Three years later, Dr Mossadegh made his revolution famous — and at the same time signed its death warrant — by nationalizing the Anglo-Iranian Oil Company. In 1953, the intervention of the CIA would bring such sacrilege to an end.

For, at that time, oil was not something to be trifled with. The West and its companies — later they would be referred to as the Seven Sisters: Standard Oil of California (SOCAL), Standard Oil of New York (Mobil Oil), Standard Oil of New Jersey (Exxon), Gulf and Texas Oil Company (Texaco), all five of them American, plus one English (British Petroleum) and one Anglo-Dutch (Royal Dutch Shell) — dominated the market. This was the time of easy profits: massive concessions granted for periods of 60 to 94 years, total control of operations, royalties accorded like charity — around 12%. Scarcely touched by the Venezuelan innovation, in 1948, of the idea of fifty-fifty sharing, the profits were colossal, at least for the oil companies: the local economies, on the other hand, gained little benefit from it. Energy at extremely low cost, with high profits, oil became the number one ingredient of Western growth.

This evolution was not without its consequences. It brought in its wake a rapid increase in oil extraction: from 500 million tons at the end of the 1940s, world production had reached 2,300 million by the end of the 1960s. At the same time, the dependence of Europe, Japan and, to a lesser extent, the United States on the Middle East was increasing: the region's share in this production went from 17% to 30%. More vulnerable than before, the West was also confronting an increasingly active nationalist movement, which made the recovery of its natural resources one of its prime targets. Such were the ingredients which, with the Arab-Israeli conflict as background, led to the explosion of the Oil **War of 1973**. There was, however, nothing surprising in this: the West had long since confronted opposition from the producers for sovereignty of their own subsoil, supervision of production and control of prices and taxation.

The means employed in regaining control of oil were diverse, from partial restitution by the companies — to avoid nationalization — to nationalization itself. To the first type belongs, for example, the agreement of 1972 by which the Sisters sold to the **Gulf emirates** 25% of participation, raising the national stake to 51%. The various competitors had been thinking along these lines for years: thus, in 1958, the Irano-Italian Association granted 75% to **Iran**, and the Nippo-Saudi-Kuwaiti agreement accorded 57% to the producers. The same went for contracts signed by Elf-ERAP with Iran (1966), **Iraq** and **Libya** (1968). The wave of nationalization launched by Mossadegh was resumed in 1961; Iraq took back from IPC 99% of its concession. The following year, **Kuwait** followed suit with 60% of the concession. Conditions in the 1970s were better. **Qadhaffi** was the first, in 1970, to combine the regaining of control with control of production and prices. A year later, Algeria did the same with the French companies. In 1972, Iraq nationalized British oil companies — but not French. The trend continued with takeovers, mostly 100%, in Iran (1973), Kuwait (1975), Qatar (1976), Bahrain (1978) and lastly in **Saudi Arabia** (1980).

But ownership is nothing without control of production and prices. This was the goal assigned to the Organization of Petroleum Exporting Countries (OPEC), at its creation in 1961. Its first victory came in 1964: royalties being added to tax on profits, the state's share went from 50 to 56.25%. Prices, however, continued to fall, to the extent that in **Syria** in 1970 one of the two pipelines carrying Saudi oil to the Lebanese port of Sidon was closed: a market depleted by the closure of the **Suez Canal** since the Six Day **War of 1967** was the perfect opportunity for Algeria and Libya to raise their prices. Agreements made in Tehran, in January 1971, raised the tax on profits from

50 to 55%. And again in Tehran, then in Geneva, prices went up in line with the dollar and the world monetary situation: in three years, the Gulf's gross went up by 70%. This record was to be smashed during the Yom Kippur War of 1973.

'There being no longer any hope of a peaceful agreement, our decision is to fight,' Anwar Al Sadat had explained, amidst general incredulity. Yet, on October 6, 1973, Egyptian troops crossed the Suez Canal, and broke through the Bar Lev Line. Arab honour was avenged, but the Israeli army recovered. It was in the midst of Israeli counter-attacks that the Arab oil-producing countries, meeting in Kuwait on October 17, decided on both a new increase of 75% and an embargo against allies of Israel. An additional increase of 115% was decided in December, in Tehran. In total, crude oil had quadrupled: from 3 to 11.5 dollars a barrel. But this enormous reassessment constituted, in fact, a simple correction of the real value of crude oil, so much had its purchasing power decreased over the preceding decades. Thus, the main event of 1973 was less the actual increase in the price of oil itself than the simultaneous takeover, by the producers, of the tariffing and the rate of extraction, a step towards the 'new international economic order' that, at the time, was the slogan of the non-aligned countries. It was, at the same time, the obligation of both the producers and the consumers to show themselves more parsimonious: the age of squandering was over, the Arab countries having thus protected the heritage of humanity itself as well as their own. It was the same story with the new readjustments in the late 1970s, which entailed both price reassessments and changes in the economy.

Yet the oil weapon was no longer what it had been. The Arab producers were encountering competition from newcomers, whose share in the market had increased (notably Mexico, Great Britain and Norway). OPEC, which in 1980 had still represented 45% of world oil production, had already, by 1986, dropped to 32.6%. As for the Middle East properly speaking, from 30.7% in 1980, its share dropped to 22% in 1986. And, in terms of exports — see table, p. 138 — the region had watched its percentage drop from 54.5% in 1980 to 40.3% in 1986. But the decrease in the shares of production and exportation was further aggravated by an accompanying slump in prices. The war between OPEC and non-OPEC producers, along with OPEC's own inability to maintain a concerted policy regarding quantities and prices, led to a steep decline: from 34 dollars in 1981, the barrel had dropped to less than 10 dollars in 1986, and has since fluctuated between 10 and 15 — which, in real terms, is less than in 1973. It took the invasion of Kuwait and the Gulf crisis for it to climb back up to $30 a barrel. But the nations of the Middle East also lost their illusions concerning the necessarily positive nature of the oil manna. In many cases, the petro-dollars were shared out in such a way as to further enrich tiny ruling classes, with transactions often as useless as they were spectacular, and investments in the capital of Western companies — only a small part being devoted to development aid, public or otherwise. Not to mention the enormous sums invested in the West: in ten years, from 1974 to 1984, capital arriving in this way in the developed countries had exceeded 350 billion dollars, 250 of which were destined for the USA alone.

Oil in the Middle East in 1986 (in comparison with 1980)

	Proven oil reserves[1]	Oil production[2]	Crude oil exports[2]	Oil exports as % of total exports	% of world crude oil exports	Oil revenue[3]
Iran	92 850[4]	2 037 (1 467)	1 454 (797)	88 (94.2)	6.3 (2.7)	6 600 (13 286)
Iraq	100 000[4]	1 877 (2 646)	1 372 (2 459)	95.9 (99)	5.9 (8.2)	6 980 (26 296)
Kuwait	91 920[4]	1 238 (1 664)	742 (1 297)	83.9 (89)	3.2 (4.3)	6 200 (17 678)
Libya		1 308 (1 830)	1 067 (1 693)	93.1 (97.6)	4.6 (5.7)	4 700 (21 396)
Qatar	3 150[4]	314 (471)	292 (466)	90.7 (95.7)	1.3 (1.6)	1 460 (5 428)
Saudi Arabia	166 980[4]	4 784 (9 901)	3 745 (9 223)	92.1 (99.2)	16.1 (30.8)	21 190 (108 174)
UAE	97 705[4]	1 309 (1 702)	1 132 (1 697)	88 (93.8)	4.9 (5.7)	5 890 (19 496)
Middle East	535 938 (361 961)	12 371 (18 353)	9 347 (16 336)			
Middle East % of World	61.6% (54.5%)	22% (30.7%)	40.3% (54.5%)		40.3 (54.5)	
Total OPEC	644 469 (435 956)	18 333 (26 879)	13 193 (22 844)	77.2 (93.8)		77 073 (286 959)
OPEC % of World	74.1% (65.6%)	32.6% (45%)	56.8% (76.3%)		56.8 (76.3)	

(1) Millions of Barrels
(2) Millions of Barrels a Day
(3) Millions of $
(4) 1 January 1988

Source: *Arab Oil and Gas Directory, 1988*, Paris.

The signal for the economic mobilization of the Arab world and of the Third World in general in 1956 and 1973, will oil, the symbol of **independence**, become a casualty of dependence? Many fear this paradox, amongst them Georges Corm, denouncing in *Le Proche-Orient éclate* the economic, social and political effects of the 'furious flood' of dollars 'shaking the most basic foundations of Arab society', the insane projects sold to 'oil monarchs that only accelerate the destruction of the social fabric of these societies rendered more and more vulnerable by decades of abortive modernization', and 'on the part of the West, blackmail of every kind, the most brutal pressure applied to countries whose apparent economic superpower is but the reflection of the depth of their underdevelopment'.

137

Oriental Jews

THE NAME given to Jews whose origins are Africa and Asia (Mizrahim), as opposed to Jews from Europe and America (Ashkenazim). Since the 1960s, their problem — called, not without a certain racism, the 'black problem' — has been a millstone around the neck of Israeli society.

The first clashes in Israel, in 1959, in the Wadi Salib district of Haifa, sensationally attracted public attention. Then came the wildcat strikes of the 1960s, and the creation of the Black Panther movement. Henceforth a subject that could no longer be avoided, the 'Second Israel' was even, in 1974, the subject of a government inquiry, whose published report exposed a scandalous system of discrimination. And, in 1977, the Orientals as a direct result of the above were a decisive factor in the victory of the right-wing coalition led by Menachem Begin. Thus, in less than twenty years, Israel had suddenly discovered both that the Orientals existed and that they were its underdogs, and that, furthermore, they were no longer ready to accept this destiny, to the extent of overturning the traditional political balance of power.

Who are these Orientals? They are often, wrongly, confused with the Sephardim; but the Hebrew word *sepharad* means Spain, and its adjective therefore refers only to the descendants of the Jews expelled *en masse* from Spain (1492) and Portugal (1496) and scattered all over the Mediterranean basin, to Northern Europe and even to America. In many ways, the Sephardim are closer to the Ashkenazim, the Jews of Europe and America, than to Oriental Jews. In fact, Orientals differ from all Western Jews, whether they be Sephardim or Ashkenazim: by the feudal, backward character of the African or Asian countries from which they come; by their essentially artisanal and commercial tradition; by their lack of any national sense and *a fortiori* of class; by the striking insularity evident in their customs and culture; by the orthodoxy of their religious practices; and by the relatively lenient fate they experienced in their adopted countries: the status of *dhimma*, however humiliating, is a far cry from the holocaust, or even the pogroms, at least until 1948 when the creation of the Jewish state in Palestine and its war with the Arab states unleashed anti-semitic riots. The latter forced Oriental Jews to opt for Israel, transported there in planes specially chartered by the Israeli government. Sometimes, the Israeli secret services accelerated the process by hatching schemes that acted as provocations, like the dynamiting, in 1950, of the Shem Tov synagogue in Baghdad.

On their arrival, these Orientals suddenly found themselves thrown into a

Western nation, historically constituted, peopled and run by Western Jews along Western lines — to a Jew from the **Yemen** or **Iraq**, both the socialist and the liberal versions are still basically Western. 'Israel', explains Elie Cohen, the head of the Dimona social services, 'wanted to live in the Western way, think like the West, have a Western education system. But, with the massive immigrations, what Israel acquired was a majority which was not Western, which did not live in the Western style, did not think like Europeans.' This is particularly true of the latest arrivals, the Ethiopian Jews or Falashas.

The Orientals' refusal to submit to this clash of civilizations has strengthened: in twenty years, they have become Israel's majority, while the clash has had repercussions into every aspect of life. Orientals — according to official statistics — monopolize the lowest rungs of the professional ladder, the lowest wages, the poorest housing, and criminal offences, as well as experiencing harsh segregation in the education system. In contrast, they are not to be found, or are present only in token form, in the management of large companies or of political parties or unions, in the Knesset or the state corridors of power.

So, who runs this nation that remains alien to them? Who has wielded this 'Ashkenazi power' which, since 1948, has victimized them? Until 1977, the reply was simple: the double equation, Labour equals pro-Ashkenazim, hence Likud equals pro-Oriental, had proved itself to be the Right's best electoral slogan. Admittedly, Menachem Begin and his colleagues were no less Western than their socialist rivals, but they had not borne the burden of the responsibility of being at the head of the state since 1948. And, just as at the time of **independence** Zionist (see **Zionism**) envoys had led the Orientals to believe that the Messiah had come in order to convince them to come to the Holy Land, in the same way, in 1977 and 1981, the rumour ran that Begin was Moroccan: to gain him their votes! The paradox is that after seven years of Likud rule, during which the Orientals saw little change in their lives, the 'miracle' would again take place during the elections of 1984, at least from the Oriental side: the main body of those attending the rallies of the Right, and of its electorate in general, came from the Jewish communities whose origins are Africa and Asia.

For all that sociologists were attesting to the 'increasing integration' of the Orientals into Israeli society, the phenomenon would still, in 1988, dominate the electoral considerations of both sides. If three-quarters of the Ashkenazim gave their votes to Labour, the Likud and the groups of the extreme Right (as well as the orthodox religious groups) managed yet again to attract three-quarters of the Orientals — including, what is more, those who claimed to be in favour of negotiation and peace.

Thus, the 'black problem' has become — and remains — central in Israel. Economically and socially, the country's development depends on the elimination of these inequalities between Westerners and Orientals which, if they continue, will threaten even the very possibility of progress in Israeli society. Politically, the Left, like the Right in 1977, cannot hope for a clear-cut victory unless it can make a breakthrough among the Orientals, a breakthrough that implies an ability (so far lacking) to make themselves heard by them and have something to offer them. As for the future: any peace process would greatly depend on a *rapprochement* between Palestinians and Oriental Jews who, the current antagonism encouraged by chauvinism apart, have much in common. The creation and work, in recent years, of Oriental Jewish movements in favour of peace demonstrates the beginnings of an awareness of this priority.

'Myself, as an Oriental, just as there are Christian Arabs and Muslim Arabs, I am an Arab Jew,' said Charlie Biton, a Black Panther leader, in the edition of *Les Temps Modernes* devoted to the 'second Israel'. And he went on: 'It is a fact that, since its creation, the State of Israel has tried to be a bastion of the West, of the **United States**, in the Middle East. Hence our loss of roots. And there will be no choice. After the signing of the peace, Israel will have to be an integral part of the Middle East, and all the efforts and tricks of the Ashkenazim will change nothing. . . .'

It was against precisely this that David Ben **Gurion** was arguing in advance, when he declared, twenty years ago: 'We do not want Israelis to turn into Arabs. We must fight against the Levantine mentality that corrupts men and societies, and conserve authentically Jewish values developed during the Diaspora.' Authentically Jewish, in other words Ashkenazi?.

Ottoman Empire

THE GROUP of countries ruled by the Turks, the Ottoman Empire emerged as a result of their expansion in the 13th and 14th centuries and came to an end in 1920, at the conclusion of the war in which it had enlisted on the side of the central powers and which brought about its dismemberment.

It was with the fall of Constantinople, the capital of the Byzantine Empire, in 1453 that the Ottomans made their presence felt. Since the beginning of the 15th century, they had held Greece, Serbia and Bulgaria, and would soon seize Asia Minor. Selim I would add the **Arab** world: Mesopotamia, **Egypt**, **Syria** and, to complete the picture, the **Arabian Peninsula**. In his turn, Suleiman the Magnificent, his successor, seized what is now modern Yugoslavia, and most of Hungary and Transylvania. At the time of his death in 1566, the Empire stretched from Vienna to Aden, from the Caspian to Algiers, encompassed the Mediterranean, the Black Sea and the Red Sea, controlled the major lines of communication and governed fifty million people of twenty different nationalities.

The decline of the Ottoman Empire stemmed from a number of factors. Some were to be found within the system itself: the often incompetent sultans, the inefficient and corrupt administration, the fact that the elite body of Janissaries had become a destructive, hereditary caste, etc. Others were the result of the reaction of sections of the peoples they oppressed: nationalist ideas were gaining strength in the Arab world, but also among **Kurds** and Armenians. Finally the Empire no longer derived the same benefits from its conquests, blocked as it now was by the strength of the great Western metropolises which, since the 18th century, had made no effort to hide their appetites. Each of them had its eye on the legacy of the 'sick man of Europe' — as Tzar Nicholas I called the Sublime Porte — and had earmarked its share.

To see this clearly, one has only to consult a map. To the West, one can see that **France** had grabbed North Africa, having already benefited from the Capitulations (since the time of Francis I) and the excuse of the defence of Lebanese Christians or the protection of Catholic sacred sites. **Great Britain** had seized, in chronological order — and with various statutes — Malta, the Pirate Coast and Gulf Emirates, Aden, Oman, Cyprus, Suez and Egypt, Sudan and Southern Arabia. As for Russia, it snatched only a single zone of influence, Persia, and even this was shared with London, which also controlled Afghanistan. Germany's influence was essentially economic and military.

But the West's designs on the Ottoman Empire were not confined to merely planting a flag somewhere: what Paris, London, Berlin and the others were after was raw materials at low prices, profitable investments for their capital, markets for their products, and the guarantee of safe lines of communication. Hence the influx of foreign capital: 9 billion francs in 1914, 54% of which were French, 25% English, 9.3% German, the rest mainly Belgian, Swiss or Italian. In Egypt, for example, it is estimated that 70% of shares and debentures were held by foreigners. Through this invasion, Europe controlled banking, the means of transport and communication (railways, ports, roads), the main services (water, gas, electricity, telephone), mining enterprises and, of course, oil. It took care, at the same time, not to foster the emergence of local industry which would hamper its own exports to the Empire. Lastly, through their nationals, their missionary societies and educational establishments, all the colonial powers struggled to become the dominant cultural influence. At the outset of the Great War, for example, France counted more than 100,000 students in its schools, colleges and universities.

The Ottoman Empire was now ripe for sharing out. The war, in which it took the side of Germany and Austro-Hungary, served as a pretext to make it official. This was the task to which the **Sykes-Picot Agreement** and the Sèvres peace treaty signed on August 10, 1920, applied themselves.

Palestinians

SINCE THE END of the Second Jewish Revolt in 135 AD, the territory known as Palestine has had various masters (Rome, the **Arab** Empire, the Umayyads, the Abbasids, the **Ottoman Empire**) and a great mix of populations. At the beginning of this century, it had around 500,000 inhabitants and relatively substantial economic activity, based mainly on agriculture (already 30 million oranges a year), an emergent industry and pilgrimages to the Holy Cities of **Jerusalem**, Bethlehem and Nazareth. The great majority of the population was Arab, both Muslim and Christian.

Like all the peoples of the region, they were to develop — under the influence of European ideas and economic upheavals — the notion of a nationalism whose frontiers would vary with circumstances: Arab, Greater Syrian . . . but above all, after the promise of the **Balfour Declaration** and the setting up of the British Mandate, Palestinian. The latter would assert itself over the years in the struggle against **Zionism**. It thus acquired all the forms of a modern nationalism that even the defeat in the **war of 1948–1949** was unable to suppress.

The Palestinian people today number 4 million men and women scattered all over the world (see table, p. 144). Three major groups stand out. Those who live in the territory of mandated Palestine (**Israel**, the **West Bank** and **Gaza**), those of **Jordan** and lastly those settled — voluntarily or otherwise — in other Arab countries. To these may be added a diaspora which emigrated to Latin America, the **United States**, etc. Of these Palestinians, 2 million are **refugees** registered by the specialized office of the United Nations Relief and Works Agency (UNRWA). They fled their villages in 1948 or in 1967. Close to 800,000 still live in camps, on the West Bank, in Gaza, Jordan, **Syria** and **Lebanon**.

We have already discussed the Palestinians of Israel (see **Israeli Arabs**), of the West Bank and Gaza. Those of Jordan are estimated at over a million, but figures concerning them are unreliable. In fact, in Jordanian official statistics, no distinction is made between Palestinians (with a Jordanian passport) and the rest of the population. The only precise details concern the refugees registered with UNRWA: over 700,000 — 300,000 of whom came from the West Bank and Gaza after 1967 — of whom 213,000 live in camps. Until 1970–1971, it was there, inside the camps, that Fatah and the **PLO** could count on the strongest support. Since **Black September**, all activity that is

The Dispersal of the Palestinian People

Egypt	35,000
Iraq	20,000
Israel	700,000
Jordan	1,150,000
Kuwait	300,000
Lebanon	490,000
Libya	25,000
Qatar	25,000
Rest of the world	200,000
Saudi Arabia	140,000
Syria	230,000
UAE	37,000
USA	100,000
West Bank	1,050,000

Source: *UNWRA Report 1988, Israeli Official Statistics, 1988*

strictly speaking Palestinian has been prohibited.

In Lebanon, the economic, social and political life of the 490,000 Palestinians was closely linked to the PLO. The resistance movement, by means of a network of mass organizations, vitalized the population. The latter furnished the PLO with its fighters, its political and administrative cadres and the workers for the industries it had set up. For these people, the PLO represented everything: national pride, physical and material security. The departure from Beirut, then Tripoli, left a shattered, defenceless population, as the massacres of **Sabra and Shatila** demonstrated. The return to Beirut and Lebanon of several thousand fighters loyal to Yasser **Arafat** has not been enough to restore to the Palestinians of Lebanon their previous confidence.

In Syria there are close to 230,000 Palestinians, all refugees. Almost a third of them exist in camps, subjected to extremely strict political control. Today, only anti-Arafat organizations have freedom of expression, and even they are kept under constant surveillance by the police.

Finally, more than 600,000 Palestinians have settled in the Gulf countries, half of them in Kuwait. This is a recent migration, going back for the most part to the 1960s, and following a classic pattern. The men leave to look for work, the families follow a few years later. The communities, although preserving their Palestinian character, have put down roots in the host country. Palestinians hold important positions, but the PLO's declarations in favour of Iraq in summer 1990 may well put them in jeopardy and weaken their consideration influence. This influence has played its part in the ongoing support the PLO receives from the Gulf countries. Rich, extremely nationalistic, sending large subsidies to the families left behind, giving financial aid to the PLO, the exiles of the Gulf constitute an influential segment of the Palestinian people.

All these groups possess a common trait: Palestinians have compensated for their frustrations by a high level of education, unequalled in the Arab world and comparable to that of Israel. The differences, sometimes consider-able, between one host country and another, do not blur the common characteristics, however. Above all, there is the profound sentiment of belonging to one people that binds the bourgeois of Kuwait with the peasant of the West Bank, the Lebanese refugee to the labourer working in Israel. They are bound to the same history. They recognize themselves in the same culture, that symbolized by the poet Mahmud Darwish or the writers Ghassan Kanafani and Emile Habibi. The PLO has been both the prompter and the symbol of this national pride.

Palestinian Dissidence

IN MAY 1983, a faction of opposition exploded into being within the PLO's principal organization, Fatah. Gathered together in this dissidence were a small number of minor leaders, including Colonel Abu Mussa and a member of the Central Committee, Abu Saleh. They belonged to those Fatah cadres who, from 1974, had been against a mini-state on the **West Bank** and in **Gaza** and against a political solution. Unlike **Abu Nidal**, who had split with **Arafat**, they had remained within Fatah for reasons of discipline or effectiveness. The signing of the **Camp David Accords** in 1978 had reunited the ranks of the *fedayeen* and forced differences to be put aside.

But, with the departure of Palestinian fighters from Beirut in the summer of 1982, the quarrel broke out again. The dissidents' grievances were numerous. They reproached Arafat for having accepted the **Fez Plan**, particularly for its seventh point, which amounted to a recognition of the Jewish state. They condemned the contacts established between Amman and Cairo, as well as with peace forces within **Israel**. Lastly, they criticized Fatah's 'non-democratic operational procedures' as well as its handling of money (corruption).

At first, the dissidents encountered a great deal of support. The confusion of the population and of Palestinian organizations after the siege of Beirut created a favourable climate for extremism. But the movement quickly became marginal. The unrealistic nature of its proposals, the absence of a real leader and its alliance with Damascus alienated sympathies. The responsibility it took for transforming the political debate within Fatah into armed resistance was a yoke around its neck. But above all, in the autumn of 1983, when the dissidence served as a cover for the Syrian troops to attack Yasser Arafat and the loyalists in the town of Tripoli (**Lebanon**), it definitively isolated itself from large sections of the Palestinian people.

Crisis broke out amongst the dissidents themselves, different groups opposed each other in armed struggle, and Abu Saleh was dismissed. In March 1985, the dissident movement took part in the setting up of the Palestine National Salvation Front (PNSF), the anti-Arafat coalition organized in Damascus. In June and July 1988, with the support of the Ba'ath Party, it took control of the camps at Shatila and Burj Barajneh, in Beirut. The dissidents, along with the Saiqa and the Popular Front for the Liberation of Palestine-General Command, refused to participate in the various Palestine National Councils. They condemned the decisions taken by the PLO at the Palestine National Council in November 1988.

Palestine Liberation Organization (PLO)

AFTER the declaration of **independence** of the State of **Israel** in 1948 and the non-establishment of a Palestinian state, the Palestinian National Movement, powerful in the 1930s, disappeared from the political scene. It was around 1960 that the Palestine question came to the fore again. A new political elite was in the process of formation, which compensated for the frustration of exile by a high level of education and an active participation in the movements then rocking the Middle East. The **Arab** regimes were forced to accept this reality and, in 1964, by a decision of the **Arab League**, the Palestine Liberation Organization (PLO) was created in **Jerusalem**.

Presided over by Ahmed Shukairy, it was under Arab tutelage, in particular that of Nasserian **Egypt**, which Palestinians trusted to liberate Palestine. Other organizations developed concurrently, including Fatah, created in 1958 by a young Palestinian engineer, Yasser **Arafat**; more radical, he wanted to be independent of the Arab countries and to rely, primarily, on the Palestinian people themselves. On January 1, 1965, Al Assifa, the military wing of Fatah, undertook its first military operation against Israel.

The **war of 1967**, the defeat of Egypt, **Syria** and **Jordan** caused a crisis within the PLO. The organization became more extreme, adopting a new National Charter (July 1968) and integrating the various armed organizations, the *fedayeen*, and, in January 1969, Yasser Arafat became president of the PLO Executive Committee. The structures of the renovated PLO gradually fell into place. The first of these was a Palestine National Council (PNC), a kind of parliament that sits approximately every two years. A third of the delegates represent armed organizations; the other two thirds represent mass organizations (students, women, writers, trade unions), independent personalities and the various exiled Palestinian communities, from **Kuwait** to Brazil. The PNC elects the Executive Committee that runs the organization. Over the years, especially in **Lebanon**, the PLO has constituted a virtual state machine (with ministers, research centres, a medical and industrial infrastructure) whose power was at its peak on the eve of June 1982.

But one should not be misled by this huge bureaucracy. If the PLO has become accepted as the core of unity of the Palestinian resistance, each organization of the *fedayeen* nonetheless retains considerable autonomy. They number around a dozen: the Fatah; George **Habash**'s Popular Front for the Liberation of Palestine (PFLP); Nayef **Hawatmeh**'s Democratic Front for the Liberation of Palestine (DFLP); Saika, based in Damascus; the Arab Liberation Front under the power of Baghdad; the PFLP-General Command of

General Ahmed Jibril, to mention only the most important. Each of these groups possesses its own armed forces, and often receives support from one or other of the Arab regimes. The PLO is therefore a non-integrated organization where the unity of the various components is constantly in question.

After the defeat of the Arab armies in 1967, the strategy of armed popular struggle advocated by Fatah took over. Having retreated to safe bases in Jordan, backed by underground cells on the **West Bank**, the Palestinian resistance movement launched operations against Israeli economic and military targets. But, very quickly, the problem of relations between the PLO and King **Hussein** arose. It was resolved in September 1970, **Black September**, and the resistance movement was expelled from Jordan. These events were to have profound consequences. The PLO withdrew to Lebanon, which became the last Arab country where it possessed military, and therefore political, autonomy. It reconsidered its position that made armed struggle 'the only route towards the liberation of Palestine', and committed itself to both political, especially on the West Bank, and diplomatic action. Finally, partly so as not to disappear from the military scene and partly out of despair, it launched itself into international **terrorism** symbolized by the 'Black September' organization.

But the **war of 1973** changed the situation and the balance of power. The Arab countries, at the summits of Rabat (1973) and Algiers (1974), recognized the PLO as the sole representative of the Palestinian people. The non-aligned countries rallied to this position and accentuated the isolation of Israel (diplomatic relations between virtually all African states and Israel were broken off). And relations between the Palestinian resistance and the **Soviet Union**, which had had their ups and downs, improved. Moscow would henceforth put all its weight behind Yasser Arafat. This breakthrough by the PLO was consolidated by the visit of its leader to the UN General Assembly in November 1974, and its acceptance as an observer member of the United Nations. Within this framework, the PLO renounced international terrorism, concentrated its military presence in Lebanon and established its political strategy after a long internal struggle between the 'realists' and the 'extremists'.

Up until 1973, the PLO had stood by 'the liberation of the whole of Palestine' (proclaimed by the National Charter) and the 'creation of a democratic state where Muslims, Christians and **Jews** will coexist', which presupposed the destruction of the state structures of Israel and the integration of its Jewish population into the new state. From 1974, at the triple prompting of Fatah, the DFLP and the Palestinians of the Occupied Territories, the PLO proposed the creation of a state based on the West Bank and **Gaza**. Without entailing the *de jure* recognition of the State of Israel, which the PLO refused, seeing this as its only card in any eventual negotiations, this new aim presupposed the effective coexistence of the two states. The PFLP refused this course, walked out of the Central Committee and, along with a few small organizations, created the Rejection Front. The confrontation lasted three years and ended, in 1977, in victory for the 'realists'.

But the situation changed. In Lebanon, the Palestinians, engaged in the **Lebanese Civil War** of 1975—1976, came out of it weakened after Syrian military intervention. This episode, symbolized by the siege of **Tel Al Za'atar** camp, is a perfect illustration of the ambiguous relations established between the PLO and the various Arab regimes: the latter did not hesitate, when their interests were at risk, to massacre their Palestinian brothers. The international background had also changed. Between 1974 and 1977, there had been a real possibility of convening an **international conference** on the Middle East, co-sponsored by the **United States** and the USSR and capable of furnishing a global solution to the Arab-Israeli conflict. This had helped the 'realists' to triumph within the PLO.

But **Sadat**'s visit to Jerusalem, in November 1977, followed by the signing of the **Camp David Accords**, destroyed this process in favour of that of a separate peace. If Egypt was to regain the Sinai, the Palestinians were only to obtain an autonomy under occupation — massively rejected by the Palestinians of the West Bank and Gaza, reputedly realists. The dynamics of the 1974—1977 situation were destroyed. Despite massive mobilization of the 'Palestinians of the inside', despite political initiatives of which the contacts between the PLO and Israeli Zionists (**Sartawi**-Peled-Avnery meetings) were hardly the least spectacular, despite its breakthrough in Western Europe, the Palestinian resistance movement had lost the initiative. On June 6, 1982, Israel, liberated on its southern front, launched the operation Peace for Galilee.

If the conquest of South Lebanon by the Israeli army took only a few days, the siege of Beirut was to last almost three months. These terrible days were to be widely reported by the international press and, like the massacres of **Sabra and Shatila**, would contribute to the tarnishing of Israel's image. Despite fierce resistance, Arafat and his followers were forced to leave the Lebanese capital. A page had been turned in the history of the PLO. Losses were heavy. The resistance movement's politico-administrative machinery, concentrated in Beirut, was destroyed and the PLO lost the capital from which it had been able to deploy an intense political, diplomatic and military activity. A more serious problem was that the leadership of the resistance movement was henceforth effectively cut off from the main body of the Palestinian people. It no longer had contact with the last sizeable group of Palestinians which had supplied it with a large proportion of its soldiers and many of its cadres. Lastly, with the departure of its fighters from Lebanon, the very idea of armed struggle, one of the PLO's crucial traditions, was affected.

For the first time since the Six Day War, the PLO was no longer present on the enemy's borders. Far from the battlefield, it ran the risk of seeing a reduction in its political clout and autonomy, and of losing the attraction it exercised for the younger generation, particularly those in the camps.

It was against this background of crisis and uncertainty that the debates on the strategic decisions of the PLO resurfaced. The outburst of dissidence within Fatah during the summer of 1983 was merely the most spectacular symptom of the new questions that had emerged.

For several years, the factions of the PLO would tear one another to pieces in search of an impossible strategy. The signing, on February 11, 1985, of an agreement between King Hussein and Yasser Arafat (see Appendix 10) revived tensions. It was fervently denounced by almost all factions of the PLO, with the exception of Fatah. The Palestinian National Salvation Front, combining Habash's PFLP, Jibril's PFLP-GC, the Fatah dissidents, Saika and **Abu Nidal**'s group, with the full support of Syria, tried to constitute an alternative solution to the PLO. But clashes between Amal and the Palestinians in Lebanon and King Hussein's repeal, in February 1986, of the Jordanian-Palestinian agreement, combined with to the efforts of the Soviet Union, ended in reconciliation. In April 1987, in Algiers, the 18th Palestinian National Council met, with the participation of Fatah, the PFLP, DFLP and the Communist Party (a member of which was elected to the Executive Committee for the first time). However, the PNSF was not dissolved and certain die-hards reject the reconciliation.

But, above all, the crisis provoked by the departure from Beirut remained. It would take the *intifada* to shake the PLO from its state of paralysis. If the organization was not directly responsible for the outbreak of the rebellion on the West Bank and in Gaza, all the demonstrators nonetheless unequivocally identified with it; the PLO thus acquired a stronger legitimacy, and the power to make the radical diplomatic and political decisions necessary. From November 12 to 15, 1988, Algiers was the scene of the 19th National Council, involving Fatah, PFLP, DFLP, the Communist Party and a few other smaller organizations; only PFLP-GC, Saika, the dissidents of Fatah and Abu Nidal's group refused to participate and later condemned the Council's conclusions.

The most spectacular decision was the proclamation, made on November 15, of the establishing of a Palestinian state which was quickly recognized by more than 90 countries, including Egypt. More important perhaps was the reference made, in the declaration of independence (see Appendix 11) to Resolution 181 of the United Nations, the famous **Partition Plan**. For the first time, the PLO ratified this UN decision that had partitioned Palestine into two states, one Jewish, the other Arab.

In its political statement (see Appendix 11), the PLO called for the convening of an international conference at which it would be a full member, based on Resolutions 242 and 338 of the United Nations Security Council (see **United Nations, Resolutions of**), and the guarantee of the legitimate national rights of Palestinans. This acceptance, for the first time, of Resolution 242, which does not even mention Palestinians, but refers simply to the 'refugee' problem, was a spectacular gesture for the benefit of Western opinion, above all of the United States. It nonetheless aroused fierce internal debates; some, particularly the PFLP, had voted against the resolution or abstained. But there was another innovation: the minority agreed to abide by the majority decisions; the sacrosanct consensus, that had paralysed the PLO, was forgotten.

Strengthened by these decisions, and its confidence in the continuation of the *intifada*, the PLO, which had been the impetus for the Palestinian national renaissance, launched a diplomatic offensive to bring about the international conference. The US's suspension of its dialogue with the PLO, and even more so, the Gulf crisis, have dealt heavy blows to Palestinian hopes. By refusing to condemn Iraq, the Palestinian leadership has alienated the moderate Arabs and given up much of the ground it had gained in international and Israeli public opinion.

Partition Plan

RESOLUTION 181 of the UN General Assembly, thus named because it determined the partition of Palestine into a Jewish state, an **Arab** state and a zone under 'special international regime' (see Appendix 3).

Adopted by 33 votes (including the **United States** and the **Soviet Union**) against 13, with 10 abstentions (including **Great Britain**), this text was the outcome, and would be the stimulus, of a long crisis. After having long been in favour of **Zionism** in Palestine, Great Britain somewhat reluctantly decided, in 1939, to alter its policy: the White Paper limited Jewish immigration to 75,000 in five years, as well as restricting land purchase. London, anxious to win over the Arabs in the face of the impending war with Hitlerian Germany, proposed, within a ten-year framework, a plan for a unitary state comprising at most a third of Jews.

But, after the war, this plan proved impracticable; the holocaust gave a tragic legitimacy to the Jewish quest for a state of their own, Many of the survivors having nowhere to go but Palestine, illegal **immigration** took place on a massive scale; the drama of the *Exodus*, and many similar ones, shocked a public whose outrage was all the greater since it had been so notably lacking during the Nazi extermination. To these factors, which made Britain's position untenable, were added the effects of Jewish **terrorism** in Palestine. The Stern group, since 1943, and the Irgun, since 1944, had been attacking British soldiers and possessions. The attack on the King David Hotel, on July 22, 1946, with its toll of a hundred deaths, stunned public opinion in the British capital. 'Bring our boys home!' yelled demonstrators, conscious of the fact that in two years, close to 150 British soldiers had been killed and 350 severely wounded.

Though anxious to maintain the British position in Palestine, particularly since it was being threatened in **Egypt** and **Iraq**, the Labour government could no longer resist pressures. On February 14, 1947, it decided 'to take the problem in its entirety to the United Nations'. In May of the same year, the latter created a special commission, UNSCOP, to look at possible solutions. A unitary state controlled by one of the two communities? Their strengths — 650,000 Jews, 1,333,000 Arabs — rendered the project illusory. The binational state proposed by the communists and the Zionist Left? The differences between them seemed insurmountable. A system of cantons? In practical terms, it was virtually unrealizable. That left partition.

14,000 square kilometres, with 558,000 Jews and 405,000 Arabs for the Jewish state; 11,500 square kilometres, with 804,000 Arabs and 10,000 Jews for the Arab state. The international zone, including the Holy Sites, **Jerusalem** and Bethlehem, would have 106,000 Arabs and 100,000 Jews. Between the two states an economic union was to be forged, jointly controlling currency, customs, railways and postal services, plus the ports of Haifa and Jaffa. Opponents of the project felt the Jews would have the best of the bargain: according to one observer, they would obtain 56.5% of a territory of which they own scarcely 7%, and where they only represent 32% of the population.

At all events, the partition plan was never put into practice. Zionist leaders, whose support for it had been purely tactical, had never given up the dream of a Greater Israel; they wanted more than the share allocated them by the UN. Arab leaders too demanded more, much more: they rejected the very idea of a Jewish state. And Great Britain, at odds with the UNO which was hoping to take advantage of the troubles to maintain its power, pushed them to attack the Zionists: after increasingly serious reciprocal attacks, Arab armies entered Palestine on May 15, 1948. This was the **war of 1948–1949**, the first of the Arab-Israeli wars.

Peres (Shimon)

TODAY the defeated leader of a vanquished Labour Party, Shimon Peres is perhaps witnessing the end of a career that has symbolized a certain kind of Israeli socialism, at once pragmatic, nationalist in foreign affairs and liberal in domestic.

Born in 1923 in Byelorussia, he arrived in Palestine at the age of eleven. His swift rise to success took place in the defence sector: attaché to the minister from 1948, then secretary general of defence from 1953 to 1959, and finally deputy-minister of defence until 1965. During this period, his political mentor was David **Ben Gurion**, Israeli Prime Minister from **independence** until June 1963, with a gap of one year. Shimon Peres remained faithful to the Old Man even when he broke away from the Labour Party, in 1965, to create the Rafi Party, of which Peres became secretary general. As such, in 1967–1968, he negotiated the reintegration of the Rafi into the new party that succeeded the Mapai: the Labour Party.

Minister again in 1969, Shimon Peres was responsible for the occupied territories before being reappointed defence minister, a post he held from 1974 to 1977 in General Rabin's government. Between Peres and Golda Meir's successor a veritable mini-war unfolded, which monopolized Israeli head-lines for some time, and played a significant role in Labour's historic defeat in May 1977. If the wear and tear of power was a major factor, if the absence of a genuine socialist alternative to the demagogy of the Right had pushed the electorate to the events of May 1977, if, finally, scandals smearing the party's ministers and leaders were the last straw, the absence of a respected leader was nonetheless crucial. Peres, no more than Rabin, could not aspire to the charisma of a Ben Gurion, or even of a Golda Meir.

Interim Prime Minister from April to May 1977, Shimon Peres was then forced to give way to to Menachem **Begin**. He assumed the leadership of the Labour Party, heading their electoral campaigns from 1981 to 1988. His line has remained unchanged: more than ever what is called for is a re-centering of the Labour Party, which, he believes, cannot regain power from the Likud unless it places itself on the same ground. Thus Labour was not ready to condemn either the bombing of the Iraqi nuclear centre at Tamuz in 1981, or the repression on the **West Bank** in the spring of 1982, or the initiation of the operation Peace for Galilee in June. This tactic of avoiding the real question would have as its consequence the Right's remaining in power in June 1981, the Left's inability to form a government alone in July 1984 and, in November 1988, a further failure.

After the experience of 'cohabitation Israeli-style, in which he was successively prime minister from 1984 to 1986, then foreign minister while Itzhak Rabin conducted the repression of the *intifada*, the Labour leader effectively led his party to defeat on November 1, 1988. However, the Labour Party participated in the ensuing government of national unity led by Itzhak **Shamir**. Ashkenazi, bureaucrat, professional minister, a mediocre orator and debater, excelling mainly in political wheeling and dealing, Shimon Peres' image is, above all, that of a socialist who excludes as vehemently as his rivals any prospect of a Palestinian state, like them giving priority to defence over diplomacy and preferring alliance with America, and, if possible, with **France**, to a concert of nations. The key to his failure probably lies there: to have proved unable to offer a genuine alternative.

Phalangist Party (Kataeb)

THE PRINCIPAL party of the Maronite (see **Maronites**) Right, the Phalangist Party was founded on November 21, 1936, by a pharmacist called Pierre **Gemayel**, following a visit to the Olympic Games of 1936 in Berlin, and modelled on Italian fascist organizations. Laying claim to **Lebanon's** Phoenician heritage, its motto is 'God, Family, Country'. The Kataeb (Arabic for phalange) declared itself against any integration of the country with **Syria**, but also took part in the struggle for **independence**.

The party did not obtain its first elected members to the Assembly until 1952. During the civil war of 1958, it was of course found on the side of President Chamoun. Organized on a pyramid model, strictly hierarchical and disciplined, the party went from 8,000 members in 1937 to 35,000 in 1942 and 70,000 in 1970. More than 80% Maronite, the Phalangist Party represents above all the middle and lower-middle classes: a third of its members are white-collar workers, another third tradesmen and shopkeepers, manufacturers or members of the liberal professions. Unlike the other Maronite forces, the Kataeb is not a feudal party organized around one of the great landed families. Its structures are modern; it is directed by a political office even if, over the years, the Gemayels' ascendancy has increased. This factor was to allow Bashir Gemayel in particular to play on the anti feudal feelings and hostility towards the great families of part of the Maronite community. The party has exercised a real, though limited, influence on traditional political life: in 1972, during the last elections in Lebanon, it gained 7 parliamentary seats (out of 99). But with the **Lebanese Civil War** of 1975—1976 and the radicalization that followed, it became the backbone of the coalition of the Right.

From 1969, the Kataeb began arming its militants who had frequent encounters with the PLO and its allies. And when, in April 1975, they were implicated in a skirmish which was to trigger off the civil war, they could muster 15,000 men, that is to say 80% of the conservative camp's forces. By the end of the year, they had begun to receive arms from **Israel** and several hundred of their fighters went for training in Israel. The conflict's switch from the political arena to the military favoured the militias to the detriment of traditional forces in both camps. Inside the Kataeb itself, the real power gradually passed to the military leader, Bashir Gemayel, the youngest of 'Sheikh' Pierre's sons.

Carried to the head of the Lebanese Forces (LF), created on August 30, 1976 to unify the fighters of the Christian Right, Bashir made it an instrument of his own power, increasingly autonomous *vis-à-vis* the political forces. The war, at first against the PLO and its Lebanese allies, then, from 1978 on, against Syria, helped him establish his authority. In the mini-state of 2,000 square kilometres that he controlled from 1977 to 1982 (East Beirut and its northern and eastern suburbs, the western slope of Mount Lebanon down to the coastline, bounded to the north by the territory of the **Franjiyyeh**s), he took over from the central authorities, levied taxes, ruled with an iron hand and had no qualms about bringing his own allies to heel.

In 1982, he was in a position to impose on the entire Christian Right his candidature for the presidential elections, supplanting his brother **Amin**, even though he was the elder. But American and Israeli support was indispensable to him, and it was in occupied Beirut that, on August 23, 1982, by 57 votes out of the 62 recorded, he was elected president of Lebanon, replacing Elias Sarkis. It was thus a warlord rather than the representative of a party who acceded to the presidency.

He was never to rule. Assassinated, he was replaced by his brother Amin. Though the latter may have enjoyed the confidence of the Phalangists, he did not have that of LF. Very quickly, differences surfaced. They were intensified after the repeal of the Israeli-Lebanese treaty in March 1984, and the death of Pierre Gemayel who had played a role of mediator between the LF and his son. Although allies in the spring of 1985 in their victory over the LF, Samir Geagea and Elie Hobeika split up in December. Clashes between their militias ended in victory for Geagea who, over the years, despite continued opposition, has consolidated his ascendancy over the LF. In 1989—1990, however, Geagea and his troops clashed with General Aoun's army, in a contest for control of the Christian enclaves.

Pogroms

FROM the Russian (devastation, destruction, from *gromit,* to destroy), the name given to the massacres suffered by the Jewish communities of Eastern and Central Europe in the late 19th and early 20th centuries.

Jewish history has frequently been marked by discrimination, persecution and exterminations. But, with the Age of Enlightenment, an emancipation movement was born. The French Revolution, the first one that is, guaranteed Jews equality before the law, thus giving the signal for change, at differing rates and with differing results, throughout Europe. A process of assimilation was even established from the beginning of the 19th century amongst European Jews, particularly in the West. Anti-semitic demonstrations of varying degrees of violence seemed to be mere vestiges of the Middle Ages.

Then, in Eastern Europe, in 1881, came the outbreak of a terrifying wave of pogroms. Not only did the 5 million Jews there have no legal status, not only did they still live for the most part in miserable ghettos, but now, following the assassination of Tzar Alexander the Good, for which they were blamed, they were ill-treated, robbed and assassinated by fanatical mobs. After Elisabeth-grad, Kiev and Odessa, the horror continued in 1882 and 1883, notably in Rostov, Ekaterinoslav and Yalta. There followed twenty years of relative peace, then a new series of pogroms, on a larger and bloodier scale, swept over Kichinev, Gomel and Jitomir in 1903, and again in 1905 when over 800 Jews were killed within the space of twelve days in west and south Russia.

The distinguishing characteristic of these pogroms was that they were organized, against a background of that widespread anti-semitism so deeply rooted in the common people of Russia and Poland, by the Tsarist government. Already, at that time, many observers testified to the encouragement given by the authorities to the mobs, to the role played by police *agents provocateurs* and to police passivity. Since then, documents have come forth to confirm the direct responsibility of the Tsar's chief ministers, first and foremost being Plehve and Witte. 'A third of them will emigrate, another third will convert, and the rest will die of hunger,' forecast the Tsar's adviser, Pobycdonotsev.

These pogroms, along with the Dreyfus Affair that took place at the same time, had far-reaching consequences. They slowed down, or even brought to a halt, the assimilation or hopes of assimilation of European Jews. They brought about a new wave of emigration, on a large scale: 4 million Jews left East and Central Europe between 1882 and 1925, of whom 120,000 went to Palestine. For the brutal resurgence of anti-semitism also, and most importantly, led to the birth and organization of **Zionism**. But, over and above these immediate effects, the pogroms of that time also gave notice of the massive pogrom that was to come, during World War II, the **holocaust** conceived by Hitler.

Qadhaffi (Mu'ammar)

QADHAFFI was born in 1938 into a family of nomads of the Syrte region, **Libya**.

He received a religious education, then, at ten years of age, was sent to school at Sebha, in the Fezzan. As an adolescent, he became a militant Nasserist, and was even expelled from his school, in 1961, for having demonstrated against the Syrian secession from the United Arab Republic. Convinced that only the army could regenerate Libya, he joined the Benghazi Military Academy in 1964 and founded a secret organization, the Free Unionist Officers. He was the master mind of the *coup d'état* of September 1, 1969, which brought to an end the reign of an aging monarch, King Idris Al Senoussi. Qadhaffi became, at thirty-one, president of the Command Council of the Revolution.

A staunch nationalist and fervent partisan of **Arab** unity, he at first followed the Nasserist line. But, after the death of the *Rais* in 1970, he became aware of its limits with the change of direction **Sadat** was making. He then developed a new theory, chronicled in the *Green Book*, conceived as different to both capitalism and socialism. It advocated direct democracy and the rejection of representative democracy; an end to wage-earning, a form of 'slavery', and with the new watchword 'Partners, not wage earners'; and the return to the natural life, to natural socialism. The explicit ideal was still **Islam** as it was at its origins, in the 7th century.

What factors influenced the Colonel's thinking? We can turn to the list drawn up by the review *Herodote* : 'His Bedouin origins linked him through his parentage to the great open spaces of the Sahara; the influence of Nasser and, as a foil, the state of Libya under Idriss I; there is also the exercise of power and the various historic situations in which he was obliged to act; and his reading and his meetings with others, but it is too difficult to unravel the intricacies of these; finally, there is Islam.'

Although a devout Muslim, Qadhaffi is first and foremost an Arab nationalist and his understanding of his religion is a very personal one, since he accepts only the Qur'an and rejects the Sunna (see **Islam**). This leads to a flexible interpretation of the injunctions. 'An important part of Islam, of Christianity and Judaism', argues Qadhaffi, 'deals with the relations between God and Man, as well as the rites. Another part concerns the relations of men amongst themselves, what they may do and what they must avoid, but only general principles are given: work for good, prevent evil, establish good relations within the family, with neighbours, treat fairly strangers, orphans, the poor, prisoners, etc. On the basis of this one can found a state or an empire, establish a republic or a monarchy, start a revolution, establish a *jamahiriyya*. In doing so, one has only to fear God, not steal and be tolerant.' From this to 'Render unto Caesar what is Caesar's and to God what is God's', is but a short step that Qadhaffi takes pains not to take; he has already been the object of numerous attacks from the Doctors of Law. But his theories allow him to consign to oblivion certain precepts like those on women: 'It was not written that they [women] should be slaves, submissive, despised and that men should be the opposite. Oppression is the result of a social process.'

Since 1987, with the breakdown of his foreign policy (particularly in Chad) and the economic crisis caused by the slump in oil prices, the Colonel has modified his pronouncements in a more realistic sense. He has re-established contact with all his North African neighbours, with **Egypt**, as well as with many black African countries. Within the country, he has undertaken a more liberal policy, marked by the return of the private sector, of small business and the destruction of prisons (in March 1988).

International terrorist and madman for ex-President Reagan, public enemy number one for the European press, Qadhaffi symbolizes the frustration of those peoples oppressed by the international order and the problems of creating an autonomous path of development.

Rapid Deployment Force

A COMBINED force made up of American army, airforce, navy and marine corps units, designed to intervene with the greatest possible speed, particularly in the Middle East.

Heir to the US Strike Command created in 1962, replaced ten years later by the US Readiness Command, neither of which had any specific regional destination, the RDF was the result of Presidential Directive 18, issued in August 1977 by Jimmy Carter, newly installed in the White House. Its mission was to be spectacularly re-affirmed on January 23, 1980, following the entry of Soviet troops into Afghanistan, on the occasion of the State of the Union speech in which the United States' president affirmed, for the first time, that his country was ready to intervene to protect its 'vital interests' in the Gulf, including oil. In March, the Force's unified command was formed, under the responsibility of General Paul Kelley of the Marines.

Indeed, at that period, American leaders felt, or claimed to feel, threatened by the headway being made in the region by the **Soviet Union**, who, from **Libya** to Afghanistan by way of Ethiopia and South **Yemen**, was surrounding the pro-Western regimes and the oil fields. It is true that with the exile of the Shah the **United States** had, in 1979, lost their main agent in the region; secure in its elite army, **Iran** had played, in the Middle East and the Gulf, a very useful role of policeman for Washington. Henceforth, the RDF would have the task of palliating this serious loss which, with the affair of the American embassy hostages, began to look like a historic humiliation. Scarcely installed, Ronald Reagan would accelerate the setting up of the RDF, with considerable means and manpower and a growing number of bases and facilities at its disposal.

The RDF's command, the Central Comand (CENTCOM) is on the huge McDill airbase in Florida, but it could well be transferred to the Anglo-American base at Diego Garcia, in the Indian Ocean. In all, CENTCOM has at its disposal 250,000 men, a force that can be increased to half a million, America's biggest contingent. It includes units from the ground forces (one airborne division, one helicopter-borne assault division, one division of mechanized infantry, one of light infantry, one division of airborne cavalry), the Marines (one unit plus a third of an amphibian unit), the Air Force (seven tactical air squadrons and two squadrons of strategic bombers) and the Navy (three groups of fleet aircraft carriers, one group of surface ships and five navy patrol squadrons). Currently, these can be in the field within three or four days notice for the first units on the spot and from four to six weeks for the last — the United States has close to 1,000 military and civil aircraft available for troop transport and around 600 units in their naval forces. But the speed of intervention depends greatly on the bases available within the region.

The formation of the Rapid Deployment Force has therefore increased the importance of the chain of bases and facilities which the American army needs as staging posts, sites for stationing troops, arms and supplies, for monitoring stations, etc. The bases acquired in Europe since the end of World War II have thus been augmented, over the last two decades: there are facilities in Morocco, the Ras Banas base in Egypt, the Masirah base in Oman, the port of Mogadishu and the Berbera airport in Somalia as well as the Kenyan port of Mombasa. Lastly there are, as well as the Diego Garcia base rented from the United Kingdom, the Israeli military bases that the United States may use, and those that Riyadh has agreed to have constructed in **Saudi Arabia**. The Gulf crisis in summer 1990 enabled the United States to deploy its forces effectively: 150,000 men, 4 aircraft carriers, 2 command vessels, 1 destroyer, 5 cruisers, 11 frigates, 310 fighter aircraft, 80 bombers, hundreds of tanks, 20 Stealth fighters and an unknown number of Patriot, Hawk, Stinger and Chaparral missiles. Washington has not hidden its desire to establish a permanent presence, with bases and ports in Saudi Arabia and the Gulf, paid for by its grateful hosts.

Reagan Plan

PROPOSALS for the solution of the **Arab**-Israeli conflict put forward by the president of the **United States** on September 1, 1982, following the evacuation of the PLO from Beirut, surrounded by the Israeli army.

The Reagan Plan was presented under exceptional circumstances. The first phase of the Lebanon war of 1982 had just come to an end, with the departure of Yasser Arafat and his troops from Beirut; their future destiny and that of Palestinians in general had become an international question of the first importance — a question that, a few days later, the Arab summit would debate in Fez (see Fez Plan). The American administration therefore had to update its position in the light of the changing situation in the Middle East, but within the framework of its general strategy.

The United States was well aware that the persistence of the Palestinian problem was an obstacle to its main objective in the region: to bring about a strategic consensus encompassing both Israel and the so-called 'moderate' Arab regimes, on the side of America and against the Soviet Union. For the White House, it was therefore a question of defining a solution acceptable to its two necessary allies, without in any way leading to the creation of an independent Palestinian state, a fortiori within the framework of an international conference in which the PLO and the USSR would take part. The solution they came up with was 'autonomy', key word of the Camp David Accords. But, five years after Sadat's sensational visit to Jerusalem and four years after the signing of the framework for peace in the Middle East, there had not been the slightest move to initiate the autonomy in question. Israel had shown itself as amenable to accepting the compromises necessary to normalize its relations with Egypt as it was intractable regarding the occupied territories: colonization, exploitation and repression had continued to increase there. Worse still, Camp David precipitated desperate measures endangering peace in the region, of which the invasion of Lebanon is one example.

Hence the dual nature of the address of September 1, 1982: in it Ronald Reagan certainly reaffirmed the United States' preference for autonomy and their rejection of a Palestinian state, but he also warned Israel against the establishment of new settlements on the West Bank. Acknowledging that the Palestinian problem is not one of 'refugees', but that of a 'people' — it was the first time since Jimmy Carter that this word had been used by an American president — Reagan proposed a two-part solution. During the first period, of five years, the inhabitants of the West Bank and Gaza would have 'complete autonomy to regulate their own affairs': they would elect — this included East Jerusalem — their own authority to whom the administration of the territories would be transferred. The second period would see the adoption of a definitive statute, 'in association with Jordan'. Matters were made quite explicit: 'The United States will therefore sanction neither the establishing of an independent Palestinian state in this region, nor an initiative on the part of Israel aiming to annex this zone or to exercise a permanent domination over it.'

Repudiating as it did the dreams of both Arabs and Israelis, the Reagan Plan naturally found itself rejected by both camps. As the main protagonists, the PLO leaders and those of Israel in fact lost no time in rejecting Ronald Reagan's proposals, as the Arab heads of state were also to do, implicitly at least, when they met at the Fez summit. Even Jordan, directly involved in the prospect of an 'association' between itself and the Palestinian body in question, spurned the American advances. It was in vain that, faced with the Palestinian *intifada* six years later, the American administration would propose a rehash of the Reagan Plan. The Schultz Plan of the spring of 1988 in fact came round to the idea of an international conference, but on three conditions: priority given to bilateral negotiations, no participation of the PLO as such, and especially no question of a Palestinian state. Challenged by the PLO, the American project was to fail, largely because of the Likud's veto. 'The only word I accept in the Shultz Plan', joked Itzhak **Shamir**, 'is his signature.'

Refugees

IN THE MIDDLE EAST, migrations are a cyclical phenomenon: **Jews** from Spain in the 15th and 16th centuries, Muslims from the Balkans and the Caucasus in the 19th, Armenians and Assyrians from Turkey after World War I, not to mention Jewish immigration to Palestine.

If the fate of **Sudan**'s million refugees remains a major preoccupation, as does that of the hundreds of thousands of **Kurds** exiled from their divided country, it is nonetheless the problem of the Palestinian refugees created by the **war of 1948—1949** and the Six Day **War of 1967** that has most abidingly marked the region. Indeed, for a considerable time, the international community was to consider the question of **Palestinians** not as a national problem calling for a state solution, but uniquely from the point of view of the right of refugees to return to their homes.

When, on November 29, 1947, the United Nations adopted the **Partition Plan** for Palestine, the country had 608,000 Jewish inhabitants and 1,237,000 **Arab**. The proposed Jewish state was to have 498,000 Jews and 407,000 Arabs. Yet the latter, at the conclusion of the first Arab-Israeli conflict, and despite the fact that Israeli territory had increased by a third, numbered only 160,000. Between 700,000 and 800,000 Palestinians had gone into exile. The overwhelming majority settled in the refugee camps set up by UNRWA (UN Relief and Works Agency for Palestinian Refugees) in the neighbouring Arab countries. In 1950, their numbers were estimated at a million.

Flight or eviction? The debate, long and heated, as to the causes of the

Palestinians' departure during the War of 1948–1949 has recently acquired important new contributions, in particular from young Israeli historians such as Benny Morris, diplomatic correspondent for the English-language Israeli daily, *The Jerusalem Post*. Years of work spent burrowing among documents, including those of the national archives of the State of Israel, led him to express grave doubts concerning hitherto accepted ideas in his book *The Birth of the Palestinian Refugee Problem* (Cambridge University Press).

In the territory conquered by Israeli troops at the time, 369 Arab towns and villages were emptied of their populations. Under what conditions? In 44 cases, the author admits he does not know. The inhabitants of 231 others left during attacks by Israeli troops and, for 41 of these, after evictions *manu militari*. In 89 cases, the Palestinians gave way to panic following the collapse of some neighbouring town or village, obsessed by the thought of an enemy attack or again by rumours spread by the Israeli army. This was particularly true after the massacre, on April 9, 1948, of 250 inhabitants of Deir Yassin, near Jerusalem, by militiamen from fundamentalist groups, especially those of the Irgun of Menachem **Begin**, who was to admit in his memoirs: 'The legend of Deir Yassin helped us to save the towns of Tiberias and Haifa. The Arabs fled in panic, crying Deir Yassin! Deir Yassin!' Benny Morris, in contrast, lists only five cases where the departure was at the injunction of the local Arab authorities.

'No proof exists', he adds, that 'the Arabs wanted a mass exodus or that they ever published a general directive or calls encouraging Palestinians to flee their homes.' On the contrary, those who fled were threatened with 'severe punishment'. At the same time, concludes Benny Morris, from the Jewish side, there existed no written plan for the eviction of the Palestinians. David **Ben Gurion**, in particular, 'always distanced himself in public from the eviction of the Palestinians. Worry over his place in history pushed him to this.'

Numerous documents nonetheless attest to the determination of the prime minister (and defence minister) of the young **Israel** to come out of the war with the Jewish state as large as possible and, in demographic terms, as homogeneous as possible. Author of Plan Dalet which, according to Benny Morris, at the end of March 1948 already showed 'clear traces of a policy of eviction on both a local and national level', Ben Gurion in July replied to Yigal Allon, who had asked him what to do with the 70,000 Arabs of Lydda and Ramleh: 'Evict them!' Shortly afterwards, in Nazareth, discovering the Arab population still present, he exclaimed: 'What are they doing here?'

Furthermore, it is undeniable that a policy was put into practice to prevent the return of refugees, which had been called for by the UN General Assembly on December 11, 1948. 'It should be clear that, in this country, there is no room for two peoples,' Josef Weitz, the director of the Jewish National Fund, had declared. It was he, in 1948, who became responsible for the 'transfer'. Rejecting the UN resolution of that year (see **United Nations, Resolutions of**)and Anglo-American pressure, Israel made it physically impossible for refugees to return: their villages were either destroyed or filled with new Jewish immigrants, and their lands distributed amongst the neighbouring *kibbutzim*. The law regarding 'abandoned property', aimed at making possible the seizure of the possessions of any absent person, legalized this wholesale confiscation.

There followed four decades of controversy fanned, after the Six Day War, by the influx of a further 250,000 refugees fleeing from the **West Bank**. The Arab regimes, claims Israel, must bear the responsibility for the fate of the Palestinian refugees, a fate they have done nothing to improve, that indeed they have even exacerbated. Utterly at the mercy of those who hire them, this cheap, malleable workforce has, it must be said, known its ups and downs amongst its Arab brothers, whose regimes are ready to repress all forms of organization, even to the extent of massacre. But the Arab world would reply that it is not a question of refugees but a national problem. And indeed, the refugees themselves have always refused any resettlement. Caught between the two arguments, the Palestinian refugees are left to rot.

Forty years after the great exodus, UNRWA counted 2.5 million Palestinian refugees, a third of whom live in its camps. In **Gaza** the proportion is as high as 80%. Without doubt it is they who would be most directly affected by the establishment of a Palestinian state alongside Israel. But how many of them are homesick, and always will be, for their family village, now in Israeli territory?

Sabra and Shatila (Massacres of)

EVEN BEFORE the end of the Palestine **War of 1948—1949**, the first refugee camps were created in **Lebanon**: some in the south of the country, others on the outskirts of Beirut. Sabra and Shatila were among the latter. Subjected to constant harassment by the Lebanese army, finding themselves forbidden all political or social activity, the **Palestinians** of the camps only began to achieve autonomy in the late 1960s, with the increase in strength of the *fedayeen*. At the beginning of the 1980s, the inhabitants of Shatila were estimated at 25,000, those of Sabra at 12,000.

The first massacre

On September 2, 1982, the last Palestinian fighters left Beirut. Bashir **Gemayel**, leader of the Lebanese Forces, and an ally of **Israel**, was elected head of state. September 14 saw the completion of the departure of the Multinational Force (**United States, France**, Italy), which had supervised the evacuation of the PLO. The same day, a charge of 50 kilos of TNT destroyed the building containing the not yet inaugurated president of Lebanon. Bashir Gemayel was no more. During the night of September 14, the Israeli Defence Forces (IDF), surrounded East Beirut, in violation of the commitments made to the PLO by the American envoy, Philip Habib. At 5 p.m. on September 16, at the instigation of the IDF, the Lebanese forces belonging to right-wing militias entered the camps of Sabra and Shatila to 'exterminate terrorists'. On the morning of September 17, Israeli soldiers, who had surrounded the camps, stood back while a massacre of civilians took place. It was to continue until the morning of the 18th. The toll: 800 dead, according to the Israeli commission of inquiry presided over by Judge Kahane; 1,500, according to the PLO.

When the facts became known, emotions ran high around the world and in Israel. Though Menachem **Begin** denounced 'the bloodthirsty plot being hatched against Israel and its government' and refused any idea of an inquiry, 400,000 demonstrators put the opposite viewpoint, on September 25, in Tel Aviv. They won their case and on the 28th, the Kahane Commission was set up to establish the truth of events.

Its conclusions threw light on part of the development of the operation, and relieved Menachem Begin of 'a certain degree of responsibility'. The report advocated the dismissal of the defence minister, Ariel Sharon, and implicated several military leaders, including Raphael Eytan, the chief of staff. But despite the searching of consciences aroused in Israel, the system effortlessly absorbed the revelations of the report which had never examined the crux of the problem: the invasion of Lebanon, the IDF's entry into East Beirut, and the alliance with the Lebanese Forces (which the Israeli newspaper *Yedlot Aharonot* described as 'organized riff-raff'). And if Menachem Begin ended by taking a back seat, Ariel Sharon has remained a powerful minister, even under the national unity governments. As for Raphael Eytan, he has returned to politics and was elected an MP in the Knesset.

The second massacre

In the spring of 1985, in Beirut, the 'battle of the camps' broke out, in other words the attack launched by Amal, the Shi'ite movement, against the Palestinian camps of Sabra, Shatila and Burj Al Barajneh. The fighting lasted several weeks, punctuated by massacres of civilians committed by Amal. '**Arab** terrorists are doing Sharon's work for him,' declared Yasser **Arafat**. On June 17, 1985, a ceasefire agreement was signed, under the aegis of **Syria**, between Amal and the Palestine National Salvation Front (PNSF), an amalgamation of the opponents of the PLO leadership. Fighting ceased. The truce proved temporary and the siege of the camps was renewed. The fighting continued intermittently until the beginning of 1988. At that time, a weakened Amal called for an end to hostilities: it declared its desire to render homage to the *intifada* on the **West Bank** and in **Gaza**. Battles now took place between Fatah and the Palestinian dissidents. The latter, backed by Syria, took control of the camps of Shatila and Burj Al Barajneh (June–July 1988). Sabra had been totally destroyed.

Sadat (Anwar Al)

BORN ON December 25, 1918 in Lower **Egypt**, into a peasant family of modest means, Sadat entered the Military Academy and graduated as an officer in 1938. In the first garrison town to which he was posted, he met **Nasser** and some of those who were to become the Free Officers. A fervent nationalist, he saw in Nazi Germany a possible ally against the British occupation: he was arrested in October 1942 as a spy for the Axis powers. In contact with the Muslim Brothers, with whom he was to maintain close links for over ten years, he was implicated in a terrorist attack and spent three years in prison. Dismissed from the army in 1948, reinstated in 1950, he took part in 1952 in the *coup d'état* that overthrew King Farouk.

During the Nasserite period, he held a series of important posts: secretary general of the National Union (the sole party, which did not play a major role) in 1957, president of the National Assembly from 1960 to 1968, vice-president of the Republic in 1964, then again in December 1969. However, he remained an unobtrusive figure, seemingly little disposed to assume the mantle of *Rais* (president) after Nasser's death, on September 28, 1970.

However, elected as the new *Rais* on October 15, 1970, Sadat ousted all his rivals and imposed a new direction on Egyptian policies. In May 1971, he eliminated Ali Sabri and the regime's pro-Soviet wing. The same year saw the beginning of the economic liberalization that would culminate after October 1773 in the *infitah*. In July 1972, he expelled the 15,000 Soviet military advisers and initiated a *rapprochement* with the **United States**. This change of direction was only possible because Anwar Al Sadat could depend on what was called the new class — middle-class bureaucrats, newly rich peasants, profiteers — which had arisen, admittedly with some difficulty, under Nasser, and which hoped to throw off the socialist yoke. This change of direction came up against strong opposition, particularly from students and workers, and the diplomatic deadlock that, despite everything, left Cairo dependent on Moscow. On October 6, 1973, Sadat launched the fourth **Arab**-Israeli conflict with clearly defined aims: to get the United States to unblock negotiations in the Middle East (see **war of 1973**). After the ceasefire on November 7, 1973, the Egyptian *Rais* re-established diplomatic relations with Washington and undertook the 'one step at a time' policy so dear to Henry **Kissinger**. The prestige he gained from the crossing of the **Suez Canal** allowed the *Rais* to speed up his *infitah* policy and to liquidate, in 1976, the single party and establish a system of 'limited democracy' with several parties. The National Democratic Party, the official organization, maintained its control of the state machinery.

But partial Israeli withdrawals from the Sinai were not peace, and Egypt was still at war. Its economic situation was deteriorating and when, in January 1977, Sadat, on the advice of the IMF, raised the price of basic necessities, massive riots shook Cairo and most Egyptian towns. Sadat then decided on his other historic initiative: he went to **Jerusalem** in November and began the proceedings that would lead to the **Camp David Accords** and the Egyptian-Israeli separate peace. Although isolated from the rest of the Arab world — most countries broke off diplomatic relations with Cairo; the **Arab League** transferred its headquarters to Tunis — he maintained his policy, counting on the support of the Egyptian people exhausted by an interminable war and hoping that peace would bring an end to the economic crisis. Concurrently, Sadat launched a major campaign against 'Soviet plots' in the Third World.

Despite massive economic aid from the United States — up from 371 million dollars in 1973 to 1.135 billion in 1981 — the social situation worsened, aggravated by the Arab boycott. It was all the more intolerable for the common people in that the *nouveaux riches*, the profiteers of the *infitah*, were flaunting their wealth. The deadlock in negotiations on Palestinian autonomy vindicated those who had predicted that the Camp David Accords were nothing more than a separate peace. The political opposition, although victimized and repressed, managed to make their voices heard. Finally, the upsurge of Muslim groups, which Sadat had greatly encouraged by granting amnesty to the leaders of the Muslim Brothers, by allowing them considerable freedom of expression, and by using them in his struggle against the Left, but who rejected his alliance with Israel, led to sectarian problems of extreme gravity between Muslims and Copts. The *Rais* then staked his all, in September 1981, by arresting 1,500 opponents of all political shades: Muslims, liberals, nationalists, communists. He even dismissed the Coptic Pope, Shenuda III. A few days later, on October 6, during a parade celebrating the victory of 1973, an armed squad of four men, belonging to a Muslim group, assassinated him.

His funeral was greeted with total indifference by the Egyptian people, an indifference in marked contrast to the place the Western media were to accord the death of the man of the Camp David Accords.

Sartawi (Issam)

BORN in 1934 in Acre (Palestine), Issam Sartawi and his family sought refuge in Iraq in 1948 as a result of the war of 1948—1949. It was there he completed his medical studies in 1960. He then went to the United States, where he became one of the country's most distinguished cardiovascular specialists. On the declaration of the Six DayWar of 1967, he decided to leave the United States and devote himself to his people. On January 10, 1967, he arrived in the Middle East where he joined the ranks of Fatah. But, a convinced Nasserite and pan-Arabist, he could not accept the organization's regionalist theories. In the autumn of 1968, he created his own Action Organization for the Liberation of Palestine.

After the expulsion of the PLO from Jordan in 1970—1971, Sartawi dissolved his group and rejoined Fatah. In 1976 he was appointed by Arafat himself to undertake an important mission: to meet with representatives of the Zionist Left. What were later called the 'Paris talks' began in July 1976. On the one side Sartawi and Sabri Jiryis, a Palestinian intellectual who had lived in Israel for a long time; on the other, General Peled, Arie (Lova) Eliav, former secretary general of the Labour Party, Meir Pail, MP, Uri Avnery and Jacob Arnon. Serving as intermediary was Henri Curiel.

These conversations, which continued into the spring of 1977, were to have far-reaching effects. For Palestinians, they marked one more step towards the recognition of the existence of Israel. For the Israelis, they confirmed, and strengthened, the existence, alongside the CP, of a Zionist peace camp ready to accept the PLO. But the limitations were equally obvious. The Israeli delegation had no official status (even though Prime Minister Rabin had been kept informed of the proceedings). And though the Palestinian group had Arafat's backing, the latter was unwilling, or rather unable, given the balance of power within the PLO, to make this public.

After Menachem Begin's coming to power, the contacts were maintained, thanks to Issam Sartawi, despite violent attacks from the Rejection Front and the denunciations of the Likud. Talks were reopened after the Palestinian departure from Beirut and, in January 1983, for the first time, Yasser Arafat met with a delegation composed of General Peled, Uri Avnery, and Dr Arnon. Some months later, Dr Sartawi was to pay for his political courage with his life: on April 10, 1983, during the congress of the Socialist

International (with whom he maintained contacts on behalf of the PLO), he was assassinated by **Abu Nidal**'s men.

Saudi Arabia

IN 1744, Mohammed Ibn Saud, a local emir from the Najd area of the **Arabian Peninsula**, signed a pact with a religious reformer to bring about, 'through force of arms if necessary, the reign of the word of God' (Henri Laoust). Mohammed Ibn Abdel Wahab had begun his preaching some years before. He aimed to restore **Sunni Islam** in its original purity at a time when the crumpling of the **Ottoman Empire** was accelerating and Shi'ism was gaining strength (Persia, **Iraq**). He rejected all non-Sunni sects, condemning dangerous innovations and the worship of saints. His doctrine, Wahabism, was to form the ideological basis for all the Saud family's attempts at constructing a state.

The first Wahabite state, which stretched as far as Iraq, was dismantled by Mohammed Ali, the Sultan of **Egypt**, in 1818. The second, less ambitious, ended in 1884. The third attempt got it right. In 1901, Abdel Aziz (who was to become known under the name of Ibn Saud), at the head of his partisans, conquered the oasis of Riyadh. After World War I, he took control of the entire Najd region and attacked his rival, Hussein, Sherif of Mecca. He defeated him and assumed the title King of the Najd and the Hejaz, controlling the two principal holy cities of Islam: Mecca and Medina. In 1932, Abdel Aziz assumed the title of King of Saudi Arabia.

During the same period, the discovery of oil and the creation of the Arabian Oil Company (ARAMCO) changed the face of the new kingdom. These two facts assured the Wahabite state, which was floating on a veritable sea of oil (a quarter of the world's reserves), a substantial income and strengthened its alliance with the USA whose companies made up ARAMCO (it was not until September 1980 that Saudi Arabia was able to assume complete control). The Roosevelt-Abdel Aziz meeting, in 1945, consolidated the Washington-Riyadh axis, which has remained till this day the touchstone of the kingdom's foreign policy. On the king's death, in 1953, Saudi Arabia passed through a period of instability marked by strikes in the oil industry, clashes with the revolutionary **Arab** Nationalist Movement and power struggles within the reigning royal family that ended with the coronation of Faisal on November 2, 1964. The *coup d'état* that brought to an end, in 1962, the absolutist regime of Imam Ahmed Ben Yahya in (North) **Yemen** and the intervention of **Nasser**'s Egyptian troops on the republican side, dragged

Saudi Arabia into a long conflict on its borders that would not be resolved until after June, 1967.

With the weakening of the revolutionary nationalism that followed the **war of 1967**, the Wahabite kingdom's role in regional and international affairs grew more important. It possessed two master trump cards, Islam and oil. Saudi Arabia, which claimed to be the faithful defender of orthodoxy and aspired to the leadership of the *Umma* (the community of believers) saw itself as an Islamic power. It used religion to secure its influence. The oldest network of relations between Muslims and the kingdom lies in the pilgrimage to Mecca, one of the five basic duties of Islam. If, in 1946, foreign pilgrims numbered only 61,000, the figure rose to 378,000 in 1971, 813,000 in 1980 and over a million by the mid-1980s. The pilgrimage not only strengthens spiritual links, it also allows an intensive Saudi propaganda complemented by multiform aid in the diffusion of Islam — conservative version — throughout the world. The formation of the Muslim World League, in Mecca in 1965, made it possible to organize a forum for the various Muslim communities. Finally, on September 22, 1969, the Islamic Conference Organization (ICO), which was joined by 40 states and the **PLO**, was created, in which Riyadh had a decisive influence (especially since 1979 with the entry of Soviet troops into Afghanistan, and the ICO's mobilization against them).

The other crucial asset is, of course, oil. After the **war of 1973**, oil profits reached their peak, allowing the kingdom, the third largest world producer after the **Soviet Union** and the **United States**, an ambitious development plan, state development aid that is one of the strongest in the world, the purchase of ultra-sophisticated military equipment (more than 20% of the GDP is devoted to arms as against 4% in France!) and the investment of petro-dollars in Western banks and companies.

However, Saudi foreign policy does not match its means. Underpopulated, the kingdom lacks an adequate workforce, skilled and unskilled, and has to import it. Its army numbers barely 70,000 men, which does not give it superiority over external forces. Since the end of the 1970s, two more difficulties have been added to these deficiencies: the challenge of revolutionary Islam, which accuses the regime of being impious (the occupation of the Great Mosque at Mecca, in November 1979, was a serious blow to the reigning dynasty's prestige); and the drop in oil demands which meant a decrease in production from 9.8 million barrels a day in 1981 to 5.45 in July 1990. During this period, oil revenues were a fifth of what they had been, dropping to less than 20 billion dollars. For the first time, in June 1988, Saudi Arabia had to float a government loan to cover its budget deficit.

Saudi policy regarding the Arab-Israeli conflict is marked by conflicting pressures: Arab and Islamic solidarity, alliance with the United States, the pressure of the **Jerusalem** question — Islam's third most important Holy Site

— and, lastly, the fear of all destabilization. A Saudi contingent took part in the military action of 1948, another backed up Jordanian troops in 1967. After the Six Day War of 1967, Riyadh granted financial aid to Cairo and Amman as well as the Fatah and the PLO. In 1973, the Wahabite state took part in the oil embargo that ended with the quadrupling of prices and the affirmation of OPEC's authority (even if, since then, Saudi leaders have done their utmost to stabilize both prices and market). After some discreet support lent to **Sadat** during his visit to Jerusalem in 1977, King Khaled, who succeeded Faisal, assassinated in 1975, condemned the **Camp David Accords** and broke off relations with Cairo. Since the assassination of the *Rais*, Riyadh has tried to promote Arab solidarity in order to reach a settlement and facilitate Cairo's return to the Arab fold following the Amman summit of November 1987. The adoption of the **Fez Plan** in 1982 was in line with this policy. Because of its weaknesses, Saudi Arabia has always maintained a prudent attitude towards other Arab powers, **Syria** in particular. Not only is contact maintained with Damascus, but the Wahabite kingdom also finances the Syrian budget, while marriages have been contracted between the Assad family and the Saudi royal family, a sort of insurance for the future.

The ceasefire in the Gulf came as a relief to Riyadh, which had feared being drawn into the conflict — especially after the Mecca clashes of July 1987, when security forces fired on Iranian pilgrims. The strengthening of the Gulf Cooperation Council, created in May 1981 and bringing together the six monarchies of the Gulf, was a means to confront all threats, including that of Iraq, militant and bristling with arms. The Iraqi menace soon materialised with the invasion of Kuwait by Baghdad's army in August 1990. Riyadh then accepted the deployment on its territory of the largest US expeditionary force since the Vietnam war. While welcoming and possibly even financing this Armada, the pragmatic Saudi government also seeks to establish diplomatic relations with the USSR.

Extending over an area of 2,240,000 square kilometres, the Wahabite kingdom numbers a population variously estimated at between 6 and 12 million. The country has a million and a half foreign workers (600,000 of whom are from North Yemen) whose numbers, despite expectations, have not noticeably dropped during the petrol crisis. Due to its wealth, the kingdom has undertaken massive works of infrastructure, industrialization (with the two giant complexes at Jubail and Yanbu) and investment in agriculture that has meant, for example, that corn production has gone from 126,000 tons in 1974 to 2.8 million tons in 1988. Political power is in the hands of the royal family — five thousand princes — who maintain it with no outside interference (but not without internal squabbles) despite the emergence of a technocratic class which wields a certain influence. The new sovereign is Fahd, who succeeded his brother in 1982.

Settlements

THE PROCESS of colonization of the **West Bank, Gaza** and the other occupied **Arab** territories by the creation of settlements began immediately after the **war of 1967**. In July, the first settlement was established in the **Golan Heights**; in September, it was the West Bank's turn, with Kfar Etzion, in the Hebron region. At the same time, Levy Eshkol's Labour-orientated government undertook the Judaization of annexed **Jerusalem**. In 1987, there were around 100 settlements on the West Bank containing 67,000 people, fifteen in Gaza (for only 2,500 inhabitants) and almost 40 in the Golan. To this must be added the 100,000 **Jews** settled on the outskirts of Jerusalem.

The central element of this colonization was the eviction of **Palestinians** and the confiscation of their lands. Making use of, when appropriate, reasons of security, laws dating from the British Mandate, or even from the **Ottoman Empire**, the Israelis appropriated more than half the West Bank's available land. As well as having a military role (*vis-à-vis* **Syria**, for example), the extremely dense sectioning-off of the West Bank and Gaza operates as a system of control and surveillance of the Palestinian population. Armed settlers, more often than not members of extreme right-wing groups, have no hesitation in coming to the aid of the occupying troops or acting as police themselves.

Two phases can be distinguished in the policy of colonization since 1967. The first developed along the lines laid down by the Allon Plan, named after the Israeli Labour vice-president, presented in June of that year. It underlined the vital importance of Jordan in the Jewish state's defence: it was there the first settlements were established. Israel did not aim primarily at the heavily populated Arab zones, even if religious movements already greatly exceeded, with the government's endorsement, the framework of official policy. In 1977, the number of settlers was reduced: 5,000 for the whole of the West Bank. A special fate was reserved for Jerusalem whose annexed Arab section found itself encircled by Jewish districts whose population reached 50,000 in 1977.

In 1974, Gush Emunim (Bloc of the Faithful) was created, a movement calling for the right of Jews to settle everywhere in Eretz-Israel. It stepped up raids and illegal occupations in heavily populated Arab zones. On the eve of **Begin**'s victory, in 1977, five settlements had been formed in this way, and their existence had been ratified by the governments of Rabin and **Peres**. The Right's accession to power speeded up the process considerably. Settlements were now created in heavily populated Arab zones, and the number of settlers rose to 44,000 in 1977. Whereas between 1967 and 1977, 750 million dollars had been invested in colonization, this figure went up to 1.67 billion for the next decade.

But the pioneer spirit of the 1930s and 1940s had run out of steam, apart from a hard core of fanatics. From the start of the 1980s, the incentive of the housing crisis was thoroughly exploited to fill the settlements. Young couples, unable to find accommodation they could afford in the large Israeli towns, were offered the possibility of homes in the urban settlements of the West Bank. Some of these are less than 30 kilometres from Tel Aviv, but cost two or three times less than accommodation there. The formation of the government of National Unity, in 1984, led to restrictions on the construction of new settlements. But the increase in the number of settlers continues; the current settlements can accommodate a million people. The government that emerged from the elections of November 1988, intended to continue colonization. It is naturally delighted at the prospect of hundreds of thousands of Jews leaving the Soviet Union and, having been denied access to the United States, resigning themselves to coming to Israel. Itzhak Shamir clearly hopes to implant a high proportion of them in the occupied territories.

The colonization process has made the Israeli occupation unique: it is not merely a question of controlling the local population but, in the long term, of marginalizing them, even inciting them to leave.

Shamir (Itzhak)

PRIME MINISTER of the government formed after the elections of November 1, 1988, Itzhak Shamir presents the typical profile of the Israeli Right.

Born in 1915 in Poland, Itzhak Yertsinski emigrated to Palestine. Like Menachem Begin, at that time still in Europe, he was a follower of Jabotinsky, the founder of the revisionist movement, a Zionist faction at once radical and fascinated by Mussolini, dedicated to the cult of force and the leader pledged to the Judaization of Palestine on both banks of the Jordan. But even such ultranationalism was not enough for Shamir who, in 1940, founded his own group, the Fighters for the Freedom of Israel, whose initials in Hebrew are LEHI. Their hostility towards Great Britain pushed them to try to form an alliance with the Third Reich!

In the archives of the German Embassy in Ankara, after World War II, a letter, dated 1940, was found from Lehi, establishing a link between 'the evacuation of the Jewish masses living in Europe, one of the conditions on which the solution of the Jewish question depends' and the establishment of 'a Jewish state within its historic frontiers'. To these Hitlerian partners, Lehi pointed out 'common interests between, on the one hand, the establishment of a new European order in conformation with German conceptions and, on the other, the national aspirations incarnated in the national military organization'. The letter pointed out that 'the creation of a Jewish state on a nationalist and totalitarian basis, linked by treaty to the German Reich, would serve German interests and consolidate its future power in the Middle East'. The letter also contained an offer to 'take an active part in the war, on Germany's side', Jewish troops trained in Europe thus being able to 'participate in the conquest of Palestine'. Lehi's fighting capacities, the letter continues, 'would not be inhibited by measures taken by the British administration in Palestine, nor by either its **Arab** population or Jewish socialists'.

Lehi's offer having been turned down by Berlin, Shamir had to be satisfied with directing its anti-British terrorist activities in Palestine: arrested in 1946, he was deported and only returned to **Israel** after **independence**. A group of which he was leader has been implicated in, amongst other things, the assassination of the UN mediator, the Swedish Count Folke Bernadotte, on September 17, 1948. It was in the 1970s that Shamir found a major role: as president of the Herut, he replaced Begin, who had resigned, as Israel's prime minister, from September 1983 to July 1984, before becoming vice-premier, then prime minister again in 1986. The deadlock created by the elections of November 1988 allowed him to lead the Israeli government.

Shi'ism

SHI'ISM is **Islam's** main dissident branch, but its differences with the majority **Sunni** are less important than the elements they have in common, above all the belief in one God and in the message of Mohammed. Shi'ism developed around a crucial question, that of the Prophet Mohammed's succession. The first caliphs, after Mohammed's death, were chosen from amongst those closely related to him. All, the Prophet's cousin and son-in-law, the fourth caliph, reigned from 656 to 661 AD. Deposed by a revolt, he was subsequently assassinated. The Shi'a, the followers of Ali, defended his descendants' rights against the official caliphs. They were, to use an expression of Louis Massignon, 'Islam's legitimists'.

Shi'ism has evolved greatly in the course of history. It split into several tendencies which define themselves according to whichever Imam, Ali's successors, they support. The place of the Imam is central to Shi'ism, since they continue the cycle of prophets who, for the Sunni, ended with

Mohammed. Amongst these Imams, Hussein, Ali's son and the third Imam, occupies an important place. In October, 680 AD, he was pursued by Yazid, the Ummayad caliph, and surrounded at Kerbala. He and his 72 companions held out for a long time, despite lack of water, but eventually he was killed. Hussein's martyrdom, his resistance to the bad caliph, play a crucial role in Shi'ite mythology. They were even used in the struggle against the Shah of Iran. Every year, during the month of *muharram*, spectacular expiatory ceremonies retrace Hussein's actions.

The divisions within Shi'ism stem not only from the definition of the lineage of the Imams, but also from their role. For the majority, particularly the Iranians, Iraqis and Lebanese Shi'ites, called Imamites or Twelvers (Duodecimians), there has been a succession of twelve Imams who derive their power from God, which makes them infallible. The last, Mohammed, disappeared in 874 AD. After having communicated with the outside world through messengers, he retired, but remained alive: it was the Great Occultation. 'The community will no longer have a visible absolute leader, until the end of time when the awaited Mahdi comes to establish a reign of truth and justice' (Yann Richard).

Another, more moderate branch of Shi'ism is Zaidism. It only recognizes five Imams whose authority stems largely from their personal qualities; it therefore does not maintain the rigid legitimism of the Imamites and rejects the dogma of the hidden Imam. Several Zaidite dynasties have ruled intermittently in history, mainly at Sana'a in the Yemen, from the 9th century to 1962.

As for the Ismailis, they seceded on the question of the succession of the sixth Imam. They were the founders of the Karmat States, and the brilliant Fatimid Dynasty in Egypt in the 10th century, of the famous 'sect of assassins' founded in the fortress of Alamut at the end of the 11th century, and of the Druze doctrine. Today, the Aga Khan is the leader of the main Ismaili community, to be found in Iran, Afganistan, India, Pakistan, etc.

Shi'ism has played a major role in the history of Islam. Often in the opposition, it was the standard-bearer of numerous rebellions against the caliph's power. But in many other cases it did not hesitate, in the name of this or that point of doctrine, to collude with the ruling powers.

Excluded from the decision-making centres of Iraq, Lebanon and Paki stan, today's Shi'ites still constitute turbulent communities. In Iran, where the Safevides made Shi'ism the state religion in the 16th century, the Shi'ite Ulemas often support the reigning dynasties. But their involvement in contestation movements has been greater than that of Sunni religious leaders — true, they enjoyed a relative economic independence *vis-à-vis* the state. The Islamic revolution and Khomeini's coming to power represented an important victory for militant Shi'ism, but its rallying cry nonetheless elicited little response in the long run in an Islamic world dominated by Sunnism.

Today, Shi'ites number more than a hundred million, concentrated mainly in Iran, Pakistan, Iraq, Afghanistan, North Yemen, the Gulf, Turkey and the USSR. In **Syria**, the Alawites are sometimes classed as Shi'ites.

Shi'ism (Lebanese)

IN LEBANON, where Shi'ites represent almost 30% of the population, the resurgence of this community was evident even before the Iranian revolution of 1979.

The Shi'ites occupy South Lebanon, the north of Beka'a, and have migrated *en masse* to south Beirut. The most underprivileged section of the population, they have often been referred to as a 'confession class'; thus, at the outset of the civil war, 40% of industrial workers were Shi'ite. However, there are also the privileged among them: great semi-feudal families in the south (Assad, Hamadeh), an agricultural middle class, traditionally linked to emigration to Africa which was considerable in the 1950s, as well as a lower-middle class.

Excluded from the sharing of political power in 1943, excluded also from the Lebanese economic miracle, the Shi'ites supplied many militants for the left-wing and extreme Left parties, particularly the Lebanese Communist Party. At the end of the 1960s, the community organized itself under the double incentive of social and political frustrations and Israeli raids in the south, which, first and foremost, struck at Shi'ites. One man was to personify their aspirations, Musa Sadr, a Lebanese from **Iran**, who arrived in Lebanon in 1960.

Settled in Tyre where he succeeded the community's spiritual leader, he broadened his field of action from the religious to the social. After 1967, his efforts took a political turn and he managed to get the state to create a Shi'ite Supreme Council, of which he became president with the title of Imam. He presented a programme aimed at mobilizing Shi'ites of all social classes: the right of access to the most important state posts; aid in the economic development of the South; defence of religion. He opposed both the traditional leaders and the left-wing parties. It was on the eve of the civil war that Musa Sadr created the Movement of the Disinherited which was succeeded by the Amal (Hope) Organization. After the **Phalangist Party**, it was the first organization that had been able to circumvent the authority of the great families, without however rejecting the confessional (see **confessionalism**) aspect of society.

Musa Sadr disappeared in **Libya** in 1978, which created a lasting antagonism between **Qadhaffi** and Lebanese Shi'ites. The movement, weakened for a while, experienced a new lease of life in 1982. Amal became involved, in the summer of 1983, in armed resistance against Israeli occupation of the south and seized control of West Beirut from President **Gemayel** in February 1984.

In 1988, two armed factions were struggling for supremacy within the Shi'ite community. There was Amal, led since 1980 by Nabih Berri, from a poor family from Tibneen, in South Lebanon, and born in Freetown in Liberia in 1949. It was there that his father had emigrated to escape from poverty and try to make his fortune. This allowed his son to undertake higher education, during which he flirted with the world of politics and, in 1963, became president of the Ba'athist Union of Lebanese Students. A graduate of law school, and of Saint-Joseph University, completely fluent in French, he took up the profession of lawyer, practising at first in the **United States**.

Nabih Berri's plan, which gave Amal a modern image, was to obtain a revision of the balance of power, and a renegotiation of the National Pact of 1943 with Maronite (see **Maronites**) leaders. He had hoped to win favour with the Syrians, in December 1985, through the agreement he signed at Damascus with Hobeika, then in charge of Lebanese forces, and **Jumblatt**. This hope was to be dashed. Since then, his authority has been contested within his own organization, and he has had to conduct fierce conflicts with the **Palestinians** and come up against the distrust of the **Sunni** community who looked askance at the encroaching presence of Amal in Beirut.

But the strongest opposition came from the Islamist Shi'ite current. If the Islamic Amal of Hussein Moussawi did not have great influence, the Hezbullah (the Party of God) had, in the 1980s, great vitality because of the Iranian revolution and the aid, both material (estimated at 7 million dollars a month between 1983 and 1988) and human — the presence of the *Pasdarans*, Iranian watchdogs of the revolution — from Tehran. Its leaders were Sheikh Ibrahim Al Amin and Sheikh Subhi Al Tufaili, the moral authority being in the hands of Sheikh Mohammed Hussein Fadlallah, who had known Imam **Khomeini** at Najaf, in **Iraq**. The Hezbullah criticized Amal for its laicism, its compromises with the Israelis in the south, and its hostility to the Palestinians. In May 1988, violent clashes pitted the two organizations against each other in Beirut, leading to the entry of Syrian troops into the southern outskirts of the town. Hostilities recommenced during the winter of 1988–1989 and again in late 1989 and in 1990.

South Lebanese Army

A CHRISTIAN, armed military force, Israeli trained and financed, which, along with the State of Israel, controls a buffer zone in South **Lebanon**.

It was in 1968 that South Lebanon was first drawn into the **Arab**-Israeli conflict, with the establishing of the first Palestinian commando units there and Israeli bombings that did not spare the civilian population. In 1970, the Israeli Defence Forces (IDF) carried out their first limited operation in the South.

The **Lebanese Civil War** of 1975—1976 was the decisive turning point. Israel established close links with the Christian villages of the frontier and, from 1976 on, began to practise a 'good fences' policy (in other words the opening of the Israeli border to 'good' Lebanese). It intervened directly alongside the Christian forces that had emerged from the disbanding of the army, in the spring of 1976, commanded by the man who was as yet only Major Haddad.

In March 1978, following a particulary bloody Palestinian raid, the IDF penetrated South Lebanon for three months. It was not until June, as a result of pressure, including that of the **United States**, that Israeli forces retreated, giving way before the United Nations Interim Force in Lebanon (**UNIFIL**). They did not, however, relinquish a strip of land, 100 kilometres long and averaging 8 kilometres wide, running parallel to the border from Ras Naqura, on the Mediterranean. This strip, which does not completely close the frontier, was assigned to Saad Haddad and his militia of 2,000, firmly officered by Israeli advisers. It was this enclave of 100,000 inhabitants (60% of whom were Shi'ite and 35% Christian) that Haddad transformed, in April 1979, into the State of Free Lebanon. He was then struck off the roll of Lebanese Army officers and charged with rebellion. On May 17, 1980, his forces were renamed the South Lebanese Army (SLA). From 1978 to 1982, there were continual confrontations between the 'Palestinian-progressives' (i.e. Lebanese National Movement) and UNIFIL's contingents.

After the Israeli invasion of Lebanon in the summer of 1982, Haddad followed the IDF in its push towards the north and moved his HQ from Marjeyoun to Sidon. He also followed its retreat, which lasted from 1983 to June 1985. The South Lebanese Army's membership, which had swollen, with Shi'ite recruits, dropped back to 2,000 and the IDF found itself almost back where it had started — except that the buffer zone now ran the whole length of the border and had to face up to a guerilla force that had demonstrated its effectiveness against the Israeli army. In January, 1984, General Antoine Lahad replaced Commander Haddad, who had died.

This buffer zone of 850 square kilometres (8% of the total surface of

Lebanon) depends entirely on the goodwill of **Jerusalem** and is permanently patrolled ·by several hundred Israeli soldiers.

Soviet Plan

THE NAME given to the proposals for resolving the **Arab**-Israeli conflict put forward on September 15, 1982 in Moscow by Leonid Brezhnev. Updated by the leadership of the Communist Party, they continue to inspire USSR policy, as can be seen by the text of the talks held by Mikhail Gorbachev and Yasser **Arafat** in the spring of 1988, whose main points can be found in Appendix 12.

Soviet policy regarding the Middle East (see **Soviet Union**) had a basic turning point: Stalin's support, in 1947, of the partition of Palestine (see **Partition Plan**). Since then, in fact, contingencies apart — good relations with **Israel**, followed by priority given to the Arabs — the USSR's attitude was to have as its basic reference point the need for the coexistence of two states, one Jewish and the other Arab, on Palestinian soil. Insisting, in the aftermath of the Six Day **War of 1967**, on Israel's withdrawal from the occupied territories, Moscow diplomacy was to place increasing stress on the national rights of **Palestinians**. The Brezhnev Plan, revived by his successors, was in keeping with this tradition.

Thus the USSR put forward six basic principles for peace in the Middle East:

1. The withdrawal of Israel from the occupied territories and the dismantling of the **settlements**;
2. The right to a Palestinian state on the **West Bank** and in **Gaza**, following a transition period of several months, under UN supervision, for the transfer;
3. The restitution of East **Jerusalem** to the Palestinian state, with the guarantee of right of access to the holy sites of the three religions;
4. The right, reciprocally recognized, of all the states to a safe and independent existence and development;
5. The cessation of the state of war. Peace and commitment on all sides, including Israel and the Palestinian state, to respect each other's sovereignty, **independence** and territorial integrity;
6. International guarantees, notably from the Security Council.

The USSR still basically defends these principles, but its attitude towards the conflict has altered considerably. 'It is essential', wrote Mikhail Gorbachev in *Perestroika*, 'to try to find a common denominator amongst the interests of the Arabs, of Israel, and of their neighbours and the other states. . . . We have no intention of ousting the USA from the Middle East —

such an idea would quite simply be unrealistic. But, for their part, the **United States** too must abandon unrealistic goals.' It is on this basis, with the aim of creating a consensus between the two super-powers, that the Soviet Union, amongst others, has developed a more flexible conception of the **international conference** for peace. While insisting on its sovereign character, Moscow refuses any imposed solution. Faithful to the conference's multilateral aspect, it accepts that bilateral negotiations may take place. Firm regarding the Palestinian presence, it leaves the task of defining the terms to the PLO. This ongoing enterprise is obviously in line with the efforts of the Soviet Union to renew normal relations with Israel. For, as Mikhail Gorbachev declared to Yasser Arafat, peace in the Middle East will stem from 'self-determination for Palestinians' and from 'the recognition of the State of Israel' and 'the acknowledging of its security interests'.

Soviet Union

IF ONE of the first acts of the Bolshevik revolution was to renounce the designs of the Tsars on the Middle East, the USSR in no way abandoned its hopes of playing a decisive role there, with, over the decades, varying degrees of success.

In so doing, the Soviet Union has pursued aims that differ noticeably from those that prompt the policies of the **United States** or, previously, of **Great Britain**. Oil, for Russia, does not have priority; it is itself an exporter of the commodity. The prospect of making substantial profits from its economic relations with the countries of the region has never materialized; the balance sheet of Soviet-Egyptian or Soviet-Syrian relations has proved negligible from the Soviet point of view. Soviet interest in the Middle East is based more on strategic and ideological considerations: within its southern belt, the Kremlin naturally hopes both to encourage the nationalist movement, which, in his time, Lenin had already identified as a revolutionary factor, and isolate, or even displace, the Western powers, who reciprocate the sentiments. Access to the warm seas was largely responsible, over the preceding centuries, for the innumerable conflicts between the Russians and the Turks; today, the question is more one of zones of influence, the influence being sought in this case by the USSR no doubt being primarily geo-political in nature. In clashes between the more or less anti-imperialist governments and the communist parties of various countries, hasn't Moscow always given priority to its inter-state relations at the expense of proletarian internationalism?

Originally of course, it was internationalism that inspired the denunciation, by the leaders of the young Soviet Russia, of the **Sykes-Picot
Agreement**. Through the minister, Sazonov, involved in the negotiations
leading up to the dismantling of the **Ottoman Empire**, the Tsar had
nonetheless managed to grab a good slice of the cake: he was to regain the
north-east of the Empire, Constantinople, the west coast of the Bosphorus,
the Sea of Marmara, the Dardanelles, as well as part of the Asia Minor coast
of the Black Sea. In the name of peoples' rights to self-determination, Soviet
communists abandoned all such claims. They went further: hostile to secret
diplomacy, they made public these arrangements, and those involving the
other powers, hitherto carefully concealed from the peoples at war. This proof
of its commitment to the struggle against imperialist pillage earned the USSR
great prestige amongst **Arab** nationalists who, at the time, were a rapidly
expanding constituency.

Secure in this halo of glory, the Communist Party (Bolshevik) of the Soviet
Union undertook, immediately after World War I, a dual effort. On the one
hand it formed closer links with the **Arab Nationalist Movement**, within
which it encouraged, with the help of the Communist International, the
creation of communist circles, even of parties, notably in **Egypt**, **Syria**,
Lebanon and above all in Palestine. It was the Congress of Baku, in
September 1920, that signalled the kick-off to this undertaking directed at all
the peoples of the Orient. But, concurrently, it also tried to establish contacts
with the existing regimes, despite the double handicap represented by their
relative control by Great Britain and their 'Islamism', little inclined to
exchanges with an atheist power. In both cases, the main object was to
deliver the most damaging blows possible to the arch-enemy: London.

It was the same motivation that, after World War II, would push Moscow
to accept the **Partition Plan** for Palestine. 'The interests of both the Jews
and the Arabs of Palestine', declared Andrei Gromyko at the UN on May 14,
1947, 'can be properly protected only by the creation of a democratic, independent Judeo-Arab state, dual but homogeneous.' But, he continued, 'due to
increasingly strained relations between **Jews** and Arabs ... the partition of
the country into two independent states' would be called for. The USSR was
to go a step further: not only was it one of the first countries to recognize
the State of **Israel**, but it also supplied it, via Czechoslovakia, with the arms
that allowed it to defeat the Arab armies that had entered Palestine on May
15, 1948. Indeed, for almost two years, relations between Israel and the
USSR were to be excellent. But the Stalinist leaders of the time feared the
influence of **Zionism** on the Jews of the USSR. So, though Golda Meyerson
(the future Meir), Israeli Ambassador in Moscow, received on the occasion
of the Jewish New Year of (September) 1948 a massive, enthusiastic welcome
in front of the synagogue, anti-Semitic reprisals, unprecedented since the

revolution, were soon forthcoming against Soviet Jews. A further deterioration in the situation occurred in 1949: there began in Hungary the series of trials that were to occur in the peoples' democracies, in which anti-Zionism, if not anti-Semitism pure and simple, played a brutal role. Tel Aviv, for its part, flirted increasingly openly with Washington (see **war of 1956**). In 1953 Soviet-Israeli relations were broken off; although re-established the same year, after Stalin's death and the denunciation of the White Shirts affair, they were never to regain the warmth of the early days.

So, from 1955, the USSR reversed its alliances, supporting the Arab National Movement and states over which it had taken control against Western imperialism, basically that of the United States which had taken over from Great Britain and **France** in the region, and against Israel, described as the USA's outpost in the Middle East. In the name of anti-imperialism and anti-Zionism, Moscow thus opened its arms to the Arab world, which was impelled towards it by Western attitudes: support for Israel, refusal to give help, including military help, to the Arabs, stubbornness in face of their economic and political demands, insistence on enrolling them into anti-Soviet pacts.

The offer was irresistible. Dating from the signing of the arms contract, in September 1955, between Czechoslovakia and Egypt, there thus began two successful decades for the USSR, which had denounced the previous (commercial) agreement linking it with Israel. Egypt, then Syria, and finally **Iraq** and South **Yemen** gradually turned towards it. Real alliances, involving multi-dimensional cooperation (economic, social, cultural and, of course, military) were formed. But the collapse was to be as rapid as the upward turn. Worse still: ten years on, only South Yemen, Iraq (officially) and — for how long? — Syria were still linked by treaty to Moscow. Cairo and Baghdad had done U-turns, seduced by the West. The Soviet Union's isolation in the Middle East appeared to be so extreme, at the end of the Israeli invasion of **Lebanon** in 1982 (see **war of 1982**), that many observers claim it has been definitively excluded from the region.

Paradoxically, the USSR's failure stems from its success: its aid helped the Arab nationalist movement to achieve its basic mission — the end of the colonial presence and the gaining of independence — losing at the same stroke one of its main *raisons d'être*. On the other hand, Moscow did not allow its Arab allies to impose on Israel respect for their rights and those of **Palestinians**. Lastly, in terms of development, the Soviet model, often transposed in caricature, while it may have guaranteed clear economic and social progress, did not live up to the expectations of the people: the inadequacy of the system, the absence of certain reforms of a democratic nature, the increasing power of the bureaucratic class and the weakness of the democratic movement precipitated, in the mid-1970s, the opening up (in

Arabic, *infitah*) to the West. 'The United States', **Sadat** was fond of saying, 'holds 99% of the cards.'

An error of judgement: the Western model has not, as yet, allowed an Arab country to 'take off', any more than Washington wanted, or was able, to resolve the Israeli-Palestinian conflict. This is no doubt the backdrop for Moscow's spectacular comeback since 1983. The American failure in Lebanon, the United States' sudden loss of credibility in the Arab world, Syria's rise in power were all cards that favoured the USSR which, within a short space of time, was able to redeploy its relations with the Arab world. It reconfirmed its alliance with the Syrian regime — like the PLO, pressing for detente between **Assad** and **Arafat** — and that with South Yemen. Over and above Damascus and Aden, the Kremlin renewed diplomatic relations with Cairo, Oman, the United Arab Emirates and Qatar and Saudi Arabia, signed huge arms contracts with **Kuwait**, arranged still bigger ones with Amman, ratified a treaty with North **Yemen**, etc. The **Soviet Plan** which, like the **Fez Plan**, draws on the United Nations Partition Plan for Palestine obtained a large consensus. And the international conference it advocates is nowadays called for, with degrees of firmness that vary from capital to capital, by the entire Arab world.

Secure in its achievements in the Arab world, Mikhail Gorbachev's USSR has been working, since 1985, at normalizing its relations with Israel, broken off in 1967. Since the secret meeting of July 1985 between the two countries' ambassadors in Paris, the gestures have multiplied, from the exchange of consular legations in 1987—1988 to the massive increase in the number of Jews authorized to leave the Soviet Union — more than 10,000 people a month in 1990. By letting its Jewish population leave, Moscow hopes to lead Tel Aviv to adopt a more flexible position over the Palestine question.

Moscow's new policy was manifest during the Gulf crisis in the summer of 1990, when the USSR roundly condemned the Iraqi aggression, stopped all arms sales to that country, voted through various UN resolutions and did not condemn the presence of US forces in the Gulf. The Soviet Union effectively backed the US, albeit strictly in the context of action by the United Nations. It also maintained a dialogue with Iraq, lay great stress on the need for a peaceful solution and reiterated its proposals for an international conference to solve the problems of the Middle East.

Strategic Consensus

THE BASIC aim laid down by **United States** leaders for their Middle East policy. The expression refers to the dual alliance that American strategists, like the British in their time, have tried to establish simultaneously: with **Israel** and the **Arab** regimes. So far, however, the project has never been realized in any lasting sense, thwarted by the Palestinian question.

Many commentators ascribe the alliance with Israel, officially designated as strategic, particularly since Ronald Reagan's presidency, to the powerful influence of the Jewish **lobby** in the United States. It is true that, on the other side of the Atlantic, the Jewish community is numerous, organized and relatively coherent politically; its electoral importance (up to 14% of the electoral roll in New York state) has long been a factor that none of the major parties or leading statesmen can afford to overlook. Its interventions, whenever differences between Washington and Tel Aviv crop up, therefore tips the balance.

Without underestimating this fact, it is nonetheless important to keep things in perspective: what unites America and Israel is, above all, the latter's uniqueness and the fact that it represents American strategists' trump card in the pursuit of their aims in the Near and Middle East. The principal economic and military power in the region, the only regime that has been politically stable in the long term, a sort of democratic, Western-style enclave set in the East, Israel represents a natural bastion for the United States, faced by both the Soviet Union and the Arab liberation movements. To defend it, Washington is, as we know (see **American Aid**), ready to sink astronomical sums in civil and military aid to Israel, tens of billions of dollars in 25 years.

A necessary condition in the economic, political and military control of this crossroads of continents, the alliance with Israel is nevertheless not enough in itself; the United States also has to stabilize and extend its position in the Arab world. From the Four Point Plan — the 1949 Economic Assistance Bill — to strategic consensus — a term brought back into fashion by the former Secretary of State, Alexander Haig — by way of the doctrines of Truman and Eisenhower, the White House has always strived to include the Arab countries in an anti-Soviet coalition. This was the meaning of the 1950 tripartite declaration (United States, **Great Britain** and **France**), of the 1951 constitution of the Supreme Allied Command for the Middle East, of the 1955 creation of the Baghdad Pact, just as it was the essence of Henry Kissinger's policy in the 1970s. And the spirit of the US proposals in the 1990 Gulf crisis is still to make the presence of the Marines in the area permanent — under the guise of a new organization.

These many plans and attempts have always encountered stumbling blocks, first a genuine desire for **independence** and then, essentially, the Palestinian question. How to convince the Arab countries and peoples of the necessity of allying with the United States (and therefore Israel) against the Soviet threat, when the real threat, concrete this time, is the total colonization of Palestine by the Jewish state supported by Washington? Impossible, apparently, at least given the present state of Arab awareness. This has rightly been pointed out by Ghassan Salameh (*Foreign Policy*, No. 3, 1983): 'Whether we like it or not, the Arab-Israeli conflict, with its vital Western aid accorded to Israel, and the deplorable fate left to **Palestinians**, has become the bane of the conflict with the West that goes far back into the historic memory of Arabs, if not Muslims world-wide. If American experts are able to forget this reality, Saudi, Kuwaiti and even Egyptian leaders live with it permanently. And even if they could forget it, the radios of Damascus, Tripoli, or even Tehran are there to remind them, every day, of the fate of Nokrashi Pasha, of King Abdullah of Trans-jordan or of Anwar Al **Sadat**, killed for having forgotten this underlying basis of political culture.

Sudan

BILAD AL SUDAN, the country of Blacks; it was thus that the Muslim geog-raphers of the Middle Ages designated the regions to the south of **Egypt**. The Egyptian monarchs conquered them, in the 19th century, on two separate occasions: between 1820 and 1822, Mohammed Ali seized the northern part of present-day Sudan; forty years later, Khedive Ismail, having taken possess-ion of the coastal region along the Red Sea, extended Cairo's authority in the south, which was to be divided into three provinces: Upper Nile, Bahr Al Ghazal and Equatoria.

But, with the conquest scarcely achieved, a huge wave of rebellion spread throughout the country. Mohammed Ahmad Ibn Abdullah proclaimed him-self Mahdi, messenger of God, raised an army of his followers, the Ansars, and, between 1881 and 1883, took control of virtually the entire country. At the time, Egypt was invaded by the British, and the retaking of Sudan by Anglo-Egyptian troops did not take place until 1898. This episode was a decisive element in the emergence of a Sudanese nationalist movement, giving birth to a huge religious brotherhood, the Mahdiyya, led by the Mahdi's descendants and which has remained a crucial factor in political life to this day.

In January 1899, Sudan passed under the control of an Anglo-Egyptian condominium, in which Cairo's role was largely fictitious. Nationalism began to impose itself after World War I, with the creation of the White Flag League. But it was mainly the two great religious brotherhoods, the Mahdiyya and the Khatmiyya (in favour of the union between Sudan and Egypt), that animated the movement through which, on January 1, 1956, Sudan gained its **independence**. A parliamentary system along British lines was set up, dominated by two parties, the Umma and the National Unionist Party, off-shoots respectively of the Mahdiyya and the Khatmiyya. But their inability to resolve the problem of the South (see below) and overcome the economic crisis led, on November 17, 1958, to the military *coup d'état* of General Ibrahim Abboud.

This dictatorship collapsed in October 1964, following a rebellious general strike instigated by the powerful Communist Party (CP). The parliamentary system was reinstated, but confronted the same difficulties as the military regime. And, on May 25, 1969, Ja'afar Al Numeiry and the Free Officers seized power. A follower of **Nasser**, the new leader set the country on a radical path: nationalization, close contacts with socialist countries, bloody confrontations with the brotherhoods. But, during the first two years of his presidency, Numeiry also crossed swords with the Communist Party. On July 19, 1971, officers of the extreme Left seized power for 72 hours: their movement was to be drowned in blood, the CP dismantled and its leaders, notably Secretary General Abdel Khaliq Mahjoub, hung.

The revolt in the South

Southern Sudan, composed of the three provinces of Bahr Al Ghazal, Upper Nile and Equatoria, extends over an area of 650,000 square kilometres, a territory larger than **France**. Far from constituting a unified whole, the South is divided into a multitude of ethnic groups: Dinkas, Nuers, Shilluks. Animists for the most part, the population is also 10% to 20% Christian. Neglected, and for long isolated from the rest of the country by **Great Britain**, these provinces developed a certain feeling of solidarity against the **Arab** and Muslim North. On August 18, 1955, on the eve of independence, the Equatoria Corps mutinied in Juba, the principal town of the South. There then began a long war that was to last until 1972, made up of ceasefires, surprise attacks, massacres; and also of foreign interference: first **Israel**, then the **United States** and, after Numeiry's accession to power, Ethiopia supported the rebels. Finally, an agreement was reached in March 1972 in Addis Ababa: it stipulated the establishment within the republic of a self-governing southern region and of local legislative and executive organs.

Peace lasted for ten years but the central authority did nothing to consolidate it: the economic and social development of the South was neglected and poverty remained the lot of most of its inhabitants. Numeiry's decision, in October 1983, to apply the *Sharia*, Islamic law, aroused disapproval that was all the stronger because the authorities had just taken the decision to repartition the South into three provinces, thus contravening both the letter and the spirit of the Addis Ababa agreement. This was the year that saw the outbreak of Colonel John Garang's uprising and the creation of the Sudanese People's Liberation Movement (SPLM) which, in a few months, extended its influence and held the army in check. This rebellion hastened the downfall of the dictatorship.

After the Addis Ababa agreement, Nemeiri had found himself alone at the helm. Several abortive *coup d'états*, stirred up by the right-wing opposition in 1975 and 1976, in particular the Umma Party and the Muslim Brothers, prompted him, in 1977, to attempt a national reconciliation. Sadiq Al Mahdi, the leader of the Mahdiyya Brotherhood, and Hassan Al Turrabi, the head of the Muslim Brothers, therefore returned to Khartoum. But the single party system was maintained, and the Sudanese Socialist Union retained the monopoly of power.

On the regional and international levels, the authorities allied themselves more and more with American strategy, intervening in Chad on the side of Hissène Habré and in Ethiopia on the side of the Eritreans. But it was above all the economic crisis and the recommencement of the rebellion in the South that brought about its downfall: famine, hidden from international public opinion, affected millions of people; the national debt rose to over nine billion dollars; the price of basic necessities soared. At the end of March 1985, demonstrations broke out against the prohibitive cost of living. The main professional unions called for strikes whose outcome, on April 6, was the constitution of a provisional Military Council that agreed to return the power to civilian hands after one year. Numeiry sought refuge in Egypt.

In April 1986, the first free elections for almost twenty years took place. Sadiq Al Mahdi's Umma Party won and set up a coalition government with the other major force, the Democratic Unionist Party linked to the Khatmiyya Brotherhood. As for the Muslim Brothers, they won fifty seats whilst the communists were marginalized. The Mahdi government has remained non-aligned in terms of foreign policy, but it has proved a disappointment in most respects. The country's economic crisis has not been tackled effectively and the government does not seem to be seeking a political solution to the war in the South. It has simply tried to gain a breathing space. The Democratic Unionist Party was provoked into resigning from the ruling coalition, and the Umma Party even formed an alliance with the Muslim Brothers, who joined the government in the spring of 1988. Growing discontent finally forced Mahdi to form a government of national unity in March 1989, excluding only Tourabi's Islamic National Front. A ceasefire in the South allowed negotiations with the SPLM concerning the holding of a constitutional conference bringing together all the different forces in Sudan. A meeting was set for July 14 to settle the final details, notably the suspension of the *huddud* (corporal punishment) prescribed under Islamic law. It was too late, unfortunately. Taking advantage of the country's weariness and the disarray in the army, General Omar Bassam

El Bechir's tanks moved in to seize power. The new dictatorship relies on only one political force, the Muslim Brothers, whose influence is felt everywhere. Strengthened by the support of certain Arab regimes — **Libya, Iraq, Saudi Arabia** — General Bechir has sabotaged all peace negotiations with the SPLM and intensified military operations.

Sudan covers a surface area of two and a half million square kilometres and has a population of 22 million inhabitants, of whom 15% to 29% are Southerners. The North is largely Muslim and Arab, but also has non-Arabic speaking minorities, such as the Nubians, Beja and Fur. The South, on the other hand, is black and animist, with a Christian minority. To the Sudanese population must be added a large number of **refugees** — a million — coming from Eritrea, Chad and Uganda. The country's resources are mainly agricultural: cotton, gum arabic. The American company, Chevron, has discovered oil in the South, which cannot, however, be exploited due to the civil war.

Suez Canal

LINKING the Mediterranean (Port Said) and the Red Sea (Suez), this waterway has always constituted an economic and strategic pawn of the first importance.

The first canal goes back to the year 2,000 BC, when Pharaoh Senustret III joined up the Bitter Lakes, which then formed a gulf on the Red Sea, to the Nile, and from there, to the Mediterranean. Abandoned and rebuilt several times, it silted up in the 8th century. It was Napoleon who, during his Egyptian campaign, once again conceived a waterway, this time direct, between the two seas. The project was realized, under Napoleon III, by Ferdinand de Lesseps: the Universal Company of the Maritime Suez Canal was created on April 25, 1859, the inauguration taking place on November 17, 1869.

For **Great Britain**, the Suez Canal constituted a vital link between London and its possessions abroad, particularly in India — it cut in half the journey between British ports and Bombay. Which is why, in 1875, the British government took advantage of an Egyptian economic crisis to buy the 177,000 shares (out of 400,000) owned by the Khedive. To this financial control was added, from 1882 on, a physical control: the British army occupied **Egypt** and the canal zone. In the latter area, British soldiers were to remain until 1954; it was only at this date that an evacuation agreement was signed between Cairo and London. Gamal Abdel **Nasser** was to go further on July 26, 1956: he nationalized the Canal Company.

A vital line of communication, the canal was naturally a pawn for the belligerents in Middle Eastern wars. It was closed for one day during World War I, following a Turkish raid, and for 76 days during World War II, after German raids. The Battle of the Canal, which Egyptian nationalists launched against the British, made it a dangerous place in 1951 and 1952. The Franco-Israeli-British operation in Suez led to its closure for five and a half months, from October 29, 1956 to April 15, 1957, after the withdrawal of the last Israeli army troops. But the canal's most significant closure was from June 6, 1967, at the outbreak of the Six Day War (see **war of 1967**), to June 5, 1975. Its reopening to navigation only came about with the disengagement agreements reached by **Israel** and Egypt from January 1974, followed by more than a year of work to get the canal back in working order, mainly involving mine clearance; there were over 730,000 mines and explosives in the canal, and almost 690,000 anti-tank and anti-personnel mines along the banks. Reopened on June 5, 1975, for the first time the canal accepted Israeli ships, before the latter were placed (through the Egyptian-Israeli peace treaty of March 26, 1979) on an equal footing with other users of the waterway.

The canal's restoration also allowed improvements to its navigability to be carried out. Its width having been increased to 160 metres and its draught to 16.2 metres, 90 ships can now pass through in a single day. Further widening is planned, at which time the draught could even reach 20.4 metres: ships of 370,000 tons laden, and 260,000 unladen, could thus pass through the canal. Although still profitable — it earns Egypt more than a billion dollars a year — the canal has in fact suffered from the relative decrease in oil tanker traffic. But the annual tonnage of the reopened canal is still clearly on the increase: from 274 million tons in 1976, it increased to 366 million in 1986. Apart from its alterations, Egypt has therefore decided on the economic development of the waterway's banks: the construction of factories and holiday resorts along the Mediterranean and the Red Sea, the creation of new harbour installations at Port Said, etc.

Sunni (Lebanese)

SUNNI Muslims, who are in the majority in the **Arab** world, are one of **Lebanon**'s three major communities, along with the Shi'ites (see **Shi'ism**) and the **Maronites**. In 1943, they made a crucial contribution to the country's attainment of **independence**. Traditionally loyal to the idea of Arab unity and to a Greater **Syria**, official Sunnism finally came round at this time to the idea of an independent Lebanon.

The Sunni are in the majority in the three main towns: Beirut, Sidon and Tripoli. The Sunni establishment, particularly the upper-middle classes, is characterized by two basic features. It does not possess a territorial base and even less a traditional power (semi-feudal or religious, for instance) over its co-religionists. Power is shared by about ten major families (as against two for the Shi'ites and two for the **Druze**), who regularly dispute the accession to the crucial post of prime minister. Amongst them are the Karamehs in Tripoli, the Salams in Beirut and the Solhs in Sidon.

Thus, their authority depends on their ability to win the support of the urban masses. This leads to a more ideological vocabulary than that employed in the countryside (and hence more influenced by Arab nationalism and Nasserism) and a partitioning of the Sunni districts. To this end, the leaders (the *zu'amaaim*) join forces with electoral agents of sorts, the *qabaday*, who set up clientship relations based on the positions of power of their patrons, be they in the government, in administration, or in the private sector. Another source of the supremacy of the Sunni oligarchy was its status as intermediary between Lebanon and the Arab economic and political world in the 1940s and 1950s. However, the upheavals that have occurred in the Middle East, whilst Lebanon and its elites have been conspicuously immobile, have eroded this role.

The election of a Ba'athist candidate in Tripoli and a Nasserist one in Beirut in the elections of 1972 symbolized the weakening of the oligarchy's domination over the Sunni population. Opinion turned more and more in favour of the Lebanese National Movement (LNM) and the PLO. Numerous organizations sprang to life, the most important of which was Ibrahim Koleilat's Murabitoun. But the war and the weakening of the great families did not, unlike what happened with the Shi'ites, lead to the appearance of a sectarian-based party; the Sunni were not homogeneous enough for that. Instead, Sunnis turned first towards the LNM then, from 1977–1978 onwards, towards the religious leaders who had up to then remained on the sidelines. The Mufti Hassan Khalid, the highest authority of Sunni Islam, took on a new role.

The departure of the Palestinian resistance movement from Beirut, in the summer of 1982, further weakened the Sunni establishment which had sealed an alliance with the PLO at the time of the signing of the Cairo agreement, in 1969, and after the events of April 1973 (see **Lebanese Civil War**). It was with some anxiety that it witnessed the capture of East Beirut by Amal in 1984 and the disarmament of Murabitoun. It then found itself excluded, in 1985, from the three-way dialogue of Amal, the Progressive Socialist Party (PSP) and the Lebanese Forces, set up to discuss Lebanon's future. On June 1, 1987, Rashid Karameh, former prime minister of Lebanon and one of the leading personalities of the Sunni community, died in an attack. He was replaced by Selim Hoss.

In Tripoli, a fundamentalist organization, the Movement of Islamic Unification (MIU), led by Sheikh Sha'aban, was formed in 1982 and went on to take control of the town. Allied to the PLO, the MIU resisted the Syrian offensive against **Arafat** in November-December 1983. After a long siege in the autumn of 1985, it was forced to open Tripoli to troops from Damascus. The MIU subsequently normalized its relations with Syria.

Sykes-Picot Agreement

A SECRET agreement reached in 1916 between **France** and **Great Britain** and subsequently ratified by Russia, to share out the **Ottoman Empire**, an ally of Germany and Austria-Hungary in World War I. Complemented by the Saint-Jean-de-Maurienne agreement which included Italy, the agreement shared out the zones of influence between the victorious powers:

- Russia retained the north-east of the Empire and, in the west, Constantinople, the West Coast of the Bosphorus, the Sea of Marmara, the Dardanelles, and part of the coast of Asia Minor and the Black Sea. But the port of Constantinople and the Straits remained open to navigation for the allied fleets;
- Greece and Italy obtained, respectively, a small zone around Smyrna to the west of Anatolia, and all the southern part of what was formerly Turkey;
- France appropriated Silesia and the *vilayet* of Adana, the Syrian-Lebanese coastal strip and a zone of influence corresponding to present-day **Syria**, as well as the oil region of Mosul that Clemenceau was to return to the British in 1918;
- Great Britain took the eastern part of Mesopotamia, the western parts being included in its zone of influence as well as the territory of present-day **Jordan**, these two zones being intended to form a state or a confederation of **Arab** states;
- Palestine was to be internationalized, only the ports of Haifa and Acre falling to Great Britain;
- Only the **Arabian Peninsula**, under Hashemite leadership, would become independent.

Clearly, the Sykes-Picot Agreement contradicted the commitments made by Great Britain to the Arabs. But their British author, Mark Sykes, had written to Lord Curzon: 'My aim is that the Arabs should be our first brown-skinned dominion — not our last colony. Arabs will react against one if one tries to lead them, and they are as stubborn as Jews, but one can lead them anywhere without the use of force if it is theoretically arm in arm.'

Like many a case of counting chickens before they are hatched, the Sykes-Picot Agreement would only ever be partially implemented. In 1917, the Soviet revolutionaries denounced the commitments undertaken by their predecessors in power. Between 1919 and 1922, Turkish nationalists, led by Mustapha Kemal, would liberate Anatolia from its French, Italian and Greek occupiers after the armistice. But, for the rest, the map thus established would supply the backdrop for the inter-war clashes that 'gave birth to nations', a framework officially established by the Conference of San Remo (April 1920), the Treaty of Sèvres (August 1920) and its ratification by the League of Nations (July 1922).

Syria

ON OCTOBER 3, 1918, Emir Faisal, son of Sherif Hussein, entered Damascus at the head of his troops. Having defeated the Turkish army, he hoped to establish the independent **Arab** state promised him by the British. But, on July 24, 1920, the French army put an end to this dream and drove him from Damascus: the French mandate for Syria began. In addition to **Lebanon**, the territory was divided into four states (Damascus, Aleppo, the Alawite state, the Druze Jebel) which would not be reunited until December 1936. On the eve of World War II, to get into the good graces of Turkey, **France** ceded to it the Sanjak of Alexandretta, something Syrian nationalists would never forgive. The French presence did not last long after the end of World War II and, in 1946, the last foreign troops left the country.

The early years of the new republic were far from peaceful. The defeat in Palestine and the failure of the Syrian troops who had intervened brought about the collapse of the parliamentary regime and the first military *coup d'état*, on March 30, 1949. For the next five years, military dictatorships were to succeed one another until the restoration of democracy and the holding of elections in 1954. They reflected the rise of new forces (Ba'athist, nationalist, communist) at the expense of traditional, conservative tendencies. The new power made approaches to **Nasser's Egypt** and the **Soviet Union**, and violently condemned the Anglo-French Suez expedition. Confronted with the pro-Western Hashemite axis between Amman and Baghdad, Syrian leaders came out in favour of total unity with Egypt. On February 22, 1958, a new state saw the light of day, the United Arab Republic (UAR) with Nasser as president and real master. But the experiment was to be short-lived: on September 28, 1961, the Syrian army put an end to it.

On March 8, 1963, a new *coup d'état* carried the **Ba'ath** to power. The first reforms (nationalization, agricultural reform) shook the established social order, arousing fierce reaction from the middle classes. However, the existing regime was replaced on February 23, 1966, by another, still Ba'athist, but even more radical. The new leaders, Dr Atassi and Salah Jedid, called for a harsh, uncompromising socialism and a hard line towards Israel. Syria took part in the war of 1967: it lost the Golan Heights, occupied by the Israeli army. Despite this defeat, it maintained a radical attitude which isolated it from its Arab partners. This policy was opposed by General Hafez Al Assad, the powerful defence minister. After long internal struggles, he seized power on November 13, 1970.

Within a few years, the new president had established his authority and that of his Alawite co-religionists, as well as that of the army, by either integrating or liquidating the various elements of political life. On March 7, 1972, the Progressive National Front (PNF) was created, composed of the Ba'ath Party, the Communist Party and three Nasserite groups. This alliance guaranteed the Ba'ath's hegemony and, over the years, the PNF lost all substance and influence. Political opposition, still represented by four elected deputies after the elections of 1973, disappeared from parliament during 1977. The small left-wing or liberal organizations could not stand up against the Ba'athist steam-roller. The only radical and potentially threatening opposition came from Sunni Muslim groups, who called for a holy war against a power denounced as Alawite and accused of being atheist. Two huge waves swept over the country. In 1973, demonstrators succeeded in having an amendment made to the new constitution, stating that 'Islam is the religion of the Head of State'. From 1977, a broader movement, against a background of political and economic crisis caused by Syria's engulfment in Lebanon and backed by terrorist actions, shook the Ba'ath hegemony. It ended in the uprising, steeped in blood, of the town of Hama, in February 1982. Since then, despite latent discontent, no force has been able to offer an alternative to President Assad's rule.

Syria took part, on Egypt's side, in the war of 1973. It won back part of the Golan and took advantage of this to normalize its relations with the United States. In 1976, Syrian troops intervened on the side of the Maronite Right in the Lebanese Civil War (see Maronites). Lebanon in fact constitutes Syria's western flank, and offers a channel of direct access to Homs and Hama. Moreover, Damascus sees it as a zone of influence, even part of 'natural Syria', snatched from the mother country by colonialism. After 1978—1979, President Assad took over the leadership of the anti-Camp David Accords Arab crusade, and tried to assume the place left vacant after Egypt's ostracism by the Arab world. Despite its troops' pitiful performance against the Israeli army in June 1982, Syria was able to turn the situation in its favour, obtaining the Israeli evacuation of Lebanon and the alliance of the rival militias. But the limits to its power were illustrated by its inability, in September 1988, to have a new Lebanese president elected. With Moscow's help, it reconstructed a military capacity that would make it a formidable adversary for Israel in the event of another war. An ally of Iran, but also of **Saudi Arabia**, hostile to the brother regime of Baghdad, it has tried to establish itself as principal interlocutor in any peace negotiations. Which is why it is anxious about developments in the situation in the Middle East. Not only did Hafez Al Assad not emerge a victor from his battle with Yasser **Arafat** but, along with the *intifada*, he helped to restore the power of the PLO, which had proclaimed the state of Palestine and obtained from the United States the opening of a 'substantial dialogue'. Damascus is particularly interested in this since, allied to Moscow by a treaty of friendship signed in 1980, it nonetheless cherishes hopes of direct negotiations with Washington which, the Golan apart, would confirm Syria's regional supremacy.

With a surface area of over 180,000 square kilometres, Syria has 11 million inhabitants. As sectarian affiliations have been omitted from official records, only an estimated breakdown is available: Sunni 68%, Alawite 12%, Christians 10%, Kurds 6%, Druze 2%, others 2%. The economy has been affected drastically by the war effort, which drained between a third and a half of a budget now heavily in the red. Since 1970, the country has been committed to a path of *infitah*, and the development of the private sector. Agriculture (cereals, cotton, beets, fruit and vegetables) and animal husbandry make up the main resources.

The agricultural reform, initiated by Nasser in 1958 then resumed in 1963 and 1966, and a certain degree of success in the agricultural sphere have guaranteed the loyalty of the rural population. Syria possesses certain raw materials (iron, phosphate, and 10 million tons of oil a year) but its industry has been confined to the processing of agricultural produce. Efforts to create an infrastructure and a sustained growth have not been able to get round dysfunctions of the economy: lack of stocks, inflation, lack of currency, bureaucracy, corruption. This has led to much debate on the respective places of the public sector and the private, which is much more dynamic. To reiterate a question from a delegate at the Ba'ath Party's eighth congress, in January 1985, is Syria a socialist society embarked on the path of capitalism?

Since then, the economic crisis has grown even worse. Basic necessities are scarce, and there is galloping inflation. Arab financial aid, crucial in absorbing the budget and balance of payments deficit, decreased from 1986, due to both the slump in oil prices and the punishment meted out to Assad for having supported Iran: the Arab countries, with the exception of Saudi Arabia, were not forthcoming with their contributions. In 1988, thanks to an increase in oil production, the situation recovered slightly.

Tel Al Za'atar

THE BATTLE of Tel Al Za'atar (The Hill of Thyme) was to be the longest, bloodiest episode in the **Lebanese Civil War**. It shocked the entire world which, day by day, followed the progress of this pitiless siege. It was to become the symbol of the Palestinian people's will to survive, of the incredible brutality of the Phalangists (see **Phalangist Party**), and also of the cynicism of the **Arab** regimes, that of Damascus above all.

Tel Al Za'atar was a huge refugee camp (see **refugees**), sheltering 50,000 people — **Palestinians**, and Shi'ites (see **Shi'ism**) from South Lebanon — situated in the eastern (Christian) part of Beirut. During the civil war, conservative militias were determined to homogenize their sector of the capital and therefore to eliminate the various non-Christian enclaves. On June 22, 1976, the siege of the camp defended by the PLO began. It was to last 52 days. It was only on August 12, after more than 70 attacks, that Tel Al Za'atar finally fell. A thousand Palestinians, many of them civilians, were massacred during the capture.

The defeat of the PLO forces allowed the remains of the camp's population to be forcibly transported to West Beirut; East Beirut became an exclusively Christian sector. But, above all, the fall of Tel Al Za'atar marked the change in the balance of power of the forces present in **Lebanon** after the intervention of Syrian troops, on June 1, 1976, on the side of the conservative militias.

Terrorism

'THE MAN of the year (1985) could well be named "the terrorist",' wrote a Paris newspaper. And indeed, never has public opinion shown such anguished obsession with terrorism. Yet, the simple question: 'What is terrorism?' finds no clear-cut answer in the statements of politicians or in specialized literature. For ex-President Reagan, it meant a new kind of warfare confronting the West, conducted variously by the Sandinistas and Carlos, Qadhaffi and **Abu Nidal**, the PLO and the Salvadorian opposition. For Yasser **Arafat** and the majority of **Palestinians**, the only real terrorism is that of the State of **Israel** which has stripped them of their lands, and for almost 40 years has continually increased armed attacks against the civilian population of the **West Bank**, in Lebanese camps and in **Gaza**. For the Israeli government and most of its people, terrorism is incarnated by the PLO which plants bombs and attacks defenceless civilians. Finally, let us not forget that Marshal Pétain and the German occupying forces referred to French Resistance fighters as terrorists.

Terrorism cannot be equated with the use of violence, to which many groups have had recourse: the French Resistance, those fighting for national **independence** or opposing some dictatorship or other. One of the first 'natural and inalienable' rights proclaimed by the French Revolution was surely that of resisting oppression. That having been said, one can, roughly speaking, designate as terrorism acts of violence that affect innocent civilian populations with the intention of creating an atmosphere of insecurity and achieving certain political objectives. Such terrorism may be the work of groups of varying degrees of organization, but also of states. The assassination of Israeli athletes at the Munich Olympic Games, in 1972, the hijacking of the *Achille Lauro* or the bomb attacks against the Vienna and Rome airports, on December 27, 1985, are a few examples related to the Middle East. Israel's strategy in **Lebanon** from 1968 of the deliberate bombing of refugee camps, or in the occupied territories of collective punishment, arbitrary arrests, torture, etc., is an example of state terrorism. Israel is not alone in this, as can be seen by the treatment inflicted by **Iraq** and **Iran** on the **Kurds**.

The hijacking of planes is one of the most spectacular forms of terrorism. Inaugurated by the Guy Mollet government on October 22, 1956, with the forced landing of the plane carrying Ben Bella and several FLN leaders from Rabat to Tunis, the practice was revived after the **war of 1967**. On July 23, 1968, the Popular Front for the Liberation of Palestine (PFLP) hijacked the El Al flight from Rome to Tel Aviv. Fatah did not resort to this type of action until after the Jordanian **Black September**. In 1973, the **PLO** and its main constituent units renounced such action; only small groups of dissidents, like that of Abu Nidal, continued to have recourse to it. There was a renewed outbreak following the Israeli invasion of Lebanon in 1982; Lebanese Shi'ite groups joined forces with Palestinian desperadoes. The sixteen-day hijacking, in June 1985, of a TWA Boeing to Beirut, then, in October 1985, of the ship the *Achille Lauro* and the Egyptian plane carrying to Tunis those responsible for this act, were the most sensational cases in this new phase of terrorism. They incited Arafat, on November 7, 1985, to solemnly condemn terrorism and all armed action undertaken outside occupied territories, a condemnation solemnly reiterated by the Palestine National Council in November 1988, in Algiers.

The taking of hostages is probably a practice as old as war itself. It is common in zones of conflict or confrontation. As, for instance, in Iraqi Kurdistan where groups of *peshmergas* repeatedly kidnapped foreign technicians. Lebanon, a country that has known every kind of discord, has in recent years become the favourite terrain for this category of act, facilitated by the disappearance of the state machine. First utilized during the civil war, the kidnappings were extended, especially after 1982, to the foreign communities. At the beginning of 1988, there were around fifteen hostages, mainly American and British, including Terry Waite, emissary of the Archbishop of Canterbury. All French hostages have been freed, the last of them — the diplomats Carton and Fontaine and the journalist Jean-Paul Kaufman — being restored to their families in May 1988. The researcher, Michel Seurat, died in captivity. There remains the case, much stranger, of the Abu Nidal group's capture of Jacqueline Valente and her two daughters, the latter being returned to their father, at the end of 1988, by Colonel Qadhaffi, while she herself was released in 1990. The Islamic Jihad, which was responsible for most of these acts, is, in fact, only a front, concealing various minor groups. Negotiations undertaken by various French governments to obtain the release of their nationals have led its emissaries to Damascus, Tehran and Beirut and have covered subjects as diverse as the role of Paris in the Iraq-Iran conflict (see **Gulf War**) or in the Lebanon **War of 1982**. Such diplomatic activities call into question the relations between various terrorist groups and certain governments.

The successive, or simultaneous support that the Abu Nidal group has found in Baghdad, Damascus or Tripoli is a matter of common knowledge. And few governments in the Middle East have abstained from enlisting the services of terrorist groups. However, it should be noted that the two main waves of non-state terrorism in the region corresponded to periods of maximum frustration for the **Arab** peoples and to political deadlocks: after 1970 and 1982. Sections of the Palestinian and Lebanese youth then saw any action as a means of expressing their frustration. To forget this means condemning oneself to failure in combating the terrorist phenomenon. Did not Reagan himself declare: 'We must recognize that terrorism is symptomatic of larger problems. . . . We must attack the problem of terrorism as a crime against the international community . . . but we must try to eradicate the causes of frustration and despair which are the breeding grounds and the incentive to terrorism'?

UNIFIL

THE UNITED NATIONS Interim Force in **Lebanon** (UNIFIL) was created in March 1978 as a result of Resolution 425 of the Security Council (see **United Nations, Resolutions of**) pertaining to the evacuation of South Lebanon after its invasion by **Israel**. Its mandate was to 're-establish peace and security' on the border and to 'help the Lebanese government to restore its authority in the region'. It has been regularly renewed since then, despite the equally regular abstention of the **Soviet Union** which has nonetheless never invoked its right of veto.

Made up of 6,000 men, including a French logistics support detachment, it has encountered serious difficulties in the field and has proved incapable of accomplishing the task assigned. Commander Haddad and the Israelis were to oppose any deployment of UNIFIL in the zone they controlled in the south. In numerous incidents the South Lebanese Army (SLA), the Palestinian-Progressives (i.e. Lebanese National Movement) and UNIFIL were pitted against each other. The later installed themselves in the north of Haddadland, but were unable to separate it completely from its Palestinian-Progressive opponents. A gap remained, in the narrow Litani Valley, around the Beaufort Castle, that allowed the two sides to cross swords: it was to be one of the principal routes of the Israeli penetration during the Peace for **Galilee** operation.

In June 1982, UNIFIL confirmed its powerlessness. The Israeli Defence Forces (IDF), in their march towards Beirut, crossed zones under UN control without being impeded. During the three years of Israeli occupation, there was a great deal of friction and UNIFIL tried to limit the effects of the policy known as 'the iron fist' on the civilian population. Perez de Cuellar, UN Secretary General, explained the peace forces' dilemma in the following way: 'For obvious reasons, UNIFIL does not have the right to prevent acts of Lebanese resistance against the occupying forces, any more than it has the mandate or the means to prevent counter-measures' (Israeli). For their actions, UNIFIL and the UN's other peace soldiers obtained the Nobel Peace Prize of 1988.

United Nations (Resolutions of)

AMONGST the innumerable resolutions passed by the United Nations on the Israeli-Palestinian conflict, several have left their mark on its history and are worthy of mention:

- Resolution 181 of the General Assembly which, on November 29, 1947, partitioned Palestine (see **Partition Plan** and Appendix 3).
- Resolution 194 of the General Assembly which, on December 11, 1948, after the first **Arab**-Israeli war, asserted the right of '**refugees** who so wish to return to their homes as soon as possible' or, failing this, to 'indemnities by way of compensation'. Both of these rights were to be repealed by twenty United Nations resolutions between 1949 and 1967.
- Resolution 273 of the General Assembly which, on May 11, 1949, admitted

Israel as a member of the UN.

- The famous Resolution 242 of the Security Council which, on November 22, 1967, almost six months after the Six Day **War (of 1967)**, acknowledged the existence and security of the State of Israel, but also made 'the withdrawal of Israeli armed forces from the Occupied Territories' the condition of a lasting peace. But, with typical UN ambiguity, the English text speaks of occupied territories. The Palestine question is still treated only as a 'problem of refugees', just as in Resolution 338 of the Security Council which, on October 22, 1973, after the Yom Kippur **War (of 1973)**, merely called on the parties in conflict 'to begin immediately after the ceasefire to apply Resolution 242 in all its provisions'.

- Resolution 2442 of the General Assembly which, on December 19, 1968, was concerned about the 'violation of human rights in the territories occupied by Israel', denounced again, throughout the 1970s and 1980s in numerous texts.

- Resolution 2535 B of the General Assembly which, on December 10, 1969, evoked for the first time since 1948 the 'inalienable rights of the Palestinian people', confirmed by Resolution 2628 which, on November 4, 1970, claimed that the 'respect of Palestinian rights is an indispensable element in the establishment of a just and lasting peace'.

- Resolution 2649 of the General Assembly which, on November 30, 1970, made explicit mention of the Palestinian people's 'right to self determination'.

- Resolution 2949 of the General Assembly which, on December 8, 1972, deemed as 'null and void' the 'changes brought about by Israel in the occupied Arab territories', a view that would later be coupled with a condemnation of both the transfers of population and the establishment of **settlements**. Thus Resolution 32/5 of October 28, 1977, stipulates that 'all measures and decisions taken by the Israeli government ... with the intention of altering the geographical status and the demographic composition in the Palestinian territories and other Arab territories occupied since 1967 have no legal validity and will constitute a serious obstruction to peace efforts'.

- Resolution 3236 of the General Assembly which, on November 22, 1974, in the presence of Yasser **Arafat** who had addressed it, recognized 'the Palestinian people's right to national **independence** and sovereignty', as well as 3237 in which the **PLO** is henceforth 'invited to participate in the sessions and works of the General Assembly in the capacity of observer'.

- Resolution 3379 of the General Assembly which, on November 10, 1975, classed **Zionism** as a form of racism.

- Resolution 3161 of the General Assembly which, on December 9, 1976, called for the 'Peace Conference on the Middle East with the participation of the PLO', a step reaffirmed by Resolution 3220 of November 25, 1977, which in turn explains, on November 29, 1979, Resolution 3465, regarding the **Camp David Accords** as concluded 'outside the framework of the United Nations and without the participation of the PLO which represents the Palestinian people', and which 'condemns all partial and separate accords which constitute a flagrant violation of the rights of the Palestinian people, the principles of the Charter of the United Nations and the resolutions adopted concerning the Palestinian question'.

The resolutions adopted since then have remained faithful to these ideas, a fundamental contradiction therefore remaining between 242 and 338 of the Security Council and the rest of the texts adopted by the General Assembly. It is this gap that explains on the one hand the insistence of Israel and the **United States** on the first two resolutions and, on the other hand, the stance of the PLO in accepting only the UN resolutions 'as a whole'. The Palestine National Council of Algiers, recognizing on November 15, 1988, Resolutions 181, 242 and 338, overcame this final obstacle. This time, Israel found itself with its back against the wall: the UN General Assembly concluded its session of December 1988 in Geneva by demanding, by 138 votes against 2 (Israel and the United States) and 2 abstentions (Canada and Costa Rica) 'the immediate start of work for the holding of an **international conference**', on the basis of suggestions made by Yasser Arafat in his speech.

United States of America

THE MOST RECENT of the Western arrivals in the Middle East, where it was never a colonial power, the United States has gradually superseded **Great Britain** and **France** to become the world's most influential country in the region. It has not yet managed, however, to set up the famous **strategic consensus**, a vast alliance in opposition to the **Soviet Union** that would include both **Israel** and the **Arab** countries.

For Washington, the Middle East's importance is primarily strategic: crossroads of three continents, meeting point of the great routes, it has been, since 1917, the southern border of the Soviet Union. Hence the military imperative: the United States needs a chain of bases coupled with regimes which it arms to make them, as in the case of **Iran** under the Shah, the local policeman of the region. But **oil** also continues to motivate American policy, as well as the petro-dollars that result from it, which, for the most part, come to be recycled on the other side of the Atlantic. The last, but not the least facet of America's ambitions is the massive market, civil and military, that the countries of the region represent for the American economy.

These objectives, which underlie all American policy in the Middle East, also determine its basic features, clearly distinguishable in the long term. First feature: the desire to eliminate Western competitors, under cover of the 'open door' policy, in order to assure itself an indisputable supremacy over other Western countries. This it has done with growing success, first after World War II, then after the Franco-British Suez fiasco in 1956 and finally with the British retreat from the Gulf at the end of the 1960s. Second feature: the attempt to form a massive regional alliance directed against the USSR and its local allies, an effort that quickly paid dividends in the north (Greece/Turkey/Iran), but has always been in vain in the south where any cooperation between Israel and the Arab countries inevitably runs up against the block of the Palestine question. Under these conditions, the Jewish state remains the White House's strategic priority. Third and final feature: the determination to resort to any means, including military, to satisfy these demands, on the one hand by supporting Israel, except in **the war of 1956**, in its conflicts with its neighbours, on the other hand by intervening, when circumstances require and permit it, against any threat of destabilization (Iran in 1953, **Lebanon** in 1958, **Jordan** in 1970, Lebanon in 1983). The aims of the USA's pro-Israeli **lobby** coincided here with the strategic aims.

These then are the aims and specific characteristics of the United States' Middle East policy, whose success can be measured during the main phases of their incursion into the region.

They had first to gain a foothold since, other than culturally, they had not been part of the **Ottoman Empire**. In the settlement following World War I, the Fourteen Points of President Wilson, who had come out against the Europeans' secret agreements, were scarcely taken into account. Any more than was the opinion of the commission formed by the Americans King and Crane who, in 1919, criticized the Zionist plan. Lacking a mandate and a sphere of influence, Washington made its first move by getting into the Middle Eastern oil business: in **Iraq** in 1927, then in **Saudi Arabia** in 1933, and **Kuwait** in 1934. Ten years later, American companies controlled 20% of Middle East production and 50% of its reserves.

With World War II the balance of power shifted. Whilst France lost its only bases in Lebanon and **Syria**, and Great Britain found itself struggling in Palestine, and consequently in the **Arab** world as a whole, the United States, on the other hand, was becoming established. In 1947, Harry Truman had undertaken to help 'free peoples who are fighting against the attempts of armed minorities to enslave them or against external pressures': in this way Greece, Turkey and Iran found themselves being lent the means to buy American arms. Saudi Arabia was securely tied up by the lend-lease of 1943.

On January 20, 1949, a new bill, the Four Point Plan, allowed money to be poured into the Arab countries.

But this proved a more difficult task. During the war, Franklin D. Roosevelt had multiplied contradictory promises, to Ibn Saud on the one hand and Zionist leaders on the other. This double game became impossible when decisions were called for: for instance, in face of Arab reactions, Washington went back on its vote in favour of the **Partition Plan** for Palestine, but did not oppose Israel in the **war of 1948—1949**. Furthermore, America ratified the Jewish state's territorial expansion, the non-creation of the Arab state and the Palestinian exile. On May 25, 1950, the United States, Great Britain and France announced that their countries, 'if they ascertained that any Middle East state was preparing to violate the frontiers of the armistice lines, would not hesitate, in accordance with their obligations as members of the United Nations or outside this framework, to intervene to prevent such a violation'. And the tripartite declaration placed on all arms deliveries the condition that 'the buyer country has no intention of committing an act of aggression against another state'.

One can imagine the reaction of the Arabs, thus forced to accept the *status quo* of the war, catastrophic for them, and to have to ask for aid with conditions whereas it was common knowledge that Israel was granted aid without strings. Their discontent explains the rejection of the Allied Supreme Command in the Middle East set up by London in 1950, and the Middle East Defence Organization which, in 1951, London, Washington, Paris and Ankara invited Cairo to join. **Egypt**'s 'No' was all the more resounding when, on July 1952, the Free Officers organized by **Nasser** took power. If the United States had made advances in the north, with Turkey joining NATO in 1951, and in the east in 1953, by putting an end to the experiment of Dr Mossadegh who was trying to regain for Iran the control of its oil, it had met with failure in the south. A new attempt, called the Baghdad Pact, was no more successful: the Turco-Iranian treaty was joined by Great Britain, Pakistan and Iran, but not Lebanon, Jordan, Egypt or Syria. Moreover, opposition to the pact stimulated Egypt's neutralist and nationalist movements which, in September 1955, signed an arms contract with the USSR.

Aware of this boomerang effect, Washington held back from the Franco-British operation against the man who had just nationalized the **Suez Canal** Company (see **war of 1956**). Staying out of things proved doubly successful: London and Paris alone footed the fiasco's extremely heavy bill, whilst the United States perceptibly improved its image. The Americans fully intended to fill the gap left by their allies; this was the aim of the Eisenhower Doctrine, described on January 5, 1957, as a programme of economic and military aid aimed at combatting the USSR's 'power policy'. But it was only accepted by Saudi Arabia, Lebanon and Iraq, where the king and his pro-Western Prime

Minister, Nouri Said, perished in the uprising of July 14, 1958. The next day, the Marines landed at Beirut and British paratroopers at Amman in order to stop things spreading. But though Baghdad joined Damascus and Cairo in its radical point of view, this was still due to the Israeli-Palestinian conflict, a constant source of anti-imperialism.

Paradoxically, the Six Day **War of 1967**, which saw Israel quadruple its territory at the expense of Egypt, Jordan and Syria, somewhat reduced the contradiction in which Washington was enmeshed, though it had nonetheless kept Tel Aviv at arm's length. Destabilizing for the radical regimes, within which it favoured moderate elements, the Arab defeat of 1967 made the USA a possible broker in a separate peace, failing the global peace that could only be guaranteed by the two super-powers together. Already evident within the framework of the Rogers Plan and the Jarring mediations of 1970, this logic was to prevail after the Yom Kippour **War of 1973**. Admittedly, the United States took Israel's side, but aside from the **International Conference** that had come to grief when scarcely opened, they were alone in proposing a plan: that of Henry **Kissinger**'s 'step-by-step', which would lead to the not so little steps of the **Camp David Accords**.

To win back these long hostile Arab countries, without in any way having to put at risk the 'special relations' existing between Washington and Tel Aviv, the United States employed during these decisive years both the carrot and the stick. The carrot was the restitution of the Egyptian and Syrian territories occupied by Israel since 1967, the Palestinian question being treated on the level of vague generalities. It was also the American economic opening up in response to the Arab *infitah*. As for the stick, it was the threat of the use of force — already deployed, after Iran in 1953 and Lebanon in 1958, in Jordan to save **Hussein** in 1970 — against any internal or external attempt at destabilization. The collapse of the Shah of Iran's regime, which had maintained order in the Gulf, was to reinforce this attitude: 'Any attempt to take control of the Gulf,' Jimmy Carter would declare at the beginning of 1980, 'will be seen as an attack against the interests of the United States, and will be resisted by any means, including military force.' And to back up the threat, that **Rapid Deployment Force** already dreamt of by the Kennedy administration was formed; and proved its efficiency in the Gulf, against Iran in 1988 and again in 1990 against Iraq.

The method was so successful that, immediately after the Lebanon **War of 1982**, Ronald Reagan could feel he held all the trumps: Israel pro-American and stronger than ever, Egypt brought round since Camp David, Jordan soon to be the same, Saudi Arabia and the Gulf in friendly hands, the PLO bleeding, Lebanon controlled by the Phalangists (see **Phalangist Party**), Iraq and Iran exhausting themselves in a bloody war. Only distant South **Yemen** and a Syria weakened by the war seem able to offer any resistance to Washington's projects. Was the strategic consensus embodied in the Rogers Plan on September 1, 1982, finally about to be realized? The reply, in the negative, was not long in coming. The defeat of Amin **Gemayel** and the Israeli-Lebanese treaty of May 17, 1983, was to rebound on the United States, whose troops had to quit Beirut. This slap in the face was also to affect their credibility with moderate Arab leaders who promptly hastened to bury the Rogers Plan and reopen talks with the USSR, back in the region in force on the side of Syria and in full control of the situation in Lebanon. It is not only in Israel that the multi-dimensional crisis worries the White House.

After fifteen years of spectacular US ascendancy, revenge for the years of Soviet expansion in the Middle East, the blow incurred in Lebanon and its repercussions appear to have caused Washington some doubts, if not as to its aims, at all events as to the method. The time seemed ripe for negotiations with Syria, to work out together a settlement taking its trump cards into account and recognizing the regional leadership of Damascus. This involved, having subdued Iran, mainly by the massive presence of the American fleet in the Gulf, accepting a ceasefire with Iraq and renewing contacts with Tehran moderates, following the path blazed by **Irangate**. Last and most important, detente with the USSR could have implications in the Middle East, by facilitating the convening of an international conference.

Having rallied in the spring of 1988, with the Shultz Plan, the Reagan administration nevertheless insisted on its umbrella character, covering bilateral negotiations between Israel and its neighbours. Following the Palestine National Council of Algiers, Ronald Reagan, on December 15, 1988, before handing over to George Bush, took a new direction. Yasser **Arafat** having, according to the White House, satisfied the conditions laid down thirteen years previously by Henry Kissinger — explicitly recognizing Israel and renouncing all forms of **terrorism** — Washington undertook a 'substantial dialogue' with the **PLO** which did not reach its conclusion. For this dialogue was interrupted in June 1990, and the Baker Plan for Israeli-Palestinian-Egyptian talks ran foul of Israeli President Shamir's intransigence. Then Iraq invaded Kuwait. The Armada deployed in the region by Washington in response was not sent just to defend Saudi Arabia or even to overthrow Saddam Hussein. Its purpose was to secure access to the oil resources, and to protect allied regimes from all internal and external threats. A solution to the Israeli-Palestinian conflict remains an essential element in achieving that very objective.

War of 1948—1949

THE FIRST of the **Arab**-Israeli conflicts, it broke out immediately after the declaration of **independence** of the state of **Israel**, on May 14, 1948. On the morning of May 15, the armies of Transjordan, **Egypt** and Syria, backed up by Lebanese and Iraqi contingents, went into Palestine.

In fact, clashes had begun to occur at the end of 1947: immediately after the UN General Assembly had adopted, on November 29, the **Partition Plan** of Palestine, a virtual civil war had broken out between **Palestinians** and **Jews**. On the Palestinian side, there was a rejection of the Partition Plan and therefore of the creation of a Jewish state. On the Jewish side, if the UN's decision seemed accepted, it was hoped it might be 'improved' to the advantage of Israel, who could occupy all or part of the Arab state, anything left reverting to Transjordan. This was also London's aim, since it was betting on King Abdullah to maintain its influence in the region.

The distribution of Palestinian refugees 1948—1949

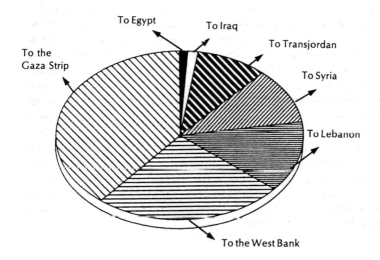

Up until March 1948, the fighting turned largely in favour of the Palestinians and their reinforcements from the relief troops of the Arab armies;

they cut communication lines, surrounded Jewish settlements and cut off the major towns, including Jerusalem. But, at the end of March, with 2,000 already dead, Jewish forces, helped in particular by Czechoslovakia, regained the offensive. Veritable massacres ensued, the most notorious of which steeped in blood the little village of Deir Yassin, where, on April 9, 1948, Menachem Begin's men killed 250 of the inhabitants, creating at the same time a panic that spread throughout the entire Palestinian Arab community. The Haganah cleared the road to Jerusalem, and seized Tiberias, Haifa and Safad. Jaffa fell on May 12, two days before the declaration of Israel's independence.

The Arab armies' entry into the war failed to turn the fighting in their favour. Though hostilities continued, interrupted by truces, until January 16, 1949, from July onwards the conflict turned in Israel's favour. Having become the Israeli Defence Forces (IDF or Zahal, formed from the Hebrew phrase meaning the same), Jewish troops now had the advantage of unusually capable commanders, with double the manpower thanks to exceptional mobilization, and a distinct advantage in heavy arms, coming mainly, by means of an airlift, from the Czech base of Zatec. This is tantamount to saying that the Soviet Union, in favour of the Partition Plan, and having recognized Israel on May 17, 1948, contributed to its first military victory. At the time, Moscow's only concern was the expulsion of Great Britain from the region.

Soviet thinking was shrewd. Beaten, humiliated by the defeat, the Arab world was profoundly unsettled. And the price London had to pay over this crisis was all the greater in that public opinion knew how things stood: 'The English encouraged us into the war', admitted the Egyptian Prime Minister, Nokrashi Pasha. Since then, the publication of British archives has even revealed that, in February 1948, a meeting took place in which Bevin, the British Minister of Foreign Affairs, decided with the Jordanian Prime Minister to use the Arab League with a view to ensuring Hashemite control over the region assigned to the Arab state by the UN. Coupled with the limitation of the territory claimed by Israel and the strengthening of the British hold over the Negev, it was London's main objective.

As it happened, Great Britain would pay dearly for the *nakba* (catastrophe in Arabic). Its man in Egypt, Nokrashi Pasha, was assassinated in December 1948, the Wafd returned to the political arena in 1950, and then, on July 23, 1952, the Free Officers took power. In Iraq too, troubles were on the increase. In Syria *coup d'état* followed *coup d'état*. Even Transjordan, which had succeeded in annexing the West Bank (or Cisjordan) to form the Kingdom of Jordan, was not spared: Abdullah, son of Sherif Hussein and grandfather of the present King Hussein, was assassinated in 1951 in the Al Aqsa mosque in Jerusalem.

But, if Britain suffered as a result of the war, the real victims were the

Palestinians. The armistice agreement signed by Israel and its various adversaries, from February 23 to July 20, 1949, ratified the enlargement, by a third, of the Jewish state as the Partition Plan had defined its borders. It went from 14,000 to almost 21,000 square kilometres, obtaining notably the **Galilee**, a strip near Jerusalem and the Negev, as far as the port of Eilat on the Red Sea. As for the Arab state, it had not materialized, Israel and Transjordan having divided the **West Bank** between them whilst **Gaza** became a trust territory of Egypt. But, above all, 700,000 to 800,000 Palestinians had to leave their homes. As the work of modern Israeli historians shows clearly, this exodus, far from having been triggered by exhortations from the Arab world to flee — no trace of any such exists — resulted from the fighting itself, during which it had become clear that, from the Israeli point of view, there was a determination to see the expulsion of the Palestinian population. This determination would continue, after the war, in the destruction of Arab villages or the establishment within them of new Jewish immigrant settlements, or again the dividing up of their lands between the neighbouring *kibbutzim*. The law on 'abandoned property' legalized this system. As for the **refugees**, the United Nations, in April 1950, would record almost a million in Jordan, Gaza, Lebanon and Syria. In December 1948, the UN proclaimed their 'right to return', which Israeli leaders however had no intention of respecting: 'We must prevent their return at all cost,' had declared David **Ben Gurion**, Israeli Prime Minister, on June 16, 1948.

With Israel already expanding, its Arab neighbours shaken, the Palestinians condemned to occupation or exile, the first Arab-Israeli conflict created the conditions of those that were to follow. Here we find the origins of the tragedy that, ever since, has steeped the Middle East in blood.

War of 1956

THE SECOND Israeli-**Arab** conflict, the Suez operation, was marked by the participation of **Great Britain** and **France**, on **Israel**'s side, in an attack against **Egypt**. This factor, which was to become deeply rooted in the evolution of the alliances between the belligerents of the earlier **war of 1948–1949**, was to have lasting consequences.

The **Soviet Union** and the peoples' democracies, particularly Czechoslovakia, had played a large part in the birth of the Jewish state and in its victory at the time of the first conflict with its neighbours. For a while, Israel had maintained good relations with them, within the framework of a non-aligned policy, but this accord did not last (see **Soviet Union**). Thus the balance between East and West in Israeli policy was quickly discontinued in favour of an increasingly open *rapprochement* with the West. Ranging from support given to the **United States** in the matter of the Korean War (1950) to making their army, ports and airports available (1951), followed by their military bases (1955), the escalation was such that, to Arab eyes, the Jewish state appeared to be a puppet of the West, which served as a cover for Israeli intransigence. For, in violation of UN decisions (see **United Nations, Resolutions of**), Israel had prevented the return of any **refugees**, had annexed the eastern part of **Jerusalem** and made it its capital, and stepped up reprisals after certain border incidents, at Kibya in **Jordan**, in 1953, and **Gaza** in 1955.

By a process of opposition, due essentially to anti-British feelings strengthened by Israel's collusion with the West, Arab leaders drew closer to the communist countries. Gamal Abdel **Nasser**, one of the fathers of what would later be called the Non-Aligned Movement, created in 1955 at Bandung, initiated this trend, which worried both Washington and London. Paris, moreover, had a personal score to settle with the Egyptian *Rais*, accused of actively supporting the Algerian rebellion whose leaders had been made welcome in Cairo. This desire for revenge was coupled with the natural amity of the SFIO (French Section of the Workers' International), then in power, towards Israel, to such an extent that the French government, like that of Great Britain, dreamed of duplicating against Nasser the operation successfully carried out in 1953 in **Iran** against Dr Mossadegh by the Americans.

A series of acts now raised tensions higher and higher. February 1955: Israeli troops attack Gaza 'in reply' to attacks. September: having been refused arms by the West, Egypt announces that it will get supplies from Czechoslovakia. October: **Syria**, followed by **Saudi Arabia**, signs a military pact with Cairo, the three countries' forces being united under the command of the Egyptian general, Abdel Hakim Amer. April 1956: **Yemen** joins the scheme. July 1956: Nasser announces the nationalization of the **Suez Canal** — it is the first time that a Third World country has successfully regained possession of one of its natural resources — whilst Paris and London set up a joint intervention general staff. October was to be the decisive month: on the 23rd, at Sèvres, the British and French secretly prepare the offensive against Egypt, after having supplied Israel with improved weapons; on the 24th, the new Jordanian Assembly joins the pact between Egypt, Syria, Yemen and Saudi Arabia; on the 29th, it is war. The operation is baptized Kadesch, recalling the wanderings of Moses and the **Jews** in the Sinai.

In no more than six days, the Israeli Defence Forces (IDF) occupied the Sinai, after having captured 5,000 soldiers and 10 Egyptian T–34 tanks. On the 31st, London and Paris bombed Egyptian targets, Cairo having rejected their ultimatum calling for a retreat from the canal zone. Five days later, despite a ceasefire decreed by the UN on November 1, French and British soldiers landed at Port Said and Ismailia. They were not to leave until December 22, under the joint pressure of the United States and the Soviet Union, who also insisted that Israel leave the Sinai and Gaza by March 14, 1957. The operation had proved to be a fiasco.

Admittedly, Israel had obtained, if not new conquests, the presence of United Nations observers at Gaza and Sharm Al Sheikh — hence free navigation in the Gulf of Aqaba and around the port of Eilat. But, for Great Britain and France, things had become much worse: the canal was closed, oil supplies hindered and, above all, the standing of the two countries in the region had been irredeemably compromised. With the exception of **Lebanon**, the leaders of all Arab states had broken with London; and the Algerian uprising was strengthened by the failure of the landing at Suez, intended to cut it off from its vital bases. As for Great Britain, its treaties with Egypt and Jordan were repealed. For the United States, which had been smart enough to oppose the Anglo-French venture though it had condemned the nationalization of the Suez Canal, its time had now come.

Thus, the second Israeli-Arab conflict, like the first for that matter, had a boomerang effect. In 1948, by pushing the Arab armies into war, London had hoped with one stroke to thwart the leaders of the new Jewish state and, at the same time, regain positions lost by Great Britain in Palestine and the region. The opposite came to pass. Similarly in 1956: the intervention, intended to suppress the nationalist upsurge and re-establish the Franco-British order, heralded the downfall of the old colonial powers and accelerated the American takeover, without in any way affecting Nasser's position. There were other contrary effects: Syria strengthened its alliance with Moscow, soon to be followed by **Iraq** where, on July 14, 1958, a revolution cut the umbilical cord attaching it to London. Lebanon and Jordan only managed to escape this evolution due to the landing of American marines at Beirut and English forces at Amman.

War of 1967

CALLED the Six Day War, the length of the military operations properly speaking, it was the third conflict between **Israel** and its neighbours. If, like its predecessors, it ended with a crushing victory for the Israeli Defence Forces (IDF) it also brought about a profound alteration of frontiers: with the occupation of East **Jerusalem**, the **West Bank**, the **Golan** Heights and Sinai, the Jewish state had quadrupled the area of its territory.

At the time, each of the protagonists blamed the other for the outbreak of war, the Western media, particularly the French, taking up the cudgels on Israel's behalf against the Arabs, as though it were some David facing a Goliath. The war of 1967 was even presented as a thundering Israeli riposte to Egyptian aggression. Twenty years on, this theory finds few defenders. Furthermore, Israeli leaders of the period have, in the meantime, modified the propaganda given out at the time. For example, General Rabin, who was the IDF chief of staff in 1967: 'I do not think Nasser wanted war. The two divisions he sent into the Sinai, on May 14, would not have been sufficient to launch an offensive against Israel. He knew it and we knew it.' Similarly, here is General Peled: 'The thesis that claimed genocide was suspended above our heads in June 1967, and that Israel was fighting for its very existence was only a bluff.'

Hostilities broke out, on the contrary, at the end of a real and disturbing mounting of tension, where each side feared the others' intentions. The climate was relatively calm when, in 1963, Israel decided unilaterally to divert the course of the River Jordan. The **Arab** riposte came in January 1964: the Cairo summit would also undertake to divert two or three of the Jordan's tributaries; concurrently, it gave birth to the **Palestine Liberation Organization**, which was formally established in Jerusalem in May, under the presidency of Ahmad Shukairy. In January 1965, Fatah sent its first armed commandos into Israel, via the Jordanian lines but with Syrian backing. Israel reacted with retaliatory raids against the Arab sites where the River Jordan was being diverted, but also against the countries from which Yasser **Arafat**'s men were infiltrating. More significantly, the general staff was organizing, according to **Egypt** and **Syria** who publicly expressed their anxiety in April, a large-scale offensive against the Arab countries. Anxiety increased on May 15, 1967, with the Israeli military march-past in Jerusalem, contrary to the armistice. So, on the 17th, Cairo had its troops stand by and, on the 18th, called for the withdrawal of the United Nations observers from Sharm Al Sheikh and Gaza, which Egyptian troops took over on the 21st. The next day, the Gulf of Aqaba was closed to Israeli ships or those transporting strategic material for Israel. In Tel Aviv, where Menachem **Begin** was entering into government for the first time, the rallying of **Jordan** (May 31) and **Iraq** (June 4) to the Egyptian-Syrian military pact, was seen as a *casus belli*.

The encircling led, the next day, to the IDF's attack. It was to be a stroke of lightning: once the Arab airforce had been annihilated (in a morning), Israeli troops took only six days to secure the Egyptian Sinai, the Jordanian West Bank and, by means of a two-day refusal to accept the ceasefire decreed by the UN and accepted by the Arab belligerents, the Syrian Golan Heights. After five months of bargaining, the United Nations, with Resolution 242 (see Appendix 4) of the Security Council, declared the need for an Israeli withdrawal from the Arab territories it was occupying, in exchange for: the cessation of fighting, the recognition of all states in the region, freedom of navigation on the Suez Canal and in the Gulf of Aqaba and the creation of demilitarized zones.

The crushing Israeli victory was, in many ways, destabilizing, as the Arab world was the first to experience. This new *nakba* (catastrophe), far from encouraging nationalism as in 1948, brought about its crisis. The wave of nationalism had of course continued into the early 1960s, notably with the independence of Algeria, the revolution in North Yemen, the armed struggle in Aden and the Ba'ath-CP coalition in Syria. It was to have certain other significant consequences: radicalization in Iraq, overthrowing of the monarchy in Libya, British withdrawal and independence throughout the Arabian Peninsula. But the trend that established itself after the Six Day War was retreat. Discredited by their defeat at the hands of the IDF, the Egyptian and Syrian regimes were also experiencing the repercussions of their domestic failures, economic and political. Once its 'independentist' aims had been achieved, the nationalist movement was naturally prey to conflicting interests, which expressed themselves in clashes in matters of agricultural reform, social measures, methods of development, of democracy, etc. The *infitah* that was to develop in Cairo and Damascus attested to the supremacy of the bureaucratic, agrarian and commercial bourgeoisie whose attitude was to be one of opening up to the West. The event that symbolized the end of an era was the death of Gamal Abdel Nasser, struck down by a heart attack on September 28, 1970, and replaced by Anwar Al Sadat.

But the tide of fate would also turn against Israel which, in 1967, entered a qualitatively new period. Up till then, the Jewish state had depended on the international legitimacy accorded it by the UN at its birth forgetting, in passing, the extension of its territory as a result of the war of 1948 and the forced exodus of hundreds of thousands of Palestinians. However, the Egyptians (with Gaza) and the Jordanians (with the West Bank) had in fact possessed the means to create an Arab state, with East Jerusalem as its capital. As of June 10, 1967, the tables were turned: Israel was now master of these territories, which it could exchange for peace. But, not only did Tel Aviv's leaders reject any realization, in whatever form, of Palestinian national rights, they took the first steps in the direction, if not of annexation, at least of colonization: the seizure of the old city of Jerusalem, the refusal to allow the return of the 300,000 refugees newly created by the war, the first Jewish settlements, violent repression, etc. If the Palestinians immediately felt the consequences of this choice, Israelis would do so later: the continued occupation of the West Bank and Gaza, the freezing of the Palestine problem, and the resulting absence of peace were to be the sources of the crisis that shook Israeli society. From inflation that at one time reached three figures to the fate of **Oriental Jews**, from the rise of Rabbi Kahane to the ever-increasing emigration of Israelis to Europe or America, not to mention the shattering of traditional Zionist values, there were few phenomena unrelated to the decision taken after the Six Day War.

'It is not true', said General Dayan at the time, 'that the Arabs hate the Jews for personal, religious or racial reasons. They see us, and rightly from their point of view, as Westerners, foreigners, even invaders who seized an Arab country to create a Jewish state.... Since we are now obliged to achieve our aims against the wishes of the Arabs, we must live in a state of permanent war' (quoted by Eric Rouleau in *The Palestinians*).

War of 1973

VARIOUSLY called the Yom Kippour, the October or Ramadan War, it was the fourth conflict between **Israel** and its neighbours. Its uniqueness stems from the breakthrough of Israeli lines, temporary as it happened, by Egyptian and Syrian troops. Although followed by an Israeli military success, this provisional victory was seen, from the **Arab** side, as revenge for the humiliations suffered in the wars of 1948–1949, 1956 and 1967.

'There being no longer any hope of a peaceful solution, our decision is to fight,' announced Anwar Al **Sadat**, in office as president of **Egypt** since November 1971. This premature declaration of war, that nobody, at the time, took seriously, demonstrates Cairo's confusion following the failures of its diplomatic endeavours. At the time, Israel still occupied all the territories conquered by the IDF during the Six Day **War of 1967**, notably Sinai. Resolution 242 (see **United Nations, Resolutions of**') of the UN Security Council, which advocated the restitution of these territories to the **Arab** countries in exchange for peace, remained a dead letter.

The Rogers Plan, presented by the **United States** in response to the war of attrition instigated by Egypt on the **Suez Canal** but with the aim of putting Resolution 242 into operation, had little more success; in September 1970, Tel Aviv suspended the negotiations initiated by the mediator Jarring two months before. In December, a peace plan in which Sadat proposed a formal recognition of Israel in exchange for the occupied territories and the return of Palestinian **refugees** against freedom of navigation on the Suez Canal, was also rejected. The Jewish state was equally unimpressed by the Nixon-Brezhnev communiqué of May 1972 which reaffirmed the 'commitment' of the United States and the **Soviet Union** 'to a peaceful solution consistent with resolution 242'.

Only the United States, the Egyptian head of state now thought, was in a position to induce Israel to negotiate. But only another war, he added, would compel the great powers to apply the pressure at their disposal on Israel. At the same time, he could silence the rumbles of popular discontent then being voiced in Egypt, where the burden of defence was becoming all the more intolerable in that nothing was happening. Such were the reasons, external and internal, that pushed Anwar Al Sadat to a 'limited confrontation' with Israel; it was with this aim, plainly stated, that, in March 1973, he combined his office with that of prime minister.

Seven months later, on October 6, the date of the Jewish holiday of Yom Kippour, Egyptian tanks crossed the canal, rushed the Bar Lev line and plunged into the Sinai, whilst Syrian soldiers advanced 5 kilometres into the **Golan Heights**. It took a week for the Israeli generals to pull themselves together, and for their tanks to regain the initiative on the two fronts. This was made all the easier since Sadat had halted his offensive. General Sharon, already exceeding orders, also crossed the canal and marched towards Suez. On the 17th, two events took place: in the Sinai one of the major tank battles of history, and in **Kuwait** the decision to set up an embargo which heralded the oil war. On the 22nd, Resolution 338 of the UN Security Council was accepted by Egypt and by Israel — which nonetheless continued its counter-offensive on the ground. A Soviet threat to send in troops, American forces on red alert: the super-powers intervened with an iron hand, as Cairo had hoped, to make Israel, which had lost close to 2,500 of its sons, see reason.

Imposing a ceasefire is one thing, constructing a lasting peace is quite another. However, conditions seemed favourable for serious negotiations. Alas, they were quickly to degenerate. And what of the Soviet-American desire to work together for a solution to a conflict that was threatening the detente then making rapid strides? Washington would opt once again for the Lone Ranger approach, Henry **Kissinger** settling for a separate arrangement which excluded the USSR. What of the political and moral crisis set off in Israel by the surprise of the Yom Kippour War? It was to turn in favour, not of the doves, but of the hawks, even bringing into public affairs, in 1977, Menachem **Begin's** men, until then always excluded from power but the principal beneficiaries of the accusations levelled against the leaders of the Mafdal — the great 'breakdown' of October. Perhaps a Europe goaded by the oil crisis would play a positive role? But the Old Continent, despite its show of intervention, would as always take a back seat to the White House. The pragmatism suggested to the Arabs by the avenging of their honour during the first days of the October War also raised hopes. But Egypt was not to be followed by its peers, most of whom, including the **Palestinians**, refused the conditions imposed by Israel.

Thus, Anwar Al Sadat's hopes were to be dashed, at least those involving international discussions under the protection of the United States and the USSR: in fact, the Geneva Conference was no sooner inaugurated than it was adjourned. Cairo was to find another road to peace, opened by the White House, one that would lead the Egyptian *Rais,* and his Israeli opposite number to the **Camp David Accords**. Even after the Yom Kippour War, Sadat was inclined, claimed Colonel Qadhaffi in 1977, to 'conclude any peace whatever with Israel, as long as he could regain the Sinai'.

War of 1982

CALLED the **Lebanon** War, where the fighting took place, this was the fifth in the history of the Middle East since World War II. It differed profoundly from those which preceded it, on three main counts: it was more an Israeli-Palestinian than an **Arab**-Israeli conflict, it proved long-lasting and, finally, it did not end in a clear-cut victory for **Israel**.

Menachem **Begin**'s launching of the invasion of Lebanon resembled Anwar Al **Sadat**'s initiating of the Yom Kippour **War of 1973** in that, if the date chosen seemed surprising, the opening of hostilities was far from unexpected. The **Camp David Accords** had led, as many observers had predicted, to a deadlock, for while the Israeli-Egyptian peace treaty was implemented, negotiations on Palestinian autonomy remained at the planning stage. The subject was of course bitterly discussed by Cairo and Tel Aviv, but with **Jordan** and, more importantly, the PLO, excluded. The assassination of Sadat, in October 1981, also brought about a firmer attitude on the Palestine question in Cairo. Unable to solve the problem at the conference table, the Israelis therefore tried to do so in the field: on the **West Bank** and in **Gaza**, where colonization and repression intensified, and in Lebanon where the operations of the Israeli Defence Forces (IDF) were now stepped up. Aware that **Egypt**'s only concern was not to compromise the regaining of the Sinai, that the Arab world was divided and the PLO relatively isolated, Israeli leaders felt they had a free hand. Throughout 1981 there was a noticeable rise in tension: the missile crisis with **Syria** in spring was followed, on June 7, by the raid against the Iraqi nuclear centre of Tammuz and, in December, the annexation of the **Golan Heights**. But, above all, in June the IDF and PLO troops based in South Lebanon began shelling each other, until the **United States** negotiated a ceasefire with the two parties.

Peace for Galilee; this was the unlikely name given, on June 6, 1982, to the incidents of the summer of 1981 — ignoring the fact that the ceasefire had been scrupulously observed by the PLO — to the Israeli military operation in Lebanon. Officially, it was only a question of affirming control of a 40 kilometre strip, from which terrorists would no longer be able to shell the north of the country. By way of this limited intervention, the IDF found itself, at the end of June (after the Syrian army had signed a ceasefire on the 11th), at the gates of Beirut. Thus began the siege of West Beirut, where **Palestinians** and the Lebanese National Movement fought side by side, whilst the Phalangists lent support — but without taking part in the fighting — to the Israeli soldiers. There seemed no end to the phosphorus bombs, napalm bombs, scatter bombs and imploding bombs that relentlessly poured down on the starving, parched west section of the town. On August 7, the American mediator, Philip Habib, declared an American-Lebanese-Palestinian agreement to allow the departure of the PLO militia, under the protection of an international contingent (Franco-Italian as it happened).

After one last wave of shelling, it was all over. On August 30, Yasser **Arafat** and the last of his troops left Beirut and, on September 15, the day after the assassination of Bashir **Gemayel**, those of General Ariel Sharon entered. On the 16th and 17th, under the very eyes of these troops, the Phalangists massacred hundreds of men, women and children in the camps of **Sabra and Shatila**. Such was the tragic end of the first phase of the Lebanon War, that of the fighting properly speaking. A second phase now opened: that of Israel's occupation of South Lebanon, which provoked increasingly extensive armed popular resistance to the point where, three years later, Tel Aviv would choose to withdraw its army.

Such, in effect, was the major, most tangible result of the invasion of Lebanon, a shambles in which, for months on end, Israel would flounder, at a cost of the lives of hundreds of its soldiers, thousands of wounded, hundreds of millions of dollars in occupation expenses, not to mention the virtually unanimous hostility of a population, essentially Shi'ite, which had given the IDF a relatively good reception in June 1982 hoping, through it, to get rid of the Palestinians. An exorbitant price to pay: was it worth it from the Israeli point of view? The benefits derived from the Lebanese affair are, on examination, far from convincing.

Security for Israel? This was the official reason for the war. In fact, the IDF was back to square one. Once its troops had withdrawn from South Lebanon, it could claim only, just as before the war, a buffer zone whose dimensions had changed little, and which remained in the hands of Israel's Christian Lebanese collaborators, General Lahad's **South Lebanese Army**.

The annihilation of the PLO? This was Ariel Sharon's publicly stated aim. 'We are here', he had declared on June 12, 1982, 'to destroy once and for all the PLO terrorists.' If the Palestinian resistance movement was not completely crushed in the vice, sections managing to get out of Beirut, it nonetheless suffered severe setbacks. It was defeated, thousands of its men dead and wounded, its military resources abandoned, what had been a virtual state machine dismantled, and, above all, the last autonomous base close to the Palestinian people replaced by dispersal into a dozen countries. These losses would have important consequences: the resurgence and intensification, manipulated by certain Arab regimes, of internal clashes within the PLO, leading to splits on the one hand and paralysis on the other. But the resistance movement would survive this new test, as it had previous ones.

A state in Lebanon that was strong, Christian and friendly to Israel? This had long been the dream of Israeli leaders. Clearly, the operation had done little to bring it about. After a period that seemed promising for Tel Aviv, during which Amin Gemayel seemed to have taken the country in hand and set it on the path to peace with the Jewish state, the course of events was reversed. So much so that four years after its intervention, Israel found itself facing, in the north, a neighbour with whom Damascus and its 'Progressive-Muslim' (i.e. Lebanese National Movement) allies had scored the winning points, the very ones that Tel Aviv and its Phalangist allies had lost. Apart from this, the **Camp David Accords** found themselves compromised, the Lebanon War having seriously damaged Israeli-Egyptian relations.

A final element, difficult to measure, nonetheless plays a considerable role in the negative assessment most observers make of the invasion of Lebanon: the damage to Israel's image. For the first time in its history, a military initiative undertaken by Israel did not appear legitimate, since it was not necessary to either its defence or survival. An already shaken public opinion was further disturbed by the dreadful pictures transmitted by the media of the seige of Beirut and, especially, of Sabra and Shatila. The repercussions were to be damaging and lasting: in Israel itself, where it gave birth to a massive anti-war movement; in the Diaspora too, where it exacerbated the sense of alienation from the Tel Aviv authorities; and finally, in Western consciousness, whose spontaneous support for Israel would be greatly curbed by a certain degree of sympathy for the Palestinian cause.

West Bank

THE WEST BANK of the Jordan was part of Palestine under the British Mandate. Occupied by the armies of King Abdullah of Transjordan during the **war of 1948—1949**, it was officially annexed on April 24, 1950; the Kingdom of

Jordan was born. Covering an area of 5,440 square kilometres, the West Bank takes in East Jerusalem and the towns of Nablus, Ramallah and Bethlehem.

Occupied by the Israeli army at the time of the **war of 1967**, the West Bank was not annexed (unlike the **Arab** section of Jerusalem). But its 660,000 inhabitants (1967 census, including Jerusalem) — in 1987, Dr Meron Benvenisti's West Bank Data Project estimated the population at 1.2 million — were to experience an occupation that totally changed their way of life and their political consciousness. As for the 250,000 people who fled to Jordan in June 1967, only a few thousand would be authorized to return home.

While practising a policy, referred to as 'open bridge', which authorizes certain contacts and commerce between the West Bank and Jordan, **Israel** has stepped up the economic integration of the occupied territories. The West Bank has become a crucial market for the Jewish state's exports. In the other direction, tens of thousands of **Palestinians** cross into Israel to sell their labour-power at low prices. From 5,000 in 1968, their number went up to 25,000 in 1971, then to 40,000 in 1979, and stabilized at around 45,000 in the 1980s.

The social consequences have been enormous: the industrial proletariat represents 40% of the active population, whilst those employed in agriculture constitute only 25%.

This reversal of conditions has provoked the disintegration of the traditional society, peasant and rural. Moral values and a way of life have been transformed. Relationships based on clientship (a system of patronage), which was the means of domination of the pro-Jordanian elites before 1967, have broken down. The increasing percentage of young people in the population and a high percentage of children attending school have aggravated this process. In a few years, a new, more nationalist intellectual elite has come to the fore, replacing its more moderate elders and confirming its support of the PLO.

All the more so since Israeli policy leaves little room for collaboration. The establishment of **settlements**, the assertion of historic Jewish rights to what Israel calls Judea and Samaria, the annexation of Jerusalem (holy city for both Muslims and Christians; it is worth remembering that a sizeable minority of Palestinians are Christian) all go to constitute obstacles. The repression exercised equally against pro-Jordanian elements, nationalists favourable to the *fedayeen* and the communists has succeeded in isolating those whom the population see as occupiers. From 1967 to 1970, all political tendencies called for the return to the *status quo* preceding June 1967; but, with **Black September** and the development of Palestinian national consciousness, the pro-Jordan elements became isolated.

In August, 1973, the Palestine National Front (PNF) was formed, bringing together nationalists and communists, and recognizing the PLO as 'sole legitimate representative of the Palestinians'. The PNF asserted its hegemony, in the spring of 1976, during the municipal elections: it obtained 80% of the seats and most of the mayoral appointments. During this period, the PNF made it possible both to affirm national identity (against Israel, but also against Jordan) and put pressure on the PLO to adopt realistic positions, in other words those favourable to a political solution and the establishment of a Palestinian state on the West Bank and in Gaza.

It was the Palestinians of the West Bank who most vigorously opposed the **Camp David Accords** of 1978 and autonomy. This was because they had concrete experience of the policy of colonization and the expropriation of land, intensified since **Begin's** victory. Political repression intensified with the dismissal, in 1982, of most of the elected mayors and their replacement by Israeli administrators. It was accompanied by routine measures taken against the Palestinians: house arrests, deportations to Jordan, administrative detentions. There were, immediately prior to the *intifada*, 4,000 political prisoners who came from the West Bank and Gaza. The only area of relative freedom was the press. Appearing in East Jerusalem, it benefited from Israeli laws, but was nonetheless subject to rigorous censorship.

The outbreak, in December 1987, of the uprising on the West Bank and in Gaza marked the culmination of a growing awareness, reflecting a strong national identity and confirming the central role of the 'inside' (i.e. inside the occupied territories as opposed to the Palestinians in exile) in the Palestinian struggle. On July 31, 1988, King **Hussein** took action by breaking all legal and administrative links with the West Bank.

Yemen

THE BAB AL-MANDEB (Gate of Lamentations) links the Red Sea and the Indian Ocean. Less well known than the Straits of Hormuz, it is nonetheless of great strategic importance, especially since the reopening of the **Suez Canal** in 1975. Indeed, it is situated in the heart of a region marked by great political upheavals: the fall of the monarchy in Ethiopia, Djibouti's accession to **independence**, the war between Ethiopia and Somalia, the Eritrean rebel movement and the many changes undergone by both Yemens. Divided for two centuries, North Yemen having fallen under Ottoman rule and South Yemen under British dominion, the two countries were reunited on 22 May 1990, with Sanaa as the capital. However the new republic will long remain marked by the past of its two regions.

North Yemen, or stability restored

Independent from the end of World War I, North Yemen experienced a long-reigning monarchy, which tried to keep the country isolated from the rest of the world. But, in September 1962, Colonel Abdullah Al Salal overthrew the Imam Ahmad Ben Yahya and proclaimed a republic. There followed a long civil war, fuelled by massive intervention by the Egyptian army on the republican side and Riyadh's active support of the monarchists, which ravaged the country until 1970.

The protagonists finally negotiated an agreement: the continuation of the republican regime; the return of the royal family to Sana'a; integration of royalists into the machinery of government. But instability persisted, with a succession of political assassinations and *coups d'état* as well as war, in 1972, with South Yemen. In June 1978 came the accession to power of Ali Abdullah Salah who succeeded in restoring stability to his country, despite the many difficulties, including another brief war with the south at the beginning of 1979.

Ali Abdullah Salah instigated a policy that maintained a balance between his powerful Saudi neighbour and South Yemen. He put down left-wing opposition with an iron hand and confirmed his government's authority in the region. Lastly, he developed close links with the **Soviet Union**, in particular in the military sphere, while managing to maintain cordial relations with the **United States**.

North Yemen has a surface area of 195,000 square kilometres. Its population numbers over 8 million, of which almost 2 million are abroad. The overwhelming majority lives in the countryside, formed into 75 tribes allied within confederations that have played a major political role. As in the south, this population is, for the most part, sedentary. An extremely poor country, North Yemen underwent a certain development due to the money sent home by its emigrants and to oil production which began in 1986; it should reach 400,000 barrels a day (20 million tons a year) by 1990. The population is 55% Zaidite (one of the sects springing from **Shi'ism**) and 45% **Sunni** (see **Islam**).

South Yemen: from radicalization to instability

Since the country's independence, at the end of 1967, and the seizing of power by the National Liberation Front (NLF), following armed struggle against British colonialism, which had occupied Aden since 1839, South Yemen's political life has received many jolts. The country opted for a socialist regime — much more radical than that chosen by **Syria** or **Iraq**, and resembling the Cuban model in some ways — and close links with the USSR.

The main leaders of the NLF were drawn from the ranks of George

Habash's Arab Nationalist Movement (ANM), which influenced an entire left-wing generation in the Middle East. The victory of the NLF's Left, in June 1969, committed the country to the construction of socialism: collectivization of agriculture and the economy as a whole, including small traders; social programmes and education; improvement in the status of women. Three men symbolize this new course: Abdul Fatah Ismail, the General Secretary; Ali Nasser Mohammed, the Prime Minister; Salem Rubaya Ali, President of the Republic. Twenty years on, two of them are dead and the third has been removed.

Involved, at the time, in an increasingly close alliance with Moscow, these leaders decided to unite the Left — in particular the Ba'athist People's Vanguard Party and the communist People's Democratic Union — to create a single progressive party. On October 11, 1978, the first congress of the new Yemeni Socialist Party (YSP) opened, but without Rubaya, executed in June following an attempted *coup d'état*.

The reign of the new leader, Abdel Fatah Ismail, was not to last: accused of having aggravated the conflict with the North and of isolating the country from its neighbours, he left in April 1980 for a gilded exile in Moscow. He was replaced by Ali Nasser Mohammed who, while retaining special relations with the USSR, sought to normalize relations with neighbouring states, including Saudi Arabia and Oman with whom Aden established diplomatic relations on October 27, 1983. From the economic point of view, the new regime improved administration and accorded a more active role to the private sector.

But internal divisions remained, fanned more by personal ambition than political differences. The return of Abdel Fatah Ismail, in February 1985, increased tension. And, on January 13, 1986, a civil war broke out in Aden and throughout the country between partisans of Ismail and those of Ali Nasser. The toll was dreadful: several thousands killed, amongst them many party leaders, including Abdel Fatah Ismail, and hundreds of millions of dollars damage.

Ali Nasser Mohammed and 70,000 of his men sought refuge in North Yemen. The new regime, composed of second-rank leaders — including the new secretary general of the YSP, Ali Salem Al Bayd — vigorously repressed its opponents. After some hesitation, the Soviet Union rallied to the victors and tried, through massive aid, to assist in the work of reconstruction — Aden represents, of course, a crucial naval base for the Soviet presence in the Indian Ocean.

Extending over an area of 333,000 square kilometres, South Yemen has slightly over 2 million mostly Sunni Muslim inhabitants, of whom 100,000 are ex-patriates. A poor, essentially agricultural country, it gets its income from a large oil refinery at Aden, the various activities of the port and the fishing potential it has developed. The recent discovery of oil is not expected to bring any appreciable income until the 1990s — by 1987, production had reached scarcely 10,000 barrels a day. Since the events of 1986, money transferred from emigrants has greatly decreased.

Yishuv

THE NAME given to the Jewish community of Palestine and the society it constructed there prior to the creation of the state of Israel.

The *Yishuv* is therefore primarily men and women whose numbers, between the first Jewish World Congress (1897) and the UN Partition Plan (1947) were to increase fifteen-fold: in fifty years, they went from 40,000 to more than 600,000; the proportion they represented in the total population increased from just over 10% to more than 39%.

Men and women, but also land: by means of the Jewish National Fund, which bought from large absentee landlords their *dunums* (one *dunum* equals approximately ¼ acre), the community extended its acquisitions, in fifty years, from 204,000 to 1,802,000 *dunums*. At the same time, the number of agricultural colonies rose from 27 to 300, many of which were collective farms, either collectively owned *kibbutzim*, or cooperative *moshavim*; in 1947 half of Jewish land was cultivated by these two types of structure, the other half being in private ownership. With 7.7% of land at the end of World War II, Jewish peasants supplied 28.3% of Palestine's agricultural produce.

The 'rejuvenation of the Jewish people through work', promised by Zionism, was accomplished in this way in the countryside, but it also took place in the towns, in industry and commerce. Starting from 100 in 1920, the industrial production index had reached almost 5,000 by 1945. The annual consumption of electricity rose from around 2 million kilowatts per hour to almost 200 million.

Industry, public services and agriculture, and British military camps, accounted for 160,000 employees, 90,000 Arabs and 70,000 Jews, whose incomes were sometimes double those of Arabs, their expenditure even greater.

The disparity thus created between Arabs and Jews did not stem only from the assets — training, technical resources, capital — possessed by the latter. It was also the result of deliberate policy on the part of the *Yishuv*: 'The necessary condition for the fulfilment of Zionism', one newspaper wrote, 'is the takeover of all the country's jobs by a Jewish work-force.' *Kibbutzim* and *moshavim*, in the name of this takeover of jobs vied with one another in using **Arab** agricultural labourers. On the walls of **Jerusalem** and Tel Aviv, founded in 1909, the posters said: 'Do not buy Arab produce! Buy Hebrew!'

But the *Yishuv*, which increased its numbers and its role within the economy, was much more: alongside the Palestinian Arab nation, it incarnated the evolving Jewish Palestinian nation, with its own language (Hebrew modernized by Eleazar Ben Yehuda), its public services, its embryo army (the Haganah, the Palmach, and the troops of the revisionist Irgun), and of course its institutions. Under the British High Commission, the legislative and executive power in Palestine, Jews were represented, as stipulated in Article 4 of the mandate, by a 'suitable Jewish body'; the Jewish Agency which, as well as distributing immigration permits, gradually took charge of the entire colonizing process. The community also elected its own National Council, the Vaad Leumi.

Three major tendencies characterized *Yishuv*. Often of socialist origins, immigrants favoured the Left: the Mapai which united the various socialist tendencies in 1930, and, further to the Left, the Hashomer Hatzair and the Poale Zion Smole, precursors of the present-day Mapam. The Histadrut union, which controlled a large part of the economic machinery, also represented a forum for them. The Right comprised a liberal tendency (the General Zionists) and an authoritarian tendency (the Revisionist Party). Lastly, the religious pole was divided between Mizrahi and Hapoel Mizrahi, who participated in the various institutions, and the orthodox Agudat Israel and Poale Agudat Israel who refused to do so. During the elections of 1931 the Left, the Right and the religious groups won respectively 42.3%, 32% and 7% of votes. The only Judeo-Arab and non-Zionist organization, the Communist Party, founded in 1922, had difficulty accommodating the contradictions inherent in its composition, aggravated by the directives of the Comintern and the 'tagging along' policy, which stemmed from it, regarding the leadership of the Palestinian movement.

Thus, the *Yishuv* already constituted a sort of state within the state. An Israel before Israel. On May 14, 1948, it gained the one attribute it still lacked: **independence**.

Zionism

FROM ZION, the hill of Jerusalem and the symbol of the Promised Land. A doctrine and a movement aiming to gather **Jews** together in Palestine in their own state, Zionism found its first political expression in 1896 in *The Jewish*

State by Theodor **Herzl**, its first coherent expression in 1897 with the Zionist World Congress, and its first victory, a historic one, on May 14, 1948, when the state of **Israel** was born.

The original basis of Zionism is of course the link that, according to its believers, unites the Jews with the Holy Land. The Jewish kingdoms founded in Palestine around 1000 BC had perished under the successive attacks of the Assyrians, the Babylonians and the Romans. The crushing of the Bar Kokhba Revolt, in 135 AD, was the signal for the departure of most of the Hebrew population. A small minority remained in Jerusalem, Safad, Tiberias and Hebron: despite the addition of pilgrims who came to join them, in particular the exiles of the Iberian Peninsula at the end of the 15th century, the Jewish community of Palestine still numbered only around 10,000 at the beginning of the 19th century. The others, all over the world, formed the Diaspora — in Hebrew, dispersion.

The memory of the 'lost homeland' and the desire to return there were for long fostered by religion alone: 'Next year in Jerusalem,' believers prayed each year. As the 18th century gave way to the 19th, the idea of the return became more political. It was Napoleon who, on campaign in **Egypt**, called on Jews to 'rally under his flag to recreate the old Jerusalem'. If this cause had defenders as disparate as the Saint-Simonians, Lord Byron, Disraeli, and the secretary of Napoleon III, it was henceforth to be embodied above all in the work of thinkers like the German Moses Hess (*Rome and Jerusalem,* 1862) and the Russian, Leon Pinsker (*Self-Determination,* 1882). The Lovers of Zion, inspired by the latter, were responsible for the first *aliya* which, between 1882 and 1903, attracted 20,000 to 30,000 Jews from the Tsarist Empire to Palestine. With these immigrants and the help of Baron Edmond de Rothschild, along with investments from other Jewish entrepreneurs, a mainly agricultural colonization of the biblical lands began. It was the Viennese journalist Theodor Herzl who supplied the movement with a theory and an organization, as well as diplomacy. The Zionist Organization with its Jewish National Fund, responsible for the purchase of Palestinian land, made the plan materialize. 'Around 1900', points out Maxime Rodinson, 'the projects of colonization were not seen, as they are today, in an unfavourable light.'

Four hypotheses formed the basis of Herzl's thesis: the existence of a Jewish people, the impossibility of its assimilation into the societies to which it had been dispersed, its right to the Promised Land and the non-existence in this land of another people who also had rights. For defenders of Zionism, such things are as self-evident as they are false for their opponents. Walter Laqueur, author of a monumental *History of Zionism*, very rightly notes at the conclusion of his work: 'This belief can be accepted or rejected: it can only be the object of rational discussion to a very limited extent.... Zionism formulated an ideology, but its scientific pretensions are inevitably less than conclusive.' And it is true that the debate over the very idea of what constitutes a Jew remains open: aside from the religion, in which not all believe, and which is no doubt insufficient in itself as a definition of a people, what would be the unifying criteria of this national presence? Racial? Territorial? Linguistic? The question of assimilation is equally controversial: though brutally interrupted by the rise of anti-Semitism at the end of the 19th century, then by the **holocaust**, it is nonetheless a very real fact. It even recommenced after the Nazi extermination. A Zionist leader like Nahum Goldmann went so far as to allude publicly to the 'danger' of a 'disintegration of Jewish communities' and their 'loss of awareness of being part of the Jewish people' (May 26, 1959). To Zionists emphasizing the continual re-emergence of anti-Jewish sentiments and deeds as proof of the need for the Jewish state, their opponents counter with the choice made by the vast majority of Jews to remain in their countries, and in many cases, to assimilate there. And finally, the problem of the right to Palestine has become all the more contradictory in the light of the interminable **Arab**-Israeli conflict: allusion to the sacred text of a religion (one of three) and to an occupation (amongst twelve) has done nothing to legitimize the unilateral claim to the Holy Land, to the exclusion what is more of another people whose very existence is denied.

Maxime Rodinson admits that 'Jewish suffering may — perhaps — justify the aspiration of certain Jews to form an independent state. But, to the Arabs, this cannot be sufficient reason for this state to be formed at their expense.' Especially, he adds, since they themselves had very little to do with the persecution of the Jews.

If its principles have been the subject of debate, Zionism has in any case undergone a certain development, as much in its influence and organization outside Palestine as in the construction, within Palestine, of a Jewish national home that became the state of Israel. The basis of the success lies both in the abject poverty of the Jewish masses in Central and East Europe and, from 1882, the new anti-Semitic wave of horrific **pogroms** as witnessed in Albert Londres' poignant report, *Le Juif errant est arrivé*. The economic exclusion of Jews was thus coupled with a violent political exclusion, by means of massacres which found a distant echo in Western Europe in the Dreyfus Affair. The disillusionment was in proportion to the illusions propagated, in the West, by the emancipation of Jews introduced by the French Revolution. 'Zionism', summed up Abraham Leon (*La Conception matérialiste de la question juive*) was born in the glare of the flames of the Russian pogroms of 1882 and in the tumult of the Dreyfus Affair, two events that reflect the increasing gravity of the Jewish problem at the end of the 19th century.'

But the progress made by Zionism was also due to the fact that the European powers saw in it an instrument: **Great Britain** in order to further entrench itself in the Middle East and protect the **Suez Canal**, Tzarist Russia to halt the spread of the revolution (many of whose leaders were of Jewish origin), Germany, whose leaders dreamed of ridding themselves of a large, influential Jewish community, the Ottoman Sultan to fill his empty coffers. To each of these potential partners, Theodor Herzl was able to show how much the Zionist project would be in their interest. Especially for London, for, as Herzl wrote in his *Journal* in 1900, 'free and powerful England, whose gaze encompasses the seven seas, will understand us and our aspirations. It is from there, we may be sure, that the Zionist movement will soar towards new and higher summits.' And his successors would do just that, above all with London which, until 1939, would remain the Zionists' main ally, even if Britain's anxiety not to compromise itself in Arab eyes meant the alliance was frequently a stormy one. But its basic foundation was solid: protecting the canal. 'England', exclaimed Haim Weizmann, 'will have a secure barrier, and we will have a country.'

It was of course from the holocaust that Zionism gained its full legitimacy and the strength to materialize. After the extermination of 6 million Jews against a background of almost total indifference, Europe and America, whose public opinion had been stunned, agreed on the need to create a Jewish state and an Arab state in Palestine. Only the first of these would ever see the light of day, corresponding, moreover, to the initial demands of the Zionist movement. But this only child carried within it the germ of the crisis that Zionism is currently experiencing. The repercussions set off in the Diaspora by the invasion of **Lebanon**, in 1982, were forerunners of things to come.

'Zionism', declared Marcel Liebman in *Né Juif*, 'runs up against a double objection, which the facts themselves continue to demonstrate. Having established as its aim the creation of a peaceful haven for the Jews, Zionism in fact created a state which has lived in constant insecurity.' The reason, continues the Belgian analyst, is the plundering of the **Palestinians** and its consequences. And he promptly adds: 'In its attempt to gather together in a single state all the Jews in the world, Zionism has been equally unsuccessful.' He concludes, regarding their children and their supposed Jewishness: 'Why should one focus on them the blinding lights that reflect the flames of yesterday? Yes, of yesterday.'

The fact of the matter is that, more than eighty years after the death of Theodor Herzl, if the Jewish state does exist, it contains only a minority, less than 20%, of the people it was intended to receive. And Israelis are not a monolithic bloc, but, as Henri Curiel noted (*Pour une paix juste au Proche-Orient*), are divided into 'two elements whose aspirations are different, if not downright contradictory. The first of these elements is composed of real Zionists, in other words those who went to Israel with the sole purpose of establishing a Jewish state there .... The second element, which forms the majority of the Jewish population in Israel, is composed of Jews who settled there because they had nowhere else to go.' Is the Zionist balance sheet a positive one?

Appendixes

APPENDIX 1
The Balfour Declaration
November 2, 1917

Dear Lord Rothschild.

I have much pleasure in conveying to you, on behalf of His Majesty's Government, the following declaration of sympathy with Jewish Zionist aspirations which has been submitted to, and approved by, the Cabinet.

'His Majesty's Government view with favour the establishment in Palestine of a national home for the Jewish people, and will use their best endeavours to facilitate the achievement of this object, it being clearly understood that nothing shall be done which may prejudice the civil and religious rights of existing non-Jewish communities in Palestine, or the rights and political status enjoyed by Jews in any other country.'

I should be grateful if you would bring this declaration to the knowledge of the Zionist Federation.

Yours sincerely,

Arthur James Balfour

APPENDIX 2
The British Mandate (Extracts)
July 24, 1922

The Council of the League of Nations:
Whereas the principal allied powers have agreed, for the purpose of giving effect to the provisions of Article 22 of the Covenant of the League of Nations, to entrust to a mandatory selected by the said powers the administration of the territory of Palestine, which formerly belonged to the Turkish Empire, within such boundaries as may be fixed by them;

Whereas the principal allied powers have also agreed that the mandatory should be responsible for putting into effect the declaration originally made on 2nd November 1917 by the Government of His Britannic Majesty, and adopted by the said powers, in favour of the establishment in Palestine of a national home for the Jewish people, it being clearly understood that nothing should be done which might prejudice the civil and religious rights of existing non-Jewish communities in Palestine, or the rights and political status enjoyed by Jews in any other country;

Whereas recognition has thereby been given to the historical connection of the Jewish people with Palestine and to the grounds for reconstituting their national home in that country;

Whereas the principal allied powers have selected His Britannic Majesty as the mandatory for Palestine;

Whereas the mandate in respect of Palestine has been formulated in the following terms and submitted to the Council of the League for approval;

Confirming the said mandate, defines its terms as follows:

Article 1

The mandate shall have full powers of legislation and of administration, save as they may be limited by the terms of this mandate.

Article 2

The mandatory shall be responsible for placing the country under such political, administrative and economic conditions as will secure the establishment of the Jewish national home, as laid down in the preamble, and the development of self-governing institutions, and also for safeguarding the civil and religious rights of all the inhabitants of Palestine, irrespective of race and religion.

Article 3

The mandatory shall, as far as circumstances permit, encourage local autonomy.

Article 4

An appropriate Jewish agency shall be recognised as a public body for the purpose of advising and co-operating with the administration of Palestine in such economic, social and other matters as may affect the establishment of the Jewish national home and the interests of the Jewish population in Palestine, and, subject always to the control of the administration, to assist and take part in the development of the country.

The Zionist Organisation, so long as its organisation and constitution are in the opinion of the mandatory appropriate, shall be recognised as such agency. It shall take steps in consultation with His Britannic Majesty's Government to secure the co-operation of all Jews who are willing to assist in the establishment of the Jewish national home.

APPENDIX 3
The Partition Plan (Extracts)
November 29, 1947

Part One: Future Constitution and Government of Palestine

A. Termination of Mandate, Partition and Independence

1. The mandate for Palestine shall terminate as soon as possible but in any case not later than 1 August 1948.
2. The armed forces of the mandatory Power shall be progressively withdrawn from Palestine, the withdrawal to be completed as soon as possible but in any case not later than August 1948.

The mandatory Power shall advise the Commission, as far in advance as possible, of its intention to terminate the mandate and to evacuate each area.

The mandatory Power shall use its best endeavours to ensure that an area situated in the territory of the Jewish State, including a seaport and hinterland adequate to provide facilities for a substantial immigration, shall be evacuated at the earliest possible date and in any event not later than 1 February 1948.

3. Independent Arab and Jewish States and the Special International Regime for the City of Jerusalem, set forth in part III of this plan, shall come into existence in Palestine two months after the evacuation of the armed forces of the mandatory Power has been completed but in any case not later than 1 October 1948. The boundaries of the Arab State, the Jewish State, and the City of Jerusalem shall be described in parts II and III below.

4. The period between the adoption of the General Assembly of its recommendation on the question of Palestine and the establishment of the independence of the Arab and Jewish states shall be a transitional period.

C. Declaration

A declaration shall be made to the United Nations by the provisional government of each proposed state before independence. It shall contain *inter alia* the following clauses:

GENERAL PROVISION

The stipulations contained in the declaration are recognized as fundamental laws of the State and no law, regulation or official action shall conflict or interfere with these stipulations, nor shall any law, regulation or official action prevail over them.

CHAPTER I: HOLY PLACES, RELIGIOUS BUILDINGS & SITES

1. Existing rights in respect of Holy Places and religious buildings or sites shall not be denied or impaired.
2. In so far as Holy Places are concerned, the liberty of access, visit and transit shall be guaranteed, in conformity with existing rights, to all residents and citizens of the other State and of the City of Jerusalem, as well as to aliens, without distinction as to nationality, subject to requirements of national security, public order and decorum.

Similarly, freedom of worship shall be guaranteed in conformity with existing rights, subject to the maintenance of public order and decorum.
3. Holy Places and religious buildings or sites shall be preserved. No act shall be permitted which may in any way impair their sacred character. If at any time it appears to the Government that any particular Holy Place, religious building or site is in need of urgent repair, the Government may call upon the community or communities concerned to carry out such repair. The Government may carry it out itself at the expense of the community or communities concerned if no action is taken within a reasonable time.
4. No taxation shall be levied in respect of any Holy Place, religious building or site which was exempt from taxation on the date of the creation of the State.

No change in the incidence of such taxation shall be made which would either discriminate between the owners or occupiers of Holy Places, religious buildings or sites, or would place such owners or occupiers in a position less favourable in relation to the general incidence of taxation than existed at the time of the adoption of the Assembly's recommendation.
5. The Governor of the City of Jerusalem shall have the right to determine whether the provisions of the Constitution of the State in relation to Holy Places, religious buildings and sites within the borders of the State and the religious rights appertaining thereto, are being properly applied and respected, and to make decisions on the basis of existing rights in cases of disputes which may arise between the different religious communities or the rites of a religious community with respect to such places, buildings and sites. He shall receive full co-operation and such privileges and immunities as are

necessary for the exercise of his functions in the State.

CHAPTER 2: RELIGIOUS & MINORITY RIGHTS

1. Freedom of conscience and the free exercise of all forms of worship, subject only to the maintenance of public order and morals, shall be ensured to all.
2. No discrimination of any kind shall be made between the inhabitants on the ground of race, religion, language or sex.
3. All persons within the jurisdiction of the State shall be entitled to equal protection of the laws.
4. The family law and personal status of the various minorities and their religious interests, including endowments, shall be respected.
5. Except as may be required for the maintenance of public order and good government, no measure shall be taken to obstruct or interfere with the enterprise of religious or charitable bodies of all faiths or to discriminate against any representative or member of these bodies on the ground of his religion or nationality.
6. The State shall ensure adequate primary amd secondary education for the Arab and Jewish minority, respectively, in its own language and its cultural traditions.

The right of each community to maintain its own schools for the education of its own members in its own language, while conforming to such educational requirements of a general nature as the State may impose, shall not be denied or impaired. Foreign educational establishments shall continue their activity on the basis of their existing rights.
7. No restriction shall be imposed on the free use by any citizen of the State of any language in private intercourse, in commerce, in religion, in the Press or in publications of any kind, or at public meetings.
8. No expropriation of land owned by an Arab in the Jewish State (by a Jew in the Arab State) shall be allowed except for public purposes. In all cases of expropriation full compensation as fixed by the Supreme Court shall be paid previous to dispossession.

Part Two: Boundaries

A. Arab State

B. Jewish State

C. The City of Jerusalem

The boundaries of the City of Jerusalem are as defined in the recommendations on the City of Jerusalem.

Part Three: City of Jerusalem

A. *Special Regime*

The City of Jerusalem shall be established as a *corpus separatum* under a special international regime and shall be administered by the United Nations. The Trusteeship Council shall be designated to discharge the responsibilities of the Administering Authority on behalf of the United Nations.

C. *Statute of the City*

The Trusteeship Council shall, within five months of the approval of the present plan, elaborate and approve a detailed statute of the City which shall contain, *inter alia*, the substance of the following provisions:

1. GOVERNMENT MACHINERY: SPECIAL OBJECTIVES

The Administering Authority in discharging its administrative obligations shall pursue the following special objectives:

a) To protect and preserve the unique spiritual and religious interests located in the City of the three great monotheistic faiths throughout the world, Christian, Jewish and Moslem; to this end to ensure that order and peace, and especially religious peace, reign in Jerusalem;

b) To foster co-operation among all the inhabitants of the city in their own interests as well as in order to encourage and support the peaceful development of the mutual relations between the two Palestinian peoples throughout the Holy Land; to promote the security, well-being and any constructive measures of development of the residents, having regard to the special circumstances and customs of the various peoples and communities.

2. GOVERNOR & ADMINISTRATIVE STAFF

A Governor of the City of Jerusalem shall be appointed by the Trusteeship Council and shall be responsible to it. He shall be selected on the basis of special qualifications and without regard to nationality. He shall not, however, be a citizen of either State in Palestine.

The Governor shall represent the United Nations in the City and shall exercise on their behalf all powers of administration, including the conduct of external affairs. He shall be assisted by an administrative staff classed as international officers in the meaning of Article 100 of the Charter and chosen whenever practicable from the residents of the City and of the rest of Palestine on a non-discriminatory basis. A detailed plan for the organization of the administration of the City shall be submitted by the Governor to the Trusteeship Council and duly approved by it.

3. LOCAL AUTONOMY

a) The existing local autonomous units in the territory of the city (villages, townships and municipalities) shall enjoy wide powers of local government and administration.

b) The Governor shall study and submit for the consideration and decision of the Trusteeship Council a plan for the establishment of special town units consisting, respectively, of the Jewish and Arab sections of new Jerusalem.

4. SECURITY MEASURES

a) The City of Jerusalem shall be demilitarized; its neutrality shall be declared and preserved, and no para-military formations, exercises or activities shall be permitted within its borders.

b) Should the administration of the City of Jerusalem be seriously obstructed or prevented by the non-cooperation or interference of one or more sections of the population, the Governor shall have authority to take such measures as may be necessary to restore the effective functioning of the administration.

c) To assist in the maintenance of internal law and order and especially for the protection of the Holy Places and religious buildings and sites in the city, the Governor shall organize a special police force of adequate strength, the members of which shall be recruited outside of Palestine. The Governor shall be empowered to direct such budgetary provision as may be necessary for the maintenance of this force.

5. LEGISLATIVE ORGANIZATION

A Legislative Council, elected by adult residents of the City irrespective of nationality on the basis of universal and secret suffrage and proportional representation, shall have powers of legislation and taxation. No legislative measures shall, however, conflict or interfere with the provisions which will be set forth in the Statute of the City, nor shall any law, regulation or official action prevail over them. The Statute shall grant to the Governor a right of vetoing bills inconsistent with the provisions referred to in the preceding sentence. It shall also empower him to promulgate temporary ordinances in case the Council fails to adopt in time a bill deemed essential to the normal functioning of the administration.

6. ADMINISTRATION OF JUSTICE

The Statute shall provide for the establishment of an independent judiciary system, including a court of appeal. All the inhabitants of the city shall be subject to it.

7. ECONOMIC UNION & ECONOMIC REGIME

The City of Jerusalem shall be included in the Economic Union of Palestine and be bound by all stipulations of the undertaking and of any treaties issued therefrom, as well as by the decisions of the Joint Economic Board. The headquarters of the Economic Board shall be established in the territory of the City.

The Statute shall provide for the regulation of economic matters not falling within the regime of the Economic Union, on the basis of equal treatment and non-discrimination for all members of the United Nations and their nationals.

8. FREEDOM OF TRANSIT & VISIT: CONTROL OF RESIDENTS

Subject to considerations of security, and of economic welfare as determined by the Governor under the directions of the Trusteeship Council, freedom of entry into, and residence within, the borders of the City shall be guaranteed for the residents or citizens of the Arab and Jewish States. Immigration into, and residence within, the borders of the city for nationals of other States shall be controlled by the Governor under the direction of the Trusteeship Council;

9. RELATIONS WITH THE ARAB & JEWISH STATES

Representatives of the Arab and Jewish States shall be accredited to the Governor of the City and charged with the protection of the interests of their States and nationals in connection with the international administration of the City.

10. OFFICIAL LANGUAGES

Arabic and Hebrew shall be the official languages of the city. This will preclude the adoption of one or more additional working languages, as may be required.

11. CITIZENSHIP

All the residents shall become *ipso facto* citizens of the City of Jerusalem unless they opt for citizenship of the State of which they have been citizens or, if Arabs or Jews, have filed notice of intention to become citizens of the Arab or Jewish State respectively, according to Part 1, section B, paragraph 9, of this Plan.

The Trusteeship Council shall make arrangements for consular protection of the citizens of the City outside its territory.

12. FREEDOM OF CITIZENS

a) Subject only to the requirements of public order and morals, the inhabitants of the City shall be ensured the enjoyment of human rights and fundamental freedoms, including freedom of conscience, religion and worship, language, education, speech and press, assembly and association, and petition.

b) No discrimination of any kind shall be made between the inhabitants on the grounds of race, religion, language or sex.

c) All persons within the City shall be entitled to equal protection of the laws.

d) The family law and personal status of the various persons and communities and their religious interests, including endowments, shall be respected.

e) Except as may be required for the maintenance of public order and good government, no measure shall be taken to obstruct or interfere with the enterprise of religious or charitable bodies of all faiths or to discriminate against any representative or member of these bodies on the ground of his religion or nationality.

f) The City shall ensure adequate primary and secondary education for the Arab and Jewish communities respectively, in their own languages and in accordance with their cultural traditions.

The right of each community to maintain its own schools for the education of its own members in its own language, while conforming to such educational requirements of a general nature as the City may impose, shall not be denied or impaired. Foreign educational establishments shall continue their activity on the basis of their existing rights.

g) No restriction shall be imposed on the free use by any inhabitant of the City of any language in private intercourse, in commerce, in religion, in the Press or in publications of any kind, or at public meetings.

13. HOLY PLACES

a) Existing rights in respect of Holy Places and religious buildings or sites shall not be denied or impaired.

b) Free access to the Holy Places and religious buildings or sites and the free exercise of worship shall be secured in conformity with existing rights and subject to the requirements of public order and decorum.

c) Holy Places and religious buildings or sites shall be preserved. No act shall be admitted which may in any way impair their sacred character. If at any time it appears to the Governor that any particular Holy Site, religious building or site is in need of urgent repair, the Governor may call upon the community or communities concerned to carry out such repair. The Governor may carry it out himself at the expense of the community or communities concerned if no action is taken within a reasonable time.

d) No taxation shall be levied in respect of any Holy Place, religious building or site which was exempt from taxation on the date of the creation of the City. No change to the incidence of such taxation shall be made which would either discriminate between the owners or occupiers of Holy Places, religious buildings or sites or would place such owners or occupiers in a position less favourable in relation to the general incidence than existed at the time of the adoption of the Assembly's recommendations.

14. SPECIAL POWERS OF THE GOVERNOR IN RESPECT OF HOLY PLACES, RELIGIOUS BUILDINGS OR SITES IN THE CITY & IN ANY PART OF PALESTINE

a) The protection of the Holy Places, religious buildings or sites located in the city of Jerusalem shall be a special concern of the Governor.

b) With relation to such places, buildings and sites in Palestine outside the City, the Governor shall determine, on the grounds of power granted to him by the Constitutions of both States, whether the provisions of the Constitutions of the Arab and Jewish States in Palestine dealing therewith and the religious rights appertaining thereto are being properly applied and respected.

c) The Governor shall also be empowered to make decisions on the basis of existing rights in cases of disputes which may arise between the different religious communities or the rites of a religious community in respect of the Holy Places, religious buildings and sites in any part of Palestine.

In this task he may be assisted by a consultative council of representatives of different denominations acting in an advisory capacity.

D. Duration of the Special Regime

The Statute elaborated by the Trusteeship Council on the aforementioned principles shall come into force not later than 1 October 1948. It shall remain in force in the first instance for a period of ten years, unless the Trusteeship Council finds it necessary to undertake a re-examination of these provisions at an earlier date. After the expiration of this period the whole scheme shall be subject to re-examination by the Trusteeship Council in the light of the experience acquired with its functioning. The residents of the City shall be then free to express by means of a referendum their wishes as to possible modifications of the regime of the City.

Part Four: Capitulations

States whose nationals have in the past enjoyed in Palestine the privileges and immunities of foreigners, including the benefits of consular jurisdiction and protection, as formerly enjoyed by capitulations or usage in the Ottoman Empire, are invited to renounce any right pertaining to them to the re-establishment of such privileges and immunities in the proposed Arab and Jewish States and the City of Jerusalem.

UN Security Council Resolution 242
November 22, 1967

The Security Council,

Expressing its continuing concern with the grave situation in the Middle East,

Emphasizing the inadmissibility of the acquisition of territory by war and the need to work for a just and lasting peace in which every State in the area can live in security,

Emphasizing further that all Member States in their acceptance of the Charter of the United Nations have undertaken a commitment to act in accordance with Article 2 of that Charter,

1. Affirms that the fulfilment of Charter principles requires the establishment of a just and lasting peace in the Middle East which should include the application of both the following principles:
    (i) Withdrawal of Israel's armed forces from territories occupied in the recent conflict;
    (ii) Termination of all claims or states of belligerency and respect for and acknowledgement of the sovereignty, territorial integrity and political independence of every State in the area and their right to live in peace within secure and recognized boundaries free from threats or acts of force;

2. Affirms further the necessity:
    (a) For guaranteeing freedom of navigation through international waterways in the area;
    (b) For achieving a just settlement of the refugee problem;
    (c) For guaranteeing the territorial inviolability and political independence of every State in the area, through measures including the establishment of demilitarized zones;

3. Requests the Secretary-General to designate a Special Representative to proceed to the Middle East to establish and maintain contacts with the States concerned in order to promote agreement and assist efforts to achieve a peaceful and accepted settlement in accordance with the provisions and principles in this resolution;

4. Requests the Secretary-General to report to the Security Council on the progress of the efforts of the Special Representative as soon as possible.

Rabat Resolution
October 28, 1974

The Seventh Arab Summit Conference resolves the following:

1. To affirm the right of the Palestinian people to self-determination and to return to their homeland;
2. To affirm the right of the Palestinian people to establish an independent national authority under the command of the Palestine Liberation Organization, the sole legitimate representative of the Palestinian people in any Palestinian territory that is liberated. This authority, once it is established, shall enjoy the support of the Arab States in all fields and at all levels;
3. To support the Palestine Liberation Organization in the exercise of its responsibility at the national and international levels within the framework of Arab commitment;
4. To call on the Hashemite Kingdom of Jordan, the Syrian Arab Republic, the Arab Republic of Egypt and the Palestine Liberation Organization to devise a formula for the regulation of relations between them in the light of these decisions so as to ensure their implementation;
5. That all the Arab States undertake to defend Palestinian national unity and not to interfere in the internal affairs of Palestinian action.

UN General Assembly Resolution 3236
November 22, 1974

The General Assembly,

Having considered the question of Palestine,

Having heard the statement of the Palestine Liberation Organization, the representative of the Palestinian people,

Having also heard other statements made during the debate,

Deeply concerned that no just solution to the problem of Palestine has yet been achieved and recognizing that the problem of Palestine continues to endanger international peace and security,

Recognizing that the Palestinian people is entitled to self-determination in accordance with the Charter of the United Nations,

Expressing its grave concern that the Palestinian people has been prevented from enjoying its inalienable rights, in particular its right to self-determination,

Guided by the purposes and principles of the Charter,

Recalling its relevant resolutions which affirm the right of the Palestinian people to self-determination,

1. Reaffirms the inalienable rights of the Palestinian people in Palestine, including:

    (a) The right to self-determination without external interference;

    (b) The right to national independence and sovereignty;

2. Reaffirms also the inalienable right of the Palestinians to return to their homes and property from which they have been displaced and uprooted, and calls for their return;

3. Emphasizes that full respect for and realization of these inalienable rights of the Palestinian people are indispensable for the solution of the question of Palestine;

4. Recognizes that the Palestinian people is a principal party in the establishment of a just and durable peace in the Middle East;

5. Further recognizes the right of the Palestinian people to regain its rights by all means in accordance with the purposes and principles of the Charter of the United Nations;

6. Appeals to all States and international organizations to extend their support to the Palestinian people in its struggle to restore its rights, in accordance with the Charter;

7. Requests the Secretary-General to establish contacts with the Palestine Liberation Organization on all matters concerning the question of Palestine;

8. Requests the Secretary-General to report to the General Assembly at its thirtieth session on the implementation of the present resolution;

9. Decided to include the item entitled 'Question of Palestine' in the provisional agenda of its thirtieth session.

Camp David Framework for Peace in the Middle East (Extracts)

September 17, 1978

Mohammed Anwar el-Sadat, President of the Arab Republic of Egypt, and Menachem Begin, Prime Minister of Israel, met with Jimmy Carter, President of the United States of America, at Camp David from September 5 to September 17, 1978, and have agreed on the following framework for peace in the Middle East. They invite other parties to the Arab-Israel conflict to adhere to it.

Framework

Taking these factors into account, the parties are determined to reach a just, comprehensive, and durable settlememt of the Middle East conflict through the conclusion of peace treaties based on Security Council Resolutions 242 and 338, in all their parts. Their purpose is to achieve peace and good neighbourly relations. They recognize that, for peace to endure, it must involve all those who have been most deeply affected by the conflict. They therefore agree that this framework as appropriate is intended by them to constitute a basis for peace not only between Egypt and Israel, but also between Israel and each of its other neighbours which is prepared to negotiate peace with Israel on this basis. With that objective in mind, they have agreed to proceed as follows:

A. West Bank and Gaza

1. Egypt and Israel, Jordan and the representatives of the Palestinian people should participate in negotiations on the resolution of the Palestinian problem in all its aspects. To achieve that objective, negotiations relating to the West Bank and Gaza should proceed in three stages:

   (a) Egypt and Israel agree that, in order to ensure a peaceful and orderly transfer of authority, and taking into account the security concerns of all the parties, there should be transitional arrangements for the West Bank and Gaza for a period not exceeding five years. In order to provide full autonomy to the inhabitants, under these arrangements the Israeli military government and its civilian administration will be withdrawn as soon as a self-governing authority has been freely elected by the inhabitants of these areas to replace the existing military government. To negotiate the details of a transitional arrangement, the Government of Jordan will be invited to join the negotiations on the basis of this framework. These new arrangements should give due consideration both to the principle of self-government by the inhabitants of these territories and to the legitimate security concerns of the parties involved.

(b) Egypt, Israel and Jordan will agree on the modalities for establishing the elected self-governing authority in the West Bank and Gaza. The delegations of Egypt and Jordan may include Palestinians from the West Bank and Gaza or other Palestinians as mutually agreed. The parties will negotiate an agreement which will define the powers and responsibilities of the self-governing authority to be exercised in the West Bank and Gaza. A withdrawal of Israeli Armed Forces will take place and there will be a redeployment of the remaining Israeli forces into specified security locations. The agreement will also include arrangements for assuring internal and external security and public order. A strong local police force will be established, which may include Jordanian citizens. In addition, Israeli and Jordanian forces will participate in joint patrols and in the manning of control posts to assure the security of the borders.

(c) When the self-governing authority (administrative council) in the West Bank and Gaza is established and inaugurated, the transitional period of five years will begin. As soon as possible, but not later than the third year after the beginning of the transitional period, negotiations will take place to determine the final status of the West Bank and Gaza and its relationship with its neighbours, and to conclude a peace treaty between Israel and Jordan by the end of the transitional period. These negotiations will be conducted between Egypt, Israel, Jordan, and the elected representatives of the inhabitants of the West Bank and Gaza. Two separate but related committees will be convened, one committee, consisting of representatives of the four parties which will negotiate and agree on the final status of the West Bank and Gaza, and its relationship with its neighbours, and the second committee, consisting of representatives of Israel and representatives of Jordan to be joined by the elected representatives of the inhabitants of the West Bank and Gaza, to negotiate the peace treaty between Israel and Jordan, taking into account the agreement reached on the final status of the West Bank and Gaza. The negotiations shall be based on all the provisions and principles of UN Security Council Resolution 242. The negotiations will resolve, among other matters, the location of the boundaries and the nature of the security arrangements. The resolution from the negotiations must also recognize the legitimate rights of the Palestinian people and their just requirements. In this way, the Palestinians will participate in the determination of their own future through:

   (i) The negotiations between Egypt, Israel, Jordan and the representatives of the inhabitants of the West Bank and Gaza to agree on the final status of the West Bank and Gaza and other outstanding issues by the end of the transitional period.

  (ii) Submitting their agreement to a vote by the elected representatives of the inhabitants of the West Bank and Gaza.

 (iii) Providing for the elected representatives of the West Bank and Gaza to decide how they shall govern themselves consistent with the provisions of their agreement.

 (iv) Participating as stated above in the work of the committee negotiating the peace treaty between Israel and Jordan.

2. All necessary measures will be taken and provisions made to assure the security of Israel and its neighbours during the transitional period and beyond. To assist in providing such security, a strong local police will be constituted by the self-governing authority. It will be composed of inhabitants of the West Bank and Gaza. The police will maintain continuing liaison on internal security matters with the designated Israeli, Jordanian and Egyptian officers.

3. During the transitional period, representatives of Egypt, Israel, Jordan, and the self-governing authority will constitute a continuing committee to decide by agreement on the modalities of admission of persons displaced from the West Bank and Gaza in 1967, together with necessary measures to prevent disruption and disorder. Other matters of common concern may also be dealt with by this committee.

4. Egypt and Israel will work with each other and with other interested parties to establish agreed procedures for a prompt, just and permanent implementation of the refugee problem.

APPENDIX 8

The Reagan Plan

Extracts from a Speech given by President Reagan
Washington, September 1, 1982

The question now is how to reconcile Israel's legitimate security concerns with the legitimate rights of the Palestinians. And that answer can only come at the negotiating table. Each party must recognize that the outcome must be acceptable to all and that true peace will require compromises by all.

So, tonight I am calling for a fresh start. This is the moment for all those directly concerned to get involved — or lend their support — to a workable basis for peace. The Camp David Agreement remains the foundation of our policy. Its language provides all parties with the leeway they need for successful negotiations.

I call on Israel to make clear that the security for which she yearns can only be achieved through genuine peace, a peace requiring magnanimity, vision and courage.

I call on the Palestinian people to recognize that their own political aspirations are inextricably bound to recognition of Israel's right to a secure future.

And I call on the Arab States to accept the reality of Israel — and the reality that peace and justice can be gained only through hard, fair, direct negotiations.

In making these calls on others, I recognize that the United States has a special responsibility. No other nation is in a position to deal with the key parties to the conflict on the basis of trust and reliability.

The time has come for a new realism on the part of all the peoples of the Middle East. The state of Israel is an accomplished fact; it deserves unchallenged legitimacy within the community of nations. But Israel's legitimacy has thus far been recognized by too few countries, and has been denied by every Arab State except Egypt. Israel exists; it has a right to exist in peace behind secure and defensible borders, and it has a right to demand of its neighbours that they recognize those facts.

The war in Lebanon has demonstrated another reality in the region. The departure of the Palestinians from Beirut dramatizes more than ever the homelessness of the Palestinian people. Palestinians feel strongly that their cause is more than a question of refugees. I agree. The Camp David Agreement recognized that fact when it spoke of the legitimate rights of the Palestinian people and their just requirements. For peace to endure, it must involve all those who have been most deeply affected by the conflict. Only through broader participation in the peace process — most immediately by Jordan and by the Palestinians — will Israel be able to rest confident in the knowledge that its security and integrity will be respected by its neighbours. Only through the process of negotiation can all the nations of the Middle East achieve a secure peace.

These then are our general goals. What are the specific new American positions, and why are we taking them?

In the Camp David talks thus far, both Israel and Egypt have felt free to express openly their views as to what the outcome should be. Understandably, their views have differed on many points.

The United States has thus far sought to play the role of mediator; we have avoided public comment on the key issues. We have always recognized — and continue to recognize — that only the voluntary agreement of those parties most directly involved in the conflict can provide an enduring solution. But it has become evident to me that some clearer sense of America's position on the key issues is necessary to encourage wider support for the peace process.

First, as outlined in the Camp David Accords, there must be a period of time during which the Palestinian inhabitants of the West Bank and Gaza will have full autonomy over their affairs. Due consideration must be given to the principle of self-government by the inhabitants of the territories and to the legitimate security concerns of the parties involved.

The purpose of the five-year period of transition which would begin after free elections for a self-governing Palestinian authority is to prove to the Palestinians that they can run their own affairs, and that such Palestinian autonomy poses no threat to Israel's security.

The United States will not support the use of any additional land for the purpose of settlements during the transition period. Indeed, the immediate adoption of a settlement freeze by Israel, more than any other action, could create the confidence needed for wider participation in these talks. Further settlement activity is in no way necessary for the security of Israel and only diminishes the confidence of the Arabs that a final outcome can be freely and fairly negotiated.

I want to make the American position clearly understood: the purpose of this transition period is the peaceful and orderly transfer of domestic authority from Israel to the Palestinian inhabitants of the West Bank and Gaza. At the same time, such a transfer must not interfere with Israel's security requirements.

Beyond the transition period, as we look to the future of the West Bank and Gaza, it is clear to me that peace cannot be achieved by the formation of an independent Palestinian state in those territories. Nor is it achievable on the basis of Israeli sovereignty or permanent control over the West Bank and Gaza.

So the United States will not support the establishment of an independent Palestinian State in the West Bank and Gaza, and we will not support annexation or permanent control by Israel.

There is, however, another way to peace. The final status of these lands must, of course, be reached by the give-and-take of negotiations. But it is the firm view of the United States that self-government by the Palestinians of the West Bank and Gaza in association with Jordan offers the best chance for a durable, just and lasting peace.

We base our approach squarely on the principle that the Arab-Israeli conflict should be resolved through negotiations involving an exchange of territory for peace. This exchange is enshrined in United Nations Security Council Resolution 242, which is, in turn, incorporated in all its parts in the Camp David Agreements. UN Resolution 242 remains wholly valid as the foundation stone of America's Middle East peace effort.

It is the United States position that — in return for peace — the withdrawal provision of Resolution 242 applies to all fronts, including the West Bank and Gaza.

When the border is negotiated between Jordan and Israel, our view on the extent to which Israel should be asked to give up territory will be heavily affected by the extent of true peace and normalization and the security arrangements offered in return.

Finally, we remain convinced that Jerusalem must remain undivided, but its final status should be decided through negotiation.

APPENDIX 9

The Fez Plan
(Extracts from the Arab League Summit Statement)
September 6, 1982

Arab-Israel Conflict

The conference greeted the steadfastness of the Palestinian revolutionary forces, the Lebanese and Palestinian peoples and the Syrian Arab Armed Forces and declared its support for the Palestinian people in the struggle for the retrieval of their established national rights.

Out of the conference's belief in the ability of the Arab nation to achieve its legitimate objectives and eliminate the aggression, and out of the principles and basis laid down by the Arab summit conferences, and out of the Arab countries' determination to continue to work by all means for the establishment of peace based on justice in the Middle East and using the plan of President Habib Bourguiba, which is based on international legitimacy, as the foundation for solving the Palestinian question and the plan of His Majesty King Fahd Ibn 'Abd Al-Aziz which deals with peace in the Middle East, and in the light of the discussions and notes made by their majesties . . . the conference has decided to adopt the following principles:

1. Israel's withdrawal from all Arab territories occupied in 1967, including Arab Jerusalem.
2. The removal of settlements set up by Israel in the Arab territories after 1967.

3. Guarantees of the freedom of worship and the performance of religious rites for all religions at the holy places.
4. Confirmation of the right of the Palestinian people to self-determination and to exercise their firm and inalienable national rights, under the leadership of the PLO, its sole legitimate representative, and compensation for those who do not wish to return.
5. The placing of the West Bank and Gaza Strip under UN supervision for a transitional period, not longer than several months.
6. The creation of an independent Palestinian State with Jerusalem as its capital.
7. The drawing up by the Security Council of guarantees for peace for all the states of the region, including the independent Palestinian State.
8. Security Council guarantees for the implementation of these principles.

APPENDIX 10

Jordanian-Palestinian Accord
(Jordanian version)
February 11, 1985

Emanating from the spirit of the Fez Summit resolutions, approved by Arab states, and from United Nations resolutions relating to the Palestine question.

In accordance with international legitimacy, and

Deriving from a common understanding on the establishment of a special relationship between the Jordanian and Palestinian peoples,

The Government of the Hashemite Kingdom of Jordan and the Palestine Liberation Organization have agreed to move together towards the achievement of a peaceful and just settlement of the Middle East crisis and the termination of Israeli occupation of the occupied Arab territories, including Jerusalem, on the basis of the following principles:

1. Total withdrawal from the territories occupied in 1967 for comprehensive peace as established in United Nations and Security Council resolutions.
2. Right of self-determination for the Palestinian people: Palestinians will exercise their inalienable rights of self-determination when Jordanians and Palestinians will be able to do so within the context of the formation of the proposed confederated Arab states of Jordan and Palestine.
3. Resolution of the problem of Palestinian refugees in accordance with the United Nations resolutions.

4. Resolution of the Palestine question in all its aspects.
5. And on this basis, peace negotiations will be conducted under the auspices of an International Conference in which the five Permanent Members of the Security Council and all the parties to the conflict will participate, including the Palestine Liberation Organization, the sole legitimate representative of the Palestinian people, within a joint delegation (joint Jordanian-Palestinian Delegation).

APPENDIX 11

19th Session of the Palestine National Council
November 12–15, 1988

Declaration of Independence (Extracts)

Despite the historical injustice inflicted on the Palestinian people resulting in their dispersion and depriving them of their right to self-determination, following upon UN General Assembly Resolution 181 (1947), which partitioned Palestine into two states, one Arab, one Jewish, yet it is this resolution that still provides those conditions of international legitimacy that ensure the right of the Palestinian Arab people to sovereignty and national independence....

Because of the *Intifada* and its revolutionary irreversible impulse, the history of Palestine has therefore arrived at a decisive juncture.

Whereas the Palestinian people reaffirms most definitely its inalienable rights in the land of its patrimony:

Now by virtue of natural, historical, and legal rights and the sacrifices of successive generations who gave of themselves in defense of the freedom and independence of their homeland;

In pursuance of resolutions adopted by Arab summit conferences and relying on the authority bestowed by international legitimacy as embodied in the resolutions of the United Nations Organization since 1947;

And in exercise by the Palestinian Arab people of its right to self-determination, political independence, and sovereignty over its territory;

The Palestinian National Council, in the name of God, and in the name of the Palestinian Arab people, hereby proclaims the establishment of the State of Palestine on our Palestinian territory with its capital Jerusalem (Al-Quds Al-Sharif).

The State of Palestine is the state of Palestinians wherever they may be. The state is for them to enjoy in it their collective national and cultural identity, theirs in which to pursue complete equality of rights. In it will be safeguarded their political and religious convictions and their human dignity by means of a parliamentary democratic system of governance, itself based on freedom of expression and the freedom to form parties. The rights of minorities will duly be respected by the majority, as majorities must abide by decisions of the majority. Governance will be based on principles of social justice, equality and non-discrimination in public rights on grounds of race, religion, color, or sex under the aegis of a constitution which ensures the rule of law and an independent judiciary. Thus shall these principles allow no departure from Palestine's age-old spiritual and civilizational heritage of tolerance and religious co-existence. . . .

Political Communiqué

. . . The Palestine National Council, being responsible to the Palestinian people, their national rights and their desire for peace as expressed in the Declaration of Independence issued on 15 November 1988; and in response to the humanitarian quest for international entente, nuclear disarmament, and the settlement of regional conflict by peaceful means, affirms the determination of the Palestine Liberation Organization to arrive at a comprehensive settlement of the Arab-Israeli conflict and its core, which is the question of Palestine, within the framework of the United Nations Charter, the principles and provisions of international legality, the norms of international law, and the resolutions of the United Nations, the latest of which are Security Council resolutions 605, 607 and 608, and the resolutions of the Arab summits, in such a manner that safeguards the Palestinian Arab people's rights to return, to self-determination, and the establishment of their independent national state on their national soil, and that institutes arrangements for the security and peace of all states in the region.

Towards the achievement of this, the Palestine National Council affirms:
1. The necessity of convening the effective international conference on the issue of the Middle East and its core, the question of Palestine, under the auspices of the United Nations, and with the participation of the permanent members of the Security Council and all parties to the conflict in the region including the Palestine Liberation Organization, the sole, legitimate representative of the Palestinian people, on an equal footing, and by considering that the international peace conference be convened on the basis of United Nations Security Council resolutions 242 and 338 and the attainment of the legitimate national rights of the Palestinian people, foremost among which is the right to self-determination and in accordance with the principles and provisions of the United Nations Charter concerning the right of peoples to self-determination, and by the inadmissibility of

the acquisition of the territory of others by force or military conquest, and in accordance with the relevant United Nations resolutions on the question of Palestine.

2. The withdrawal of Israel from all the Palestinian and Arab territories it occupied in 1967, including Arab Jerusalem.

3. The annullment of all measures of annexation and appropriation and the removal of settlements established by Israel in the Palestinian and Arab territories since 1967.

4. Endeavoring to place the occupied Palestinian territories, including Arab Jerusalem, under the auspices of the United Nations for a limited period in order to protect our people and afford the appropriate atmosphere for the success of the proceeding of the international conference towards the attainment of a comprehensive political settlement and the attainment of peace and security for all on the basis of mutual acquiescence and consent, and to enable the Palestinian state to exercise its effective authority in these territories.

5. The settlement of the question of the Palestinian refugees in accordance with the relevant United Nations resolutions.

6. Guaranteeing the freedom of worship and religious practice for all faiths in the holy places in Palestine.

7. The Security Council is to formulate and guarantee arrangements for security and peace between all the states concerned in the region, including the Palestinian state.

The Palestine National Council affirms its previous resolutions concerning the distinctive relationship between the Jordanian and Palestinian peoples, and affirms that the future relationship between the two states of Palestine and Jordan should be on a confederal basis as a result of the free and voluntary choice of the two fraternal peoples in order to strengthen the historical bonds and the vital interests they hold in common.

The National Council also renews its commitment to the United Nations resolutions that affirm the right of peoples to resist foreign occupation, colonialism, and racial discrimination, and their right to struggle for their independence, and reiterates its rejection of terrorism in all its forms, including state terrorism, affirming its commitment to previous resolutions in this respect and the resolutions of the Arab summit in Algiers in 1988, and to UN resolutions 42/195 of 1987, and 40/61 of 1985, and that contained in the Cairo declaration in this respect.

The Palestinian National Council expresses its deep gratitude to all the states and international forces and organizations that support the national rights of the Palestinians, and affirms its desire to strengthen the bonds of friendship and cooperation with the Soviet Union, the People's Republic of China, the other socialist countries, the non-aligned states, the Latin

American states, and the other friendly states, and notes with satisfaction the signs of positive evolution in the position of some West European states and Japan in the direction of support for the rights of the Palestinian people, applauds this development, and urges intensified efforts to increase it.

The Council notes with considerable concern the growth of the Israeli forces of fascism and extremism and the escalation of their open calls for the implementation of their policy of annihilation and individual and mass expulsion of our people from their homeland, and calls for intensified efforts in all arenas to confront this fascist peril. The Council at the same time expresses its appreciation of the role and courage of the Israeli peace forces as they resist and expose the forces of fascism, racism, and aggression; support the people's struggle and their valiant *Intifadah*; and back our people's right to self-determination and the establishment of an independent state. The Council confirms its past resolutions regarding the reinforcement and development of relations with those democratic forces.

The Palestine National Council also addresses itself to the American people, calling on them all to strive to put an end to the American policy that denies the Palestinian people's national rights, including their sacred right to self-determination, and urging them to work towards the adoption of policies that conform with the human rights charter and the international conventions and resolutions and serve the quest for peace in the Middle East and security for all its peoples, including the Palestinian people.

APPENDIX 12
'Mikhail Gorbachev's Meeting with Yasser Arafat'
Soviet News, April 13, 1989

Mikhail Gorbachev had a meeting in the Kremlin on April 9 with Yasser Arafat, the Chairman of the Executive Committee of the Palestine Liberation Organisation.

The interlocuters were unanimous that more favourable conditions have been forming lately for a settlement of the Middle East crisis.

The prospects of overcoming the crisis were studied from broad positions of the present world development. 'The deeper the new thinking will enter the consciousness of the world public, political life, the quicker a new political situation will form in the world in which it will be easier to solve conflict including regional problems,' Mikhail Gorbachev said.

He said that given a profound dialectical understanding of the new thinking there is no contradiction between a policy based on it and the interests of every people, including those struggling for their independence, for an independent choice of national development. On the contrary, such a policy expands the possibilities of approaching in a new way the most complicated problems which had defied solution for years and decades. In an atmosphere in which prospects of ridding mankind of the nuclear danger are taking shape it is the more intolerable that there remain trouble spots, bleeding wounds, which it is simpler to cure.

Yasser Arafat stressed that the Soviet Union's course in the world arena pursued in the spirit of new thinking facilitates the solution of the main international problems and improves conditions for settling regional conflicts as well.

On behalf of the Soviet people Mikhail Gorbachev expressed solidarity with the Palestinian people's selfless struggle. The Palestinians are a people with a difficult destiny. But it is not alone in upholding their just cause. The Palestinian people has extensive international support and this is the earnest of the solution of the main question for the Palestinian people — the question of self-determination. Just as recognition of the state of Israel and taking its security interests into account, the solution of this question is a necessary element of the establishment of peace and goodneighbourliness in the region on the basis of principles of international law.

The upsurge of the Palestinian popular movement has now become a key impulse for searching for practical solutions leading to an all-embracing settlement. The potential of this mass upsurge is in its profoundly democratic nature and ability to stay away from the road of extremism despite the provocative and cruel repression by the occupiers. This gains for the movement ever greater international support and sympathy in most diverse circles, Mikhail Gorbachev said.

The search for a solution of the Middle East problem should be based on negotiations, on an equal and business-like dialogue and not an armed force and the desire to dictate, he went on.

The Soviet Union, Mikhail Gorbachev said, persistently works for a just and all-embracing settlement with due account for the interests of all — both Arabs, including Palestinians, and Israel. It is prepared to interact constructively with all the participants in this peace process.

The Soviet view of the essence of the settlement, he said, is the following:

The withdrawal of Israeli troops from territories occupied in 1967 — the west bank of the Jordan, the Gaza Strip and the Syrian Golan Heights — is the key precondition of a settlement.

The Palestinian people has the right to self-determination in the same measure as it is ensured for the people of Israel. How the Palestinians will exercise this right is exclusively their own business.

An international conference under the aegis of the United Nations Organisation is the most effective mechanism of a settlement. Recognition by all its participants of resolutions 242 and 338 of the United Nations Security Council and the lawful rights of the Palestinian people, including the right to self-determination, should become the legal basis of the conference.

The conference should be attended by representatives of all the sides drawn into the conflict, including the Arab people of Palestine, and also the permanent members of the United Nations Security Council.

The conference presupposes most diverse forms of interaction of its participants. As to the role of the permanent members of the United Nations Security Council, it will be to create a constructive atmosphere for the conduct of talks at the conference. For this purpose, in particular, they can collectively or individually table proposals and recommendations.

The invitatons to all participants in the conference are to be sent by the United Nations Secretary-General.

Mikhail Gorbachev showed an understanding attitude to the idea of a single Arab delegation at the international conference.

Mikhail Gorbachev and Yasser Arafat exchanged views on various constructive ideas which could facilitate the preparation of the conference, its convocation and fruitful work.

The Soviet Union is not against intermediate measures and stages on the road to an all-embracing settlement. But they should be considered and carried out within the framework of the conference and in linkage with its end aims.

Success depends in many ways on the great powers, first of all the USSR and the United States. The Soviet approach provides for a combination of adherence to principle and realism, account for the viewpoints and interests of all sides related to the conflict. The point is to achieve a balance of interests.

One of the components of the normalisation of the situation in the Middle East must be the ending of the arms race there, the more so that it is acquiring a new nature in connection with the appearance and means of mass destruction and rockets with an enhanced range in the possession of the conflicting and warring sides.

Mikhail Gorbachev noted the importance of inter-Arab accord on the main questions of the Middle East settlement. The development of Syrian-Palestinian mutual understanding is acquiring special importance.

Yasser Arafat stated that the Palestinian people has always thought highly of the Soviet Union's invariable support for its inalienable national rights and of the Soviet efforts towards an all-embracing Middle East settlement.

The meeting passed in a business-like and constructive atmosphere characteristic of the long-established friendly relations between the CPSU and the PLO.

APPENDIX 13

Declaration on the Middle East
by the European Council

June 26–27, 1989

The European Council has examined the situation in the Middle East conflict in the light of recent events and of contacts undertaken over several months by the Presidency and the Troïka with the parties concerned, and it has drawn the following conclusions:

1. The policy of the Twelve on the Middle East conflict is defined in the Venice Declaration of 13 June 1980 and other subsequent declarations. It consists in upholding the right to security of all States in the region, including Israel, that is to say, to live within secure, recognised and guaranteed frontiers, and in upholding justice for all the peoples of the region, which includes recognition of the legitimate rights of the Palestinian people, including their right to self-determination with all that this implies.

   The Twelve consider that these objectives should be achieved by peaceful means in the framework of an international peace conference under the auspices of the United Nations, as the appropriate forum for the direct negotiations between the parties concerned, with a view to a comprehensive, just and lasting settlement.

   The European Council is also of the view that the PLO should participate in this process.

   It expresses its support for every effort by the permanent members of the Security Council of the United Nations to bring the parties closer together, create a climate of confidence between them, and facilitate in this way the convening of the international peace conference.

2. The Community and its Member States have demonstrated their readiness to participate actively in the search for a negotiated solution to the conflict, and to cooperate fully in the economic and social development of the peoples of the region.

   The European Council expressed its satisfaction regarding the policy of contacts with all the parties undertaken by the Presidency and the Troïka and has decided to pursue it.

3. The European Council welcomes the support given by the Extraordinary Summit Meeting of the Arab League, held in Casablanca, to the decisions

of the Palestinian National Council in Algiers, involving acceptance of Security Council Resolutions 242 and 338, which resulted in the recognition of Israel's right to exist, as well as the renunciation of terrorism.

It also welcomes the efforts undertaken by the United States in their contacts with the parties directly concerned and particularly the dialogue entered into with the PLO.

Advantage should be taken of these favourable circumstances to engender a spirit of tolerance and peace, with a view to entering resolutely on the path of negotiations.

4. The European Council deplores the continuing deterioration of the situation In the Occupied Territories and the constant increase in the number of dead and wounded and the suffering of the population.

It appeals urgently to the Israeli authorities to put an end to repressive measures, to implement resolutions 605, 607, and 608 of the Security Council and to respect the provisions of the Geneva Convention on the Protection of Civilian Populations in Times of War. They appeal in particular for the reopening of educational facilities in the West Bank.

5. On the basis of the positions of principle of the Twelve, the European Council welcomes the proposal for elections in the Occupied Territories as a contribution to the peace process provided that

- the elections are set in the context of a process towards a comprehensive, just, and lasting settlement of the conflict
- the elections take place in the Occupied Territories including East Jerusalem, under adequate guarantees of freedom
- no solution is excluded and the final negotiation takes place on the basis of Resolutions 242 and 338 of the Security Council of the United Nations, based on the principle of 'land for peace'.

6. The European Council launches a solemn appeal to the parties concerned to seize the opportunity to achieve peace. Respect by each of the parties for the legitimate rights of the other should facilitate the normalising of relations between all the countries of the region. The European Council calls upon the Arab countries to establish normal relations of peace and cooperation with Israel and asks that country in turn to recognise the right of the Palestinian people to exercise self-determination.

Bibliography

HISTORY AND GENERAL
Juan R. I. Cole, Nikki R. Keddie (eds), *Shi'ism and Social Protest*, Yale University Press, 1986.
Albert Hourani, *Arabic Thought in the Liberal Age*, Oxford University Press, 1970.
Michael C. Hudson, *Arab Politics: the Search for Legitimacy*, Yale University Press, 1977.
Walter Laqueur, *The Struggle for the Middle East*, Routledge and Kegan Paul, London, 1970.
Georges Lenozowski, *The Middle East in World Affairs*, Cornell University Press, London, 1980.
Giacomo Luciani (ed.), *The Arab State*, Routledge, London, 1990.

THE ARAB-ISRAELI CONFLICT
Neil Caplan, *Futile Diplomacy, Arab-Zionist Negotiations and the End of the Mandate*, Cass, London, 1986.
Jacob Coleman Hurewitz, *The Struggle for Palestine*, Schocken Books, New York, 1976 (first edition 1950).
John and David Kimche, *A Clash of Destinies: The Arab-Jewish War and the Founding of the State of Israel*, Praeger, New York, 1960.
Yaacov Shimoni, *Political Dictionary of the Arab World*, Collier MacMillan, London, 1987.

ISRAEL
Amos Elon, *The Israelis*, Adam Publisher, Tel Aviv, 1981.
Simha Flapan, *The Birth of Israel: Myths and Realities*, Pantheon Books, New York, 1987.
Yehoshafat Harkabi, *Israel's Fateful Hour*, Harper and Row, New York, 1988.
Shlomo Swirski, *Israel: The Oriental Majority*, Zed Books, London, 1989.
Tom Segev, *The First Israelis, 1949*, Collier MacMillan, London 1986.

PALESTINE
Geoffrey Aronson, *Israel, Palestinians and Intifada*, Kegan Paul International, London, 1990.
Alain Gresh, *The PLO: The Struggle Within*, Zed Books, London, 1988.
Alan Hart, *Arafat, Terrorist or Peacemaker?*, Sidgwick and Jackson, London, 1984.

Rashid Khalidi, *Under Siege: PLO Decision-Making During the 1982 War*, Columbia University Press, New York, 1986.

Zachary Lockman and Joel Beinin (eds), *Intifada*, South End Press, Boston, 1989.

Benny Morris, *The Birth of the Palestine Refugee Problem, 1947–1949*, Cambridge University Press, 1987.

THE BIG POWERS AND THE MIDDLE EAST

T. Bose, *The Superpowers and the Middle East*, APH, New York, 1972.

Michael Cohen, *Palestine and the Great Powers, 1945–1948*, Princeton University Press, 1982.

Paul Findlay, *They Dare to Speak Out*, Lawrence Hill and Co., Westport, 1985.

Galia Golan, *The USSR and the Middle East*, Cambridge University Press, 1990.

Stephen Green, *Living by the Sword: Americans and Israel in the Middle East, 1968–1987*, Faber and Faber, London, 1988.

William B. Quandt, *Camp David: Peacemaking and Politics*, The Brookings Institute, Washington, 1986.

Yaacov Ro'i, *Soviet Decision-Making in Practice: The USSR and Israel 1947–1954*, Transaction Books, London, 1980.

EGYPT AND SUDAN

Tim Niblock, *Class and Power in Sudan*, Macmillan, London, 1987.

Charles Tripp and Roger Owen (eds), *Egypt under Mubarak*, Routledge, London, 1989.

John Waterbury, *The Egypt of Nasser and Sadat*, Princeton University Press, 1983.

JORDAN

Amnon Cohen, *Political Parties in the West Bank under the Jordanian Regime, 1949–1967*, Cornell University Press, London, 1982.

LEBANON

Michael Jansen, *Class and Client in Beirut*, Ithaca Press, London, 1986.

Jonathan Randal, *The Tragedy of Lebanon*, The Hogarth Press, London, 1983.

Kamal Salibi, *Cross Roads to Civil War*, Ithaca Press, London, 1976.

Kamal Salibi, *A House of Many Mansions: The History of Lebanon Reconsidered*, IB Tauris, London, 1988.

THE GULF, IRAN AND SAUDI ARABIA

Shahram Chubin and Charles Tripp, *Iran and Iraq at War*, IB Tauris, London, 1988.

Fred Halliday, *Arabia Without Sultans*, Pelican Books, London, 1974.

Fred Halliday, *Revolution and Foreign Policy, The Case of South Yemen 1967–1987*, Cambridge University Press, 1990.

Robert Litwak, *Security in the Persian Gulf, Sources of Inter-State Conflict*, IISS, London, 1981.

Hanns Maul and Otto Mick, *The Gulf War*, Pinter, London, 1989.

R. K. Ramzani, *Revolutionary Iran*, John Hopkins University Press, London, 1987.

William Qaundt, *Saudi Arabia in the 1980s*, The Brookings Institute, Washington, 1981.

IRAQ

Hanna Battatu, *The Old Social Class and the Revolutionary Movements of Iraq*, Princeton University Press, 1978.

Marion Farouk-Sluglett and Peter Sluglett, *Iraq since 1968*, KPI, London, 1987.

Cardri, *Saddam's Iraq*, Zed Books, London, 1989.

SYRIA

John F. Devlin, *The Ba'ath Party*, Hoover Institute Press, 1976.

Patrick Seale, *The Struggle for Syria*, IB Tauris, London, 1986.

LIBYA

Jonathan Bearman, *Qadhafi's Libya*, Zed Books, London, 1986.

KURDS

Gerard Chaliand, *People Without a Country: The Kurds and Kurdistan*, Zed Books, London, 1980.

Index

Macmahon, Sir Henry, 114
Magnes, Judah, 91
Mahdi, Sadiq Al, 185
Mahjoub, Abdel Khaliq, 184
Maimonides, 103
Marienstras, Richard, 100
Marx, Karl, 103
Massignon, Louis, 172
Mauroy, Pierre, 44
McFarlane, Robert, 79, 80, 81
Meir, Golda, 86, 152, 179
Mendès-France, Pierre, 30
Mendelssohn, 103
Meyerson, Golda, see Meir, Golda
Mitterand, Francois, 43, 44
Mizrahi, Rachel, 93
Moawad, René, xx, 120
Mohammed, Ali Nasser, 218
Mohammed, Imam (9th century), 173
Mohammed, Prophet, x, 84, 85, 172, 173
Mollet, Guy, 194
Morris, Benny, 161
Moses, 85, 103
Mosley, Oswald, 114
Mossadegh, Dr, 53, 77, 134, 135, 200, 206
Moussawi, Hussein, 175
Mubarak, President Hosni, xvii, xx, 33, 75, 131-2
Mukhtar, Omar Al, 121
Mussolini, Benito, 121, 171

Nabulsi, Suleiman, 64
Nahas Pasha, 32
Napoleon, 2, 32, 40, 186, 221
Napoleon III, 117, 221
Nasser, Gamal Abdel, x, xi xiii, xiv, 5, 12, 13, 18, 33, 47, 57, 64, 68, 70, 82, 83, 86, 104, 121, 122, 132-4, 156, 164, 166, 167, 184, 186, 188, 190, 191, 192, 200, 206, 207, 208, 209
Neguib, General, 68, 133
Neher, André, 103
Nicholas I, Tsar, 141
Nimrodi, Yaacov, 80
Nir, Amiram, 80
Nixon, Richard, 79, 81, 109, 125, 210
Nokrashi Pasha, 183, 204
North, Oliver, 80, 81
Numeiry, General Ja'afar Al, viii, x, xiv, xviii, 184, 185

Orwell, George, 55

Pail, Meir, 166
Peled, General, xvii, 30, 92, 95, 96, 148, 166, 208
Peres, Shimon, vii, xx, 75, 80, 87, 97, 151-3, 170
Pétain, Marshal, 194
Picard, Elizabeth, 30, 120
Picot, 41, 50, 52, 68, 117, 127, 142, 179, 189-90
Pinsker, Leon, 2, 60, 221
Plehve, Tsarist minister, 155
Pobyedonotsev, Tsarist minister, 155
Poindexter, William, 80, 81
Pompidou, Georges, 43

Qabus, Sultan, 11
Qadaffi, Mu'ammar, x, xiv, 121, 122, 135, 155-7, 174, 193, 195, 212
Qleibi, Chadhli, 6

Rabath, 5
Rabin, General, 72, 86, 92, 152, 166, 170, 208
Radjavi, Massoud, 78, 108
Rafsanjani, President, 57
Rahane, Rabbi, 124
Rashid, Sheikh, 10
Reagan, Ronald, xvi, xviii, 35, 43, 79, 80, 81, 82, 100, 124, 125, 157, 158-60, 182, 193, 195, 201, 202, 241-4
Reza, Mohammed, 77
Richard, Yann, 173
Rocard, Michel, 44
Rodinson, Maxime, 85, 103, 221, 222
Rogers, xiv, 201, 202, 210
Roosevelt, President Franklin D., 124, 167, 200
Rothschild, Baron Edmond de, 2, 221, 226
Rouleau, Eric, 210
Rufeisen, Daniel, 101

Sadat, Anwar Al, xi, xvi, 26, 27, 33, 45, 46, 47, 65, 70, 131, 132, 134, 136, 148, 156, 159, 164-6, 169, 181, 183, 209, 210, 211, 212, 239
Sadr, President Bani, 56, 78
Sadr, Musa, 174
Safavi, Ismail, 76

Zed Books Ltd

is a publisher whose international and Third World lists span:

- **Women's Studies**
- **Development**
- **Environment**
- **Current Affairs**
- **International Relations**
- **Children's Studies**
- **Labour Studies**
- **Cultural Studies**
- **Human Rights**
- **Indigenous Peoples**
- **Health**

We also specialize in Area Studies where we have extensive lists in African Studies, Asian Studies, Caribbean and Latin American Studies, Middle East Studies, and Pacific Studies.

For further information about books available from Zed Books, please write to: Catalogue Enquiries, Zed Books Ltd, 57 Caledonian Road, London N1 9BU. Our books are available from distributors in many countries (for full details, see our catalogues), including:

In the USA
Humanities Press International, Inc., 171 First Avenue, Atlantic Highlands, New Jersey 07716.
Tel: (201) 872 1441;
Fax: (201) 872 0717.

In Canada
DEC, 229 College Street, Toronto, Ontario M5T 1R4.
Tel: (416) 971 7051.

In Australia
Wild and Woolley Ltd, 16 Darghan Street, Glebe, NSW 2037.

In India
Bibliomania, C-236 Defence Colony, New Delhi 110 024.

In Southern Africa
David Philip Publisher (Pty) Ltd, PO Box 408, Claremont 7735, South Africa.